I Worked Alone

I Worked Alone

*Diary of a Double Agent
in World War II Europe*

LILY SERGUEIEW

Edited by MARY KATHRYN BARBIER

McFarland & Company, Inc., Publishers
Jefferson, North Carolina

LIBRARY OF CONGRESS CATALOGUING-IN-PUBLICATION DATA

Sergueiew, Lily.
I worked alone : diary of a double agent in World War II Europe / Lily Sergueiew ; edited by Mary Kathryn Barbier.
       p.   cm.
Includes bibliographical references and index.

ISBN 978-0-7864-9613-6 (softcover : acid free paper) ∞
ISBN 978-1-4766-1717-6 (ebook)

1. Sergueiew, Lily—Diaries.   2. Women spies—Great Britain—Diaries.   3. Spies—Great Britain—Diaries.   4. Women spies—Europe—Diaries.   5. Great Britain. MI5—Biography.   6. World War, 1939–1945—Personal narratives.   7. World War, 1939–1945—Secret service—Great Britain.   8. World War, 1939–1945—Secret service—Germany.   9. World War, 1939–1945—Secret service—Europe.   I. Barbier, Mary.   II. Title.
D810.S8S379   2014   940.54'850941—dc23   2014033735

BRITISH LIBRARY CATALOGUING DATA ARE AVAILABLE

© 2014 Michele Jimeson and Mary Kathryn Barbier. All rights reserved

No part of this book may be reproduced or transmitted in any form or by any means, electronic or mechanical, including photocopying or recording, or by any information storage and retrieval system, without permission in writing from the publisher.

Cover photograph: Nathalie Sergueiew, alias Lily, in 1944 (Security Service, National Archives UK)

Printed in the United States of America

McFarland & Company, Inc., Publishers
Box 611, Jefferson, North Carolina 28640
www.mcfarlandpub.com

To the memories
of Nathalie "Lily" Sergueiew
and her husband
Colonel John Barton Collings
and to her nieces,
Corinne Sauty de Chalon Liard
and Irène Sauty de Chalon Schaeffer

Table of Contents

Editor's Acknowledgments	ix
Editor's Preface	1
Author's Original Preface	2
I. Beirut to Paris, 1940–1942	5
II. Paris, 1942–1943	73
III. Madrid, 1943	139
IV. Gibraltar, 1943	183
V. England, 1943–1944	196
VI. Lisbon, 1944	244
VII. England to Paris, 1944	274
Editor's Notes	305
Editor's Bibliography	308
Editor's Index	309

Editor's Acknowledgments

I first learned about Nathalie "Lily" Sergueiew when I was doing my dissertation research. She was one of several double agents who contributed to Operation Fortitude, which provided cover for the Normandy invasion that commenced on 6 June 1944. Lily's experience is unique because most double agents were men. When France fell to Germany in June 1940, Lily became determined to do her part to boot the German occupiers from French soil. She decided that the best way to do this was to become a double agent—to offer to spy for the Germans when in fact she intended to work against them.

There are several people who deserve my thanks because, without them, this book would never have seen the light of day. First, I would like to thank Colonel John Barton Collings, who loved Lily deeply and devotedly and held on to her books and this manuscript after she died. Unfortunately, he passed away in November 2013 before I was able to finish this project. I would like to thank his daughter Michele Collings Jimeson, who grew up hearing about the love of her father's life—Lily. Michele contacted me when she discovered Lily's "things" in her father's attic. She graciously allowed me access to them and purchased a copier and helped me photocopy Lily's memoir. In addition, Lily's niece Corinne Liard gave me access to the novel, *Jean*, that Lily wrote and refers to in her memoir.

I would like to thank Dr. Gary Myers (my former dean at Mississippi State University) and Dr. Gregory Dunaway (my current dean at Mississippi State), who awarded me HARP grants that helped fund my research trips for this project. Thanks also go to Dr. Alan Marcus, my department head, who has supported both my research and my presentation of it at academic meetings, and to my department colleagues and friends at Mississippi State, who have patiently listened to me talk about Lily and her experience.

I would also like to acknowledge the support of my family who has been subjected to repeated anecdotes about Lily and her adventures. Special thanks go to Dr. Dennis Showalter of Colorado College, my mentor and friend, who has offered me encouragement and sage advice every step of the way.

Special thanks also to Dr. David I. Hall, JSCSC, King's College London, for his support and encouragement as I worked on this exciting project.

Editor's Preface

Nathalie "Lily" Sergueiew—aka Treasure, Solange, Tramp—was a travel writer, an adventurer, a romantic, a patriot, and, for a brief period during the Second World War, a double agent. She was a strong, confident woman who lived during a time when men were dominant in society. Although the majority of spies and double agents were men, some were women. Recently, scholars have called these women heroines. At the time, however, society did not always treat them kindly. After all, only a certain type of woman, like Mata Hari, who used her feminine wiles to hoodwink men into revealing state secrets, would become a spy. Obviously, female spies were immoral, sexual sirens who set out to entrap unsuspecting men. They slept their way to information. Men who employed the same tactics were suave, debonair, and admired.

Not all women conformed to the stereotype. Some, like Sergueiew, were patriotic and did not think twice about engaging in a profession that would allow them to contribute to the defeat of the enemy. Unfortunately, she was more focused on kicking the Germans out of her beloved France than in getting along with her British employers, which brought her into conflict with the "cold" British men and women with whom she worked. The two sides—Sergueiew and the British—had different motivations and different perspectives. Their failure to understand and completely trust each other led to the dissolution of their relationship within a short period of time—seven months. Despite the unceremonious severing of their relationship, Sergueiew made a major contribution to the Allied war effort.

A writer before the war, Sergueiew continued to write during and after. She broke the rules and kept diaries that chronicled her experiences from the end of 1940 when she decided to become a double agent to the frustrating delays that she experienced along the way as she tried to bring her plan to fruition, to her work with the British, and finally to her return to France as a member of the M.M.L.A., French army. Along the way, she encountered incompetence, received training in encoding and decoding, invisible writing, and wireless transmission, had serious health problems, and suffered a loss, the result of a broken promise that tainted her relationship with her British employers and fostered the distrust that both sides experienced.

After the war, Sergueiew decided to write a memoir, originally entitled *I Worked Alone: Diary of a Double Agent*. In 1966, Sergueiew's mother had part of the diary published in France with the title *Seule Face à l'Abwehr*. The English version, *Secret Service Rendered*, was published two years later. In January 2010, I acquired a copy of Sergueiew's translated, unedited memoir. What follows is Lily's own words. I have provided clarifications for the reader when necessary, but I want to let Lily speak for herself. Therefore, I have made spelling and grammatical corrections only when necessary to help the flow of the narrative.

Author's Original Preface

To gather this material scattered in notebooks has made me live again all these months of disappointment when, very rapidly, I lost, one by one, the illusions which, for three years, had given me force and faith to bring my work to an end. For those who will read what follows, it will be but a book, pages, words. For me, it has been something different. I had to live through it. When I doubted, there was no one to give me confidence; no one to assure me it was worthwhile and that I was right. It was as though I was walking in a black tunnel. But what does it matter now; it's finished. Maybe I'm wrong to try to make a book out of it.

It isn't facts I have tried to relate. I have rather attempted to show what one feels, what one experiences, what one thinks when doing what I did. A writer can invent facts a hundred times more thrilling, he can show sharp emotions, but he doesn't know what it *really* is. I don't wish to make a detective story out of it. I could have exaggerated situations; it wouldn't be difficult. But I want it to be a document. There will be people whom it will interest; it will give them an idea of different methods of espionage, the working of certain Secret Services, personal reactions and the advantages one can draw out of certain situations. It will interest experts. As to the rest of the public, I didn't have them in mind when writing.

To make this story clear, it is better that the reader should know from the beginning what I myself learned much later, i.e., the functions and rank of some of the characters. The German Service of Information (S.R.A.) had its H.Q. at the Hotel Lutetia, Boulevard Raspail, in Paris. At the head of it was Colonel Winter; his immediate aide was Major Emilee Kliemann[1] (alias Killburg, alias Kylberg, alias "Monsieur Jean"), chief of the "Air Section" of this Service. The others belonging to this Service were: Pragel, who took Kliemann's place from August 15, 1944, on, Fuchs, Gerard and Overbeck. The latter had been at the head of the S.R.A. for the South of France (Marseille) and was killed in a railway accident, after which his place was taken by Graff.

The recruitment of agents, who were to communicate with the Germans after these had eventually fallen back from France, began as early as 1940. Major Kliemann, who had been my "boss" for two years, was an Austrian. He was not a member of the Nazi Party, and, curiously enough for a man occupying his situation, he didn't like the Germans. Yvonne Delidaise, Kliemann's mistress, was a "good girl without principles." Since her mother was German, she didn't consider it wrong to betray France which was only half her country. Her brother, Richard Delidaise, alias Dugratien, born in 1912 at Hensy, in Belgium, was, in 1935, barman at the mess of the 104th Air Base in Le Bourget. According to his sister, he was already working for the Germans. Immediately after the occupation of Paris, he entered

Major Kliemann's service as chauffeur-interpreter. From October 1940 to January 1941, he went through a radio course at number 70 Avenue Foch, after which he became instructor at the S.R.A.

All the names of persons and places in this story are real. If for one reason or another I didn't want to give someone's name, I put initials or a name without a surname, but never have I used fictitious names.

—L.S. (ca. late 1947)

I

Beirut to Paris, 1940–1942

BEIRUT, 1940

Babs lifts up the shaggy truffle of his nose; his liquid-amber eyes look at me inquiringly. Standing on his hindlegs he looks over the window-sill into the garden. His comprehensive eyes seem to say: "Everything's O.K. The neighbour's cat doesn't venture near. I see to it! No beggars trying to get in. What worries you?"

Mechanically I run my hand over his wiry coat. "You can't understand," I tell him. "In your kingdom there is peace, but France is defeated!" And harshly I repeat: "Defeated!"

How many days is it since that evening—late in the evening, almost night—when a doctor friend of ours came in haggard faced saying: "France has capitulated! France isn't fighting anymore!" I was in bed. Pulling up a wrapper, I rushed to the hall where my friends had preceded me. I heard Leone D. say: "It isn't possible!" A silence fell when I appeared. Three dismal faces turned towards me.

"What is the matter?" I asked.

It's then, that the doctor came forward and said: "France has capitulated—France isn't fighting anymore!"

And, before I knew what I was doing, I had slapped him across the face. "It is not true! France will never capitulate—NEVER, do you hear?" and slamming the door, I ran out. Well, it was known the next day that the Armistice was signed. Then, for a short while, we were dissidents.

During that time we lived in the exaltation and hope that the fight would be continued in spite of everything: IN SPITE OF THE TREASON of the ones and the cowardice of the others; that regardless of the occupation of France, the seizure of the metropolis, the fight would go on overseas, wherever there would be a Frenchman. And then Syria and Lebanon, in turn, had signed the Armistice.

That is what I am thinking of, looking at the garden. And everything seems confused in my mind, for I cannot accept the fact of France vanquished. My brain refuses to imagine Paris crowded with Germans: feld grau[1] uniforms strolling along the Champs-Elysées, or sitting at the terrace tables of cafes, the Swastika floating instead of French colours. I feel that, up to now, I have not hated them, but at the thought of Germans parading their masterdom about Paris, I shake with powerless rage and hatred. It is not possible that, because a government has signed some paper, all those who want to fight for their country, who are ready, are strong and have not yet had a chance, should be obliged to lay down arms. There must be some sort of solution. But where? Which?

The garden is motionless, crushed under the mid-day sun. Noises from Beyrouth[2] come from the distance. October is here; it is hot; the sky is cloudless. The twisted mimosa-tree is in blossom again. The thick apricot-tree is casting a round shadow in which we hung a hammock. The flowers have died from lack of watering. "Our" flowers we were so proud of, Leone and I (but, really, we had other things to do besides watering them) and their heads droop mournfully at the end of dried-up stems. Only the thin fountain-jet continues to spout in the centre of the basin and the goldfish to turn round and round. The leaves of the banana-trees are splitting and I notice that we have forgotten to pick the oranges.

All the office-friends I have met today are gloomy, depressed. I asked: "What are you going to do?" To this all of them reply with a shrug of discouragement. Lieutenant G. said to me: "I'll return home and plough my fields." As he is a career officer, I protested: "You cannot quit the Army at such a moment. You haven't the right to do it!"

To that he retorted: "What can a defeated army do with its officers?"

I wish I were a man! It seems to me I would have known what to do!

It is feared there may be trouble in the army. Too many unoccupied, idle men: soldiers who have left everything to fight and who are told about the defeat before they have had time to take up arms. Cases of soldiers refusing to salute their officers on the street occur more and more often. There has been fighting between civilian Lebanese and French soldiers.

I've given up going to the Medical Faculty and neglect the dispensary. Now all that seems so useless. I tell myself that I have remained in Beyrouth and graduated for my S.B.M. diploma to join the Expeditionary Corps which was to leave for the Balkans.[3] Now, all my efforts have been in vain. And here I am alone, worthless, so far away, so very far from France, from Paris. The whole length of the Mediterranean separates me from them. I don't even know if I should like to return—at the mere thought of Paris OCCUPIED, all desire vanishes. On the other hand, I hate the easy life out here when I think of the privations they endure over there. Last winter, I know, has been very cold. What will this one be like? I am without any news from my family. I'm torn between the desire to return to them and the temptation to go over to Palestine. More and more army men join the dissidence.

I had an idea, which seems so impossible that I hardly dare to consider it. I think of it since two days. At night, in bed, the lights out, I make plans and everything seems quite simple! But in the morning, by broad daylight, my schemes appear to me mad or childish. There are things one reads about in books, but which do not happen in real life.

I am alone. No one in whom to confide, whom to ask for advice. On the other hand I have the impression that if I explained what I intend to do, one would laugh at it. Having written this sentence, I realize that, without noticing it, I have made a decision: to try my luck. Here is my idea. During my foot trip from Paris to Warsaw, I got acquainted with a journalist from the Baltic provinces by the name of Dassel—Felix Dassel. He had been interested in my wanderings and had written articles about me. I saw him again during temporary stays in Berlin. Then I made a sudden discovery. Under the pseudo-journalist was hiding the recruiting agent of the German Intelligence. This was three years ago. I haven't seen him since. It's of him I am thinking: to get enlisted into the German Secret-Service and then perhaps to be able to help those who carry on the fight. How? I don't know yet. The dimly outlined scheme is already taking shape.

Yesterday, I was telling myself that perhaps I ought to go to the British Embassy to explain the possibilities I have, tell them what I intend to do and come to an agreement with them. But this morning, having thought it over, I have regretfully given up this plan as being too risky. The Embassy is sure to be strictly watched, and I should be marked down from the start.

I get on my faithful "Tott '38," my lovely "duralumin" bike and followed by Babs, I take the road along the sea, amid olive-trees which leads to Saida. We don't go very far. A short cut through an olive grove brings us on a beach of white sand. There is no one in sight except, in the distance, an armed sentry who seems to have been put in that quiet spot to remind one of war. The soldier doesn't trouble us.

Babs frolics in the waves. Laying "Tott '38" at my feet, I sit down on the warm sand. I say good-bye to everything surrounding me: to the blue sky, the vast sea, to the locusts, to the vibrating air, to the majestic Lebanon, raising its peaks behind me, to this country where I have been happy and which I am about to leave. For it is done: I have applied for repatriation and am to embark the day after tomorrow. It seems so near!

The infamous Babs, Lily's beloved dog, who was the source of problems between Lily and the British Secret Service, held by Lily's father, Serguei Vassilievitch Sergueiew (KV 2/466, The National Archives of the United Kingdom).

NOVEMBER 23RD, 1940

The *Mariette-Pacha* with all its bulky mass towers above the deserted quay. A little farther on, the *Champollion* raises its gray silhouette. The engines have just been set in motion and are sending a throb through the whole vessel—like an awakening animal. We are not moving yet, but we are going to. Leaning against the bulwark, I am crushed by the compact multitude of soldiers and officers crowded on the deck. They are sixteen hundred men, returning to France. How much this departure differs from an ordinary one! No crowd gathering on the piers: no friends, no relations waving good-bye, no hands extended, no farewell.

The decks of the *Mariette-Pacha* are so silent that one might think they are deserted. One is quite surprised to see these hundreds of khaki uniforms at a standstill and these hundreds of set faces all turned in the same direction. Down below, on the pavement of the quay, two sailors are coming towards us. A policeman marches in front of customs. The gangway has been lifted some time ago. I am looking at the water, in the narrow space between the pier and us, beating the side of the ship. The water reflects the sky and appears infinitely distant. The windlasses are revolving making a din releasing the cables which link us to the land. The sailors unfasten the moorings from the spur-posts and pull them aboard. We are kept fast by a single cordage. Slowly, the bow of the *Mariette-Pacha* leaves the quay. The last cordage stretches, tightens, comes out of the water sending up a shower of drops—like a shaking dog. For a few moments the ship remains like that—a tight rope between us and Lebanon. But we have veered about sufficiently. Now the windlasses reverse, the cordage loosens, hangs like a gigantic skipping-rope. The sailor, on the quay, unfastens its end and letting go drops it into the water wherein it sinks.

I gaze at the liquid band; it is getting wider and wider until, finally, it ceases to be a band—to become the sea. The sailors on the quay, having performed their duty, are going away without waiting to see us start. The *Champollion* has already got the advance. Beyrouth grows, stretches out as the distance increases. The great Seraglio rises about the roofs. The mountains which appeared cramped seem to rise. I can see all of the blue road zigzagging between the fir-trees. Up there is Aley, then comes the narrow pass, beyond which one goes down to the plain of the Becka. Then, it is Anti-Lebanon and Damascus. Then, the desert. "No, no," I say to myself, "I mustn't regret anything!"

And I look at Beyrouth which now is decreasing. Through the railing Babs is looking too. We are alone on the deck because the other passengers don't want to miss their lunch. Already, I cannot distinguish the houses. The town is nothing but a light spot at the foot of the bluish mountains. Little by little, the sky and the water converge on the land crushing it from above, from below, clipping off more, reducing it to a narrow strip which gets thinner and thinner, becomes dim, hazy, disappears. The sky and the sea, having engulfed the land, close up over it forming an immense blue Infinity.

November 26th

The weather has kept fine ever since we have left. One scarcely notices that the air is getting fresher. I spend my days on the upper-deck avoiding the first-class and promenade-deck, for the purser has taken a sudden and violent dislike to Babs and me. I am travelling in the "2nd Intermediate." Just fancy! Wheedling about that, calling it "2nd intermediate." Why not simply say "3rd class?" It is over there, at the stern of the boat, quite at the back near the engines. One must go down innumerable iron steps—one could say break-neck-ladders—to reach the cabin I share with the cook of an attaché, two other women and hundreds of cockroaches! Every evening I have to hide Babs to take him to my cabin because my enemy, the purser, intends to keep him on the upper deck. Aviators from the next-door cabin help me by their complicity.

On the boat, however, there is a general mix-up. Sometimes we get ahead, and sometimes it's the *Champollion*. We share the risk to blow up on a mine.

November 27th

I got the permission to settle down on the quarter-deck. I have spread out my rug in a quiet corner and am lying in the sun. I try not to think. I banish from my mind the riddle of tomorrow, the reminiscence of yesterday. Suddenly it seems to me I see a spark on the horizon. I rub my eyes and look again. I see it again once, twice, three times.

Then I notice that the commander and all his staff are leveling their spy-glasses at a spot in that direction. Passengers, on other decks, have stopped their stroll and are gazing intently. It's just after ten o'clock. A few moments pass. It seems to me I can see tiny black specks growing rapidly. Half an hour elapses. Already I can distinguish the outline of naval units. Those who have spy-glasses say the battle-ships are going at full speed; it shows by the black smoke spreading low on the surface of the water. The rumour is they are Italian units on the run before the Britishers. Presently dull gunshots can be heard: fire tongues flash in rapid succession from the warships.

As they draw nearer to us, the noise increases and men running about the deck can be seen. Nine grey vessels are heading for us. Their guns are firing at some invisible enemy. From beyond the horizon, other cannon-shots are fired. Shells drop around the Italian ships; they drop into the sea with a splash and raise sheaves of water. A plane comes whirling overhead. The anti-aircraft polka dots the sky with numberless tiny black puffs. I look at the Champollion ahead of us, dangerously bending to starboard, dragged down by the weight of two thousand spectators, all crowded on the same side of the ship.

It appears that the Italians have first ordered us to get out of their way and then to stop. We are there, in the middle of the battle, like two clumsy mastodons, turning round and round. Enthusiasm is boundless on board our ship. Everybody sides up against the Italians. Soldiers have climbed on top of the life boats and up the rigging. They are calling out indications to the invisible shooters: "More to the right!"—"More to the left!"—"Missed! Oh! D..... it! Oooh!"

Suddenly one of the officers exclaims: "Quick, look here, one of them is hit!"

I turn round in time to see the stern of a ship sinking into the sea. That was quick work! Its disappearance is greeted by a storm of applause. By degrees, the Italians have taken shelter behind us. Ahead of us the horizon disappears behind a curtain of artificial smoke. Another unit outrides us by starboard. The Italians have vanished; the cloud of smoke is dispelling. The Britishers seem to have given up their pursuit. It has been going on for nearly two hours. We resume our course. Some way farther we come across a burning vessel. A recognision plane is hovering above it. We pass.

Babs is stretching himself. But I am displeased with Babs. At every shell passing overhead with a whizz, he flopped down and closed his eyes. He has not proved gallant!

November 28th

The wind sweeps the rough surface of the sea carrying the foam and lashing it against the smoking-room windows. In the distance, the familiar silhouette of Notre-Dame de la Garde outlines white against the black sky, rising high above the chalky cliffs. Huge breakers crush against them. For an hour we have been trying to enter the port of Marseille. The *Mariette-Pacha* rolls and pitches. The furniture creaks. Through the wet panes the horizon goes up and down. It is freezing outside: -14 degrees.[4] The deck is slippery. Icicles hang along the cables and the riggings.

Inside, too, it is cold. There are few people in the smoking room. A few soldiers—their collars turned up, their kepis on and their noses red—looking through the window at the slowly approaching coast. The door opens to admit a newcomer; a blast of icy wind slams it behind him. The other passengers are still in their cabins, packing or sea-sick.

As time passes, the smoking room fills up. I study the surrounding faces and try to guess what goes on in their minds. These are Frenchmen going back to France—to defeated, occupied France—with the intention of doing … what? Has he accepted the defeat, that fat ferocious major, with his black moustache? Has he submitted, this sunburned, sad looking young Lieutenant? Has he surrendered, this rough, prematurely bald soldier? And this Air Force sergeant, rubbing his hands—numb with cold—has he given up too? Have they all accepted, these returning men, to live as tolerated citizens in a country which is their own? I try to imagine them in civilian clothes—anonymous amongst an anonymous crowd. But, maybe, behind these blank eyes expressing nothing but weariness at waiting, plans of fight and sabotage are ripening. Perhaps, these soldiers returning to be discharged only want to be free to fight the better. Maybe, they too, are returning in order to serve their country, serve it to the end, until the last German has left the soil of France. Suddenly I feel less lonely … bound by a common aim to all these strangers.

December 1st, 1940[5]

At last I am seated in a 3rd class compartment. We are ten. Luggage is everywhere: in the nets, under the benches, beneath our feet. And on my lap: Babs. The passengers are waiting in silence for the train to start. Many of those people have already known three, four such departures. They went as far as Lyons, Moulins, and then were driven back by a counter-order, or because the rail-track was not clear. They were parked for days and finally sent back to Marseille. It might be the same thing this time. They are resigned; haven't they known the "exodus?" They wait in silence.

I close my eyes. The excitement of the return: the landing from the *Mariette-Pacha* onto the quay swept by the freezing Mistral; five days spent in an unknown town crowded with discharged soldiers, where all the hotels were full; the luck to have found a room all to myself thanks to the friends of a Corsican lieutenant I had met aboard. A sordid room, on the third floor of a port brothel. Those unforgettable nights, stretched all dressed on an iron bed with filthy sheets. And Babs bristling and growling at the door some drunkard tried to open; unsteady steps along the dark, narrow passage; cries on the stairway, swearing of a drunken female. At dawn, as the bleak day-light entered through the curtainless dirty window, things one by one emerged from the darkness: the chair with a board replacing the broken seat, the iron washstand and its chipped basin, a ring of dirt round the border. And then, in the centre of the floor, my tan leather suitcase and hat-box like lost islets in the midst of these unfriendly surroundings. All this has worn me out. For three days I haven't washed and scarcely slept at all. To cheer up, I remind myself I was lucky enough to have been able to get on this first train. I owe it to a letter of recommendation of the High Commissioner Puaux to the Prefect of the Bouches-du-Rhône. But, already, all this appears like a bad dream. Wearily I lean against the hard back of the seat trying to think about the future, about tomorrow, about Paris I'm going to see again, about my people.

I didn't notice when the train started to move. My neighbours are silent. Gradually I doze off. And I see Paris as I left it in September 38.[6] The familiar aspects of the city rise in my mind, one by one, sights one notices so little when there, but which acquire such significance when one is far away. Then, I try to picture the actual Paris: the Champs-Elysées empty. All the shops closed. The deserted café terraces. The closed restaurants. The emptiness of a dead city sounding hollow under the German heel. I don't doubt for a moment that all trade, traffic, business have ceased in the conquered capital. I feel sadistic pleasure at the thought that the conqueror will be frustrated of Paris' luxury, gaiety, night life. There will be nothing for them, nothing but hatred, silence, and contempt.

The train rolls on with jerks. Babs is getting impatient and wants to move to another place. The passengers have taken out their provisions; they eat and talk. Gradually, one

I. Beirut to Paris, 1940–1942

gets acquainted, for who knows how many days we'll have to spend together. I go to sleep again. A jolt wakes me up. We are in Lyons. The night is dark. Everybody is concerned. "It's here they have unhooked us last time," says a fat woman. Our chief of convoy reassures us. We are allowed to go to the restaurant. The place is warm, light and noisy. Only now, I begin to realize that I am in France, back after two and a half years of absence.

I'm hungry but have no ration-tickets. In Marseille I was given small squares of coloured paper and was told that they were good for a fortnight. Not knowing how to use them, I left them all at the restaurant. A young blonde—my compartment neighbor—offers to give me some, but I refuse not knowing their value. I eat some soup and an apple. We are off again. At 1 a.m. we stop at St-Germain-des-Fossés. Our railway carriages are unhooked and side-tracked. It is bitterly cold. Time drags. Now and then, the blonde girl and I take a run on the platform to get warm. The station-bar is open but it isn't heated. The only beverage to be had is lukewarm mint-tea.

We return to our compartment and try to sleep. I put my suitcase and my hat-box between the benches and stretch upon them. Holding Babs close to me, I doze off. I dream of Beyrouth, palm-trees and warm sand. But the sand gets cold, the wind starts blowing, and I wake up, frozen stiff. And so it goes until 7 o'clock, when our train is hooked on and we resume our journey.

Moulins. Here I come across the first German France: Frozen soldiers, furious to be disturbed at such an early hour. Outside everything is covered with frost. It is -17 degrees.[7] We are called out and counted over like cattle. What puzzles me is that the Nazi-officer begins, addressing us, by the word "Bienvenue." Which means "Welcome." Coming from a German, I find it impertinent.

We have been warned it is forbidden to carry letters, but I could not make up my mind to destroy the ones I have in my pockets. There is one from a gendarme to his fiancée. One, from a waiter to his mother; one from "madam Lavatory" to a niece or sister. One from a Marseille porter to his brother, and so on. Nine letters: all of them to unknown people—from people I do not know.

We go through the customs formalities in less than an hour but our luggage is not searched. The Germans seem to be in a hurry to return to their well-heated offices. Our train starts again. We all look at each other: how lucky! We are over the demarcation line. My heart is full of joy and sadness with a shade of apprehension.

Post scriptum. I have found out the answer as to why the Germans were "welcoming" us; in our compartment an old spinster whose surname Bienvenue was at the head of the list.

SAME DAY—LATER ON

The agony of these last hours! The watch seems to slow down and the train to crawl. After having left Moulins, we were informed that we would be detoured by Dijon. There we would have to wait for the Paris train leaving tomorrow. Then we are told we'd be hooked onto a through freight train which eventually should bring us to our destination at about 10 p.m. We agree to everything without comment, unable to discuss for sheer weariness. However, we haven't been deviated or unhooked, and suddenly, in one of the stations, I see: Fontainebleau. Only sixty more kilometers, and it will be Paris! Good Lord! It seems miles away!

And then we are there: the Gare de Lyon![8] I step out on the platform, hesitating, feeling so stupidly upset. I find myself face to face with a fat jovial porter whose red face contrasts with the blue colour of his cover-all. "Had a fine journey?" he asks me. His face shines, his mouth spreads into a wide smile showing gold teeth.

Such a joy overcomes me all of a sudden that I fall on his neck and kiss him. He is amazed. Confused, I try to explain: "It's three years I haven't seen Paris. That I've been away from France. So, you see, you … you represent all that!" He nods his head knowingly. Without understanding, it flatters him to think he represents France although I must seem crazy to him.

The station clock says 3:35 p.m. The man collects my luggage. As there are no taxis, he'll carry it to my home. We plunge into the underground. Babs is in my arms, well concealed in my coat. In the rush, the handle of my suitcase breaks. The porter catches it by the straps but in turn they give way. I am so happy, nothing could disturb me. We proceed. One more change—at the Gare-Saint-Lazare—and we are at Brochant, and home. The concierge throws up her arms on seeing me and shrieks with joy, exclaiming: "Oh! Mademoiselle! Won't your Mother be happy!" But I make her promise not to tell Mummy I have come back: I want to get the benefit of the surprise.

The flat is empty and cold. In places the wallpaper is puffed with dampness and hangs. In the bathroom the towels are damp. I am terribly hungry. In the kitchen the larder is empty. I find a piece of Genoa-cake in the cupboard. Although it is stale, I am on the point of eating it, when it strikes me that it may be a ration on which they reckon, and I leave it. There is also some jam at the bottom of a jar. That is all.

It is half past four. Mummy and Daddy won't be back before seven. To pass the time, I unpack the presents I have brought: 2lb. coffee, salami, two large cakes of soap, some sugar, rice, cigarettes, a big box of Damascus candied fruit and a Syrian dressing gown.

The key turns, the entrance door opens. Mummy comes in. She holds the milk-can—with half a pint of skimmed milk. Stopping she looks, flabbergasted, at Babs who examines her with surprise, distrust and a certain amount of discontent. I rush up to her, seizing in time the milk jar which she is dropping. Mummy laughs and cries, repeating over and over again: "You … you … you…" between kisses. And even would she want to say something else, she could not do it because of the kisses I am showering on her.

We are now reunited, all the three of us—or rather: all four, because already Babs is part to the family. We are in the dining-room with closed doors and the small electric heater switched on. In spite of that, we keep our coats on, and our breath makes a dense steam in the cold air. Mummy brings out some preserved eggs and Daddy opens a bottle of Champagne. It's quite a celebration! A real festive day.

December 27th, 1940

I didn't want to do anything before Christmas. I have allowed myself three weeks of holidays—deceptive three weeks during which I have renewed contact with Paris. How different is reality from what one dreams. The German occupation has but little altered the outward aspect of the city. Cafes and restaurants are crowded with Huns. Dealers compete as to who will sell "them" more things. The "Boches" are rifling the perfumery-shops, buying up all wine and liquors they can get at, as well as silk underwear and stockings. Everybody talks about "black Market." I don't quite realize yet what it is. I haven't found the collusion against the enemy I had expected. "Each one for himself" seems to be today's slogan. I am disappointed.

I. Beirut to Paris, 1940–1942

If I succeed in my enterprise, I shall be alone, utterly alone. I won't be able to trust anyone and shall have to beware of everyone. The letter is written. I have turned it over and over again, read and re-read it. There is but one sentence that counts: "I intend returning shortly to Syria." I do not suggest, not do I offer anything. That is the bait. On these few words depends the future.

It has to work out. All my will is concentrated on it. I can just imagine Dassel (as it is to him I am writing) receiving my letter. I can see him tearing the envelope: "Hey! It's from Lily!" Reading, and then coming to that sentence: "I intend returning shortly to Syria." "Hmm! Hmm! Hmm! Interesting, very interesting. There may be something in it." That is how it will be, because it must be so.

I remember the time, before the war, when Felix and I were friends. Am I now going to exploit his friendship in using him against his country? It is for him to decide. If he chooses to make use of me against France, I don't need have any remorse. This is his chance. I stick to my plan and the purpose of my letter. Presently I go out, up to the Avenue de Clichy and to the mail-box. I don't register it: an ordinary letter ... a very, very, ordinary letter.

January 17th, 1941

Three weeks have gone and still no answer. There are days when I doubt my luck. So many things may have happened: my letter got lost; Dassel has moved, or has enlisted, or is dead. But I shake my head. I know it is not so. No, he is alive and has received my letter. Well, I must wait. Patience!—I'll need a limitless amount of it if I want to succeed.

To kill the time I go to a hospital where a friend of mine—a surgeon—is willing to admit me into the operating room. The patients are mostly wounded soldiers. Many are amputated: men who are young, robust, strong, and have lost an arm, a leg, or both sometimes. And the defeat weighs heavier when I see the price we have paid ... in vain.

January 21st

"A pneumatic for you." Mummy hands me the thin blue envelope. The writing doesn't suggest anything to me. I tear off the perforated margin. There are only two lines: "Should like to see you tomorrow 11 a.m. at Maxim's. Felix."

I feel my heart stop, while a cry of triumph and victory rises from the depth of my being. However, I am able to conceal my joy. My hands are not shaking when, folding the message, I put it in my pocket. And to Mummy asking: "Good news?" I reply casually: "A girlfriend who wants to see me."

Tomorrow belongs to me!

January 22nd

I arrive half an hour before time. When I realize it, I take a walk round the Madeleine, but the pavement is slippery. It is terribly cold. I enter the "Trois Quartiers"[9] where I rush through the departments without seeing anything.

God! How nervous and frightened I am! I am scared to death to mess things. I try to think of something else and reach Maxim's at five past eleven. Felix is already there, to the left of the revolving door. For a few seconds we look at each other without speaking. Then he gets up and stretches out his hand: "Good! Very good. You look fine and happy. Come, sit down." Felix has changed. His thick blond hair—without losing any of its opulence—has turned grey. He has grown stouter, has more wrinkles and resembles Goering less.[10]

The terror I felt a short time ago has left me, never to return again. I have a vague feeling that the game I am up to surpasses me, that its issue is settled in advance, that I have nothing to fear. Dassel is no longer a friend. He's a chess pawn I have to move to win the game. I take a place on the red velvet seat beside him. "I expected to see you in uniform," I say.

"In uniform? Surely, you don't mean it."

We talk about all kind of things: his wife, his children, the war, Berlin. But we both know that it isn't what has brought us here—only he doesn't know that I know!

He makes a sign to the waiter and asks me what I'll take. He speaks bad French and makes coarse jokes. I suddenly feel ashamed, infinitely ashamed for the obsequious waiter, ashamed for the Frenchman he is, ashamed to be sitting at one table with a German. And I am humiliated by the contempt which perhaps the waiter has for me. It is stupid pride, I tell myself. I must get used to it, for God knows I shall have to trample it!

"And what do you thing about the British?" asks Felix without seeming to attach any importance to his question.

This is what I was waiting for: the anodyne sentence that will link all the rest. I had so often imagined the way he'd say it, that now, hearing, it, I don't know if it is his voice, or the voice of my mind who utters it. Although I've thought of it a lot, I refrained from preparing an answer. I was too afraid it would seem artificial. I say: "I think that I owe those bastards because I have been obliged to interrupt my journey. It is they who have drawn France in the war. They are the cause of our defeat! And then, I am fed up, fed up, I tell you! I am sick of being hungry, of being cold! You understand why I want to go back to Syria. Do you understand it?" And to brace myself up, I swallow my port.

Dassel is turning between his fingers his half-filled glass, staring at it. He lifts it, puts it down again and faces me. "Don't let's beat around the bush! You're too smart for that. You've guessed what I am driving at?"

I look at him an instant before I say: "I hate riddles."

"Do you want to work with us against the British?"

"I don't wish to remain in France."

"Who is talking about remaining in France? You want to go to Syria? Excellent idea. You can be very useful to us over there."

"I thought you offered me work *against the British*? What have they to do with Syria?"

He pats my hand with a protective air: "France doesn't exist anymore, my dear. War is between Germany and England."

"What am I to do?"

"Report on the movements of troops. Traffic between Palestine and Turkey. Activity of the Beyrouth harbor, and so on. The particulars will be given to you before you start." He said: "Will be given to you"—as if the question was settled. He was right.

"All right. I accept."

We shake hands and he says: "I knew it!" And to the waiter: "Garçon, a bottle of Champagne."

"Babs, come quick, look here: this hand—the right one—is French, English, in short allied. This one, the left … let me whisper it in your ear: it's the Fifth Column! And look: the right hand shakes the left one: "Pleased to meet you." Now, the left clasps the right one:

"Ach! Du lieber Freund!"[11] And they both work together." Babs appreciates the game and tries to snatch alternatively my hands. I take him on my knees, on the drawing-room sofa, and I say in his pink ear: "It's a fine game, it's a grand game but, you know, if we lose it, we'll lose our lives … mine, at any rate."

I must get accustomed to this thought: death. I must accept it entirely, totally, so that it can never stand between the risk and me—interfere with my work. Then, everything will be easy—once apprehension of death is eliminated. Tomorrow I am to see Dassel at the same place.

January 23rd

"Had a good night's rest? Not too nervous?" asks Felix.

"Nervous? What about?"

"That's right. You've got steady nerves. So much the better. Let's get to the point. Can you come with me to Berlin?"

"When?"

"Tomorrow."

"Difficult."

"Why?"

"You know that I am staying with my parents. It won't be difficult to find some excuse to get away from Paris for a few days: see a girl-friend in the country, for instance. Only there is that it's my birthday on the 25th and no one would ever believe that I'd go away that day. All the more, I haven't mentioned it yet."

"Right you are. Do you think you could get away on the 26th?"

"Yes."

"Then, that's settled. Now you need a permit and some money. Presently, one of our girls will bring the papers you'll have to fill out. Everything will be ready by Saturday."

Shortly after, a *Gretchen* arrives. She is tall, fair and resembles Greta Garbo. I have to fill-in two large sheets of endless questions. And all the time, there is that waiter hanging around. God! How ashamed I am! Greta Garbo leaves with all *my curriculum vitae*. We remain for a while. I am in a hurry to go home. I'll not see Felix again before he returns to Berlin. He'll come to meet me at the Zoo-Bahnhof station when I arrive. (Everything goes too well!)

January 24th

I told Moussia[12] my secret. My little sister neither seemed scared, nor did she ask questions. "Are you sure it'll help?" was all she said.

"Irch Allah!"[13] I answered with a reminiscence of Syria.

"Can I help you?"

"No. That is to say: yes, you can. I should like to move to your flat this evening. At home, I have told them I'm going to spend a few days at a girlfriend's. I have to take the Berlin train tomorrow morning, at seven. I'll ask you also to take care of Babs while I am away."

"You can leave him."

JANUARY 26TH

The alarm rings. Babs growls. I sit up in my bed trying to understand where I am. Memory returns. In the dark I grope for the switch, put on the light. It is a quarter past five. My room is cold because of the open window. The apartment is asleep. The house is asleep. Outside the night is dark and it is freezing. I am dressed in a jiffy and thrust my pajamas in a small suitcase. I verify my papers and count the money "Greta Garbo" had brought me yesterday.

Through the half-open door appears Moussia's sleepy little face. "Have made some coffee for you. Come quick and drink it." I scold her and go to the kitchen where it is warm. I swallow in a hurry the barley beverage, which they call coffee, and eat a piece of tobacco-coloured bread.

A silence follows. I don't know what this journey has in reserve for me. I don't tell myself that, maybe, all this is chimerical, crazy. My only thought is to get in time to the station, get my ticket, and find a seat in the train. Babs is restless—as always when he sees a suitcase. His eyes implore me. My caresses are useless. He looks at me reproachfully. I hate when Babs looks at me like that. I also hate to leave him behind. The time has come to leave.

"Take care of yourself and succeed," says Moussia, kissing me good-bye.

"I shall succeed."

Then, bending, I lift Babs and say, holding him in my arms: "I'll come back. And when I'm back, we shall have progressed. And so, little by little, we'll haul in the rope. Good-bye and be good. I entrust you to my little sister."

Snow covers the Avenue Henri-Martin and makes the night less black. A few dim silhouettes make haste towards the underground. An anonymous clock strikes six. I hurry. Inside the underground time suspends its flight; there is no longer day, nor night, evening, nor morning. I reach in time the Gare du Nord, take a ticket and find a seat. The train starts. How little this journey resembles last month's. From my first-class compartment I look at the landscape unreeling before my eyes. In spots the snow has melted; the wet meadows and hedges shine.

It is a splendid day. I remember dreaming of all this in Syria, longing for the gentle green slopes of the meadows, the limpid brooks bordered by stumpy willows, the grayness of the bare trees and this pale rain-washed sky. Over there, in Syria, under the burning sun, casting blue shadows, I felt the nostalgia of the autumn mist, of the rustling dead leaves in which sink the feet. Nostalgia of the grey winter clouds, of spring, of delicate buds bursting open, of the tiny tender green leaflets—varnished, fragrant, unfolding, spreading, covering everything: trees, bushes, ground. Now, it is for the sun I crave. My thoughts turn to Damascus—green oasis on the border of the yellow desert; to Aleppo, raising its citadel in the dazzling sky to Palmyra with its palm tree groves.

Brussels—Liege—

I must put some order in my ideas. I must work out a plan of action. I'll have to make "them" accept the idea of meeting in Ankara. I think it will be easy enough for me to do this trip, as I have a cousin in Turkey. There I shall get in touch with the British! I already know Moran, at the British Embassy. He will tell me what to do and who to see. This is, I think, the best solution.

We reach the border by night. The train stops. Everybody has to get out. I stand in line, my red pass in the hand. No difficulties whatsoever, although the employees are gruff and irascible. My suitcase is superficially examined. In spite of that, I have the impression that everyone is looking at me. People must wonder why I am there and draw conclusions. As time passes, my uneasiness increases and I wish I could disappear under the earth. At last, escorted by S.S., we are authorized to return to our compartments.

Outside, the dawn is breaking and all is white with snow. I have slept, stretched out on the seat, and remember vaguely people coming in during the night. I believe someone even tried to sit on the place beside me, because I remember kicking. Groping in the dark, I tidy my clothes, then lift the blind which goes up with a jerk flooding the compartment with garish morning light. It's early yet, not quite half past seven. The train is late.

I examine my travelling companions: two civilians and three officers. The civilians must have gotten on to the train recently; they are wide-awake and start a conversation as soon as I have pulled up the blind. They are stout and fat, with heavy jaws, thick noses and highly-shaved napes. One has close-cropped hair. The other is bald, with a kind of part in the middle smoothly brushed down fringe on top of his head. Both carry leather portfolios. Business-men, no doubt.

The three officers sleep in different positions. The one near the window, with fine-quality boots, has crossed his legs and propped his chin on a clenched fist. This makes him a prognostic jaw and gives him a ferocious look. The middle one, slouching on the seat, has stretched his legs in front of him and folded his arms. His head is lowered on his chest, and I can only see the top of his skull and his fair thinning hair. At each breath, his head lifts slightly with a deep snore. The third officer is snoring on a high note, head thrown back and open mouth. He is extremely young, despite his two decorations, despite his grade of lieutenant, despite the little moustache he must have had difficulty to grow. His hands are white and slender. He has rosy cheeks, and a curl hangs over his childish forehead. I try to guess his age: sixteen at the utmost? At this very moment, he wakes up, meets my gaze and sits up, vexed, trying to put some order in his appearance. He seems furious to have been seen asleep. So furious, he is on the verge of tears, and I doubt he is even fifteen.

We are nearing Berlin. I look out of the window and only begin to realize where I am at the sight of a snow-covered aerodrome, where the aeroplanes resemble huge night-moths. I am in the heart of Germany. Lots of people would give a great deal to find access to it. I am sorry not to have gotten in touch with the British yet to take full advantage of the opportunity. There might be things I could do already. But I tell myself, one can't have everything. One has to sacrifice the less important in order to get the most important. It's possible I'll have to remain inactive for a long time and get firmly established in the place and acquire freedom of action. I'll have to gain insidiously "their" confidence—sometimes at the price of hard concessions. I'll have to lie, lie... That's what worries me: I loathe lies! Shall I be able to pull through? It seems to me that if, some day, "they" tell me abruptly: "You are double crossing us!" I'll reply: "Yes."

Around me the travelers are beginning to stir. The officers are putting on their fur-lined coats; the two civilians have left the compartment and are standing in the passage. It's twenty-five past nine. The train slows down, then stops. I get up and pick up my suitcase. My legs are numb and my back is stiff from twenty-five hours on the train. Outside the cold seizes me. I look around for Dassel and don't see him. It's useless to wait; he has not come. I am not surprised; it's too early for him. I go down the steps and am in the street. Everything is white with snow—a snow different from that of Paris: dry and brittle. The tyres have crushed and polished it; the road is hard and glistening.

I pass under the railway-bridge and turn on the Kurfürstendamm. To my great surprise, there are taxis, but I decide to walk. Although the Fasanenstrasse is quite near, my hands are frozen when I reach the No. 68. I climb up to the fifth floor and ring the bell. Dassel himself opens the door, and Sigrid, his wife, is behind him.

"There she is at last!" exclaims Felix. "We are waiting for you."

I look at him, as if I expected to find a change since last time. But he still has the same air of propelling his belly. He still smokes using glass cigarette-holders. Presently, he'll take out a dozen of them, will put them on the table, clean them, stuff a bit of cotton-wool into each one to filter the nicotine and then arrange them in an empty cigarette-box: his provision for the day. I remember every gesture of his.

Sigrid hasn't changed either. The same small-featured narrow and pale little face. Same blond hair she has never cut. She is wearing it up, parted in the middle and pulled back tight. The children, on the contrary, have grown. Suddenly, I sense the awful feeling that I have no hatred towards them, and that, nevertheless, I am going to do them harm. I brush away this thought with wrath. Has war ever spared individuals? I recall my humiliation before the waiter at Maxim's. I remember the cold in all houses; the rutabaga at all the meals; the swastika on the Eiffel-Tower and on the Chambre des Députés. I carry in myself the hatred of a whole nation for the nation which has vanquished and enslaved her—a hatred which sweeps away all scruples, all personal feelings.

The flat is heated. Sigrid brings in some coffee. "It comes from Paris," claims Felix. The bread is white. There is butter on the table.

At eleven o'clock I meet Reichart: Herr Doktor Reichart. He walks in, shakes briskly my hand and tells me to sit down. We are in the dining-room: he, Dassel and myself. Reichart rubs his hands, numb with cold, blows on them to warm them up, then looks at me through his glasses with round pale-blue short-sighted eyes. He is about thirty-seven or forty years old, has a chubby face with red cheek-bones and pimples. His nose is slightly turned up; his thinning hair is light-brown. He glances at Dassel—a glance which seems to ask: "Do you think that she'll do?"

Dassel turns to me and says: "Herr Doktor does not speak French. I'll translate."

I could easily do without his translation, but I welcome it, because it will give me time between the questions and the answers. Besides, this is a mere coming in contact. Dassel, in a few words, explains how and when he met me, tells "Herr Doktor" about my foot and bicycle travels, wherefrom he draws conclusions of physical endurance, spirit of adventure, love of risk and heaps of other deductions—all to my advantage it appears. Reichart, without taking his eyes off me, nods approvingly. Under his scrutinizing gaze, I am on a culprit's stool. I seek strength, and find it, recalling images of Paris as it is at present: with hunger, cold and rutabaga prevailing. I defy his gaze looking straight into his eyes. Felix has stopped talking. Now Reichart addresses me in slow, measured terms: "You fully realize and have thought over what you are doing: entering the German Espionage Service?"

"Yes."

"You know there is no issue out of it, that the least digression is punished by death. You know that?"

"I do."

"Are you decided?"

"I am decided."

"Why do you want to work for us?"

Felix's translation gives me a few seconds respite and I reply: "War is between England and yourselves. Had I chosen England, I wouldn't be here. Playing off your card, I stake on the winner. This is the most evident. I could also add that I follow the lead of my sympathies, but I am aware that such a statement is valueless, although Felix can certify it. To tell you that I hate the British doesn't mean anything, unless you take my word for it, in which case you'll understand why I wish to work with you."

All the time Reichart is nodding in approval of what Dassel is translating—and all the while his eyes gaze at me. "All right," he says at last after a silence. "I shall refer it to my chiefs and see you tomorrow!"

Dassel accompanies him out. I remain alone. For a moment I close my eyes. I let myself go against the back of the chair. The entrance-door bangs. I sit up and smile at Felix who is coming back. "Well?" he says, patting me on the shoulder. "Pleased?"

"I don't know. He is very laconic. What do you think?"

"My dear, he is simply delighted!"

"He certainly hides it well!"

"It's a trick of the profession!"

It's true: the profession. My profession from now on. I too will learn to conceal—not to show anything. I don't go out as we have mutually agreed that I must avoid being seen.

January 28th, 1941

10.30 a.m. Reichart is here. He smiles as he holds out his hand. Good omen. He wants to know if I have thought of my plan of action. For me, two points are essential: to be able to go to Ankara and that it should be he who suggests it. I explain that before I met Dassel again, I had intended returning to Syria, where I thought of working as a nurse. My passport was issued in Beyrouth and stated I was a resident of that town. So I don't think there will be any difficulty in getting a visa. If need be, I could say I am returning there to get married.

"This seems a good idea. But, do you really intend getting married? This might be embarrassing."

"No, it would only be a pretext. All means are good. Isn't it so?"

He looks pleased: "Well, that's that: O.K. for the first part. Now, when over-there: to keep in touch? The simplest and most logic way: through the unoccupied zone. We can provide you with addresses."

"This solution isn't without handicaps. First: time—letters take ten to twelve days. Then, should anything develop in the Mediterranean area, I'd be cut off."

"That's right." His short-sighted eyes run over the map spread on the table in front of us. "A neutral country ... Bulgaria.... The most convenient for us would be Budapest."

I shrug my shoulders. "Why not simply Berlin?" I ask.

Lifting his eyes, Reichart gives me a dirty look through all the thickness of his lenses.

"Don't you know anyone in Ankara?" puts in Dassel. "Turkey would be the ideal place."

Last night, while Felix was rather drunk, I slipped an allusion about that cousin I have in Ankara, suggesting I could easily visit him. Now, he doesn't remember. He imagines the idea is his own, and I let him believe it.

"I do," I say evasively, "but I don't see that it can help. What do you want me to do? Send you letters at my cousin's address?"

"No. But you could go to see him. We could meet there." Dassel is quite carried away by "his" idea, explaining it to Reichart who listens with interest.

"I believe, you've got something there," finally says Reichart. And turning to me: "What do you think of it?"

"I think it's a good idea. Nothing could be more inconspicuous as to visit my cousin, being so near. But the Turkish police are a nuisance. The least move of a foreigner is watched. Impossible to meet in a café. Ankara is so artificial! One feels in it like in an aquarium."

"We could stop at the same hotel," says Dassel.

"It would be almost unavoidable. To my knowledge, there are only two of them: the Ankara-Palace and the Bellevue."

For two hours we discuss the "pros" and "cons." Particulars are worked out, such as an address and a code for counter-orders. "Sincere condolences" would mean "Impossible to come," in case I were prevented from keeping a date. The use of the pigeon-holes at the Ankara-Hotel to signal the numbers of our respective rooms, by leaving in them a note addressed to some nonexistent X, written on a bright coloured paper. And so on, and so on. Everything is decided and fixed, even the day of our first meeting: three months after I leave Paris.

At last the gathering is broken up. My head is bursting. My nerves are on edge. I have the sensation as if walking in a dream, or reciting a lesson rehearsed over and over again. After Reichart's departure, Dassel approaches the money question. But I am too tired and indifferent to bother about it. Therefore, I agree to everything he offers, simply drawing his attention to the fact that it might make me appear suspicious if I was known to carry too much money with me. He agrees and suggests 4,000 francs for my journey and 10,000 francs to take with me. If prices have not increased too much, over there, it will be sufficient to cover my expenses until we meet again.

I retire early to my hotel. In the large double-room with its windows looking over the Kurfürstendamm, I go to sleep without dreams, forgetting everything, the mind empty of problems and of doubts, accepting in advance this future I have set in motion, but which, some day, I might not be able to control.

—⚹—

Berlin, January 29th

There are two more men, besides Dassel and myself, around the dining-room table. Two newcomers, resembling old hawks. Without being introduced, they sit down, open their leather portfolios, take out phials, glass-tubes, paper, blotting paper, cotton-wool, tooth-picks, and immediately set to work. This is my first lesson in sympathetic ink writing.[14] It is quite an event! It counts in one's life!

I write it down here like a cookery recipe: One dissolves an antipyrine tablet of 0.1 in a tablespoonful of alcohol at 45°. Then one takes a little cotton-wool and rolls it tight round the end of a tooth-pick. Dipping it in the sub mentioned solution, one uses it for writing, holding it lightly and employing white, not too thin and un-glazed paper. It must dry for half an hour. After that one dips it in an alcohol-bath, then puts it between two sheets of blotting-paper placed on the marble of a mantelpiece, under press, and it dries again for two hours.

I go through the first part once, twice, three and four times. First it's the cotton-wool that doesn't hold; then, I press too hard when writing, or it is the end of the tooth-pick which scratches the paper. At last, the attempt is declared satisfactory and I am told to bathe, dry and press my sheet of paper. Tomorrow Felix will take it to the laboratory where it will be examined. I find this proceeding complicated. It demands time and is messy.

At 1 p.m. Reichart comes to take me out for lunch at Kempinsky's. Dassel is expecting the visit of a French officer from Headquarters whom he doesn't want me to see. It is freezing today: -24°.[15]

PARIS, FEBRUARY 2ND, 1941

With an irresistible dash, Babs leaps at me nearly throwing me off my feet. I have to put down my suitcase, sit in the middle of the hall on the floor and take him in my arms, to show him that my happiness at being back equals his. How I missed him during these six endless days! He licks everything he can reach of me, moans and wriggles with joy, rolls on the floor, wags the black stump of his tail. When his effusions are a little calmed down, I am allowed to kiss Moussia.

"Satisfied?" she asks.

"Yes. Everything is O.K., but Gosh! How very unpleasant it was!"

FEBRUARY[16]

This morning I go to the Prefecture of Police. I buy a stamped paper, fill it out and present it at the visa section. But there I am told that my motive is not valid and that, besides, they are not allowed to accept applications that are not accompanied by a German authorization. So I return empty handed. I am not worried about the authorization. I shall immediately write to Felix. Taking advantage of the house being empty and my parents out, I compose a letter in sympathetic ink, as I was taught. It takes me the whole afternoon. First I have to dilute the 80% alcohol, then go and buy some antipyrine. Only at the fifth stationary store do I find the right paper. As I am about to begin, I notice that the cotton-wool is of bad quality (with small bits of wood in it) and I have to go down again. Finally, I can get to work and everything runs smoothly. Nobody comes to interrupt me. Slowly, the time passes. The sheets are already two hours under press. Carefully I remove the heavy volume, lift the blotting-paper. The paper appears gently corrugated! I crimple it and angrily stamp it down. After three days' patient efforts, my letter can go at last. I have used a quart of alcohol. So I add a post scriptum telling Dassel that his system is no good. Now there is nothing to do but wait for the answer.

FEBRUARY 27TH 1941

Time passes and Felix does not answer. I have sent another letter. Meanwhile, I continue to work at the hospital. But though I don't want to admit it, Felix's silence worries me. What if "they" should have changed their mind?

APRIL 7TH, 1941

I am in the dumps. Everything goes wrong. Today the Germans have invaded Yugoslavia and Greece. I think of all my friends in Belgrade, in Sarajevo, in Dubrovnik, of all these peasants who have received me with outstretched arms, who have taught me to love their country. At the hospital, mother Abbot, to cheer us up, has brought up the prophecies of St. Odile. And though we don't believe in them, they cheer us up!

Still no answer from Dassel. What on earth is he doing?

April 30th

"My dear old fellow, not hearing anything from you, I suppose that you have changed your mind. I haven't. I am leaving in a few days by my own means. Shall see you some time. Best wishes and good-bye." I sign and, without reading it over, close the envelope and go out to post the letter. I am furious, and this time for good. All the more because I have not the least intention to leave "by my own means."

All I can do is to go for a week's visit to a friend in Brittany—a week of riding over hills and downs, under a fine rain, through woods that smell of pine, of wet earth, of decaying last year's leaves; rides without purpose, from which we return, Babs and I, mud covered and with huge appetites.

Gertrude Walter's (alias Mlle Yvonne's) message reaches me there. The letter is six days old; it gives me an appointment for today at the Café du Rond-Point. She says she has an urgent communication for me; she gives me her telephone number: Littre 34-46. Nuts to her: she'll have to wait. I don't intend leaving before three days.

May 12th, 1941

All Gertrude Walter wanted to tell me is not to leave on any account. Dassel is due to arrive very shortly. Ouf! I really have been scared! I did believe for a moment that everything was finished. Now, there only remains to wait.

May 23rd

Collet has passed in Palestine with his Tcherkesses.[17] I envy him. I recall Collet: his rugged face with a small bush-like black moustache. His rough manners: a real soldier. The first time I met him was at the French Embassy at Ankara. After that, I saw him again at Antioch, at Beyrouth. I trained for nursing with his wife. This reminds me of the surprise parties, the picnics of the last term between students and nurses. Syria … the blue sky … and once more nostalgia of the sun seizes me. A prohibited subject.

I return to the daily reality. How lucky that winter is over! By and by the chilblains[18] have disappeared; we have discarded the ski trousers and exchanged the heavy boots for ordinary shoes, which seem so wonderfully light on the feet. The heads have emerged from the hoods which the cold has imposed on fashion. On the market, the rutabaga's reign is finished. The flat has emerged in a terrific state from the heating crisis. All the walls are covered with "blisters." Large dampness spots decorate with the most fancy designs and colours the wallpapers which used to be plain and now hang sadly here and there. But now winter is over and all this is only a bad dream.

June 5th, 1941

Lately the B.B.C. speaks so much about German airports in Syria that it looks as if it was preparing the public opinion for a so-called "defensive" action of Great-Britain.

June 8th

It's done. The British have entered Syria. This means the Syrian plans are up. Will "they" still need me? Oh God! Let me have my chance!

June 10th

A message from "Mlle Yvonne" (alias Gerda Walter) informs me of Felix Dassel's arrival and asks me to telephone him tomorrow before 11 a.m. AT LAST!

—⚏—

June 11th

Have telephoned. She (Yvonne) will arrange an appointment for me tomorrow.

—⚏—

June 12th

It's raining. On the Champs-Elysées, the shining asphalt seems to be liquid. The processions of umbrellas streams before the wide panes of the Hungaria. Waiting has a bad effect upon me. How different life seemed to me on that September day of 1938 when I was leaving this same café to realize a dream that remains unachieved. 38—39—40, and now 41. How time has fled since I left. I returned. I shall always return, whether I want it or not—sooner or later, from far or from near, as if I were held by a rubber band. The swinging door revolves. I was watching it. Yet I only see Dassel when he is in front of me.

He is still fatter than he was in January and slightly drunk, as usual. Without introduction: "Sit down and hold tight," he says. "Where do you think we want to send you?"

"I don't know."

"To Australia!" I remain unmoved. "Is that all the effect it makes on you?" He seems disappointed.

"What do you expect? Me to dance? Or jump?"

"Do you accept?"

"Of course."

"When can you come to Berlin?"

"Now, if you want."

"That's perfect. I'll settle the question of the pass and you could start on Tuesday, for instance."

"O.K. And Syria? Finished?"

"Finished."

"Why didn't you answer my letter? I wasted a quart of alcohol on it."

He laughs: "I know. We'll have to change the system. Alcohol is sacred! But the reason you did not get my answer is that I was away: twice in Finland and once in Istanbul."

I bring him back to the question of Syria, because that scheme was so convenient, and I hate to give it up. I must get accustomed not to get attached to plans: more suppleness, better adaptation. All the same, it's a pity. As to Felix, he is not pleased with the Syrian events, but proves to be a philosopher: "After all, the British and the French can wear themselves out one against the other. It's always that for us!"

"And U.S.S.R.? We hear lots of rumours."

His face becomes grave: "There will be fighting."

"Then it is not a false alarm?"

"Did you really believe that?"

"I don't know. But many think so."

"The fools!"

"When?"

"Perhaps in a few days."

"You'll attack?" He only nods. "But what is your interest in creating a new front?"
"Don't you understand that for months the Russians have been mobilizing all their forces?"
"One speaks of fifty-two divisions."
He laughs: "If it were only that! But there is at least twice as much."
"And do you expect it to be easy?"
"A cinch!"
I accompany Dassel to the Reynold's where he has stopped and have dinner with him.

June 13th

This morning Dassel has introduced me to E. who will act in future as liaison between him and myself, or better, between me and the German Espionage Paris Branch. It'll be he who will bring me my papers after Felix leaves tomorrow. I shall follow on Wednesday. I have received 2,000 francs for travelling expenses.

June 16th

E. arrives with a desolate expression and empty hands. The "Monsieur" who was to bring him my papers hasn't showed up. Neither is he at his home, and E. does not know his office telephone number. It is a M. Mercier, 12, Rue Beaujon. I reassure him and go down to the corner "bistro" to ring up Mlle. Yvonne.

2:30 p.m. Very few people are inside the Café du Rond-Point des Champs Elysées. Yvonne appears in a flowered gown, a tiny fox under her arm. She introduces him to me: Mouki. I tell her about my troubles. She promises to arrange everything. She leaves first; we avoid going out together. I look at her as she goes, rolling her hips, highly perched on her heels, the fox trotting at the end of its leash. Funny girl! French? German? The appearance is German: her fair skin, light blue eyes, her blond hair parted in the middle. The mind is French—sparkling—more than that, it is the Parisian bagout,[19] the quick retorts, sometimes slang.

June 20th

My affairs don't advance. Everything seems so complicated. In Syria the British don't advance either. I scold Babs because he doesn't like rutabaga. And then I have remorse, because in a few days I shall leave him again and he'll be desperate.

"This evening, Babs, I'll take you to see a picture with tigers and monkeys." He likes this kind of films. When a lion is shown approaching the camera, becoming larger and larger until he fills the whole screen, Babs bristles, growls and then ducks under the seat with a yelp of terror. It is too large for him!

June 22nd

Without any war declaration, the German army has invaded Russia. It has happened! One has the impression that the storm that was hanging in the air has burst. I regret not to be in Berlin; I should like to have seen the first reaction. Anyhow, our Australian projects are obviously unrealizable.

June 24th

We feed on the news of the B.B.C. in spite of the German jamming. So far, there hasn't been yet any serious collision between the Russians and the Germans. The "Boches" advance without encountering any resistance. How far will they go?

A pneumatic from Yvonne (Gerda Walter) asking me to be at the Rond-Point at 6p.m. My papers are ready and I am leaving this evening. Instead of her, it is E. whom I find in a dark corner of the café. He hasn't anything with him and is waiting for somebody who must bring my pass. We wait—half an hour—an hour—an hour and a half—an hour and fifty minutes.

"There he is at last!" exclaims E.

I see a civilian advancing towards us. He is of medium height, dressed in a brown suit, wears a felt hat of the same colour and carries a dispatch case under the arm. He nods to E., takes his hat off and kisses my hand. This seems strange coming from a German. E. simply introduces him as "The Major."[20]

"Sorry. Much late. Much occupied. Pray you, sit down. Here papers." He speaks bad French, but without hesitation. His hair, slightly graying at the temples, waves on the top of his head and is parted on the left side. His gold signet is initialed: E.K. He's got regular features: his eyes are a shade between hazel and green; he wears a small brush moustache, nicotine tinted, and has false teeth. He explains to me, as well as he can, that the person whom Felix put in charge of my papers has left on a mission. "Our friend Engelhardt has not given sufficient instructions," he says. Engelhardt? That's amusing! So Felix is travelling under the name of his friend Gory, the Baron Engelhardt!

The "Major" continues, telling me he took it upon himself to have some German identity papers made out for me. I am interpreter in the German Army! Because, according to a recent decree, the pass is no longer sufficient and the passage of the border must be entered in the passport, which, in my case, must be avoided at any price. Anyhow, I have missed my train for this evening. When I leave the Major, it is past 8 o'clock.

At home, Mummy awaits me impatiently: "What news?"

"Tomorrow morning."

Poor Moune! She lives in fear. She hasn't much faith in my luck. Above all she doesn't see the utility of my enterprise, and I cannot explain it to her. I can only have faith. Was I right or wrong to warn her? Had I the right to let them take the risk—her and Daddy—without knowing it? That's why, some time ago, I told her. She was horrified. "What do you think you can do, alone, against them? You are mad!"

And a few days later, Daddy knew about it too, but each of them separately, without knowing that the other one knows. I want to be sure of their silence. I want to see how long they will keep my secret. Daddy is skeptical, but with him, curiosity has the upper hand. Sometimes he tries to question me, but I very rapidly discourage him. And I ask him once for all never to speak of it again.

June 25th

Trying journey, very much like the last one, except for the scenery outside; it is summer. On the frontier, I don't have to leave the train. Don't I belong to the German army? The station at Kola has been hit by two bombs which have carried off the rails on the right and on the left on a distance of ten meters. The gauge is already repaired. The walls and roofing bear witness to the damage. And then, like last time, it is Berlin. I go directly to Dassel.

"Well? What do you think of it?" are his first words.
"Well played! Is everything according to your wishes?"
"Absolutely."

But a few minutes later, while she helps me unpack, Sigrid confides: "It is awful. We didn't expect at all that the Russians would resist. Felix is terribly upset. It keeps him awake at night!"

I sense a somber joy. This "something" that's gone wrong, this unexpected "something," this hitch, however small, is the first against which stumbles the undefeated German power. Who knows if it doesn't mean the end of their uninterrupted, inhuman, unexplainable progress?

June 27th

How changed is Berlin since January! Everywhere queues before the shops. Hardly any uniforms in the streets. The men one sees are old, or looking ill, or very young (14–15 years old). All the others are on the Eastern front. Petrol is running short; cars are rare. On my last visit I had been struck by the large number of taxis. Now they have practically disappeared. Facing the Gedächnisskirche stands a house partly demolished by a bomb. A few months ago, the damage would have been immediately repaired. Today it remains as it is, gaping with its empty windows; labour is unavailable. The new front has drained Germany of all her available manpower. From the bottom of my heart I wish that they never return.

Berlin, June 28th

The German radio gives no war news. The silence is heavy with suspense. One doesn't know what to think. One can only suppose. One fears, one hopes, and everybody awaits Sunday—tomorrow—because tomorrow we will know at last: so it has been announced.

The weather has changed; it is raining. I don't go out, spending all my time at Dassel's. He is away the whole day. When he comes home, in the evening, he seems worried. He answers with a shrug of the shoulders the questions Sigrid and I ask him. "We'll know tomorrow" is all we can get out of him. It leaves us disheartened.

I haven't seen yet anyone concerning my business.

Sunday, June 29th, 1941. Berlin.

It began early this morning and lasted the whole day through. Though it is Sunday, we are up much earlier than usually. I shall not soon forget this day which has been like a long agony. Together with the others, I live from "Sondermeldung" to "Sondermeldung,"[21] knowing hour after hour the renewed apprehension of a victory for them, which would mean a disaster for us.

I force myself into laughter: I pretend to be happy, to rejoice with them, while my contracted nerves jerk painfully at every drum beat and are ready to break at the trumpet sound which precedes and follows each communiqué. Now it's over. I am back in my room, have put out the light, and feeling safe that nobody can see or hear me, give way to the strain which has become too great. With my head buried in the pillow, I sob until I am out of breath, as I sobbed when I was five years old and had a grief too big for me. Then, exhausted, I fall asleep without even undressing.

BERLIN JUNE 30TH, 1941[22]

In spite of the successes announced yesterday by the German radio; in spite of the figures—an impressing amount of figures!—stating the destroyed tanks, the occupied localities, the kilometers of advance, the prisoners made, the planes brought down, in spite of all this, Felix doesn't seem fully satisfied.

"A desertion. A mutiny, no matter where, at the rear, in any small lost village. That is what we need. Why don't they announce it? That is what I'm waiting for! Instead, they give figures and figures! To hell with their figures! Who believes them? I also can make some up." And furiously he paces up and down the drawing room. Then he questions me about France, public opinion, the progress of collaboration.

"My dear man," I say to him. "You'll never be able to get anything out of the French. All your courting is in vain. You believe that you have set them up against the British with the Syrian propaganda. But they say: "Better that the English should occupy Syria than the Boshes." You make concessions. They puff out their chests and say: "They need us," or: "They are afraid of us." If you freed their prisoners to gain them to your cause, they still say: "They have nothing to feed them with." And if you'd liberate France, they would think: "They lack of men to carry on the occupation; they need ones who are here." But never, NEVER, will you be able to persuade them that any measure you could take would be taken in a sense of friendship. They hate you; this cannot be reasoned."

"But are there any who still believe in the British victory?" asks Felix.

"I don't know if they *believe* in the British victory, but more than ever they are for the British."

So after all, Bialostock has not surrendered. The two Russian armies which were encircled in that town did not capitulate! It has been a slaughter, if the figures given by the Germans are correct. Felix is ready to cry with rage, while he restlessly paces through the drawing room. "The fools! The fools!" he repeats. "What need had they to get themselves killed when it was so easy to surrender? And we who are coming as liberators!"

Every day I stand in endless lines with Sigrid. Since a fortnight, there are no more potatoes. On account of the large amount of it that the Germans eat, it's a hard privation for them. Regarding vegetables and fruit, it's worse here than in France. Everything can only be had with tickets, and even so isn't obtainable every day. In Paris, this year, we have a profusion of strawberries, cherries, raspberries. Here all this is a rarity, nearly a luxury!

Everything is terribly expensive, even if you don't take in consideration the exchange rate. Yesterday I wanted to buy a tiny little bunch of marigold: 85 pfennig. It used to be 10 pfennig. In Paris it costs 8 times less. Here for a tiny carnation one has to pay 54 pfennig. At home, I buy every week a whole bunch of them for a little more than half that price. And everything is in the same proportion. In the lines, people are colourless, grumbling, and often insult each other. The weather is still bad; a fine rain is falling.

Still nothing has been decided for me. Felix says that everybody has left for Russia and that there isn't a soul left in Berlin. "If you were taken ill, you wouldn't ever find a doctor to look after you!"

JULY 1ST, 1941

The bridge game is at full swing. As usual, I am losing, because my thoughts are very far away. This evening Felix has invited a friend, prepared a "cruchon"—mixture of white wine, vodka and soda water to which are added a few slices of lemon and strawberries.

Everybody is gay. During a few hours, we forget the war and tomorrow's uncertainty; during those too short instants, I shall blot out of my conscience the notion—always so acutely present—of being among enemies, on the watch out, careful of every word, of every gesture, of every expression of my face. They believe I am their friend, but I am here to spy upon them, to betray them. If they find it out, they'll have no pity. It is like a temporary truce among the four of us infinitesimal atoms in the universal conflict.

"Five no trumps!" Felix gives us a glance of triumph and of challenge.

Coming from far away through the air, the space, through the thousand noises of the towns the music announcing the special communiqués comes softly from the radio. Dassel throws his cards on the table, jumps to the instrument and turns it louder. The sounds of the brass band fill the room. Stronger than the noise of the music, I hear the disorderly beating of my heart. We are silent. In a few seconds we shall know. Then suddenly, I feel that I am getting pale. I am sure everyone will notice it. Then they will understand. I can't leave my place. Still holding the cards, I feel my icy cold hands become moist. These "Sondermeldungen," in three days, have utterly shattered my nerves. Each time a panic apprehension seizes me.

"What is the matter?" asks Felix.

I heard the communiqué in a dream (nothing striking: some localities taken). I didn't notice Dassel resume his seat and pick up his cards. He looks at me, wonderingly, then bursts out laughing, offering me a clue without knowing it: "My word! You're drunk! Look at her; she's as white as a ghost!"

I make a frantic effort to smile an answer: "You know I'm not used to drinking!"

July 8th, 1941[23]

"The 20,000 Russians surrounded in Minsk have killed their political commissars and have surrendered," has just announced a special communiqué.

"Hurrah! Hurrah!" yells Felix at the top of his lungs. He seems demented. His eyes protrude. Out of breath he has to sit down. With elbows on the table and his face in his hands, he repeats over and over: "At last! At last!" I am stupefied at the violence of his emotion. Finally, he sits up and looks at me. I see tears in his eyes.

"Do you realize what it means? THE-REVOLUTION-IN-THE-RED-ARMY! For days and days we awaited it! We could not understand what was delaying it. Thank God! It has happened at last. Now that it has begun, it will spread like wild fire. The example of Minsk will bring about new revolts, will cause other mutinies. God be praised! Now everything will go well." Under the sway of emotion, he has spoken. He has given himself away, showing the bluff of all he had pretended and simulated and concealed. Why should he mind disclosing this in front of me? Now "everything will go well," as he says. Now he holds a reality. What does it matter to him to acknowledge his former fears and doubts? He can afford to tell me: "I have lied to you: I told you that all went well, when all went wrong; that we were sure of success, when we doubted of tomorrow. Now everything is all right—you've heard it for yourself."

I suddenly feel very tired. Why struggle any longer? They seem to succeed everywhere; nothing seems to resist them. But I drive this thought far from me. Even without hope, even in vain I shall fight. I follow Sigrid to the kitchen. Sigrid only sees the war in so far as it affects her household. Minsk's capitulation fills her with joy.

"At last, Felix will be able to sleep tonight! He was so terribly upset all these days. You understand: nobody expected they'd (the Russians) resist. We thought that they would all surrender and pass on our side. Now, Felix says that everything will run smoothly."

—∞—

JULY 5TH, 1941[24]

Although nothing has been done on my account, I have decided to go back to Paris, pretending that a longer absence might seem strange. And Felix has agreed. He says that the plan of sending me to Australia still holds, but as "serious events are preparing in the Far East," it is possible that all communication with Australia will be interrupted at a day's notice. "In which case, we have no interest to send you there. You will be more useful here," he declares.

—∞—

JULY 6TH

At last, I go back with the instruction to "wait." The journey seems endless, so great is my haste to leave Germany and be again among my own people. At the frontier station of Herbesthal,[25] the loud-speaker announces the defection of thirty-two thousand Russians with their whole equipment; they have joined the Germans. And I think: "Keep on talking! It's the last time you're forcing me to listen to you. You can take my word for it!"

—∞—

JULY /TH 1941[26]

Paris: sunshine, hand-carts full of flowers. I live again. And then, to learn that the story of Minsk was a tremendous bluff, fills me with joy. On the other hand, extracts from German papers which appeared in the Paris press describe Minsk's capture "street by street, house by house"—which is nothing like the "surrender" announced by the German radio.[27] Must the Germans already, after only ten days of Russian campaign, recur to such lies to maintain their morale?

In Paris I find a complete change in the public opinion. The general apathy has reverted into exaltation. A new hope has risen—indefinite yet—but which has awaken the people from the lethargy in which they were slowly sinking. One notices it most in the crowds, the lines at the market. Even the anti-communists wish for the victory of the Soviets, seeing in it a chance of salvation for France.

And July passes. I wait patiently. August arrives, seeing the German advance in Russia, the fall of Smolensk. The war in Persia.

While the Germans fortify feverishly the North coasts of the Atlantic, in Paris revolt is fomenting. Riots, assassinations and sabotage multiply. The "Boches" reply by executing hostages. Posters appear on the walls of the town. First white ones, with the picture of the guilty patriot—posters which promise a large reward to anyone who would help in finding the fugitive. An hour after their display, the photo on the poster has been scratched off. Then appear the others: the red and yellow ones, bordered in black, with their lists of names of the executed hostages. The yellow posters are for the "enemies of Germany," patriots who were found in possession of prohibited arms, information agents of de Gaulle, saboteurs. The red ones are for Jews and communists.

Little posters guarded by policemen to prevent their destruction—how much hatred they stir up! The crowd goes by in silence; the eyes read the names and the faces harden from contained powerless hate, but which some day will repay hundred fold. In the whole of France "Resistance" awakes, ripens. It is still scattered, uncoordinated, but it exists.

August 25th, 1941

I am still waiting. A pneumatic from Mlle Yvonne: She wants me to call her up tomorrow.

August 26th

Yvonne has made an appointment for me with the Major who I already know.

August 27th

Since three quarters of an hour I am waiting at the terrace of the "Triomphe." I have absorbed two grape juices and prepare to order a third one, when I see him alight from his car. The Major comes directly towards me and, seemingly unaware that he is late, tells me that the person he wanted me to meet cannot come today.

In the meanwhile, Paul Collette tries to kill Laval and by ricochet wounds Déat. Both have a near escape.[28] Japan and the United States are getting restless. Von Papen, in Ankara, is agitating. In Russia, the Dnieper dams are blown up. In Paris, the cost of living increases. Butter, on the black market, rises from 85 to 120 francs. Meat to 70 francs a kilo. The bread is getting darker.

August 30th

Another pneumatic from Yvonne while Hitler is meeting Mussolini!

September 2nd, 1941

At the other end of the wire, Mlle Yvonne gives me an appointment for 6 o'clock: "It is a man of a certain age; he wears spectacles, a brown hat and yellow gloves. If you don't see him, ask the waiter for 'M. Dupont.'"

The weather is fine. Through the empty space between the two wings of the Trocadéro appears the Champ de Mars, the silvery Seine, dominated by the Eifel Tower. The chestnut trees of the Avenue Henri Martin are turning yellow. Babs likes to romp about in the dry leaves, to roll in them when I am not looking, to throw them up in the air and bark—bark very loudly.

At the terrace of the Kleber, a few idle customers warm themselves in the evening sun. As I approach, I examine the half-dozen men sitting at the tables. Not one of them fits Yvonne's description. Nevertheless, I go without hesitating towards an individual with thinning hair, and a face marked by a large scar. "M, Dupont." What an Irony! Can one imagine face more German! On my approach, he gets up and gives me a chair. I smile and ask: "Camouflage?"

"Camouflage?" he repeats, not understanding.

"Yes. Where are your gloves?"

"My gloves? In my pocket. Why?"

"That's it. I have been told that I would recognize you by your spectacles, your brown hat and yellow gloves. Now, your hat is under the table, your spectacles in their case and your gloves in your pocket. So that's why I ask: camouflage?"

He laughs: "I have not been told that these would be the reconnaissance signs."

"It doesn't matter. The main thing is that I have recognized you."

We chat about indifferent things. Then he asks: "Shall we walk?" We stroll without aim. Just before leaving the Etoile, he says: "Would it suit you to go to Dakar?" And without waiting for an answer: "Do you think it's feasible?"

"If you have a sufficiently good motive, yes."

"We have one."

This is all I'll know this time. I return home with the name on the lips: Dakar, and a terrible desire to let my imagination loose. But I forbid myself to think about it: no plans, no dreams.

September 3rd

His name is von Winter—at any rate the one he told me.

At 10.30 a.m. I arrive at the Fouquet's. He is already there. He, at least, is punctual. But he is also laconic. All that I learn that morning is that "they" want to send me to Dakar under cover of a "commercial thing" as he says. He doesn't explain more of it, saying that he awaits the arrival from Berlin another personality. We are to meet on Saturday.

September 4th, 1941

It is the third letter I send to Bessie, my English cousin. This is the essential of the text, inserted between family news: "I have been invited twice by the new owners of the place where we have spent a summer together. They have offered me a very important job. As I don't personally need it, I thought it might interest your people. But not knowing where to find them, after all these upheavals, I should like you to give them my address asking them to look me up." The signature is illegible. The names of my grandmother and my aunt which I mention should allow her to identify me—as the handwriting is not mine either.

I have a very high opinion of my cousin, as much from the point of view of character as of intelligence. I rely upon her entirely and am sure that if she can help me, she will do it. Now, the only place where we ever spent a summer together is Tchecoslovquia.[29] The new owners of Tchecoslovaquia are the Germans. It seems to me that she cannot fail to understand the meaning: "I have twice been invited by the Germans. They have offered me an important job. Not needing it personally, I have thought that it might interest the British (she has no family in France). But not knowing where to find them after all these upheavals, I should like you to give them my address, telling them to look me up." I hope that she will contact the Intelligence Service (she knows many people at the War Office), and that perhaps they will be able to get in touch with me and advise me for my work.

The first letter was sent from the unoccupied zone over a month ago through a friend who works at the Finance Ministry and was returning to Vichy. The second I sent under double envelop, with an enclosure of 5 francs, to an address that had been given me. This third one will leave with a nun who will conceal it in her "cornette."[30] *A Dieu vat...*

September 6th

Lunched at Prunier's. Today the ice is definitively broken between von Winter and myself. He has just discovered that I know one of his University friends, a certain Jansen, Attaché at the German Embassy in Belgrade, whom I have met at some friends.' Instantly, his reticence disappears. He becomes nearly talkative. So far, he had always refused to approach the subject of the war, stealing off at the faintest allusion I made of it. Today, he makes the first step. "What do you think of the situation in Russia?" he asks me.

"It is a surprise for everyone," I say frankly. "And I believe that your position is not an easy one."

"A very difficult one," admits von Winter. "At the beginning, I thought it would be a question of weeks. But soon after the beginning, I understood that two forces were opposed: on our side, the rapidity of advance, on their side their rapidity of destruction. And so far, they have been the strongest! We have also been deceived by their prodigious camouflage; all our reckonings concerning their presumed armament turned out to be wrong."

I ask: "If you took Leningrad?"

"It would be of no value to us, except to impress fools. All our losses in men, material and time, our entire advance, bring no compensation whatsoever; we find no supplies, no shelters, no support. We cannot even employ the prisoners in our rear, as their very presence is a great danger, without speaking of the sabotage. The capture of the smallest village represents a loss, never a gain. I have fought in Russia in 1914–1917. I've had my hands frozen. Yet, at that time, the towns were untouched and we found supplies as we advanced. I am terrified at the thought of what awaits us next winter. It is well that the young ones who are fighting over there don't know what is coming to them."

I say again: "Here, public opinion has greatly changed since the beginning of the war with Russia. People have regained hope."

"I know," he says. "One of my friends was in Vichy on the 22nd of June. Everybody was wearing three-coloured cockades, and one could hear people say: 'Now the Germans are done for, and we are saved!' Do you think America will declare war?"

"I believe so," I say.

"I don't think so," he retorts. "You'll see that they will apply Monroe's doctrine, take advantage of the war to enrich their country. 'America for America!'"

"I doubt it," I say. "From the fact that America retains the major part of the world's gold, it is not in her interest to see you win the war and replace gold monetary unit in Europe by, let us say … carrot slices! The new order, a united Europe which would be self supporting, is not what America needs. Her advantage lies in a dismembered Europe, in which each country would trade directly with her, in prejudice of one another."

But von Winter doesn't agree. So I change the subject: "And Japan?" I ask. "Was its occupation of Indo-China in your interest? The press here may well try to persuade the public that the "cession" by Vichy of Indo-China to Japan is nothing but a Franco-Japanese "friendly collaboration" against the unavoidable British aggression; the effect produced on the French public is most unfavorable to you."

"I don't know. There might be some reasons which I ignore. But the whole thing seems rather obscure."

"Japan doesn't seem in a hurry to help you!"

"It might make up its mind to attack Russia in the spring—it might also betray us. In any case, the war it has undertaken against China is without issue; Japan will never be able to win it."

"And Turkey? Will it be able to remain outside the conflict?"

But here he balks. "It is a subject which has no immediate interest—no interest whatsoever."

"You astonish me," I say. "There are the Straits, the way to Mossul, to Suez."

"When I say 'no interest,' I could as well say 'too much interest.' It is a crucial subject, and I prefer not to discuss irritating questions."

A little later, I say: "Do you truly believe that if you had not attacked Russia, it would have attacked you?"

"It's very difficult to tell. We knew that we would have to fight it in two or three years. We didn't want to give it time to get ready. When we attacked it, we thought it was weak, and that it would be a matter of a few weeks. We wanted to have finished with it before throwing all our forces against England."

"In short, Russia has played the same trick on you as Italy to France. It paralyzed your troops along the frontier?"

"Exactly!"

"But what was Russia's interest to make a pact with you? Your interest was obvious: to guarantee your security in the East, while you were clearing up the West. But Russia's? Didn't it realize that your victory meant a threat against it? That your increasing power, your expansion were a danger to its frontier?"

"You see," says von Winter, "it is very difficult to answer this question. In '39, we could suppose that Russia's weakness obliges it to submit to our claims. Now that we know its strength, the hypothesis falls. Was it in order to advance its borders by occupying Poland, and so, be able to dissimulate the fortification work going on in the interior? Was it to give itself time to complete its armament? Was it because, no more than ourselves, could Russia foresee the crushing defeat of France, and hoped to see us wear ourselves out in a war in the West? All these suppositions are possible, but none is certain. Russia is, and shall remain for us, as the Sphynx, an enigma."

Another time he also says: "Churchill is supposed to have said, speaking of us: 'I let them win battles, but we shall win the war.' Will we be victors? No doubt. Perhaps! But it won't be yet tomorrow, and it will not be a great, a magnificent victory. We shall be exhausted, ruined, economically and in men, perhaps more defeated, than the defeated."

"Do you earnestly believe in the possibility of an invasion of England?"

He avoids the question and only says: "The time of sea supremacy is passed, and the time of the air mastery is opened. Don't forget that the largest airport is Tempelhof."

"Why then, if, as you say, you have the air supremacy, do you risk your troop transports in the Baltic? Why don't you use transport airplanes? Is it on account of petrol shortage?"

"Petrol! There is no shortage of petrol! We have Roumania."

"That isn't much: one single vulnerable point. And which is continually bombarded."

"We have reserves."

"Nevertheless, I think that it is easier for you to foresee their end than the end of the war."

He shrugs his shoulders wearily. I often feel him stubborn and unwilling to answer. The conversation veers off to the Vichy Government, and I ask him what he thinks of it.

"It is exactly what we had in Germany under Hindenburg, of whom Petain is a replica: something representative and inconsequential, a convenient façade, behind which we can act at our leisure."

A little later, I remark that the Versailles Treaty has, since 1918, made possible the actual war by surrounding Germany with disparate countries artificially constituted, such as Tchecoslovaquia and Poland, or else by weakened countries such as Austria and Hungary, who were to become an easy prey, whereas a strong country would probably have stopped Germany's expansion. Von Winter answers that it was difficult for the men who dictated this treaty to foresee twenty years ahead France's decadence, as well as the incredible audacity of Hitler, who would always gamble on the hesitation of the Allies to reduce one after the other all these puppet countries.

"But above all," adds von Winter, "what the Treaty of Versailles could not foresee, is that by disarming us, they put us in the obligation of renewing the whole of our armament, replacing the old by a new one, provided with all the latest modern inventions, to which we owe the superiority of our arms over the arms of all countries we have defeated one after another."

We continue to discuss the matter in the hall of his hotel while we drink coffee. It is only when I am about to leave, that he mentions "my affair." As usual, he is very laconic and only tells me that it has to do with oil importation. The staff is French. But for more information, I must meet a "journalist," who will come from Berlin on the 15th. Von Winter drives me home and leaves me at the corner of my street.

P.S. Today Paris-Midi announces three new executions in reprisals for the stabbing of a German soldier.

September 8th, 1941

The German radio announces the capture of Schlusselburg[31] and the encirclement of Leningrad. To brace up my courage and chase away the "cafard,"[32] I read the "Campaign of Russia" by Tarle,[33] wherefrom I copy the following passage, taken from a letter of Count Worontsoff, dated June 5th 1812. May his prophecy come true for a second time, after 129 years!

Worontsoff, at the time Ambassador of Russia in London, wrote to Alexander I: "Even if, at the beginning, they (the military operations) are unfavourable to us, we can win by persisting in a defensive war and by retreating. If the enemy begins to pursue us, he is lost, because, as he gets further away from his supply bases and ammunition depots, and as he breaks into a country without roads, short of food, of which a Cossack army will deprive him by encircling him from all sides, his situation will grow worse and worse and, eventually, he will be decimated by the winter, which has always been our most faithful ally."

As I am copying this passage, I am struck by a certain similitude with what von Winter told me a few days ago, and which I scribbled down as soon as I got home. I must be more careful in the future. This habit of writing will play me a dirty trick one of these days!

September 13th

The Germans advance towards Kiev. Odessa still holds. We feed on the news from over there. The smallest slackening in the German advance brings back hope that it might be at last the final stop. But soon again they progress at a jump, and we sink in discouragement. Will anyone ever stop them, and how far will they advance? This evening, I am dining with von Winter.

"Do you still believe that America will not enter the war?" I ask him, as coffee is served.

"Yes," he answers. "Americans are too much of businessmen to get involved in anything as risky as war."

"But then, how do you explain the incident with the Greer?[34] Even according to your propaganda, America is trying to provoke a casus belli.[35] Why should she, if her intention wasn't to enter the fight? On the other hand, it seems to me that an America at war would present less danger for you, than an America so-called "Neutral," and which would put all her war production at the disposal of your enemies. Do you believe that her active war potential would be superior to her potential of aid to Great Britain? I suppose, it would depend on the strength of her navy."

"It wouldn't be so much her military power," says von Winter, "which is weak and chiefly distant—that would be dangerous in case of a war declaration by America—as the morale effect. It would not only stimulate our enemies, but would create resistance in the occupied territories. Who knows if Japan would not let us down and if other countries would not desert us? It would also be most demoralizing for our troops, which are fighting and are exhausted."

"How are things going on the East front? You have advanced lately."

"Oh! What nonsense! You know as well as I do the value of propaganda. Things are going badly, worse and worse every day."

"I am terrified at the thought of what will happen this winter."

"No, not so much this one, but the next, the one in two years!"

"Do you expect to be able to hold out that long?"

"We'll have to. In the end, we'll be victorious, but, economically, Germany will be ruined, and with her the whole of Europe. That is why final victory will belong to America, without her having been obliged to fight."

"Don't you think that in this war, not only time, but also petrol are factors of the victory? This winter, when the snow will have immobilized the tanks, the fighting will go on in the skies. Will you have sufficient gasoline?"

"For the time being, we have Roumania, and soon we'll have Odessa. Then the Caucasus will belong to us."

I look at him in amazement, wondering if he is pulling my leg, ignorant of geography, or believes I am! However, I only say: "The Caucasus is far away."

"Not so very, and when the Russians will have lost Odessa, their power will be much diminished." Speaking about food supplies, von Winter says: "With the reserves provided by the conquered countries, we can pull through the winter; after which time we'll need the African resources."

I ask him what he thinks of Weygand.

"Weygand and de Gaulle are one and the same. They are real Frenchmen. However, dissidence is not dangerous to us because the actual France is a decadent degenerate nation (he pronounces "deguenerate"). Dissidence would have been a threat if the French had not substituted for patriotism their personal interests, lucre and fear. See, we have devaluated their money, but because we pay them prices which are twice or three times higher (although in reality they do not represent even the quarter of the actual value), they prefer to sell things to us, and let their own people be short of everything. Our Occupation force in France is a handful of men unable to fight: reformed for old age or ill health. And it is sufficient so great is the fear inspired by the green uniform! This is only possible in France. I tell you they are "deguenerated!""

This evening, in bed, I think over von Winter's last words. I recall the German soldiers guarding the gates of Paris. It is true that nearly all of them are old, and wear spectacles, or squint; it is true that they are like dwarves! Those one meets in the metro, in the streets—less numerous than before—are no better. Could von Winter be right? Are we afraid? Is a green uniform on a scarecrow sufficient to make us bend our heads? But no, the day of the revenge has not come, and until then, we must be silent and have patience.

September 18th

Kiev is encircled. Its fall is imminent. This morning, the walls of the metro are covered with new posters announcing the execution of ten hostages, amongst which a boy of nineteen and an old man of seventy-two. If some day I should weaken, if I were ever on the point of abandoning the struggle, saying: "What's the use?" I'd think of you, bloody little posters, with your lists of men who were shot; and if, for a reason which I cannot imagine, my hatred of the Germans should diminish, the thought of you alone would be enough to make it tenfold.

September 20th

Kiev has fallen, and the Germans advance. Twelve new executions. From this evening on, we are "punished": curfew at 9 p.m. for Paris and the departments of Seine and Seine-et-Oise. I find this measure idiotic, as it only strikes the restaurants, theatres and cinemas. There are rumours—but are they true?—that last night, two German officers were hanged on the iron gates of the Abattoirs de la Villette (Slaughter house), with the inscription: "Meat without tickets." Agitation is growing.

September 23rd

Von Winter seems pleased this evening. "Things are going very well," he says, unfolding the paper in which the fall of Kiev is announced in large characters on the first page. We are at the terrace of the Ermitage, at Plessy-Robinson. The sun is going down. The air is transparent, light. From below are rising sounds of dogs barking, distant calls. It is the first time that I see von Winter so gay. I have only known him pessimistic.

"Yes," I say, "it'll be a fine victory if you manage to destroy Budenni's forces. But if they escape you, it's nil, and you'll have to begin all over again."

"Yes, but I believe that this time we hold them." A little later he says: "It is very difficult for us, at the present moment, with the Luftwaffe." I don't ask why, and he adds himself: "The Russians are very good pilots; their anti-aircraft are good; and the objectives are very far apart and scattered."

Only at the end of the meal does he mention our business. "I think," he says, "that it will be difficult for you to go to Dakar."

"Didn't I tell you so from the very first day you spoke about it? It is nearly impossible to travel at present without a serious motive—so much the more to go to such a neuralgic spot as Dakar where I really have no pretence whatsoever to go!" I know that what I am going to add will decide the future. This minute is mine. I stake my whole game on it. It means: win or lose. But I shall win—I must win. I want to win. The same certitude fills me now as when I sent off my first letter to Dassel, basing all my plans on his problematic answer. Therefore, I continue in an indifferent voice: "It would be easy for me to go to Portugal, to Australia, to England. I have relatives there and nobody would be surprised that I should want to leave France. But Dakar!"

Will he bite at the hook? He must! And von Winter asks, without seeming to attach to it any importance: "Do you believe it would be possible for you to go to England?"

"Yes. Why not? People go there every day, and I have a cousin in London."

He doesn't answer anything, and I don't add anything either. The seed is sown. I must give it time to sprout.

—⚭—

SEPTEMBER 30TH

I have seen von Winter only for a short time. This evening, the project of Dakar has been definitely given up.

"What interests us at the present time," says von Winter, "is Cairo and London."

"Cairo is as inaccessible as Dakar, and for the same reasons," I tell him. "As for London, that is much easier."

"How do you propose to do it?"

I pretend to consider the question for a moment, not to seem to have prepared it beforehand, and answer: "I could go to Lisbon, where I have a cousin, an aunt and an uncle. Once there, I would declare that I don't want to return to France and would ask to join my other English cousin. I would say that I want to serve on the side of the Allies, that I am ready to do anything. I am a nurse. Maybe I could work in a hospital. What do you think of it?"

"Yes, but will you be able to return?"

I consider it a moment. Then: "I can see only one means. Enter the British Service of Information and have them send me over to France."

"That's an idea. And how about money? You'll need quite a lot."

"I couldn't take much with me without appearing suspicious. But nothing would prevent me from taking jewels with me and from selling them openly in London. I would say that I have inherited them from my grandmother."

"Very good! Excellent!" On this we part. He'll refer it to "his people in Berlin." Our next meeting is on Tuesday.

—⚭—

OCTOBER 7TH, 1941

It is while walking in the Parc of Saint-Cloud, flooded by the last rays of a setting sun, that von Winter announces the ultimate decisions: "They" want me to go to Lisbon for a fortnight. If I succeed, I must go from there to London. If I fail, I am to return. Von Winter doesn't seem to attach too great an importance to a possible failure.

I shall receive a sum of money for three months (partly in notes, partly in jewels). Also a few addresses where I can write. "And an address in London, where you can find a person, in case you are short of money," he says. "Does it suit you?"

"No."

"Why, no?" he asks, surprised.

"For the simple reason that if I suddenly found myself in London in possession of money "fallen from nowhere" it would seem most suspicious. Don't you think so? Because I shall certainly be watched—in the beginning, at any rate. I would be much better if you gave me an address in the free zone, in Portugal, or in Spain, where I could write, under double envelope, a letter to my Mother asking for money. You would send it to me in small amounts at a time, as if it were she who sent it."

"Just perfect," he says. "That's excellent! And now, here is what you'll have to do:

1. We want to know all the objectives reached during the last bombardments of London.
2. The supplies: abundance, repartition, shortage of products.
3. Arrival of convoys from America. Ports of arrival, tonnage, material transported.

Is it understood?"

"Yes. The two first points seem easy. But the third one looks more complicated. How do you want me, being in London, to know what is arriving, and where?"

"By the maritime agencies, the railroad offices. When transports arrive, there are perhaps twenty-five or fifty ships that dock at the same time. The passengers hasten to get their tickets, chat, and the agencies are informed."

"All right. In any case, I'll do all I can."

We have dinner at a little place called "Au lapin frit."[36] It's a farewell dinner: von Winter "passes me on" to the "Major" whom I have already met on several occasions. England isn't von Winter's "department." Besides, he is recalled to Germany.

"I'm afraid things don't take a pleasant turn for me," he says. "I don't share 'their' views." He shrugs his shoulders. I shall not see him again.

—⚉—

October 8th 1941

Have been at the Prefecture de Police.
Two conditions are required to obtain a passport:

1. An exit permit from the occupation authorities,
2. A letter from the Portuguese consulate granting the visa.

At first sight, it seems easier than I had presumed.

—⚉—

October 9th

We must meet, the Major and myself, at Dupont, Place de Clichy. What a strange place for an appointment! It is half an hour past the rendezvous time. Outside, life seems to be centered round the familiar statute of _____.[37] At the other side of the square, the Café Wepler, transformed into a "Soldatenspeisesaal,"[38] shows its white barriers guarded by policemen. The passersby are obliged to step down from the pavement and walk in the middle of the street. From a distance, they can admire at their leisure the sardines, the butter, the slices of sausages, the steaks with fried potatoes which the German soldiers remorselessly devour. Why shouldn't they? Aren't they the masters? And the windows are bare of curtains, so that those who are hungry can tell themselves that, had we won the war, we too would have something to eat.

Time goes on and nobody appears. I'll have to wait for an hour, perhaps for two, and when he'll come, I shall not have a single word of reproach, not a movement of impatience; I shall smile in a most natural way.

"Good evening! How are you?" I look up. Mlle Yvonne is in front of me. She is alone. "I am very annoyed," she says, sitting down. "At the last moment, he told me he couldn't come."

Lily's Carte d'Identité issued by the Prefecture de Police and dated 20 November 1941 (KV 2/466, The National Archives of the United Kingdom).

"I am sorry," I say. "It'll be for another time."

"Come and have tea with me tomorrow, and we'll fix another appointment." And she gives me her address at Vanves,[39] explaining to me how to get there.

October 10th

Yvonne—who has definitely given up her pseudonym of Gerda Walter—lives on the upper floor of one of the large modern buildings of the rue. The flat belonged to Finns and has been requisitioned. We've had some trouble to get there, Babs and I; it is so far.

Yvonne receives me clad in a dressing gown, while Mouki runs towards Babs with joyful yelping. They are both so buoyant that we are obliged to put them out on the terrace, which forms the roof of the house. Yvonne brings in the tea on a big tray. The condensed milk and the pineapple jam are from Portugal. "The Major has just returned from Lisbon," she confides, "and has brought me lots of things."

I try to make out her role. She pretends to be the Major's secretary, but I don't know why. She does not make the impression to be that "officially," … rather his "petite amie."

We fix an appointment for 5 p.m.

October 13th

Winter is here. It has set in after a day of rain and cold. The sun has appeared again, but a different sun: paler, remoter. The air is filled with the smell of dead leaves, rotting on the wet earth, of damp bark. But one is without illusions. One knows that the fine days for which one had hoped will not come back. The winters of 40 and 41 will join hands over a miserable cold summer. The great offensive against Moscow is launched. It is the last effort of the Germans to take possession of the Russian capital before winter sets in.

After another appointment, numerous telephone calls, I am at last in the presence of the Major. He comes to fetch me at the Café du Rond-Point, where I am waiting for him … since two hours. Or, rather, it is Yvonne who comes; the Major has remained in the car. I get in the back seat. The Major drives. Yvonne sits in front beside him. They speak German. Yvonne turns to me: "It is late; we shall keep you for dinner. Is it all right with you?"

The car follows the Champs-Élysées, goes down the Avenue Foch, enters the Bois de Boulogne. We stop at the Cascade. Everything is closed and seems deserted. Nevertheless, my companions knock. The door opens and I see at once that they are usual customers.

A table is fixed for us in a corner of the empty restaurant. The proprietor himself bustles around us. While dinner is getting ready, we have some aperitifs. I am cold; there is no heating, naturally. The large desolate dining-room with its dark corners renders the cold more bitter. And, besides, I am nervous: I am facing two new adversaries whom I don't know, of whom I ignore everything. I had gotten used to von Winter, and von Winter leaves tomorrow.

Everything has to be done all over again: dissipate a new distrust, win a new confidence, appear to their eyes the way they want to see me; be sufficiently indifferent and yet sufficiently interested in their work. And above all, not to appear as an enigma, show nothing which could in the least, puzzle them. I approach the subject that has brought me here in a simple way, as a conversation which I should be continuing. "I must admit frankly that I don't know anymore where I stand. All seemed to get settled with von Winter, and then, suddenly, he tells me that he is leaving and sends me to you. Where do you come in?"

"Von Winter has told me about the 'possibilities which you present,' but I should like to hear about them from you personally."

I tell him once more about the plans we had elaborated with his colleague and about the trumps I retain. But he wants more details. He wants to know how it is I contacted von Winter, and through whom. All he knows about it is, that one day he received orders to arrange a meeting between us, without knowing what it was about. I tell him about Dassel, whom I have known for eight years. He seems satisfied. He asks me where I was at the beginning of the war. I tell him in Syria. As he doesn't insist, I have the impression he believes I was there on a mission. I don't correct his mistake.

"I am interested by your projects, but they have to be revised," pursues Major Kliemann. "Yes, I intend to send you to Portugal, but the question demands to be studied and must be carefully thought over, as I strongly doubt that, coming from the occupied zone, you will be authorized to go to England."

I can see already that it will take a very long time, that it will drag ... for weeks ... perhaps for months! Shall I have enough patience to go on waiting? I have been waiting such a long time already: nearly a whole year! And once again, I feel the treacherous grip of discouragement ... but I drive it back.

Major Kliemann asks me a quantity of details about my actual passport. "Delivered in Syria. That is good. It shouldn't mention at all your stay in the occupied zone. One could invent something in the free zone."

"It would be very risky," I say. "Just think of the difficulty of camouflaging a whole year at a cross examination of the British Security. It would be easy for them to make inquiries in the other zone. What would have been my means of existence? What kind of work? With whom? And the neighbours? And above all, what would have been my object of returning from Syria if it were not to join my family? No, I think you are mistaken. It would only appear natural that I should have spent all this time in Paris."

"You may be right. We'll have to think it over."

Yvonne, who has not taken part in the conversation has been yawning for some time and shows signs of impatience.

"Well," says Kliemann, "we'll be going home. You can both wait for me in the car. I'll join you presently, as soon as I have paid."

Yvonne gets up and walks towards the door. I am about to follow her, when the Major puts his hand on my wrist forcing me to sit down again. He leans forward and, fixing me right in the eyes, asks pointblank: "Why do you want to work for us?"

Someone else has asked me the same question before him. It was in Berlin. I look at him a moment in silence, then I smile: "Major," I say, "you are an intelligent man. How much would my answer be worth to you? I can tell you that it is out of conviction, or according to my principles, or because I love Germany, or else because I hate the British. But if I were your enemy, if I were here to harm you, to spy upon you, to betray you, do you believe that my answer would be any different? So, will you allow me not to answer?"

He has a brief laugh: "It's true, you are right!" and releases my wrist.

Yvonne who has come nearer during this short colloquy, shrugs her shoulders and says in German: "You ask idiotic questions!"

We start home. The streets are like black gulfs in which the car advances gropingly with the short tentacles of its black-lights. Suddenly, Kliemann pulls the brakes and turns back towards me: "Do you know Morse?"

"No."

"You'll have to learn it." He starts again the car. We stop at the corner of my street. "Yes," says he, continuing his thought, "I think that with you some twenty lessons will be sufficient. You'll learn quickly. Then, there will be the ciphering. You already know the secret writing?"

"Yes, but the proceeding doesn't seem very good to me."

"Well, we shall see."

And turning to Yvonne, he asks her to warn Richard, so that I can begin my lessons as soon as possible. "Richard in Mlle Yvonne's brother," he explains to me. "He'll be your teacher in the beginning."

Before I leave them, I take the rendezvous with Yvonne for Friday.

October 16th 1941

At the next table, a feldgrau captain with a shaved nape and congested face is holding hands with one of these women whom one would not like to call French. As soon as I have formed this judgment, I reproach it to myself. What right have I to throw the stone at this woman, when I am seated between Yvonne and Kliemann?

The "patronne" lifts the curtain which separates the kitchen from the restaurant, and comes towards us. "My little Yvonne!" she exclaims. "A whole week since I last saw you! I was wondering what had happened to you. And how is 'Monsieur le Major?'"

"Well. Thank you, Mme Boris," answers the latter. "Say, Mme Boris, I need your help. Can you get me clothing points?"

"How many?"

"About fifty."

"I'll give you the name of a friend who works at Frank's. You can see her on my behalf."

"You're an angel, Mme Boris! Will you also give us some chocolate cream like the other day?"

"There will always be some for you, you know that!" She returns to the kitchen.

It is the first time that I come to the Maisonnette. The narrow rural style brick façade is hardly noticeable from the much obstructed rue de Passy. The interior is arranged with good taste. The panels of carved wood, the pictures, the fruit dishes, the rare bottles on the centre table, make you forget that there are no windows, and that one is in a transformed court-yard. One can get anything at the Maisonnette: out of season strawberries, mayonnaise, 'frites,' fresh cream and real coffee. One can get anything at the Maisonnette if one can afford to pay. Therefore, all the tables—or nearly all—are occupied by the uniforms of the "occupants."

Our meal is excellent. Kliemann likes to eat well and while he eats, he doesn't speak—not about business in any case. Coffee? "Fine." Mme Boris comes herself to take off the table cloth. Now the room is nearly empty, but for a couple of lovers in a corner, but they pay no attention to us. The Major puts his elbows on the table, leans forward. "Please, will you repeat what relatives you have abroad? I want to be sure not to make a mistake."

"A cousin in England; she is British. Another cousin whom I believe to be in Lisbon; he is Polish and a diplomat. An uncle and an aunt in Madeira. My sister is in Algiers. In Istanbul, I also have a cousin. And finally, an uncle in Australia."

"Good. What interests us for the moment is the diplomat cousin and the English cousin. Very good that. Why do you say about your cousin that you 'believe him to be in Lisbon?'"

"Because it is possible he joined his Government in London."

"That's right. But how can we know that?"

"If he is in Lisbon, he would be with his Portuguese aunt. I could write him, but would you be able to forward my letters?"

"Nothing is easier."

"What I would suggest is not to hurry things in the beginning. Just to prepare the ground. To tell him that I have the intention to leave France and to join my cousin Bessie. Could he let her know? At the opportune moment I would ask him to help me. In the meantime, as every discreet and respectable diplomat, he would have chatted. It might come to the right ears. Later, I could explain all the difficulties I had to get away!"

"That isn't a bad solution. One could always try."

"And do you know what I have thought about the passport? I thought of going to the free zone to get it. I'm sure that my Lisbon relatives will help me get a Portuguese visa. Oh! An idea! Wait…. Yes, I've got it. You know, the aunt of my cousin, the one I mentioned before, is an old ailing lady. I could give as pretence that I must go to nurse her: I am a nurse. Let me think…. One ought…. I've got it! My own aunt, her sister, would have to write me asking me to come, telling that it is most urgent. This would certainly enable me to obtain an exit visa. What do you think of it?"

"Yes, but how would she reply to you? There is no postal communications between the occupied zone and foreign countries."

"I would have to spend a month in the free zone. One can write from there."

"It would seem suspicious that you should have obtained a pass. Bear in mind from now on that someday you will have to account for all your doings and moves."

I shrug my shoulders: "The passes can be bought like nothing on the black market. You know perfectly well that the Germans themselves sell them."

"That's true."

"So, what do we decide?"

"I think that we must begin by writing this letter to your cousin, as you have said. That will be a test. We'll see what comes out of it, and where he is. As soon as you have begun your training and are half ready, we can get to the second half of the programme. For if you obtain your exit visa, it is delivered only for 90 days, and in these three months you will have to get your other visas—Portuguese and Spanish—have finished your instruction and have left. It doesn't give you much time, as you can't wait to the last day to leave France. Such a lack of eagerness could seem suspicious. So, for today, it'll be all. Write the letter to your cousin and give it tomorrow to Yvonne. I'll have it forwarded."

October 17th 1941

Meet Yvonne at the Rond-Point des Champs-Elysees and give her the letter for Janio.[40]

October 29th

"The Morse code, as you know, translates letters into a series of dots and dashes. As soon as you will know the Morse equivalent for every letter, i.e. the number of dots and dashes of which it if formed, you'll have to forget that you have ever seen these signs written and only retain them by sound. I believe that the best way to remember the Morse signs is not following the alphabet, but by juxtaposed groups. You have

E .	- t	a .-	-.n
I ..	--m	u ..-	-..d
S ...	---o	v ...-	-...b
H			
K -.-	.-. r	w .--	--. g
X -..-	.--. P	l .-..	..-. f
		Y -.--	--.- q

The c, j, z are not matched. You'll have to remember them separately."

I listen carefully to the explanations of this first lesson. Yvonne has left us the dining room. Richard is a man of about thirty, with auburn hair and a slight lisp. Unlike his sister, he speaks very bad French.

"Now," he pursues, "I'm going to send you a series of letters with the manipulator. You must get accustomed from the very beginning to distinguishing the dots from the dashes. I'll do it slowly to start, and you can keep the alphabet before you!" He has a small buzzer which seems very archaic, and a battery. Every time he presses on it, it makes a more or less prolonged shriveling.

It is much less difficult that I had expected. After a short time, I can do without the book; and after half an hour, Richard passes me his manipulator and dictates me letters. At the beginning, my dots sound like dashes, and my dashes continue one into the other. After an hour, I have a violent headache and don't know anymore if, in the ordinary alphabet, the b stands before or after the m! I have to cry for mercy.

"It isn't bad for today," declares my professor with satisfaction. We have learned the value of three lessons. If we go on like this, in a month you'll be able to transmit and take messages."

"If I haven't been taken to Charenton[41] before that. My head is splitting!"

"It's a question of habit; you'll get used to it. I'll see you tomorrow, at the same time."

November 3rd 1941

Today, Paris has woken up under snow. Never has winter been so early. In Russia, Kharkov, Kursk have fallen one after the other. Simferopol and Theodosia are in the hands of the Germans. But in front of Moscow, their advance is held back by Tver and Mojaisk.[42] Japan continues to be carefully provoking.

Rumour says that Petain has personally written to Hitler on the subject of hostages. At any rate, the second hundred executions consecutive to the murder of the commandant of Nantes, Lt Colonel Hotz, and the commandant of Bordeaux, have been suspended. Amongst the uproar of the war, the chaos, the hunger which threatens France, seemingly indifferent to all of it, every day I take the metro to go to my lesson.

The first two were at Yvonne's. But it is so far, that Richard has told me to come to his place. It is nearly opposite to the house of Balzac, at No. 48 bis, rue Raynouard. I ask for M. Delidaise and the concierge, without glancing at me, grumbles: "Fifth floor!" I take the lift. Richard himself opens the door and shows me into the dining room. A young wolf dog—or more exactly a she-dog—comes to have a sniff at me. "Down, Sigrid!" says her master. But Sigrid seems to be more frightened than fierce.

The lesson begins. I write; then I transmit under his dictation. According to Richard's advice, I have spent the time in the metro trying to read everything in Morse. "Defense de fumer"[43] now appears to me only as: Ta, tit, tit-tit-tit, ta, tit-ta.... And so for all the rest. When I succeed in forgetting that all this is part of a definite plan which, if it succeeds, will be a weapon against the "Bosches," when I succeed to forget the uncertainty, the problematic success, then I enjoy it thoroughly.

The pleasure to learn, to acquire new knowledge—different from all I had before! I enjoy this satisfaction in spelling every word. During the years of my wanderings through Europe and the Near-East, my brain has undergone a forced rest. Today it responds willingly to the effort I demand of it, absorbs everything like a sponge and registers all faithfully.

This morning we have begun the figures; it isn't any more a question of memory but of hearing. Suddenly, Richard begins to laugh, because he has noticed that I count upon my fingers.

"Don't count," he says.

But as much as I try, quite unwillingly, now for the dot, now for the dashes, something in my head makes "One-two-three, one-two-three-four, one-two." The second half of the figures, i.e., 6, 7, 8, 9, 0 is much more complicated, and I am amazed when I think of the work that my brain does. For I count the dashes, add them to 5 and make the addition! ... = 2 + 5 = 7 Ta, ta, ta, tit, tit = 3 + 5 = 8 If I counted the dots, it would be still more complicated as I should have to subtract them from 10. - ... = 10 - 4 = 6 I am beginning to feel quite lost, when a ring of the bell, shortly followed by the appearance of the maid's head in the half-opened door, interrupts the lesson.

"It's Monsieur Loiseau."

"Ask him in, Suzanne," says Richard.

The Loiseau in question is a German of sporting appearance, middle height, with chestnut hair and wearing a trench-coat. Richard introduces him as "My professor." The latter bows: "Also, wie geht's?"[44] and without waiting for an answer, he seizes the manipulator and sends me a serial of letters at what seems to me, a terrific speed. I look at him open mouthed. "What then? You not talking?"

"But, Monsieur, I am only at my third lesson," I answer with much dignity.

"Ach! This not quick thought!" And losing all interest in someone so nil, he throws the manipulator over to Richard.

The lesson is finished. "I shan't see you for some days," says my professor, "as I am moving. As soon as I'm settled, Yvonne will let you know."

"I hope that it won't be too far."

"No, Neuilly. In the meantime, so as not to forget too much, do as I told you—in the metro and at home with a book."

"There is nothing to forget!" M. Loiseau says ironically.

I give him a dirty look and leave.

The fact is that he has deprived me of my marvelous confidence, this bird of a bad omen ("L'oiseau" in French means bird). I had the impression that everything was going on so well, and Richard said that I was learning quickly. And now this other one seems to expect me to be doing already hundred! Because he did go quickly! Is it possible that some day I'll be able to go as quickly as that? I feel discouragement gaining me and am full of doubts. And now I am going to lose a whole week!

-.-. .-. .--. .-. .. .; .; .... Mechanically, I translate in Morse code the words that meet my eyes.

I walk in the snow which already begins to melt—I walk dragging my feet. My shoes leak and I have Chilblains. I tried to get a "bon," but it was refused to me. I have asked once more: another refusal. Without being discouraged, I have tried for a third time … with the same lack of success. The other day, as I was at the rue Jacquemart for my ration card, I made a fourth request.

"Why insist, when you are told no?" grumbled the employee with a nasty look.

And this morning I have received my fourth refusal. What shall I do now? Buy some at the black market? It seems the only solution possible. What a chance that Babs doesn't need shoes!

November 5th 1941

"It's for you," says Daddy putting down the receiver. "Mlle Yvonne."

I go to the phone. "Hello?"

The voice comes from far away, very indistinct: "Listen. You must absolutely go to Richard's this afternoon. Our 'friend with the little moustache' wants to see you. He'll come. It's urgent."

"All right. But I thought that your brother was moving?"

"Tomorrow. He is still there today."

"O.K."

I have the whole morning to make suppositions and try to guess what he wants from me. Have they changed their mind? Have they discovered something? What? I'll know presently. I cannot fix my attention on dots and dashes, while Richard only thinks of his new house. Everything goes wrong. I get impatient. My professor gets cross. I try to learn from him why the Major want to see me, but he pretends not to know.

Kliemann turns up at the end of the lesson, very excited. He puts his leather portfolio down, takes off his hat and coat, sits down and seizes my arm. "Reichart is in Paris!" he exclaims.

I don't see anything extraordinary in Reichart being in Paris. Above all, I don't understand Kliemann's agitation. "Ah?" I say.

"Yes. He wants to see you."

"Ah?" I repeat for the second time.

He shakes my arm. "Don't go on repeating 'Ah!' like that. Say something. I won't allow it! You must choose: with whom do you want to work? Him or me?"

"Truly I don't care! But I should like to see you come to an agreement between yourselves, so that I would know what I am doing because you don't seem to know it. And this situation last since January! I have made two useless trips to Berlin. When I want to leave, I am told: "Wait!" I see successively lots of people, who all make plans, the ones more chimeric than the others. And who finally disappear! Dassel, Reichart, von Winter, and now you! Do you all work against each other?"

"So far as I am concerned, I'll tell what happened. After your second journey to Berlin, Felix's plans were altered due to circumstances, and he let you down. Two months ago, Reichart rang me up asking me to put you in connection with von Winter. So far, I was only an intermediary. I ignore what happened with von Winter, but one day he was recalled. Before that, he came to see me and told me you didn't interest him, but if I thought I could employ you, he was willing to pass you on. That's when I saw and questioned you, and understood at a glance what could be obtained from your English and Portuguese relations. I have elaborated a plan of action. Now that I have thrown its bases, that we are training you, Reichart wants to have you back. It is impossible to work in these conditions. I want to keep you, if you accept." Persuasive, begging, he leans over me, pleading: "You prefer to remain with me, don't you? And besides, the work we have undertaken interests you? Think of the future, of our successes, of our victory. Because we shall succeed, we'll vanquish—you and I—and that depends upon you. But to begin with, you must help me."

"What must I do?"

"Tell Mr. Reichart that the plans I have made interest you and that you would like to see them succeed. It isn't necessary to speak about the passport complication. He wants to see you tomorrow. I have accepted an appointment at 11 a.m. at the Marignan bar."

I agree. The question being settled, Kliemann seems reassured and relaxes.

"Your letter to your cousin Janio has left directly for Portugal. But I should like you to write him another one. I'll give you an address where he can answer you."

With many "Ifs" and "In case of," we discuss the pros and cons of our plans, their probabilities and chances. It depends of so many things. Is my cousin in Lisbon? If he is there, will he consent to make the necessary moves? And if he is willing, will he be able to do them? Has he the sufficient backing for it? And even if he does succeed in reaching Lorenzo, the chief of the International Police, the almighty master on whom everything depends, will the latter grant the visa?

11 o'clock. At the bar of the Marignan, no sign of Reichart. I wait until 11.45 and go home without having seen anyone. I suspect Kliemann not to have trusted my decision to remain with him and to have told Reichart that I either couldn't or didn't want to see him. At any rate, Reichart hasn't come.

November 8th 1941

"Reichart has left," announces the Major rubbing his hands.

"He didn't come yesterday," I remark. "What did you tell him that he didn't come?"

Kliemann raises his thick eyebrows in a perfect semblance of indignant surprise: "What do you mean? What are you suggesting?"

"Oh! Nothing. In any case it has no importance whatsoever, as I had decided to remain with you."

He squeezes my hand with satisfaction. "So you are not displeased? Not cross? You needn't regret Reichart. You'll see the fine work we'll do together."

November 14th

The interruption has not been a long one, and today I've had my ninth lesson.

Richard has moved to 73 rue de Lonchamps in Neuilly, in a sort of wooden cottage surrounded by a large garden. Babs has found in Sigrid an enthusiastic playmate and together they ravage the soaked and uncultivated flower-beds. Then they come tearing into the house, covered with mud and leaving everywhere the prints of their eight paws.

Richard and I discuss things without coming to an agreement. The Major wants me to take with me a wire-less transmitter. I must therefore learn to transmit. I agree on that, but I protest against having to take with me a radio. It will be wonderful enough if I manage to get into England, without complicating everything and making it still more risky by the presence of a radio in my luggage. I don't even know if I'll be authorized to enter the United Kingdom.

"It would be better if you showed me to transform an ordinary radio into a transmitting set and told me what are the necessary parts to make one."

"For that I have to ask the "Dr." We'll see!"

I never know if by "Dr." he means his professor or the Major. In Germany every other man is a "Herr Doktor."

Richard shows me a small radio of a current model and turning it over explains how he transformed it into a transmitter. "I have used it during the early part of the war until the occupation. I've had several searches at my place; my radio examined, but nothing was ever discovered." He seems quite proud of it.

November 20th 1941

The general offensive is launched in Libya. London says it is the result of five months' preparations.

In the corner room, at Richard's, my manipulator is now branched on the radio, which, in turn, has been connected with a similar buzzer in the adjoining room, the Delidaise couple's bedroom.

"Love," Richard's wife—he pronounces "Leuve"—is there in permanence, or on watch, with another pupil of whom I know nothing, except that his first name is "Roger." The groups of letters which I send are transmitted to the next room where Roger takes them. After a while, we switch: he transmits and I take down. We don't go very fast either for us; we are both only beginners. Nevertheless, we know already the typical presentation of a message, as we shall have to send some day.

KA to say: "Attention, I begin," repeated twice, then the dash followed by the number of letters; another dash repeated twice, then the groups of five, with a space between each group and at the end: dash, AR, AR. So far, it's all.

I am nervous because my neighbor doesn't separate his groups and gets me all confused. Today, Richard has taught me what to do if I don't understand or cannot hear well: I must interrupt my series of dots and ask for repetition by sending two rapid tit-tit. I spend my time interrupting and asking Roger to repeat, until he gets so mad that he sends me a very dirty word!

Friday, November 28th 1941

This week, new posters have appeared on the walls of the metro; they promise a reward of 200.000 francs for helping to find two young Belgians who murdered two Gestapo agents in Tournai. We also know from the newspapers that attempts by dynamite have been committed in Paris.

Saturday, November 29th

There has been an extraordinary bulletin issued by the German H.Q. stating that "according to instructions, the occupation troops have evacuated Rostov, in order to submit the civilian population of this town to exemplar reprisals for having committed acts of hostility in the rear of the German armies!!!" It's the first time that I hear such an explanation given to the loss of a position!

WEDNESDAY, DECEMBER 3RD 1941

A new murder, yesterday, in the XIIIth. district, where curfew has been ordered at 6.30 p.m. Posters threaten the Parisians with new sanctions if the culprits of the attempt of the night between the 2nd and 3rd haven't been discovered before the 6th.

DECEMBER 5TH

Japan answers by a refusal to the American memorandum. War is getting nearer.

Another attempt in the VIth. district. Contrary to what could be expected, no sanctions have been taken this evening.

Yvonne has moved out. I went to see her at her new flat, place du Palais-Bourbon, 8. She has taken a maid, a Breton, who has a baby from a German. Yvonne considers it as her "moral obligation" to help out this girl, who has given a future soldier to the IIIrd. Reich. Her name is Annick. The baby, thin and covered with scabs, spends its days in its pram in the dark kitchen full of unwashed plates and dishes. The dog Mouki is ill; he has a meningitis, can hardly stand on his legs and soils everywhere.

DECEMBER 6TH 1941

"Starting from zero hour England will be at war with Finland, Rumania and Hungary," has just announced the B.B.C.

SUNDAY, DECEMBER 7TH 1941

It has just been announced that Japan has attacked the American bases of Hawaii and Manila.

DECEMBER 8TH

The United States and Great Britain are at war with Japan.

My lessons are very irregular. I believe that Richard is more interested in black market traffic than in teaching me Morse! Several times I went there uselessly. "Monsieur begs to be excused; he has been obliged to go out" Suzanne tells me on such occasions. At the third time, I got cross: "He has my telephone number! He could let me know." And I have complained to Yvonne. I told her that I wouldn't return there under such conditions. Since then, either Richard or his wife, or Suzanne telephone me if there is to be no lesson. It happens twice or three times weekly. It all drags on in the most exasperating way.

Today is the first day of the curfew at 6 p.m. Rush in the metro. But people take it lightly. It is so much better than hostages.

TUESDAY, DECEMBER 9TH

America strikes back: Formosa and Tokyo are bombed. Is England going to withdraw its fleet from the Mediterranean in order to send ships in the Pacific? What will be Japan's attitude towards Russia, and Russia's toward Japan?

Sunday, December 14th 1941

Hitler has declared war on America.

The "punishment," which consigned us at home daily at 6 p.m., is abolished. At the same time, the radio announces that new attempts have been perpetrated yesterday. In reprisal, the Jews of the occupied zone have been taxed 1 million francs, and one hundred new hostages are going to be shot. It is going to make trouble.

December 15th

New attempts rue des Victoires and at Villejuif. Half of my lessons are spent discussing the latest events with Richard. I tell him that I don't see what benefit Hitler can get out of a war with America, especially after having promised his Armies that everyone would be home for Xmas 41. And Xmas is in ten days! Richard answers that by this new war declaration Hitler shows to the World, and to Germany, that he is stronger than ever, and is not afraid to face a new enemy as powerful as America. On the other hand, from now on, the German submarines will be able to sink American conveyors and transports, no longer neutral. And thirdly, the United States are much too far away for Germany to fear a direct action on their part.

"And if the U.S.A. should use England as a base?"

Richard laughs: "The u-boats control the Atlantic, and soon there will not be a single town left in England, thanks to the Luftwaffe!"

December 17th

The Berlin radio announces that in the East the German army proceeds to a straightening of the front in order to reduce the distances and to establish winter headquarters. Extensive action is not possible anymore on account of the bad weather. The retreat is affected according to pre-established plans. I feel that this will cause another discussion with Richard. I love to make him lose his self-control by asking him insidious questions.

December 18th

The shortage of coal is felt more and more. The cost of living increases from day to day. Butter is at 185 francs a kg. A short time ago, it was at 120 francs.

December 20th

I have asked Yvonne to come to Richard's. She is late; it is half past twelve when she arrives. "Will you have lunch with me at "La Maisonnette?" she asks me. "We'll talk over eating."

Madame Boris greets her as usual with outstretched arms. There are but few people at this time of the day. I start immediately on the subject: "I'll tell you what it's about. I cannot continue to do nothing, I mean—not to work. It may surprise you, but I'm no millionaire!"

"Oh! But, of course! Aren't you paid? It is absolutely necessary. I'll talk to 'our friend' with the little moustache. Ring me up tomorrow."

I hesitated a long time before taking this step. But eventually I decided that to appear selfishly interested would seem quite normal to them, whereas indifference would look suspicious. That is why I asked to be paid, and it was difficult for me to do so. I am not interested in money; I hate to have to ask it from them, to be obliged to accept it from them is humiliating. To ease me mind, I tell myself that they are paying me to work against them.

December 25th

Christmas! Daddy was able to get (at what price!) half a goose. It was tough, but had a "festive" taste. I decorated a tiny Xmas tree. Christmas 1941!

January 1st 1942

New Year has entered hesitatingly in a desolate, gloomy Paris, with its squares deprived of their statues. The bare pedestals seem a silent reproach to the passers-by for not having been able to defend the memory of Victor Hugo, Balzac, Lavoisier, who made the glory of France. Petain made a melancholic speech.

January 2nd 1942

Yvonne has given me the Major's reply concerning my salary. I shall get 3,000 francs a month, paid in advance. "Does it suit you?" she asked.

"It does," I replied, although I know they generally pay their reserve agents 6,000 francs! But I don't care, as long as I can live in the meantime.

January 8th

After an interruption of two weeks, I return to Richard's. From the Neuilly bridge, tramping in melted snow, I have to follow Longchamps street. My worn out shoes leak.

Richard has just returned from Berlin.

"Are you bringing us good news?" I ask him.

"They exaggerate everything over here," he answers. "People misinterpret the strategic withdrawal on the Eastern front, so eager are they to see us make a false step! They are quite ready to proclaim it a Russian victory. As if they didn't know that to stabilize a front one fortifies a line, then falls back on it. That's what our army is doing in Russia. It has already occurred in 1916-17."

"Maybe," I say. "But it would seem more logical—when one has a front of 3,000 kilometers, that one is at thousands of kilometers from one's supply bases, that the temperature is—50 degrees, or even -60 degrees—it would seem logical that an Army should establish its winter quarters in towns (or, at least, in what remains of them) and not in open fields. At present, these towns: Toola, Kalooga, Kalinin, Klin and in a few days, Orel, Koursk, Kharkov,—you are losing them one after the other. And Libya? Is it also a strategic fall back? And if so, is it in Tunis you intend to establish your winter quarters? No, believe me, leave propaganda to the mass of imbeciles. You know me well enough. You know that I am, as much as yourselves, interested in your victory. You see me restless because I see you losing your grip and should like you to assure me of the contrary."

Suddenly, Richard's bluff falls, leaving him depressed. "Everything is going wrong," he admits. "However, in North-Africa, we still hold Sollum and Al-Faya."

I get up and go to the map pinned on the wall. "Look. You are encircled at Tobruk, but Tobruk is supplied by sea. You have no fleet in the Mediterranean. For you it's a question of a few days!"

He looks thoughtfully at the map, as if seeing it for the first time. "It is worse than I expected. They say in Berlin that in a month there won't remain a German in Africa! As for the British, if they enter in Tunisia, I suppose that the French will declare war."

"If it happens, it will be like in Syria. But it's improbable; you don't believe it yourself! The French, in Africa, are more pro–British than pro–German, or, if you prefer: more Germanophobe than Anglophobe. And there are ninety-nine chances to one that they would join de Gaulle rather than you. Why didn't you destroy England when it was time yet?"

"Yes: why! But everyone makes a mistake some time or other!"

The rain has stopped and I walk home. Richard's defeatism has cheered me up. At the Porte Maillot I am surprised not to see any German soldiers. Then I remember having been told that since a few days earlier the gates of Paris are no longer guarded by the Wehrmacht. Paris is rapidly losing it "undesirable" guests.

January 12th

I am furious with myself. This morning, when I came to the corner-room where I usually work, I saw a man's grey felt hat on the table. Five minutes later, Richard came to fetch it. Apparently, it was "Roger's" hat, for it was he who was in the next room. I recognize him by the way he transmits; he always forgets the intervals between the groups. And from the moment Richard came to take away the hat, I've been furious with myself.

It annoys me to know nothing of my correspondent, except his Christian name, his voice (which is quite ordinary) and the rhythm of his transmitting. Now, there is one more item: the grey felt. And I tell myself that I ought to have done something to see his face if it were only a glimpse. Perhaps the hat might have helped me, but Richard gave me no time. Anyhow, what could I have done? I don't know; that's why I am annoyed at myself. I have the impression I've missed an opportunity.

January 16th

Hurray! The hat is there again. I look around for inspiration. The table cover has a fringe. I tear off a thread and slip it under the ribbon of the hat, at the back, in such a way that only a tiny bit of it shows. I try to imagine the gesture of a man putting on his hat. He takes it by the front part and puts it on his head. He wouldn't notice the thread. If he looks at himself in a mirror, he still won't see it. But if Richard comes to fetch it and puts it down the wrong way, he might notice it. The door opens and Richard comes in.

"If you don't mind, we are going to work in the next room today."

"Not at all," I say, but inside I think to myself: "on the contrary" for that way the hat won't be moved.

Richard leads me onto the landing, while my "Neighbour" passes through the communication door.

"Next time," says my professor, "you'll take a real transmission. Be on time. I'll begin at 10 o'clock sharp."

"Do you think I'll know how?"

"I don't see why not! I have chronometered you; you do 60. Next transmitting shall be only at 45."

"O.K."

I hurry to the underground. I know that Roger hasn't left yet. Unless he walks home, he is bound to take the metro. And the Pont de Neuilly station is the terminal: one direction and only one platform to watch. I feel in me the instinct of a hound!

I settle down on a bench under a light, to have a good view of all the passengers who will come by. Roger is obliged to pass in front of me, and as I have a very sharp sight, if the bit of thread is there, I cannot fail to see it. A train enters the station. The automatic gate closes, people get into the carriages. During a few minutes the platform remains deserted. The metro leaves and a new rush of passengers hurry in.

I let another train pass, and then a second one, and a third. It is thirty minutes past twelve. I have examined more than grey felt, but none had my mark of distinction. I begin to feel discouraged. He may have passed by without my seeing him, or he may have picked the thread off his hat, and if it's so, I can wait until tomorrow. "One more metro," I say to myself, "and if I don't see Roger, I shall go." The metro leaves the station. Another comes. Nobody. "This time, it will be the last." Two more pass. Still no one.

With a sigh of resignation I decide to go. Passengers are becoming fewer. There are longer intervals between the trains. It is late. I am waiting for the next metro; I'll take it. In front of me, a man is waiting at the edge of the platform, reading a magazine. Instinctively I look at his back. He has a dark-blue rain coat. Suddenly I start; a bit of white thread shows above the hatband of his grey felt.

The train enters the station. "Roger" gets in among the passengers. I follow. Nearly all the seats are free. Carelessly, I sit down facing him. He looks up, then resumes his reading: a cheap detective story. I can examine him at leisure. The man is below average height, about 28 to 30 years old, brown hair, graying at the temples. He is clean-shaved, thin-lipped, with drooping corners. He wears two narrow ribbons in the buttonhole of his overcoat: the Croix de Guerre and the medaille militaire[45] (The swine!) and a small aviation badge: encircled wings.

We reach the Etoile station, where I change. I hesitate a moment. Shall I follow him up? What's the use? Besides, he might notice it and if some day we meet at the rue de Longchamp, he would recognize me. My curiosity satisfied, I go home.

—⚞—

January 20th 1942

Yesterday, the Russians have recaptured Mojaisk. It is lucky the German defeats have no effect on my professor's mood. He is only interested in his black-market deals, leaving to the Nazis the honour of getting killed for a "Greater Germany." I asked him the other day why he had not enlisted, to which he replied he was much too precious as a radio-instructor, as they were very few.

This morning I arrive a quarter of an hour in advance. I am rather nervous at the thought of having to take a "real" transmission. Richard gives me the wave length, and I start looking for it. Then he tells me the call sign. I write it down.

"They are going to call during ten minutes, so you have plenty of time to get ready. After that, there will be a dash; then KA, twice; a dash; then the number of letters; again a dash and then: the message. Is it clear?"

"Yes," I say, and I feel my nervousness increasing.

Richard looks at his watch. "It is time; they must be there. Look for them."

Slowly, I turn the knob. I hear various sounds intermingled with music, but amongst all the dots and dashes, I am unable to make out a single letter.

"Well, you had it!"

Again I pass it, because I didn't recognize the call sign. Richard gets angry. "Can't you hear it?" He sets it for me.

I listen with all my ears, but am desperate to see that I cannot distinguish the three letters which compose the call sign. My ear perceives them as ONE continuous sound. My hands are moist. "Steady," I say to myself. "Be calm. I have ten minutes before the message begins. It will be no different from the one I take and send every day. All that is nothing but imagination." And the ten minutes are over.

"Look out!" says Richard.

I hear a different sound. "It must be dash," I say to myself, because I have also forgotten how a dash sounds! "After that, it'll be KA." So I write KA in advance. Then, shamelessly, I squint at Richard and copy from his sheet. He is much too busy to notice what I am doing. About the middle of the message, I recognize an A, then a B, an S … unless it's an H—I always mix them up. Then O. I. I skip a letter, putting a dot instead. Now I am started. I forget my nervousness, my panic vanishes, and I finish honourably. Rich throws a glance at my copy book.

"Well, you see, it wasn't so terrible! You even haven't so many mistakes!"

I let an "ouf" of relief. My hands are still shaking while I gather my belongings.

"The next transmission will be after tomorrow. It is every two days. Be on time."

February 28th, 1942

New American contingents have arrived in North Ireland. Here everybody thinks it means an Anglo-American invasion on the coasts of France. If only it could be true! I wish it so much that I don't stop to think what my position would be should it happen. I probably would be arrested and accused of working for the "Boches." Everything would be against me. I would have no proof of the contrary. But what would it matter, if France were free and our people no longer starving.

March 3rd 1942

A distant and prolonged rumble interrupts the end of the B.B.C. bulletin. It is not quite half past nine. I open the window. A thunderstorm? It can't be; there is a full moon. Beyond the fluffs of little white clouds, myriads of stars twinkle in the darkness of the night. An explosion is heard very clearly, followed by others. No possible doubt; there is shooting! "An ideal night for an air raid," I say to myself at the very moment when the first flare lights up in the sky. It is there, motionless, like a huge lantern hanging above the town. Everybody is at the windows, forgetting the black out. The dark blocks of houses light up with luminous rectangles, outlining human silhouettes.

Before the first flare had time to go out, others light up. Strangely enough, the sirens keep silent. The explosions sound in rapid succession. Our window-panes are rattling. One clearly distinguishes the deflagration of bursting bombs from the shooting of the A.A. guns which is very scarce. The sky is buzzing with low flying planes, appearing and disappearing between the clouds. The luminous rays of the projectors try in vain to pierce the low ceiling.

Very soon their lights go out. The scenery is fairy-like. The houses seem to be covered with silver roofs. The vault of heaven is dotted with balls of fire which slowly float adrift.

I go down in the street. It is crowded with people. The "concierge" is in the street; the chemist from the corner too, as well as the mild-woman and the laundress. Here comes the baker. The houses empty; everyone wants to hear the news.

"The British! The British! Here they come at last!" are shouting the people, oblivious of all caution, as if to have English planes above and around them, and the night as ally swept out all fear.

"Hurrah for the English! And to hell the Boches!" shouts a workman. And as, in spite of all, people look around, scared, he adds: "Don't worry; they can't hear us. They have all hidden in the shelters."

Somebody has brought out a map of Paris. One can see as by broad day-light. I count nine flares in the sky. People try to orientate the direction of the attack.

"Billancourt is getting it!"

"Listen!" says somebody, as a chaplet of bombs blows up. "Tomorrow there will be nothing left of Renault's works."

"It will be that much less left for the collaboration," says another.

"I pity those who are working in rotation tonight!" says a third.

"They knew what they were doing," he is told. "It's war!"

A machine-gun goes off over our heads. The street empties. Shutters bang. I go back home, draw an arm-chair to the open window and, with Babs on my lap, watch to the end of the bombardment. Babs tries to sniff the flares; he stretches his neck. He wonders if it's any good to eat. The explosions are getting weaker, more distant, more spaced. The last flare goes out. Babs has gone to sleep, his nose under his hind-paw. The sky has cleared up; the clouds have melted away. Windows are being closed everywhere. In the distance, beyond the roofs, a red glimmer tints the sky where the factories are burning. It is almost midnight.

March 4th 1942

This morning I go to see the premises of the disaster. It takes me two hours and a half to get to the Sevres bridge because the metros are so overcrowded. People go there as on a pilgrimage. At the "correspondence" of Glare St Lazare, I have to stand in line for an hour. On reaching its destination, the metro adds the tide of newcomers to the crowd already stationed there. Near the entrance, a bomb going through the ground has opened a round hole with sliding edges.

Outside, the sight is incredible: roofs have been torn off; calcinated beams, trees, uprooted or broken like matches are scattered all over the place; half of an armored tank is caught in a tree. The ground is littered with broken tiles, crushed glass and various rubbish; the pavement is upturned; through the holes and the cracks of the shattered walls the eye catches glimpses of the collapsed walls. Small size tanks from one of the work-shops have been projected in all directions by the force of the explosions. A mocking crowd passes under the sullen glance of helmeted German soldiers on watch. Had the Germans been able to prevent the Parisians from going to Billancourt, they would, no doubt, have done it, but it would have meant to consign all Paris.

"That's some work!" approves a workman who has brought with him his whole family.

I cross the Sevres bridge, blown up in two places, and walk along the Seine, on the other side of the Ile Segain. The Sevres railroad has received a direct hit. The rails have been blown up on a length of six or seven meters. The crater is not very deep; nevertheless, the violence of the explosion has blown down three houses on the opposite side of the road. As I pass these ruins, a plaintive chirrup makes me lift my head. A tiny canary is perched on top of the demolished wall! Nearby, a broken cage is lying on the ground.

"Poor little thing!" says a man near me. "If I could catch it, I'd put it with my own. If it remains here, it will die of hunger, or be eaten by a cat." Carefully, he approaches the small bird. The wee creature observes him with glossy, bead-like eyes, without stopping its sad chirrup. The man picks up the bird, without it trying to resist. It doesn't know freedom; freedom has no value for it.

On the island, two gas-tanks have been shelled and this spray of petrol spurts in all directions. There is but little damage on the other side. I reach the bridge at Issy-less-Moulineaux. The war-houses on the island have had their share. Masses of truck frameworks have been more or less flattened out. I cross the Seine and stop for a moment in front of a seven-storied building, of which nothing remains but three walls and the roof. It's extraordinary what a small heap seven stories and all their contents make after they have collapsed. In front of another house—smaller but in the same condition—a woman is telling another one: "To think that I'm here in front of my home and can't even go in to take a handkerchief out of my cupboard!"

Going further on, I succeed in baffling the German sentries and find myself in the very midst of the bombed buildings. Through the wide breach of a gaping wall, I enter the inside of a factory work-shop leather belts torn away, twisted machinery lying on the ground, steel superstructures twisted into huge corkscrews like spirals. The air is heavy with the smell of burned rubber and paint, choking with petrol and oil smoke. In some places tires are still burning, in others they are smoldering, spreading thick and acrid fumes. Soot is falling from the sky. As I advance, I notice that the workshops have been systematically demolished one after the other. The methodic, regular destruction must have been affected from a low altitude. Yes, that's some work, and well done too! As that other one said.

March 5th

As Richard is tidying the papers scattered on his desk, I catch a glimpse of a sketch which I recognize as being that of the Renault factories from the peculiar curve of the Seine at that place, and also by the shape of the Seguin Island. I conclude that he too must have been there.

"How were the fireworks over here?" I ask.

"It wasn't very pleasant," he says, thrusting his papers in a drawer and putting its key in his pocket. "Anyhow, they have missed their aim; the only victims are civilians."

"Did you go there?"

"Yes."

"Have you been inside?"

"I have."

"Ah? And you find that it's demolished?"

"Completely."

"Oh? I have been assured of the contrary. Well, it's too bad!"

My lessons are not satisfactory. I take them two or three times a week, very irregularly, with long intervals of sometimes eight days, just because Richard happens to have gone to Savoy, or has been busy with some black market deal, or got involved in a mercury business.

It takes about half an hour by the metro and ten minutes by foot to reach the rue de Langchamp; that means an hour and a quarter travel for fifteen minutes work. It can't go on like that.

March 10th

Richard came yesterday to our flat to fix an additional aerial and to check Daddy's radio. I want to try to work at home, but Richard does not think that it can be done, as our radio isn't good enough. And he is right; this morning I try vainly to catch the call sign. I'm quite sure it isn't my fault, for now I generally find it without help and without mistake.

March 11th

"Just imagine!" says Yvonne whom I haven't seen since Billancourt. "We were going out of a restaurant, which was rather noisy, when we suddenly heard: boom! boom! boom! Remembering a stale joke, I shouted: "Look out! Here come the British!" and burst out laughing. At the same moment: ploof! goes a rocket: ploof! another, and planes all over the sky!! And shooting everywhere. I did not expect to have guessed so well. Do you know what we did? The restaurant was in a basement; it was a good shelter. So we hurried back to it and waited for the end of the show … drinking champagne! Still, aren't they swine!"

"Yes, swine "they" are!" I say with conviction thinking of the people who drink champagne while others are killed.

"I should like to see 'Moustache,'" I add a moment later.

It is thus that, gradually, "Our-friend-with-the-little-moustache" became "Little-moustache," then simply "Moustache," as we had come by mutual agreement, to call very irreverently Major Kliemann.

"He is very busy just now. Is there anything I could do for you? Do you need money?"

"No, it isn't that. It's about these Morse lessons. They are absolutely worthless. It's a loss of time. I want him to know it. The day to leave will come. It will be decided quite suddenly. 'Moustache' will think I'm ready, whereas I shall know nothing. It's not a game, neither for your Secret Services nor for me. The whole thing is too risky to embark on it rashly. And that is what your brother doesn't seem to understand. It is what I want 'Moustache' to know."

Yvonne looks annoyed. "I know," she says. "Richard takes things too superficially. He has already been reprimanded more than once. I shall speak about it to 'Moustache.' In the meanwhile, will you come and take your transmissions at my place? My radio is good."

"All right. I can always try."

March 26th

Babs gambols like mad on the forbidden lawn, barking at the trees, rolling in the new young grass. The sun is hot. Around the lake, the yellow iron chairs have re-appeared. I draw up one to the water-edge and seat myself. The calm surface of the lake reflects the opposite bank, the great motionless pines, the pale cloudless sky. A duck passes breaking the reflection, which re-forms itself after it's gone. Round the bend, retire the island, a boat manipulated by a single rower, progresses slowly. How quiet everything is: no people; hardly a car from time to time. And the air is light; everything is green, fresh, new. I should like to remain here, motionless, for a long, long, time. I would like to forget that there is a war on, that there is hatred, that there is fighting. Not to hate would be so good.

When I was a little girl, my sister and I used to come with our governess and row on this same lake of the Bois de Boulogne. How we loved it! We were somewhat scared, but we felt the equals of the ducks. When we passed amongst them, they hardly took any notice, except to avoid the oars. Sometimes, we brought them some bread. They fought in the water, chasing each other and ducking, round droplets rolling down their oily feathers. The boldest ones—and they were many—came out of the water onto the bald grassy bank to get crumbs out of our hands. Suddenly, I feel sorry not to have brought any bread. A few ducks are precisely rambling around in search of something to eat, looking in my direction.

Funny, how everything is just as it was twenty years ago, even more than that. These ducks are other ducks; yet they are exactly like those of the past. And the pine-trees on the other side of the lake are the same pine-trees; the island is the same island; the bridge is the same bridge. Perhaps, I'll return here when I am an old lady, and everything will be then as it was at the time of my childhood—as it is now—everything, except beings like me.

Gradually, my mind returns to the only thing which preoccupied me at the present moment: the nearest future. Because the weather is so fair, and everything breathes of peach, I let my imagination drift off, as drifts that little white feather lazily floating on the water. Let us suppose that I do leave France. The Germans haven't discovered anything about me, have entrusted me with a confidential mission, and I reach Madrid. What am I to do then? I see myself in the office of the British military attaché. I don't ask myself how I got there. I'm not concerned with that detail at the present. I take it for granted that I get there, and once there, I tell him everything. What "everything?" Well, everything from the beginning: my hike to Warsaw, my accidental meeting with Dassel, and then, years after, the war, my decision to continue the struggle by my own means. I smile. It seems romantic and a little foolish! (That's how it was, nevertheless!) Then how I enticed Dassel. Then how I met von Winter, then Kliemann, then, how I came to Madrid.

How does the attaché react to my tale? Every time I tell myself this story—for this is not the first time—he reacts differently. Sometimes, he gets up, shakes my hand and congratulates me. At other times, he wants to have positive proofs. I have none to offer, and he has me arrested. But the worst is when he refuses to believe me and sends me away. What do I do then? All my work has been in vain. Where am I to go? Neither forwards, nor backwards; all the bridges are cut! Generally, when I reach this point of my thoughts, I stop and try to think of something else. But today, I skip the "cordial" hand-shake and the "congratulations" and dwell on the two other possibilities.

"If he asks for proof." Suddenly, I burst out laughing to myself. Why, he'd have to be a fool. What positive proofs would I be carrying with me? So there remains the "if he doesn't believe me" alternative. He'll have to believe me! Suddenly I feel capable of an irresistible force of persuasion, of a limitless willpower. He will believe. It may take some time; there'll be verification, investigations. I shall wait. I shall wait, as I am waiting now, tirelessly, knowing that, eventually, I'll win. I'll wait until he tells me: "I believe you." Then I won't answer, but inside me a voice will sing "Allelluia!"

I stretch out my legs. The arm-chair is hard, but the weather is so wonderful. How tired I am of waiting, ever and ever waiting, without anything positive, anything sure in view. If I knew that I had to wait for two years.... But not to know it. That is the horror of the situation. I feel the slow and constant erosion of my nerves. At home, I am sulky, violent, and always impatient. Is this waiting to last forever?

April 1942

My transmissions at Yvonne's give no results. I went there five or six times. Generally, she wasn't home. Annick, the maid, must have received orders; she closed all the doors without my telling to do so and left me alone.

The dog Mouki is recovering, but has remained an idiot, and soils everywhere, worse than a pup. I have given up my visits to the Place du Palais Bourbon, as half of the time, the radio was out of order. Now, I am waiting again. "Moustache" seems to have lost all interest in me. Anyhow, he is in no hurry to see me!

I look desperately for lodgings without finding any. I want to settle on my own, to keep my parents clear from my activities. I have always hinted to Yvonne that I didn't get along at home. More than once, has "Moustache" asked me what tale I serve at home and how I explain the money he is giving me. I told him that my parents never questioned me, but that, to be on the safe side, I had spread rumors that I was dealing with black market. That satisfied him.

June 1942

Since Monday, all the Jews must wear a yellow star on their left lapel. The other day, seeing a queue in our street and having nothing to do, I went and stood in line, thinking that I might perhaps get something interesting. I had omitted to ask what they were selling. When, looking up, I saw that I was in front of a furrier's shop! Somewhat amazed, I asked my neighbor: "What is the line for?" "They are giving out insignias to the Jews." And I had waited twenty-five minutes for nothing.

June 15th 1942

I have, at last, found lodgings.

June 22nd

Laval has made a speech, in which he wishes "with all his heart" the victory of the Germans. He enjoins the French workmen to enroll for work in Germany, "in order to hasten the victory, which will release our prisoners and set them at liberty!" The reflections one hears in the streets are in the style of, this one: "Now, the traitor Laval has thrown down his mask. He no longer pretends to speak as a Frenchman, but reveals his pro–Germanism." People deduce from the speech that the lack of man-power is getting worse and worse in Germany. It brings us a new hope.

June 26th

I had to get really mad to force an interview with "Moustache." As I arrive this morning at the Place du Palais Bourbon, Yvonne is out, but Annick informs me that "Monsieur" is "in conference" in the library. She shows me into the drawing room. A few minutes later, someone else comes, whom she locks up in the dining-room. The next one will have to go to the bath-room!

The door leading into the library is not thoroughly closed, but the walls are so thick that, in spite of that, one hardly hears the murmur of voices. Mouki comes to greet me. He must have recognized "Moustache's" voice, for he raises his ears, turns his head to the library, then takes off, stumbling, towards the library door, pushing it slightly with his nose, and sneaks into the next room. Through the door, now ajar, every word reaches me distinctly, and I immediately prick up my ears, the subject seeming of interest. After five minutes eavesdropping, I start feeling uneasy. Would it not be better, safer, for me to go away? If "Moustache" discovers, or even suspects that I have overheard this conversation, it is difficult to foresee what his reaction might be. But I can't make up my mind to waste such an opportunity and decide to remain. To give myself a countenance, I pick up a book within reach and start turning the pages. It is a sumptuous edition of a pornographic work. I look at the pages without seeing them, all my attention concentrated on what is said in the next room.

Apparently, Kliemann is giving his ultimate instructions to one of his agents, who is ready to start. The latter has bought—in his name but for the account of the German Secret Services—a certain number of fishing boats, which have been restored and are ready. The unknown interlocutor is to go to Libreville, in French Equatorial Africa, to organize there a shark—fishery. This is the "camouflage." The true aim is to scatter fishing-boats on the route of the British supply convoys coming from Brazil and putting in at Lagos, before continuing to South-Africa. Kliemann's agent is to mark the tonnage of the ships, their number, the speed of the convoys, the strength of their escort, etc. It appears from this conversation, that the location where the fishery is to be installed is not electrified. The transmission-post the spy is to take with him will be run by a battery. Kliemann explains how he will have to attach it onto his car in order to charge his battery. The Major advises him to "go out driving aimlessly around in the evenings." After this, he recommends caution, enjoins him to mistrust everyone and warns him of the efficiency of the Intelligence Service. I feel that the conversation is coming to an end.

Suddenly, there falls an impressive silence. The moment I have been dreading has come. "Moustache" must have noticed the open door. The throbbing of the blood in my temples hurts. I keep up turning slowly the pages and glancing at the sub-titles which I do not see. My back is to the door. Yet I know that Kliemann is on the threshold. I sense him watching me. The silence is excruciating. I can feel Kliemann approaching, although I cannot hear him, owing to the thickness of the carpet.

"I am going to scream in a moment," I think to myself. "I can endure it no longer."

"How do you do?"

I start with a cry. It relieves me. "You have frightened me!" I say, pressing a hand to my heart. "Moustache" looks at me and his gaze is very cold. I continue angrily: "I don't find it funny to startle people like that! From where did you come out?"

"You didn't hear me coming?" he asks, adding: "How long have you been here?"

"I don't know exactly. Annick told me you would be coming soon. I found this book; it's ripping!"

"Moustache" starts laughing. "Well, you're lucky to have found this book," he says.

"Yes," I say. "Waiting has seemed less long!"

His distrust has vanished. He assures me he is doing all that's necessary to get my pass. As no answer has come from my Polish cousin, the Major has decided that it will be better to manoeuvre from the free zone.

The first thing that catches my eye, this morning, at Richard's place, are photos of fishing-boats on the walls. They had been there for some time, but I have never paid much attention to them. Today, I look at them, because of yesterday's overheard conversation.

"Are you leaving on a cruise?" I ask Richard.

"Not I; one of my friends. He is going out fishing."

"That's grand! With the shortage of fish and the black market prices, he couldn't do better!"

"It won't be eating fish," says Richard.

"What for, then? What kind of fish?"

"Sharks."

I open my eyes as wide as I can: "Sharks? But there are no sharks along the coasts of France! You're pulling my leg!"

"Not at all! I never said it would be on the French coast."

"In that case, your friend will have to go as far as the Indian Ocean, or to Australia, or South-America."

"Or Africa," adds Richard.

"If you like." And I ask: "What is he going to do with his sharks, if one cannot eat them?"

"They give oil. Their skin is used for making shoes and bags. It brings a lot of money!"

July 19th 1942

The deportation of foreign Jews has begun. This morning, at the corner of Avenue Mozart, I notice a truck parked along the curb. Two German soldiers are on guard. The truck is crammed full with men. Their faces are ashen, bewildered, haggard. Some of them hold bundles. Others are empty handed. The passers-by look at them with compassion and hurry on, because of the armed soldiers. I ask a housewife, returning from the market, with a sack of lettuce, "Who are those people?"

And she answers, in a whisper, without turning her head: "Jews 'they' are taking God only knows where."

I too pass by, without glancing back to spare them at least the sensation of trapped animals. The Jew hunt is systematic. Children are taken from their mothers, and wives separated from their husbands. Rather than go through such hell whole families commit suicide. A Rumanian doctor, who used to come to our hospital and had lived in France for twenty years, killed his wife and children with an injection; then followed them in death. There have been other instances where workmen's families having no means have chosen a more brutal way: the father slaughtering his wife and children before opening his veins. Women throwing themselves out of windows with their children in their arms. The same scenes of horror repeat themselves and multiply. At the Vel d'Hiv—turned into a concentration camp—thousands of children and women are herded in appalling hygienic conditions.

Houses and apartments thus vacated are looted. Hatred towards the oppressor grows from hour to hour. Whatever result the German hopes to obtain by these drastic measures, there is one consequence he obviously hasn't thought of. He has made a "martyr" of the Jew.

July 28th

"Allo? Yvonne? I hold you at last? It must be the tenth time I'm ringing you up. Don't worry. It'll be the last. Will you please give the following message to Moustache: The day after tomorrow a girl friend of mine is going South. She is going there 'like that.' You know what I mean? I am going with her. That's all. I just want Moustache to know that I won't be here."

"Why ... you don't mean ... you quit?"

"Have it that way if you like. In other words, I don't like to be made a fool of. I am sick of it."

"Listen. I'd much rather you'd talked to him yourself," says Yvonne at the other end of the line. "I am always getting hell for the others."

"It's useless. I've tried three times daily for a week to get him on the phone. It is always the same. He is not there, or has just left, or, else, if he is in—he is in conference. You can see for yourself that for a year and a half nothing has been done. So let's call it quits and part on friendly terms."

Replacing the receiver with a sharp click, I end the conversation. The "friend who is going away" only exists in my imagination. A lie is my intention to break up with Kliemann. The only true thing is that I am fed up with all of it. On my way out, I throw one franc and fifty centimes on the counter. The proprietress of the café gives me a broad smile. She knows me. It is seldom that I come less than four times a day to telephone. This morning she must think seeing me so cross: "Something has gone wrong with her love affair." Something has gone very wrong, but it has nothing to do with love.

Next day

At noon I find a letter under my door and recognize Yvonne's hand-writing.

"My dear Napoleon," I read, "abate your wrath and come to see Moustache this afternoon at five o'clock. And above all, tell your girl-friend that you are not leaving with her. As ever yours, Josephine." Once I had signed my letter to Yvonne: "N" as for Napoleon and since then, when corresponding, she calls me Napoleon and I call her Josephine.

Babs sniffs at the envelope. As everything coming from Yvonne, it must smell of Mouki. "What do you think of it, Master Babs? Are we to consider this invitation as a good or a bad omen?" Babs smiles with all the length of his honest dog's mouth. "So you think we can be optimistic? All right. At any rate you'll come with me this evening."

"Good afternoon, Miss." Annick greets me. "No one is in as yet. But Miss Yvonne rang up to say she was coming immediately."

I settle down in the drawing-room. Babs rushes up to Mouki, as to an old friend, but I notice that very soon he walks away from him and doesn't respond to his advances. Jumping on my lap Babs considers from there the stumbling creature that Mouki has become. "Poor old Mouki," I say to myself. "It would have been better had he died from his meningitis."

Minutes pass slowly. I count up five. I count ten. At fifteen, I get up to go. "Annick, I am leaving. You will tell 'Mr. Moustache' that I've waited for him quarter of an hour. Please note that the time is 15 minutes past five. You will also remind him that I am still leaving tomorrow evening and that if he has anything to tell me, he had better hurry up."

And out we go, Babs and I. In reality I am not at all so sure of myself. I am even rather worried. I have always been so subdued, so patient. What is going to come out of this new tactic of mine? But really and truly, I cannot endure any longer.

JULY 30TH 1942

Who can be knocking so early at my door? I open and find Annick.

"I come early to be sure to find you," she says. "You should have heard the row Mr. Moustache made last night when Mlle Yvonne told him you had come and gone."

"At what o'clock did he come back?"

"Oh, it wasn't quite eight."

"That means he was only three hours late."

"Anyhow, he has sent me to tell you he wants to see you absolutely this evening at six. He is sure to be there."

"All right. But if I waited 15 minutes yesterday, today I shall only wait ten. You can tell him so."

When Annick has gone, I remain alone, imagining with apprehension the coming interview. I feel I am venturing on an unknown ground, which can be dangerous. Major Kliemann has—according to the consecrated term—always been very "correct" with me. So have I with him. And, suddenly, I reverse this atmosphere of civility into one of threats and blackmail. From subdued I have become arrogant. And I start wondering if I am firmly enough established in the place to dare risk this new tactic. We shall see. Come what may. When I arrive at six o'clock at the Villa Boileau, I get the surprise of my life to find the major in the drawing-room.

"Really," he says impatiently, "I find that you might have waited yesterday. You knew that I had to talk to you. I was detained by other business. You are not the only one. It was no reason to go away." It is the first time he uses that tone with me.

"No," I say.

"No what?"

"No, I did not wait. No, I shall not wait. No, you shall not continue to treat me as if I were an old rag." I started the sentence with apprehension but, gradually, I worked myself up and reach a real fury. I see his eyebrows rise as his surprise increased. They are so broad, his eyebrows, and so thick that you can't not notice their change of level.

"Listen. To begin with"

But I do not let him continue. "No, I am not going to listen to you. And it is precisely why I am here: To tell you that I'm fed up, that you can look for someone else."

While I was speaking, he has been fumbling in his wallet taking out an orange piece of paper, which he now hands over. "Your Pass," he says. "If you wish to leave us and go to the free zone, you needn't smuggle yourself in, as Yvonne told me you intended doing. You can use this." Then, smiling, he adds: "But I am sure you are not going to forsake your work. Come on. Don't be angry any more. You see that I have got you your pass."

It is my turn to smile as my artificially roused anger dies out. "You are right. I care more for the success of our enterprise than you think. But put yourself in my shoes. Wouldn't you be fed up?"

"I know. It's dragging on. But these things' always take a long time to organize. So now you have your pass. You'll go to the free zone—I believe it's Marseille you have chosen?—and I do not want to see you again until you have come in touch with your Portuguese relatives. If possible, get them to write you a letter calling you urgently to Lisbon. Then you shall be able to go with it to Vichy and start proceedings over there. Your permit is valid for a month."

—⁂—

August 3rd 1942

Babs, his truffle crushed against the pane, where it forms a ring of mist, looks at the landscape running before his eyes. With half-closed eyes, I think of that temporary liberty towards which I roll. More illusive than temporary as the absence of the feldgrau uniforms will be but apparent; for, in the free zone, as well as here, the Germans are as numerous, if not as obvious.

At Moulins, we pass the line of demarcation between the two zones. I have with me five letters which I have inserted in the folded "Pilori," left carelessly on the table, before the window. I am hoping that the German control which is to come will not be interested by this well known pro–Nazi newspaper. Nevertheless, I feel slightly nervous. Yvonne has given me an address. In case I should get into a jam I must insist on having notified a certain Mme Marty-Chanclos. Fortunately everything goes well and the train starts on its way.

Holding Babs' leash in one hand, my suitcase in the other, I go down the wide stone steps that lead from the station and follow an avenue lined with plane-trees. I do not know Marseille and go haphazard towards the centre. All the hotels are filled up. At last I find a room at the "Hotel de la Poste."

Immediately I set off to work. First of all: a wire to my aunt. I tell her of my intention to leave France and explain that in order to obtain an exit-visa, I must have a letter from her "requesting my presence at the bed-side of a dangerously ill aunt." To this I add that it doesn't oblige her to anything and she must not fear that I shall encumber her by my presence. The telegram is difficult to compose as, because of the censorship, it cannot show too clearly the "bluff" of my plot. On the other hand, should my aunt take seriously my offer of "coming to nurse" her sick sister, she would certainly refuse to let me come.

Over and over I change the text. When the wire is ready, it has 305 words. Next, I write a letter to my Polish cousin and another to my English cousin (in case she did not get the three first ones). I end by a last one to a friend who lives near Bristol. Each of them I ask—in veiled terms—to help me get to England once I'll be out of France. I haven't yet decided at what precise moment I'll inform the British of my plans. Sometime I think the best would be as soon as Madrid. Sometimes, that it should be better to wait until I am in England, because of the Germans, that are everywhere. I am afraid that if the British facilitate my entry to England, it might arouse the suspicion of the German Secret Services. To conclude, I write a detailed letter to explain my wire. It'll go air mail. All this writing takes me two days. At the post office, when I hand my telegram, an amazed official asks if I am not making a mistake, if I am not giving him a letter. It is so long.

And now there is nothing else to do but wait.

—⁂—

August 10th

While waiting for the answers, I have come to live at La Ciotat. I've made some friends here: an architect and his girl-secretary, and Marcel, the proprietor of the "Auberge de Louvteau." The Auberge is at the end of the pier, facing the Aresenal. The food is good. Marcel, the Algerian, is a smart guy. When talking to the people, I am astonished to see how their way of thinking is different from ours of the occupied zone. One could believe they were from another country ... speaking the same language.

The Germans, for them, are something distant, detestable in principle but real. One might think that the occupied part of France does not belong to their France, that the French of the North of France are even another nation than the French of the South. They have a feeling of resentment against the Northern provinces because the food conditions are better there. As if we had chosen to "be occupied," as if it was our fault that the invader had grabbed the richest part of France.

August 12th

The answer from Portugal has arrived. I still can't get over it. Written from Madeira it is due to the sententious pen of my uncle, telling me that he cannot possibly ask me to come because, in the first place, he can't take a decision for his sick sister-in-law in regard to the care that must be given her; in the second place, he is not entitled to dispose of her house; and thirdly, he advises me in all earnestness to go to the American Consulate and, with their help, to get a British visa. "With this visa," the letter continues, "you will have no difficulty in obtaining an exit-permit from France as well as a transit-visa for Portugal and Spain."

This letter throws me into a raving fury, until laughter has the better of me. It really is too funny to advise me to apply for a British visa—on what??—I have no passport. And to think that in 305 words my dear uncle did not grasp the situation. What illusions they have kept those whom the war hasn't touched.

Before leaving Marseille, I write my uncle a second letter in which I lay out clearly everything. I dot the i's and cross the t's. And to hell with the censorship. It may think what it pleases. I tell my uncle that: (1) I have no intention of taking care of his sister-in-law; that (2) I am not expecting a 200 f.; that (3) I have means for my living; and (4) that his letter would not bind him in any way but that for me his invitation is of the greatest importance as it will allow me to "get out of hell." I ask him to send his answer to Vichy.

August 13th

Vichy: hurrying people with leather portfolios under their arm; quantity of office-boys, of small ministerial officials, their elbows protected by lustrine half-sleeves, homely pimply faces, short-sighted, spectacled eyes, pale complexions: a world in itself of etiolated scribblers. And then this other category—always neighbouring the first one: the invalided of the First World War—one-armed, one-eyed, one-legged, for whom are reserved secondary jobs in the governmental machine: concierges, ushers, awaiting their retirement ... and a pension. The few rare patients, who have come down for a cure, circulate with slow, timorous steps, lost in the unwanted crowd that has invaded their domain.

All the hotels have been requisitioned and are transformed into Ministries. One is amazed to see the number of these. A ministerial universe has sprung up like mushrooms.

Even small hotels of doubtful appearance have placards announcing: "Ministry of this"—"Ministry of that."

So here I am in Vichy. Fortunately, I know the fiancé of a friend who works in the Finance Ministry. He gets me a room, which is lucky for all the hotels are crammed, and the best the billeting office can offer me is a 2-d class berth in a parked railway car on a side-track near the station. And now that I am in Vichy, I don't know by which end to start. The obliging young man, who has already come to my rescue, advises me to go to the Sub-Prefecture. The Sous-Prefecture has her quarters in a Swiss-chalet–style villa. I am received by a short, limping man who smiles when I tell him pointblank: "I like to get a passport and an exit-visa."

He seems to find it highly comical. "In any case," he tells me, "you'll have to start with the State Police."

I feel already better to know where I have to begin. At the State Police, the officer who receives me inquires what documents I have to support my request.

"None."

He looks perplexed and directs me towards one of his colleagues. "And why do you want to go to Lisbon?" asks the latter.

"Well," I tell him, looking as if I were about to cry, "my dear aunt is very, very ill. She is asking me to come and take care of her. I am a trained nurse. My poor aunt's condition is hopeless, you know." I give a big sigh. "She is afflicted with _____. It is terrible."

The police agent nods in sign of comprehension.

"And then I must also tell you that I am her heiress. She has no children. She has no one in the world." My interlocutor is getting more and more compassionate and interested. "That is why she requests me to come. But it must be without delay. You understand it, don't you?"

He does understand. "I'll tell you what you must do. You are going to send her a wire telling her to go to the French Embassy where she is to apply for a visa for you. This application will be forwarded to you through the Embassy, and we shall then deliver you a passport."

"But that's impossible," I say. "My aunt is dying. She cannot even hold a pen."

He scratches his nape thoughtfully. "That's annoying; most annoying. And she cannot write, you say. And you tell me she is alone?"

"Quite alone." Then I venture a suggestion. "Maybe a telegram would be sufficient? She could dictate it to her maid who would take it to the post office. Would that do? Would it be sufficient?"

"It will have to be sufficient, although you know, telegrams from sick aunts … I too can send you some!"

"Yes, but not from Lisbon."

"No, that's true."

As I am about to leave, I remember another question. "Is it O.K. if the telegram is addressed to me but c/o someone at the Ministry of Finance?"

"Why? Have you no address in Vichy?"

"No."

"But then, where do you come from?"

"From the other side."

"Paris?"

"Yes."

"How?"
"The best I can."
"I see. That means you'll have to go back."
"Yes."
"Over there, nothing doing?"
"Nothing."
"Well. It's understood. Come again to see us as soon as you've got your telegram. And take care passing the border."

I write a last letter to my uncle, asking him to send me a wire—the wording of which I am sending him—and to send it to the address I'm giving him. The message says only: "Aunt seriously ill. Come urgently." I leave the signature to his choice for the answer.

After this, I agree with Robert C.—my friend's fiancé already mentioned—should a letter come for me to his address to forward it to me somehow to Paris. But if it is a telegram, he must not send it on but notify me as quickly as possible.

—⚡—

AUGUST 16TH

Back in Paris, I find the city gloomier than ever. People look sullen and tired. The traders are disagreeable, the shop-girls rude when, humbly and with great politeness, you risk to ask for some object of current use, which they don't have.

—⚡—

AUGUST 17TH

I ring up Yvonne. This time Moustache wants to see me at once. "Well?" asks Yvonne at the other end of the line. "How goes?"

Funny how two short words "how goes?" can mean a lot of things. It can be interpreted as "Have you been successful? Have you had a nice journey? Did you get into trouble? Are you brining back good news? Is there any hope for the future?"

And I answer: "O.K."

With a slight restriction in tone Yvonne says: "So? Anyhow, we'll see."

She has interpreted my "O.K." by: without a catastrophe, I've obtained no definite result. No trouble, but no good news. And all that was contained in the two brief sentences: "How goes?"—"O.K."

Moustache is there. He comes to me with outstretched hands. "Well?" he questions.
I simply shake my head.
"No?"

He knits his brow. He is disappointed. We go to the drawing-room and I explain everything in detail. He listens attentively and makes me repeat certain points.

"I have the impression that my uncle will do nothing," I say to finish. "He is afraid, afraid to take a responsibility, afraid of compromising himself. I think we can cut him out. As to my cousin, I have learned that he is in London."

Major Kliemann is deep in thought. "The outstanding facts are," he says finally, "1. That according to what you were told by the State Police, everything depends upon the 'urgent call' from your aunt. 2. This 'call' is legally valid in form of a telegram. 3. That your uncle refuses to send it to you." His face brightens as he squeezes my hand. "Why! It's perfect. We shall be your dying aunt." He starts laughing.

"It's elementary art. Give me the address where you asked your uncle to wire you his answer. You shall have your telegram in a few days. This is settled. Let us proceed. I'll start immediately to get you another pass. As soon as you are informed that your telegram has come, you'll leave for Vichy. You'll get through the necessary rigmarole and shall obtain— so I hope—a passport, the exit permit and the Portuguese visa. As soon as you'll return to Paris, you'll enter our Radio school to receive there the finishing touch—it'll take but a fortnight.

"In the meantime, knowing the number of your passport, I shall entrust someone very reliable we have in Madrid to obtain you a transit through Spain. I have thought it over and have decided that it will be easier for you to get your Portuguese visa from Spain. I could, of course, easily get you one by means of connections we have in Lisbon, but I do not wish to make use of them as one can never be sure of the Portuguese and there could come more harm than good from it."

"What about those people of yours in Madrid? Are you absolutely sure of them? There'll be no leakage?"

"None whatsoever, you may be sure of it. Should there be the slightest risk, I wouldn't chance it."

"All right. There is another question. Could I get the 'finishing touch' right away? I'm afraid I'm not as advanced as you expect."

"All right. I'll see to it no later than tomorrow with Mr. Vogel. Ring up Yvonne two days from now."

"Vogel? Is that Loiseau?"

"Yes, I've forgot you've already met him. He'll be your instructor." As he accompanies me to the door, the major lays his hand on my shoulder. "I am pleased with you, Lily," he says.

AUGUST 18TH, 1942[46]

Everybody talks about the British attempt at Dieppe. In spite of what the German propaganda says, it seems to have been successful, but not without losses. The "pro-Nazis" consider it as a "landing," which has failed, and rejoice. The "pro-British" see in it a "general rehearsal," full of promises, and rejoice too. Everyone believes it to be what he wishes the most.

Once again I take the way to the rue de Longchamps. Babs recognizes the entrance of No 73 and, in sign of joy ... lifts a hind paw. I ring the bell and go in, greeted by the bark of the German sheep dog Sigrid. I have not seen Richard since April but everything is now as it always was. Sigrid is not quite so fat. Richard isn't changed. Susan, the maid, is the same; so is Pierre, her husband.

"Loiseau has just called up," says Richard, "to say he'll be here right away."

Five minutes later, Vogel comes in. Elegantly dressed, shoed in brown buckskin with thick soles, smiling, he has in spite of the dimple in his right cheek, something cold, something cruel in his glance. Something very lucid too. I distrust him. He is the only one in whose presence I don't feel safe.

"Hullo," he says, examining me with a mocking air. "You very much learn, since last time?"

"Absolutely nothing," I say, remembering the vexation he had inflicted upon me at my third lesson.

"Ah, so? Then Richard not good professor?"

"On contrary, Richard good professor but I not good pupil," I say, imitating his pidgin French.

"You laugh my French speak? Sehr gut. Von jetzt an, warden wir deutsch sprechen."[47]

"You mock my Morse, so I mock what I can. It is never very charitable for a professor to make fun of a pupil."

We get into his car and take off.

"Where are we going?"

"Radio school."

"Where is it?"

"You shall see."

We drive through the Bois-de-Boulogne, come to the Muette, follow the boulevard Montmorency, turn into the rue de l'Assomption and stop at the corner of the rue du Dr. Blanche, No 77. The elevator takes us to the 5th floor. My companion rings at the door on the left of the landing. A moment later, steps resound inside and the door is slightly pushed ajar. Having been identified, we are admitted into the apartment.

Vogel introduces us: "Herr Grün, one of our professors—Miss Lilly."

"Everything is ready," says Herr Grün, leading us into a spacious library, summarily furnished, excluding the book-shelves partly stripped of their volumes,—with a large table covered with green India-rubber moss cloth and with leather arm-chairs of the same colour.

On the table, a Radio-transmitter-receiver set in a small suitcase has been prepared. I have never seen anything like it, and it seems to be very complicated. I take off my coat and settle down. Grün leaves us.

"Well," says Vogel, "let's begin with the alphabet."

And getting hold of the key, which looks much more "comfortable" than the one used by Richard, he sends a dash and a dot ... and then folds his arms.

"N," I write and also fold my arms.

"Fancy!" he says. "You know that. I'm sure that last time you didn't know. And this?"

I write F, put down my pencil, and get up.

"What are you doing?"

"Going away."

"Going? Why?"

"Because, Mr. Vogel, I haven't come here to have fun."

"But you told me yourself, you didn't know anything."

"Yes, from your point of view, what I know amounts to null compared with your knowledge. But you know perfectly that I have been Richard's pupil for six months. So even if he were a very bad professor and I a very stupid pupil, you might suppose that I have learned something more than to distinguish an "N" from an "F."

"O.K., O.K. You needn't get mad. Sit down. I am going to send you groups of letters."

A moment later, he takes out his watch, puts it in front of him on the table and starts to chronometer my speed.

"Fifty," he says. "It's not so bad but it isn't sufficient. I should like you to do seventy."

We have been working for an hour and a half. It is passed midday now.

"Tired?" Vogel inquires.

"No."

It is one o'clock. We are still working.

"Tired?" my professor asks again.

"No," I say once more.

So "Loiseau," giving up the hope of having me ask for mercy, heaves a sigh of resignation: "Listen. Perhaps you are not tired, but I am hungry."

The lesson comes to an end.

August 19th 1942

9:00 a.m.—I arrive almost at the same time as my professor and the lesson begins immediately. Vogel has very soon discovered my weak points—the "Y" and the "C"—and he makes me work on them. He is a good professor. Richard hardly ever made me work on figures. Now, Loiseau dictates to me whole exercises of numbers. He has a lot of patience—more than I have—and makes me start over and over again whenever there is something that doesn't go well. I think that under his tuition, I shall learn very quickly. After three lessons, Vogel has passed me on to Grün who, from now on, is to be my professor. Vogel's profession does not seem to be tuition. He is "their" technician.

Grün is a placid and somewhat sleepy chap, of about thirty five years, with a flabby, wax-like face. He is learning Spanish. With him I start learning the manipulation and the construction of the Radio-set. There are lots of knobs to turn, and I get all mixed up.

September 2nd 1942

Robert C. has just let me know by inter-zone post-card that a telegram is awaiting me in Vichy. I run down the staircase four at a time—and rush to the corner "bistro."

I dial the N Littre 42.10.

"Zimmer 344," I tell the standard operator.

"Ein Moment, bitter."[48]

I wait. It is the secretary who picks up the receiver: "Wer spricht?"[49]

"Fraulein Lily."

A few minutes go by; then I hear Moustache's voice at the end of the line. "Good morning."

"Good morning. News from the aunt."

"All right. I'll do what is necessary. See Yvonne Monday."

That is all. I hang up the receiver.

"Fine weather on the barometer of the heart," the bar-woman must think, seeing the smile which accompanies the two francs I put down on the counter for the phone call.

"We resume our adventure, my Babs," I say to my frizzy, passing a hand against the hair of his back. "Soon we'll be off on a trip again." At the word "trip," Babs pricks one ear. When I say that he "pricks" it, it's a way of speaking for the ears of my little mongrel are naturally standing up. "It doesn't matter," I tell him by way of consolation. "My ears stick out too. It's a sign of personality." But Babs doesn't worry in the least about his ears. He goes into the next room and brings me a slipper. "No, we are not going yet. Take it back to its place," I tell him. Obediently he carries it back to the closet.

This evening, strolling down the Champs-Elysees, I run against a barrage in front of the Marbeuf underground station. "What's going on here?"

"It's nothing. Simply the exit of the Marignan—the Soldatenkino. That's why this entry to the metro is exclusively reserved to the "Herrenvolk."[50] We, the defeated, have to cross the avenue and take the metro on the other side," explains my friend Solange who accompanies me.

"Nuts to them. If they imagine I'll go out of my way."

"You won't be allowed through," Solange assures me. "There are policemen and plain clothed detectives all over the place."

"We'll see."

"I'll wait for you down on the platform," says prudent Solange.

I advance resolutely alone. I don't know exactly how I'll go about it. As I am about to enter the mouth of the metro, a man in civilian clothes, with a felt hat and his collar turned up, stops me. "To the other side," he says gruffly. I look at him as if I did not understand. He has a doubt. More politely he asks: "Have you a pass?"

I have a sudden inspiration: "Foui. Foui. Pien sur. Foulez-fous foir?"[51]

A servile smile lightens up his face. "No, no, it's not necessary, Fraulein. You can go." My awful German accent did the trick.

"How did you do it?" asks Solange when she joins me on the platform of the metro.

"I said: "Halifouzikapilaminouzikowski." As he could not make it out, he let me pass. Next time you can try it."

September 23rd

I had to pester relentlessly Moustache to get my pass; it was ready since three days. It is valid till the 21st of October. I am off again.

Marseille, September 24th, 1942

It's raining here. What a difference with the last time. I am here illegally. I ought to be in Vichy and I am in Marseille. The reason for it is that I want to try to spend a few days with my sister in Algiers. I do not know if it will be possible, but it's only from here that I can attempt to take the necessary steps.

September 30th

I have time to waste. I try to make it a holiday. Unfortunately, these are wet vacations. This morning I leave La Ciotat for Vichy. Posters divulge the new law, claiming all workmen for labor in Germany. Riotous mobs. The gardemobile had to intervene.

Vichy, 2nd October 1942

Once more I am engulfed into the labyrinth of Ministries. I dive head forward into the imbroglio of official papers and the bureaucratic chaos. Moustache's telegram from Lisbon in hand, saying: "Aunt Theresa dangerously ill. Come urgently." And signed with my aunt's name, and then I go to the State Police. The cable looks authentic and, really, what does the State Police care? A "dossier" is made up for me and inserted into a large envelope, which I have to carry to the Sous-Prefecture myself.

After half an hour's waiting, the same envelope is handed back to me—slightly thicker—and I am told to take it to the Ministry of the Interior, 7th Bureau, "Hotel de Russie" to get a signature. In spite of the incalculable number of officials, clerks, paperjacks, scribblers, they seem to be short of office boys. Therefore, I am compelled to perform the functions of that being considered too humble to exist in Vichy.

At the Ministry of the Interior I am told: "Come again in a few days."

"Impossible. I must ab-so-lutely see that gentleman."

"What gentleman?"

"The one who gives his signature."

"What for? You do not even know him."

"The Prefect said so. He told me to insist."

"In that case," and the clerk goes back to the bureau.

"Will you come in," he says returning a few minutes later.

"So it is the Prefect who has sent you?" a middle-aged man asks, looking at me from above his spectacles.

"Yes, personally, and he insists on my getting this signature immediately to enable me to take further steps," I say with assurance.

"You have a very nice little dog. I had one like him. What is his name?"

"It's Babs."

Babs jumps on the gentleman's knees and the gentleman signs my papers. I can go. As I am about to open the door, the old man says: "And you know, the Prefect is absent from Vichy. But you have a very nice dog." And he smiles.

Now I turn my steps to the Ministry of Foreign Affairs. It is for Laval to say "Yes" or "No." But Laval has just left, as it is noon. Moreover, it is Saturday—therefore, nothing more can be done today. Even Vichy keeps to the "semaine anglaise."[52] Tomorrow is Sunday, and then comes Monday. Monday too is a holiday for the Vichy people.

In Vichy and in the neighbourhood black-market restaurants abound. We have lunch at Gannet, Robert and I. Here is the menu: Hors-d'oeuvres—sausage, ham, radishes, sardines. After that, we have: partridges, veal escalopes with mushrooms, potatoes—suttees, salad, cheese, apricot-tart. Fruit: peaches. Wine. Coffee. Bread—as much as you like, and all the rest without ration tickets. I can hardly remember when I ate so well last time.

Tuesday at last. The Ministry of foreign Affairs has given an "avis favorable."[53] With my precious envelope held fast in both hands—the envelope has considerably increased in size—I dash to the Ministry of the Interior and am quite astonished to hear that my part as a "messenger-boy" stops at that. My "dossier" is to go—without my participation—to the Hotel du Parc" for a signature. From there, it will be returned to the Ministry of the Interior to finally stand at the Sous-Prefecture where I can pick it up in eight days.

October 10th

I wasn't able to book a seat on the Marseille train. As I stand in the corridor, a porter whispers to me: "Do you want one?"

"Yes."

"It's expensive," he warns me.

"How much?"

"Fifty francs."

Well, I'm lucky.

II

Paris,
1942–1943

ALGIERS, OCTOBER 16TH, 1942

Four days spent in Algiers. What a relief. Blue sky, fine weather and, above all, the feeling to have the protecting width of the sea between us and "them." I have seen Pep. I spoke to him. Pep is the only one whom I trust enough to confide in and ask for advice. Pep—up to his quite recent resignation (he was too disgusted with Vichy)—was with the 2nd Bureau. He listened to what I had to tell him and then asked: "In reality, what do you expect from me?" And as I don't reply at once, he adds: "I can tell you that you are playing a difficult and dangerous game. You know it. As well as you are aware that you are too deep in it to pull out. What else do you want to know?"

"Have I been right?"

"Yes, if you succeed. No, if you fail."

"I see. Is it always like that with this kind of work?"

"Yes. Expect neither thanks nor gratitude. You will be "dropped" the day they have no use for you unless you are suppressed. Be ready for deception, for treason."

"I know."

"Then it's all right."

"Can't you tell me anything more? Give me an advice that would guide me. I have told you what I have done; it has worked. I told you what I intend doing. Will it work? I am somewhat at a loss."

"You are going to work with the British?"

"Yes."

"That is the safest. Distrust the organizations, so called "Resistance"; they are rotten with double-agents. Avoid them. Don't breathe a word until you have contacted the British in Spain."

On deck of the boat which is taking me back to France, I ponder what Pep has told me. I am dissatisfied. I should have preferred to hear him tell me what to do, and not what not to do. I feel utterly lonely, in an endless labyrinth leading to the Unknown. Pep seemed to believe there would be soon a landing in Algiers. He is not the only one. I have heard it from different sources.

"What chances would the Allies have if they landed here?"

"That would depend on who would land. If the Allies have intelligence enough to let the Americans disembark in North Africa, these will be well received—at least they wouldn't meet much opposition."

But I fear should the British make a landing, they wouldn't be welcome; the thought of Mens-el-Kebir and Dakar is vivid still.

It is sad to return to France. Everything there is grey and feldgrau.

October 20th Vichy

Vichy once more. Again I pick up my passport, which is ready since the 14th and has been waiting.

"You don't seem to be in a hurry, lady," remarks the functionary of the sub-prefecture, handing it over to me.

October 22nd Paris

Hardly back to Paris, I dial the number Aut. 65-06 and when I hear Yvonne's voice at the other end of the line, I say: "Hallo, it's I."

"Hurray. Well, is it yes? Or is it no?"

I keep her a few seconds in suspense before saying: "YES."

"He will be pleased. Can you call me up again tomorrow early in the morning because I shan't see him before late tonight? He's sure to want to see you right away."

"Righto."

October 23rd

The appointment is at 10 o'clock at Yvonne's place. "Moustache" comes a little late.

"Well," he says, stretching out his hand. Without saying a word, I give him my passport. He looks it over rapidly, verifies the dates on the exit visa. "Good. Very good. Three months," he adds, "that gives us plenty of time."

"I went to the Spanish Embassy in Vichy," I tell him, "but I was informed that they only deliver diplomatic visas and that I had to get mine either in Lyons or Marseille. I would have gone there, had not the validity of my pass expired the day before last."

"It doesn't matter," says Kliemann. "It is preferable for me to make the application through the Foreign Ministry of Spain, backed up by a friend of mine in Madrid."

"Is it safe? It might transpire."

Moustache is offended. "I told you already that the people I employ are reliable and that I wouldn't risk compromising a successful enterprise by an imprudence. Remember that. In the meantime, you are going to continue your lessons with Herr Grün. I'll tell him to accelerate your training."

The last violent bombardments of Genoa, Milan and Turin seem to forebode in the nearest future the resumption of action in North Africa. We live on hope. It is extraordinary how tenacious hope can be. Every month one expects something decisive to happen next month, something that will put an end to the abhorred occupation, to hunger, to privations, and, above all, to inaction, something which will permit action, fighting once more. And as nothing ever happens, we find excuses, reasons to put off to later, to next month, that what we are waiting for.

Hope does not decrease. It seems to draw its strength out of despair itself. There is but one thing which worries me personally. It is that war should end before I had time to do anything. It is not that I'd want the war to last a single second longer to enable me to fulfill my plans, but I'd like to see their accomplishment before it is too late.

Maybe it is with the idea of possibly "getting stuck" that I undertook to write these notes. I fully realize my imprudence, but I fear less to see them fall into the hands of Germans than to be some day accused by our own people of having worked for the enemy. This, I couldn't bear. It is true that if the war ended, it wouldn't matter what happened to me ... if only it were over.

Guy, my brother-in-law, was to come to Paris at the end of November. He has a job with Lemaigre-Dubreuil of the "Huiles Lesieur Co." Today, he informs us in a laconic interzone card that his journey is put off.

This morning, arriving at Rue de l'Assomption, as I am about to enter the elevator, a man wants me not to close the door; he too is going up. Although there is nothing particular about him, something tells me that he is going up to the same place as I. "What floor?" I ask before pressing the button.

"Fifth."

I was right. Not wishing to walk in with him, I press on the 3rd knob, get out and let the man continue by himself. Slowly I go up the two stories and, having given him time to enter, I ring the bell.

My lessons are very irregular. I am getting used to the set and take down without difficulty the training transmissions. But I could do better. I should like to know how to take apart and then put again together the radio. I cannot understand why they are putting it off until the last moment, the most important thing ... unless they've changed their minds.

November 6th, 1942

The British have started their offensive operations in Egypt. Rommel is falling back. The British have advanced 200 kms and announce the capture of 2,000 prisoners. In Gibraltar, 120 Allied ships are reported. People in the street are smiling.

November 7th, 1942

Madagascar has definitely capitulated. In Africa, five divisions of "gallant macaronis" are encircled.

Sunday, November 8th

Daddy has switched on the radio and put it very low as it is too early yet for the French program of the B.B.C. I follow absentmindedly the Polish emission, but suddenly I start, listening intently.

"It can't be possible," I say.

"What can't be possible?" asks Daddy lifting his eyes from the paper he is reading.

"I thought I understood they said that the Americans are in Algiers. Wait. Listen."

Daddy pricks up his ears, but the transmission has come to an end. "You must have misunderstood. Anyhow, we shall know in a few minutes."

We wait, our eyes riveted to the box from where the voice will come, holding in our breaths, hoping—not daring to believe. At last. The news. I was right. No mistake about it. The Americans have landed in North and in French-Occidental Africa. No details are given. The speaker's voice quivers with emotion.

General Giraud is Commander in chief of French Forces in North Africa. He is said to have issued instructions for the French to join the Americans against the Axis. Roosevelt made a speech (in French) to affirm that the United States had no views on the French territories of North Africa and that his American troops came to the rescue, as friends, to free Africa from a common enemy. General Eisenhower issued instructions to French armies on land, on sea and in the air. Will they be followed?

"Daddy," I say. "It's the end of the war. Just think: the END of the nightmare."

"Let us say: the beginning of the end," he admits cautiously. "It can go on for a very long time."

Mummy is anxious, uneasy. For her, the liberation of Algiers is equivalent to bombardments, disorders, and Moussia is over there. My little Mother, for whom every joy seems to be lined with anxiety. When I go, that which will be the crowning to my efforts, will be a new source of worries and concern for her.

I walk along the streets for the house is too narrow a space to hold my overflowing joy. I think of my little sister over there, in a liberated country at last. And I feel happy for her.

(Later on the same evening)

I am anticipating tomorrow's lesson. It will be fun. Grün will be mad.

November 9th, 1942

Algiers and Oran are occupied by the Allies. Petain has said: "We shall defend ourselves … is the order I give." I am surprised at that as I consider that Petain, in spite of all, is honest and loyal. I can't believe he is a traitor. Just an old man.

I arrive to my lesson as usual. Grün looks sour and frowning. His colleague, whom I have nicknamed "Zazoo," is in a sarcastic mood.

"Well, what do you say about this African parody?"

"They are up for another Dieppe," I say casually.

"That's it. Exactly what they can expect: a second Dieppe."

But I drop the subject for I am too pleased, too enthusiastic to be able to feign indifference and am afraid of betraying myself. Grün is irritable and I am so absentminded that I make endless mistakes, both in receiving as well as in transmitting. Babs must feel the electricity in the air for, having jumped twice on the table, he finishes by upsetting the inkstand. Grün gets angry and the lesson is curtailed.

Tuesday, November 10th

The occupation of the free zone by the Germans is doubtlessly but a question of hours. The news today:

(1) The "traitor" Darlan has been received with all the honours of the war by the High Commandment of the American forces in Algiers.

(2) Petain has taken up the supreme Commandment of the French ground, air and sea forces.

Wednesday, November 11th

Hitler has chosen the day of the Armistice of the "other" war to decree the occupation of the whole of France. There is no longer a "Free Zone"—or supposed free. My lessons are suspended for a few days.

Thursday, November 12th, 1942

I was standing in line since 8:30 this morning, in front of a shop where an arrival of vegetables was expected. At half past eleven, a truck unloads a score of baskets containing … lettuce. Having waited all that time, I decide to have patience a little longer. At the stroke of twelve, the shop closes. There are about thirty people in front of me and over two hundred behind me. In the hope of a new arrival, I keep my place in the queue. At 3:00 p.m. the delivery starts again. By the time my turn arrives, there are but two crushed lettuces left at the bottom of the first basket. Behind me a poor old woman laments "to have waited all this time and be obliged to return empty-handed. What shall I give my old man to eat?" Without making a great sacrifice, I leave the two faded lettuces to the old woman and walk away.

Friday, November 13th

Hour by hour, we follow the development of the events in Algiers. To know that the Germans have been beaten, makes it easier for us to endure privations. The Allies on their way to Tunisia have taken Bougle and Bone. Berlin denies the arrival of parachutists in Tunis, which makes us suppose that it is true. Darlan launches an appeal—(better late than never.)—to the Mediterranean Fleet, bidding them to join the Allies. The British capture Bardia and Tobruk. Toulon remains "outside" the German occupation.

November 14th

Mekill and Derua are taken, opening the road to Bengazi to the British.

I have resumed my lessons. Grün is in an execrable mood. We exchange few words. I apply myself to my task.

"You have improved," remarks Grün gruffly. In spite of that, he seems in no hurry to teach me something new. Each time I ask him to explain me the construction of my radio-set, he waves me off: "We have plenty of time. Later on."

From this I gather that Moustache hasn't told him to accelerate my training. And if so, that Moustache himself hasn't decided yet of the precise date of my departure. Maybe they haven't even decided if they would send me at all. This situation is getting on my nerves. I phone to Yvonne several times a week, to inquire if Moustache has done anything about my Spanish visa. She answers evasively that "he is seeing to it," without telling me anything precise.

Wednesday, November 18

Petain has named Laval his successor and has conferred him full-power rights. Petain's address raised general indignation on the street and in the metro. At the beginning of this week, a curious fact occurred. Immediately after having communicated Darlan's nomination to the post of Chief of Civilian Administration in Algiers, the B.B.C. read de Gaulle's declaration, saying that he and the Free-French Government do not recognize the recent nominations of Darlan and Giraud and take no responsibility for the consequences that may arise. It looks like an Anglo-American family-quarrel. De Gaulle is supported by the British and Giraud by the Americans. Since then, the Americans have reversed, and Roosevelt has declared—without blaming Eisenhower—that Darlan's nomination is but provisory. It's difficult for us to make head or tail of what's happening.

November 27th, 1942

This morning, as I am getting out of bed, Mummy rushes into my studio: "You've heard the news?" And without giving me time to say "No" or "What is it?" "The whole Fleet at Toulon has been scuttled."

I look at her in disbelief. "What? Why? Toulon was a free town—the Germans were not there."

"They have tried to overtake the Fleet by surprise and to get hold of the units anchored in the port. They didn't succeed; the Fleet was scuttled," explains Mummy out of breath for having run in the street.

"Hurray!" I shout. "Hurray! Hurray! They didn't surrender. The "Boches" didn't get them."

"You are pleased?" asks Mummy, not quite knowing whether to rejoice or be grieved. "The whole Fleet is at the bottom of the sea."

But I only see one thing: our seamen have not capitulated. The honour of the French Marine is safe. I ask for some details but there are none yet. So I dress and, leaving Mummy, go to my lesson.

"What do you think of the last events?" I say to Grün, as soon as the door of the study where we work has closed behind me. I try to put on a catastrophic air which I hope looks natural.

Grün gives me an unexpected explanation: "They have sunk the ships because the British were going to seize them. It is idiotic; if they had called us to their rescue, we would have defended them against the British."

"Yes," I say, "why didn't they call for your help? You would have come."

December 2nd, 1942

In Tunisia, the Allies trample, without advancing. In Cyrenaica, the British regain "their breath" in front of El Azeila. In Russia, the Germans have lost some ground in front of Stalingrad. Everything seems to slow down and the Liberation, which at a time seemed imminent, becomes once more problematic and in a distant future.

December is on, bringing back the distressing fuel problem. Shall we see, as last winter, the walls sweat with dampness, the papers hang unglued, the ceilings crumple, dropping plaster on the floor. Some think this winter won't be so hard, the black-market having got organized since last year.

Finally I got Moustache on the phone. "What has happened to you? You seem to forget that my passport expires in a few days. I am not at all ready. And you, have you done what you were supposed to do?"

"Everything is ready. Don't worry. Come to see me tomorrow at 3:00 p.m. I'll warn Yvonne."

December 18th

"How very impatient you are," says Moustache. "One might think I am forgetting you, whereas I have been busy with your concerns. The authorization to deliver you a Spanish visa awaits you in Lyons. You see that everything is done."

"But my exit-visa expires the day after tomorrow," I say, getting desperate by now.

"The day after tomorrow? It's not possible. It says, 'Three months.' You surely are mistaken."

"There, look for yourself: "passage at frontier must occur before the 20th of December." The 20th of December is day after tomorrow."

"So it is, indeed. But it doesn't matter as it's only your exit visa that's overdue. You can have it renewed. And, provided you have your passport, the Spaniards will issue you a Spanish visa. They have orders from Madrid."

"You think so?"

"I am perfectly sure of it."

He hasn't convinced me. Nevertheless, as I leave Paris this evening, I shall be in Lyons tomorrow morning, and if the Consulate doesn't close on Saturdays, I might still get my visa.

"I'll leave this evening," I say resolutely.

"Impossible."

"Why?"

"I have no pass for you and it takes at least 48 hours to get one."

Crossing my arms, I gaze at him in silence. "Are you pulling my leg?" I say at last. "And if you are not pulling mine, whose leg is it you are pulling? How many times shall I have to renew my visas? And what reasons shall I give to account for my lack of eagerness to leave Paris when I have the possibility to do so? Is it you who are going to provide me with motives? Is it you? Even in a month's time, I can't go—not even in two months' time. I am not ready—NOT READY—do you understand?" Then, recovering my calm, I say: "Good bye."

But Kliemann doesn't even let me take a step towards the door. "It is my fault," he says, hanging on to my sleeve. "I admit. I confess—but don't go. During the last weeks, I have been positively overrun with work. But I assure you that this overdue visa is of no importance whatsoever. Take my word for it. It won't happen again—I promise you. Should they ask you anything at the Consulate, you will say that you have been ill and could not go before. But they're not going to ask anything. And in Vichy, you'll get it renewed without difficulty, once it has been granted to you. You shall have your pass in three days. Yvonne will take it to you."

I shrug my shoulders with lassitude. What is the use of arguing? I am well aware that, whatever happens, I won't give up my part, not for anything in the world. And even if I must wait ten years, ten years I'll wait to reach my aim.

December 21st

Moustache is not there. He is not coming. But Yvonne has the money, the instructions and the pass. "As agreed, your Spanish visa will be delivered to you at the Spanish Consulate in Lyons. Moustache wants to know when you intend leaving."

"Right after Christmas. It would be useless going before. The Consulate will be closed for the holidays."

December 22nd

I go to see my doctor-friend: "Doc, I have a favour to ask you. Can you give me a medical certificate, saying that I underwent an operation … let us say, on the 23rd November. It is in order to obtain a visa."

The Doctor smiled. He knows the value of medical certificates nowadays; he knows operations … when a piece of an adhesive tape stuck on the belly of a man saves him from being sent for compulsory labour to Germany. He knows that bandages wrapping a head have saved more than one from concentration camps. He knows of hospitals sheltering creatures hunted by the Gestapo. Without asking any questions, he makes out a certificate of a "surgical intervention" and, holding it over to me, he says: "Take it to the police station and have my signature legalized." When accompanying me to the door, he taps me lightly on the shoulder with an India-rubber gloved hand, saying: "Good luck, old girl. Don't get me too involved if you can help it."

X-mas 1942

Yesterday Darlan was murdered in Algiers. Both the B.B.C. and Radio-Paris keep silent not knowing what version to offer the public.

On the Christmas day, I should like to forget politics, war and hatred. In my studio, I have a tiny Christmas-tree, which I have decorated. At the top, there is the traditional silver-paper star. The presents are wrapped in brown paper, as it is impossible to get white paper. In spite of everything, there are presents—that's the principal. The candles on the tree are from a church. Later on, there will be a high-tea-dinner-buffet-supper, to which all those invited will have brought their contribution. It is almost as in time of peace. Even Babs will get his present: a rubber ball. Such a rarity.

Same evening, towards night

The candles have burnt out. The melting wax has dotted the sheet with yellow round spots. My guests have left in time to catch the 11 o'clock metro. The air is heavy with the scent of fir and candles. Babs has gone to sleep, his ball between his paws. How many more Christmas-eves before we are a free Nation again?

December 28th, 1942

It is freezing in Lyons. Wrapping my coat tighter around me, I hurry on in search of the Hotel du Tourisme. A traveler in my railway compartment gave me this address "in case they might have a free room." The hotel is not far from the station though it is far enough to get my hands frozen.

"We have no vacancies," says the hotel proprietor.

"Not even for one night? Anything would do. I have just arrived and am leaving tomorrow morning."

The man examines me and then consults the register book. "There is a bathroom, if you won't mind."

"Shall I have to sleep in the bath?" I ask in awe.

"No, there is a folding bed." I follow him to the first floor. He pushes a door open and I find myself in a narrow bathroom where all the free space is occupied by a camp-bed. "At least I'll have some running water," I think to myself philosophically.

"The pipes are burst," says the proprietor as if guessing my thought. "The frost. You'll have a can of water brought up to you."

"That's just my luck." The bathroom is between two rooms and has no window. If lacking ventilation, the room at least is not too cold.

I go out to try and find a restaurant. But all those I see advertise such unattractive menus that my hunger vanishes. I walk into a "bistro" where they serve me a beverage made of roasted barley and beans, of which only the colour reminds one of coffee—the taste evoking no reminiscence of it. On the saucer—a lozenge of saccharin. In Paris, they don't give you any since already a long time.

December 29th

Despite the attraction of my bathroom without water, I get up early and go out in search of the Spanish Consulate. To my great relief, it is open. I feared they might be closed between Christmas and New Year. I hand over my passport and explain that I have come for the visa the authorization for which they must have received from Madrid.

The clerk at the office-box consults a file in his drawer, sorting out a telegram. He compares the two names. "Yes, the authorization is here."

I sigh with relief. "Good. Can I have the visa right away?"

"I can't deliver you any visa."

"Why? I don't understand. You've just told me that you have the authorization."

"Your exit-visa is expired."

"I know it, but the passport is valid. I have been ill, I've undergone an operation. There, you see, I have a certificate. My exit-visa will be renewed."

"I regret," replies the clerk calmly, not even glancing at my medical certificate. "Your exit-visa is overdue. I cannot deliver you a Spanish visa. Besides," he added, "even if it were still valid, the situation would be the same. Your visa has been delivered before the occupation of the free zone and since then the Spanish frontier has been closed. Now a special permit is necessary and I very much doubt you'd obtain it."

It is useless to discuss. I can see I'm getting nowhere. Hurrying along the street, I curse Moustache. He was so sure—and, as always, he did not know. I enter a café to get warm, if one can pretend to get warm in an unheated place. Having in front of me an "Erzatz" of some kind, I start thinking matters over. What is to be done? Go to Vichy and endeavour to get my exit-visa renewed? If what the Spanish official told me about the closing of the border is true—and I am inclined to think it is—it is more than probable that, without backing, I shall get nothing in Vichy. Suddenly, I remember someone I have met in Marseille; he is director, or sub-director at the Marine Transports. Perhaps he could lend me a helping hand?

So off-"nach" Marseille!¹

—⚋—

December 30th, 1942

I have bought a "reserved seat" from a porter, at a black-market price as it is currently done. So I have been able to doze vaguely during the night. It is not so cold in Marseille. After having taken the wrong street a few times, I come at last to the house I'm looking for. The offices are open and Mr. C. is there. "Oh, yes, he remembers me. Can he do anything for me?" I tell him my trouble: operation, visa overdue, refused Spanish visa and, over there, beyond the frontier the "rich aunt," whose heiress I'm supposed to be, dying, while expecting my arrival.

"Could you not help me? Don't you know anyone who could?" I plead.

Mr. C. ponders. "I know the Prefect of the Bouches-du-Rone. Wait a moment. I think there is something I could do but the person I have in mind will only be here on the 5th, after the holidays. Can you wait till then? At any rate, on the 5th, I could tell you with certainty if yes or no something can be done. Where can I get you in case I have an answer before that time?"

"I'll be at La-Ciotat at the 'Auberge de Louveteau.'"

What a change in La-Ciotat since I stayed there last time. The lovely sea-bathing place is transformed into barracks. Feldgrau uniforms everywhere. The hotels, boarding houses, villas are all under requisition, occupied by the Germans.

I enter "Le Louveteau." Marcel, the owner, is behind the counter of the bar. All the tables are occupied by soldiers. On seeing me, Marcel represses a slight motion of surprise, but doesn't say a word. I go up to the counter.

"Can you put me up?" I say in a whisper, very quickly. And then, aloud: "How are you?"

"All right, cousin. And yourself?" and he adds under his breath: "Go into the kitchen. We'll fix you up."

His wife receives me cordially. "What do you say to that?" she says, pointing her chin towards the room from where resound thick, Teutonic voices, intermixed with the tinkling of glasses striking against each other, the noise of forks and knives and the tune of German Lieders. I shrug my shoulders.

"We've had them for two years already. You can consider yourselves lucky."

Marcel joins us. "Listen," he says rapidly, "we have not the right to put up anybody at the hotel. We are requisitioned. But, if you don't object, you could share our daughter's room, and we'll say you are my wife's cousin."

"Yesterday I spent the night in a bathroom," I said laughing, "and you ask me if half a bedroom would suit me? Thank you, Marcel, you are a good friend."

Later on in the evening, when the curfew has obliged the soldiers to return to their quarters, and the bar thus emptied, leaving a battle-field, Marcel, his wife and myself gather in the kitchen around the stove where the fire is dying out.

"What brings you here?" Marcel inquires.

I tell him about my interview with his brother-in-law.

"He'll fix it for you. He has connections and, besides, he is a good guy."

The silence of the night is broken by a passing patrol. For a moment, the heavy tramping of "their" boots stops outside the door. We don't move. The steps recede.

—⚋—

December 31st, 1942

I have borrowed from the cook her box Kodak. I make it into a parcel wrapped in newspaper, tied with a coarse string. I make four holes in the paper: one for the lens, one—for the little window where the number of the film appears; one—for the releaser; one—for the screw which revolves the spool. With my parcel under my arm, I take the train for Toulon. Toulon being restricted area and the station guarded, I'll have to alight one stop before Toulon. Here I take the bus which brings the workmen to the port and passes unnoticed.

Not knowing Toulon, I start by losing my way. At last, at the end of a narrow lane, I perceive a barricade and go in that direction. It is a hastily built construction of piled up sand-bags, kerb-stones, broken pieces of furniture, legs of chairs and tables, and bits of barbed wire. Beyond the barricade, the lane leads to the port. The water is covered with a thick black layer of oil, cart-grease and burnt paint in which are floating buoys, broken oars, an overturned life-boat and a lot of rubbish. The sea-air is heavy with the stench of petroleum. Over there, to the right of the pier, I discern the masts and the funnels of three sunken ships. I'll try to take a photo of them. To come nearer to my aim, I have to cross a dockyard with barracks here and there. A high iron gate separates the dockyard from the quay against which the scuttled vessels were anchored. In front of the submerged ships, a German sentinel is on guard, striding up and down. If I succeed in getting near the gate, I can take a "snap" when the soldier's back is turned.

Unfortunately, a gendarme is following me. I feign to be strolling, then I pretend to shake sand out of my shoe. The gendarme passes by but remains in proximity. He really is a nuisance. We reach the gate at the same time. The "boche" sentry throws us a scornful glance without interrupting his pacing. I look pensively at the remains of ships emerging out of thick water. At a short distance, the gendarme is looking too. He seems in no hurry to go away. I must find out his intentions.

"Such a pity," I say, gazing at the twisted iron mass emerging from the water.

"Right you are, Mademoiselle. It is a pity. The whole French Fleet is at the bottom of the sea."

He keeps silent because of the sentry coming back towards us. As soon as the Boche is out of ear-shot, I go on: "Had they any chance to act otherwise?"

"How should I say? They ought to have. I mean to say, they could have surrendered in Algiers."

"You were right in saying ought."

"Hush," he says, throwing around an anxious look. "If anyone should hear you." In short sentences, interrupted every time the German approaches, he relates the events of the tragic dawn of the 27th November. "The ships were anchored with their fore-part towards the pier. It takes a certain time to manoeuvre them. Many had no fuel. No, it was then too late. It ought to have been done when the Boches started occupying the free-zone."

The German sentry seems to pay no heed to us.

"I'd like to take a photo of these ships," I say.

"Yes, it would be easy from here if one had a camera," says the gendarme.

"I've got one," I say, indicating the parcel under my arm.

"That?" he queries incredulously.

Suddenly he looks at me with terror: "Don't do that. They shoot people for less than that. It is strictly forbidden and you are not even from here."

"Listen," I say. "Go to the corner of this building and get busy for three minutes re-adjusting the leather-straps of your leggings. If you see anyone coming, just start whistling 'I am alone this evening'; it's a tune everyone knows."

"But I don't."

"Well then: 'The Madelon.'"

His face brightens: "Right-ho. I know that one." But he immediately asks with concern: "What about the sentry?"

"I'll see to that. I'll wait until the Boche has his back to me."

I give the gendarme time to reach the barracks; the soldier has turned on his heels and is off to the far end of his guard-march. I take a snapshot from between the bars of the gate and am about to take another, when a terrified "Madelon" rises in the air. I turn round and see a German officer coming in my direction. The sentry on the quay has but a few strides to make before he turns round and walks back. Quickly I take the second photo. Then, putting casually my parcel on the ground, I bend to tie the lace of my shoe. The German officer has stopped and is watching me. Replacing my parcel under my arm, I go away strolling leisurely along the gate. The German shrugs his shoulders and enters the barracks.

My friend the gendarme has disappeared. Ten minutes later, when leaving the dockyard, I see him emerging from behind a heap of sand. "Good Lord. You've given me the fright of my life. What possesses you to photograph forbidden things?"

1943, January 1st

I celebrate the New Year in company of some casual friends. We make pancakes with dark-grey flour and water. We pour grape-juice over them. Marcel procured us a chicken and I have brought a bottle of "Ersatz" champagne for which I paid 88 francs. Behind the closed shutters, one hears but little of the uproar raised by the drunken Germans celebrating their "Neues Jahr," their Victory close at hand and the future domination of the "Gross Germany" over the world.

It is late as I hurry home. The curfew has been set back for today. On the solitary quay, an icy wind lashes my face. I pass in front of the Christmas-tree which the German army has erected for her sons. Facing the sea, shaken by the gale which has torn all its ornaments, it raises a mournful silhouette, reminding one of a scarecrow. A sentry is on guard to prevent possible sabotage.

January 4th, 1943

The dining room at the Louveteau is empty—except for two German soldiers sitting in a corner. They have ordered a better meal than the one to which their mess ticket entitles them. They have asked for some wine and are half drunk. One of them gets up and, a glass in his hand, comes towards me with an uncertain gait.

"You understand German?"

I hesitate, then answer: "Yes."

"Oh. Splendid." He says. "My name is Karl. My Kamerad is Fritz. Our anniversaries[2] are on the same day: today. I am 24 years. He is 30. Come, drink a glass with us. Bitte, do not refuse. He also, everybody." He adds, beckoning to Marcel and his wife.

We gather round a table. Karl fills the glasses and passes them on. Both of them lift theirs in a toast. Marcel throws me a questioning glance. I raise my glass very high and say: "A la victoire des Alliés."[3]

"What does it mean?" asks Fritz.

"It means "Prosit" in French."[4]

"Oh, very good, very good. How have you say? Alafik…?"

"A la victoire des Allies."

"Ja. Ja. Alafiktoartesalje. Alafiktoartesalje. Des ist colossal. War fur ein Wort."

Marcel, his wife and I can hardly control our laughter. But Fritz and Karl shout so loud to the victory of the Allies, that we are obliged to silence them for fear of a passing patrol might hear them.

January 5th

The day is bright but cold. As I have nothing to do and nowhere to go, I spend the greater part of my time in the hall of the Louveteau, reading newspapers and, from time to time, chatting with soldiers. Sometimes it is interesting. A moment ago, I got the German version of the capture of Toulon told by a soldier who had taken part in the action.

He told me that the alarm had been given at three o'clock in the morning; the news had spread that British ships were in view of Toulon and were going to attack. This soldier and his pals were immediately sent by truck to Toulon. He didn't see any British. He thought they must have fled. But some of the French units were already burning. After Toulon had been taken, all the Germans who had participated in this action had the right to buy 2 kg of coffee at 60 fr per kilo. The coffee came from the Arsenal of the Marine.

It's also at the Louveteau that I met the commander of a submarine, which I know is at the bottom of the water. He told me that he was arrested at 5 o'clock in the morning when he was in his bed. It was an officer of the S.S. who came and said to him—in faultless French: "You do not recognize me, Commander?"—"I looked at him more attentively," went on the naval officer, "and I recognized him. He had been a sailor on board the ship under my command at Dakar."

The door of the Louveteau opens letting in a gust of cold air and the noise of the dockyard. A man stumbles in. He wears a brown suit and a black felt hat pushed backwards. His starched collar is too tight for his thick red and sunburned neck. He isn't used to wearing a collar. You can see it by the way he continually inserts in it his finger and tugs at it, lifting up his chin.

"What good luck brings you?" greets Marcel who seems to know him.

The newcomer leans with all his weight against the counter of the bar. "I've heard there's an English girl staying here," he says in a thick voice with a silly laugh.

"What is this nonsense?" protests Marcel who is getting worried. "Who told you that?"

"You sly dog," says the drunkard. "Everybody is talking about the English lady." His uncertain glance hovers across the bar, empty at this hour, then rests upon me. "Why, by Jove, there she is. I knew it," he exclaims coming towards me, swinging on unsteady legs. "Miss, I present you my respects. You must know that I admire the English people. A cheer for England. To hell the Germans." And to Marcel who rushes to make him shut up: "Bring us some champagne. Two bottles of champagne—three bottles. By Jove. This asks for a celebration." Then, bending towards me, he asks confidentially: "Where do you come from? London?"

"I assure you that you are mistaken. I am not English. I come from Paris."

"Tut. Tut. Tut. You—a French girl." And them, with an air of reproach: "You distrust me. It's quite comprehensible—you do not know me. Well, well. I am not going to ask you anything. Only, will do me honour to have a drink with me?" He beckons to Marcel, urging him to bring the bottles. Marcel looks at me inquiringly. I shrug my shoulders. The cork pops, the champagne bubbles. The stranger raises his glass to my health, to my success, to the health of the King of England, to the victory of the allies. Except for this, he doesn't say a word and his eyes don't leave me. From time to time, he murmurs in ecstasy: "An English woman. A real English woman."

The door opens with a crash and German soldiers perform a noisy entry. The drunkard puts a finger to his lips and whispers: "Hush," throwing at me a glance of complicity.

I get up and say: "Good bye and thank you for the champagne."

He winks significantly and urges: "Be sure to hide well."

Later on, I ask Marcel: "Who and what is that frantic creature?"

"He is a vineyard owner. But he seldom comes down to La Ciotat."

"Do you think all this might cause you harm?"

Marcel shrugs his shoulders: "Your papers are in order, aren't they?"

January 7th

Marcel has phoned to his brother-in-law, but the friend has not returned. I cannot wait indefinitely and am very annoyed. To pass the time, I go strolling aimlessly to the beach of La Ciotat. Alongside the road, the Germans are fortifying the coast with blockhouses and casemates.

"It doesn't look too solid," I say to M. who accompanies me and is an architect. "Is that the way a wall is built, even a concrete wall, without foundation? Simply placed upon the ground. The first flow of Mistral will turn it over."

"It does seem built in spite of common sense," says M., "and has no more protective value than a stage-scenery made out of paste-board."

… And that is the Mediterranean Wall.

This evening at the Louveteau, at a table next to mine, six young soldiers are eating in silence. They look so young, so immature, clad into large uniforms with too wide collars that I cannot help but ask them: "How old are you?"

One of them jumps to his feet, makes am impeccable salute and, speaking in the name of all, says blushing: "I am the youngest. I am fourteen years and eight months old. My pal, here, is the eldest. He is sixteen and three months."

Children. Their beardless faces look drawn with fatigue and are covered with dust. I try to find a question which won't sound too direct. "Do you like La Ciotat? Are you going to remain here for a long time?"

"No," says the one who has already spoken. And he adds, not without pride: "We leave tomorrow for the Russian Front. We have already received our equipment and our skis." His neighbor jostles him in the elbow and my interlocutor blushes. He has forgotten that the orders are not to talk.

I say reassuringly: "It's fun skiing. Do you like it?"

He answers candidly: "I do not know: I have never tried it. But I'll learn very quickly." And that's what "they" are sending to the Russian Front: boys aged 14, a pair of skis and no knowledge how to use them.

II. Paris, 1942–1943

January 8th 43

"I can get your exit visa renewed, but to do so, I must send your passport to Vichy. That will take at least 8 days but I can promise you that it'll be done," says M. "Can you leave me your passport for a week?"

I think rapidly—I do not like the idea of letting go my passport. Who knows what may happen? The fellow to whom he will entrust it might lose it, or he can be arrested, or he may die, for all I know. And then everything will have to be started over again. Still, I must have that visa renewed one way or another. Anyhow, I'll have to come back to Lyons for my Spanish visa. "All right," I agree. "I shall leave the passport with you and, as soon as you get it back, you'll send me an inter-zone post-card to notify me."

January 10th

There has been an attentat[5] in Marseille and the curfew has been advanced to 6 o'clock. I have to wait four hours at the railway station.

January 11th

The return journey has been awful and bitterly cold in an unheated train. I have caught a bad bronchitis with a terrible cough. On my arrival and before going to my flat, I call Moustache on the phone. I am so angry that I give him no time to ask questions. "I knew that nothing would come of that trip. I told you so. You always are so perfectly sure of everything. Are you satisfied now? I've lost a fortnight doing nothing."

"We'll talk about it presently," says the major annoyed. "Can you be at twelve o'clock at the "Deux Maggots" at St. Germain?"

"Yes," I say angrily replacing the mouth-piece with a bang.

Moustache walks in at 27 min. past 3 o'clock, and sits down next to me as if nothing was amiss.

"You are late," I remark sourly.

"Am I?" he says surprised.

"You are."

He doesn't answer, but orders grog. When the waiter has gone, he turns to me. "Well, what is it that went wrong?"

"Everything."

He lifts his eyebrows in sign of surprise and doubt. I tell him all about my problems, which he seems to find quite natural and rather amusing. "It doesn't matter," he says at last. "Give me your passport and I'll have it renewed here."

"But I have told you that I left it at Marseille."

"Oh. I didn't grasp that. It's bad, very bad. You ought never to let your passport out of your hands. You'll have to go and fetch it immediately."

"Where? From Marseille?"

"Of course. Isn't it where you've left it?"

"But why won't you let me have it renewed there?"

"Because I do not know that Mister C. And I do not trust people I do not know."

"Then I shall need a new pass."

He looks at his watch: 32 min. past 4 o'clock. "I think I can still do it. When is there a train leaving?"

"Tonight, at ten o'clock, I believe."

"All right. Go home now and wait. Yvonne will bring your pass."

I don't even have time to see Mummy. It is Annick, Yvonne's maid, who brings me the paper. Two more sleepless nights, in prospect, on the train.

Marseilles, January 12th 43

C. seems surprised to see me walk into his office.

"I thought you had left yesterday."

"I have left … and come back. On returning to Paris, I met someone who can get me my visa renewed immediately. So I came to fetch my passport. I hope you won't bear me a grudge for having disturbed you for nothing?"

C. looks annoyed and discontented. Also the facility with which I cross the demarcation line must seem rather queer to him. The hell with it. Anyhow, it's the last time I go to Marseilles. "All right," he sighs, "when do you want it?"

"I'd like to leave by the evening train."

"Let's see. Can you come back at 5 o'clock? I'll have it ready."

I was able to get a seat in a second-class compartment. I can hardly wait to be back. Unconsciously, I examine my left-hand neighbor and, suddenly, recognize him. "Oh," I say, "an old acquaintance."

"What a surprise, dear friend," exclaims the Count de Gueydon.

His "dear friend" amuses me. I used to play with his children before he played his "swindler's trick" on my family. After that, we lost sight of him until the time when he reappeared as an ardent propagandist for the "New Europe" and the "New Order." He talks on the "Radio-Paris": propaganda transmissions intended for Canada.

"It's abominable," he says, "being obliged to travel 2nd class. But I think, I may be able to settle this slight misunderstanding as soon as the ticket-collector comes. This seat is all I have been able to get." Still the former snob.

"I don't see anything so terrible in travelling second class. I always do."

"But no, it can't be possible. Decent people do not travel 2nd class. You will allow me to get you a 1st class seat," he says, seeing the train-controller at the end of the passage.

I can see him take out a few notes from his wallet and press them into the controller's hand. "Come," he says, "everything is settled." And not waiting for my consent, he gets hold of my suitcase.

Curiosity more than anything else makes me follow him. We have seats facing each other. I can examine him at leisure. He is quite bald now and his single goggle is still as protruding as ever. On the other, he wears a black patch. Gueydon wears a thick, too conspicuous tweed, a gaudy tie, shoes with over-thick leather soles. He talks loud; he wants to be heard.

"What have you done during the war?" I ask him.

"My DUTY. Then, there was Dunkirk. The British treason. I was wounded. Taken prisoner. We were evacuated to Germany. With open wounds, losing my blood, I had to walk for days and nights, At last, a hospital. I was covered with wounds. You see. I lost an eye."

"Do you mean, you have lost it at the war?"

"Where else do you think?"

"I thought," I said innocently but rather meanly, "you got it knocked out winding a car."

Gueydon nearly chokes, suffocated with anger. "Well…. After all…. Sure…. I have never said the contrary. In short, I was telling you I was covered with wounds."

His neighbor tries to conceal his increasing hilarity behind a newspaper, but the jolts of his abdomen betray him. My vis-à-vis turns his head away blowing his nose noisily. Gueydon is furious but goes on with his palaver: "As I was saying, wounds all over. In Germany, I was very well attended to by excellent first-rate surgeons. They treated me most correctly."

"That was the least they could do," I interrupted him very rudely, "after having made such a mess of you."

"You don't like the Germans; you are prejudiced against them. Perhaps you would prefer to see here the British?" he says with a look of challenge addressed to all the compartment.

"And if it were the case, could I answer 'YES' here, in public?" I ask him.

He shrugs his shoulders and starts on another subject.

January 13th

Kliemann pockets my passport with obvious satisfaction. "I feared it might have already gone to Vichy, or that something had happened to it. I'll keep it for you; it is safer. In a few days, you'll go and see a friend of Yvonne's. I know him too, but everything will be arranged through Yvonne, as I do not want it to be known that you have anything to do with me. My plan is made. The gentleman I am talking about is an intimate friend of Laval. He knows all the people at the Hotel Matignon. With an introduction from him, you'll get any visa you want, all the more a renewal."

"Very well," I say. "But how will I later explain to the British that I was able to get that visa in Paris?"

"Why should you worry beforehand? We have plenty of time to find some plausible explanation."

January 26th

Yvonne's pneumatic says: "Dear Napoleon, I must talk to you business. Come this afternoon.—Josephine."

"Here I am," I say, entering without ringing the bell.

"It's about our 'Plot' to get you a visa," she says laughing. "Here is what we have concocted with Moustache. I am going to give you the name of one of my friends. I have spoken to him about you. He is warned. But above all things, don't mention the major. This friend of mine doesn't suspect that you know Moustache. He lives in Rue de Varenne in the house next to the Hotel Matignon. I have written his address on this bit of paper. His name is— Mr. Genty. I've taken an appointment for you tomorrow at 2 o'clock."

January 27th

It is Mme Genty who opens the door. "My husband hasn't yet returned. But if you will kindly wait a little, he won't be long."

I wait in the drawing-room, which is pretentious and cold. I am beginning to be fed up by all this running about for this passport. Why not let the Germans do it themselves?

After all, it's their concern that I should go. Maybe. But I am as interested as they are—if not more.

The entrance door bangs. I hear a murmur of voices and a tall man walks into the drawing-room. "Please excuse me. I have been detained," he says, offering his hand.

Yvonne had told me that Genty is 42. He does not look it.

"We'll go down immediately and I shall introduce you to one of my friends. You may rest assured that I'll do all I can to satisfy the Major."

"The Major?" I say, astonished, Yvonne and Moustache having both instructed me to pretend not knowing him.

"Yes, Major Kliemann, who has so warmly recommended you."

"It must be a friend of Yvonne's. I am so sorry to say I do not know him."

"Oh. I thought…. Anyhow, it doesn't matter. If he thus recommends a friend of Yvonne's without knowing her, he must know what he is doing. He is a charming man. He has been infinitely obliging. He never refused us a pass for the free zone or a permit for my car or an authorization to circulate after curfew. I am only too happy, if I can, to help him in turn."

Mr. Genty accompanies me to the Hotel Matignon, which is quite near. At the main gate, he waves a friendly hand to the porter, who bows. In the big hall, the usher recognizes him and greets him as "one belonging to the house."

"Is Mr. Guillaume there?"

"Yes, sir."

"Will you wait here a moment?" says Genty, turning to me.

As I take a seat, I see him push a door open without having been announced. I look around. There was a time when good taste prevailed. What a lovely private residence it must have been. Through the windows, I see a garden with very old trees, well cared for lawns.

"Come along quickly," says Genty whom I didn't hear walk in.

I follow him into the room where I saw him disappear a moment ago. A young man gets up from behind a large writing-desk. "Mr. Guillaume—Mlle Sergueiew," introduces Genty. And addressing Mr. Guillaume, he adds: "Mlle Sergueiew has been recommended to us by a highly important personality. Therefore, dear friend, as I have told you, I hope that you will do your utmost to give entire satisfaction to her demands."

Turning to me, he apologizes: "Unfortunately, I shall be obliged to leave you. I am going away and shall not have the pleasure of seeing you again. But I am sure that Mr. Guillaume will solve all your problems."

After Genty's departure, I explain to Guillaume what I expect of him.

"Do you care particularly that your visa should be renewed in Vichy?" he asks after having listened carefully.

"I think it would be the simplest, as they have all my records over there and as anyhow, I'll have to go to Lyons to fetch my Spanish visa."

"You may be right. Leave me your passport and ring me up towards the middle of next week,"—he consults a calendar—"let us say, on the 2nd of February."

January 29th

Yesterday, the B.B.C. announced that a communication of "the greatest importance" would be made at 3 o'clock this morning. Everybody was told to listen. We were all terribly excited and impatient. Surely they'll announce a general offensive or perhaps even the invasion. Mummy has verified twice her two alarm-clocks: the one that works only when it is "lying on its face" and … and it is always fast. And the one that only works when it's "upside down" and is generally slow.

Daddy has set his alarm at 2:30, allowing half an hour to time his radio, and didn't sleep at all for fear of oversleeping. Having no radio at home, I spent the night at my parents' flat and, trusting the three alarms to wake me, didn't hear any of them. The last minutes are the longest. At last, we are going to know. And what do you think they tell us? That Roosevelt, Churchill, de Gaulle and their Staffs have met in Casablanca. The hell with them and where they meet. One doesn't disturb people at 3:00 a.m. to tell them that. Also today, the crowd in the street look tired, and faces wear traces of insomnia: dark rims under the eyes, and in quarrelsome mood. We all think the B.B.C. has played on us a joke of doubtful taste.

February 2nd 43

I ring up Guillaume, but he tells me that the man who was to see to my visa in Vichy is on leave and has just left. He won't be back before the end of next week. I must ring him up on the 11th. In the meantime, I go on with my radio lessons without any conviction, as these lessons are merely a sort of training.

February 5th

The Russian advance is progressing. At Stalingrad, General Paulus has surrendered. Hitler has just promoted him to the grade of Marshal.

The winter in Paris is still mild. People go on grumbling, rationing increases, and prices are going up steadily. The "black market" is flourishing: butter is 500 to 580 fr per kilo. Coffee—2,000 fr/ kilo. Oil, from 800 to 1000 fr/ litre. Tea—6000 fr. per kilo … when one can get it. Woolen tissues—1500 to 2300 fr. per meter. Gold breakage is at 400 to 425 fr. per gram. The sterling pound is at 4800 fr.

February 8th

The Russians have taken Kursk and are progressing. By now, the Germans have lost almost all the territories conquered during 1942.

February 11th

I ring up Guillaume. He isn't there.

February 12th

I ring up Guillaume. He had just left.

February 13th

I ring up Guillaume. He doesn't work on Saturdays.

FEBRUARY 15TH

I ring up Guillaume. He does not come on Mondays.

FEBRUARY 16TH

I ring up Guillaume. He is at a conference.

FEBRUARY 17TH

Ring up Guillaume. He is busy.

FEBRUARY 18TH

Ring up Guillaume. He hasn't come yet. I call him up again; he has just phoned to say he wouldn't be coming today.

FEBRUARY 19TH

I dial Littre 07-30, and when I get the Hotel Matignon at the end of the wire, I say to the standard operator in a ferocious tone: "Could you give me information? On what day of the year is Mr. Guillaume to be found in his office?"

"But, Madam, he is there," she answers quite bewildered.

A moment later, I hear Guillaume's voice: "I am sorry. I was told just now that you have telephoned several times during my absence. Can you come to see me at 2 o'clock?"

At the Hotel Matignon, Guillaume has asked for the connection with Vichy, Hotel du Parc, Presidence du Conseil. In the meantime, he says to me: "I want to telephone in front of you to the chief of Mr. Laval's Cabinet so that you should know exactly what I am going to tell him."

"Allo—is it you, dear colleague? This is Guillaume speaking. Yes, Guillaume from the Hotel Matignon. I have a favour to ask you. Can you hear me? Splendid. I was saying that I have a favour to ask of you. I have here, with me, Mlle Serjiens, no, Sergulier, I mean … Serguieux. Wait a minute, I am going to spell it."

He spells. Then: "This young lady has been recommended to us by someone very important. Do you hear me? I am saying 'very important.' No, no, it is not she who is "very important." She is recommended by someone very important. That's it. She will call on you and explain her case personally. I'll be thankful to you to do whatever you can to help her. That's right. Thank you. Good-bye, dear colleague."

He hangs up. "There. It's done. One hears very badly. I apologize for this 'very important' misunderstanding. I didn't mean to say you are not important, but it was difficult to explain on the telephone … and I would have had to give details. Well, there only remains for you to go to Vichy. Do you wish me to make you a reservation on the train and in a hotel in Vichy?"

"Thanks. You're very kind, but I do not know yet when I shall leave, nor by what train."

SAME DAY

"Yvonne, where is Moustache?" I say when I've got her on the line. "I haven't been able to reach him at his office."

"He'll be here at 7 o'clock. Is there anything you want me to tell him?"

"Yes, if you see him before that time, tell him I must have a new pass for Vichy—I must have it right away."

"All right. But try and 'phone again towards 7."

At 9 o'clock, when I get Moustache on the 'phone, he asks me to come and see him tomorrow.

FEBRUARY 20TH

I can hardly believe my eyes when, on reaching Yvonne's place that morning, I find Kliemann there. I'll have to make a mark on my calendar. As far as I can remember, it is the first time the Major isn't late for appointment. He closes the door of the drawing-room behind me and we settle down on the silk-upholstered divan.

"Well, is everything all right?"

"Guillaume has—in my presence—telephoned to Vichy, introducing me to Laval's Chief of Staff. They are expecting me. I need a pass."

"You'll get it. So that is settled. Now, how are you getting on with your transmitting? What's you speed?"

"Sixty the last time it was chronometered."

"I'll have to see Grün. You haven't started yet with the ciphering?"

"No."

"You must do that."

"I don't even know how the radio works. And should something burn out or break."

"What kind of set are you actually working on?"

"The one in a leather suitcase."

"I see. It isn't what you'll take with you when you go."

"Why can't I be trained on the set you intend to give me? I should at least be used to it."

"Because we haven't got one. It hasn't been yet constructed."

"When did I meet you first, Sir?"

"In October 1941. Why?"

"Oh. Simply because we are in February 43. That makes a year and five months. I should have thought you'd have time enough to have one made."

"To tell the truth, we haven't decided yet what model we are going to give you. Vogel has tried a few, but they didn't prove satisfactory."

"It's about time you made your choice. And as we are talking about it, can you tell me under what camouflage you intend to give me a radio to take with me? It's not a trifle you can smuggle unnoticed—especially in war-time."

"That's the very thing over which we cannot make up our minds. One of our agents took to England a radio concealed in a gramophone. It's true he was of Portuguese nationality, which makes it different. Besides, most probably we won't give you a set before we are sure that you will get a visa for Great-Britain. When it'll be certain, I'll bring you over a radio, either to Madrid or to Lisbon."

"What will you do if I fail to get to England?"

"This too has been foreseen. We shall keep you in Lisbon where you can be very useful to us. If you are refused the Portuguese visa—which might happen—we can still make use of you in Spain, although we do have a sufficient number of agents there. Or we can send you to North Africa, where you have a sister I believe?"

"Yes."

"We are not short of alternatives, as you see—but the main aim remains LONDON."

"And to begin with—Vichy. When will I have my pass?"

"I shall see to it this afternoon and you'll have it on Monday, or Tuesday at the latest. Will that do?"

"That means the 23rd. I'll leave right away."

"All right."

―⚍―

February 25th

It's only today that I've received my pass.

―⚍―

February 26th

Formerly, train passengers used to talk among themselves. It made the time pass quicker and the trip seem shorter. Nowadays, everybody keeps to his corner; everyone distrusts his neighbor. Who knows with whom one travels? The fact of having a demarcation line permits makes one appear suspect. How did one get it? Surely this one is a collaborator, unless he is a militia. The best is to hold one's tongue.

We arrive at Moulins: the demarcation line. I am less sure of myself today, as I have quite a number of letters in my suitcase, too many to have even attempted to conceal them. I have nine of them which I have promised to mail from the ex-free zone. Most are very thick letters, for, when one is lucky enough to find an "opportunity" to get a letter through to the free zone—an "occaz" as we say, who doesn't warn you: "Write on cigarette paper, for I have to put your note into my hollow tooth."—one takes advantage of it to write everything that an inter-zone post-card cannot hold—which means a lot.

Usually when I carry correspondence, I take precautions and it has always gone all right. But this time, there were just too many. In my compartment are six men, a woman and myself. It is the first one in the passage. A "Kraut" peeps in, telling us to have our papers ready. Obediently we take out our orange-coloured passes. And officer and a soldier come in, accompanied by a woman. The officer examines the permits, compares them with a list he has, and passes them to the soldier to be stamped. It is quickly done.

"No papers? No letters? No books? No newspapers?" he asks the passengers.

No one has anything. Everything seems all right.

"Shall I search them a bit?" the woman in grey asks the officer.

"Yes, do," he replies.

"The fiend," I curse her under my breath. I can just see what will happen: my letters discovered, and 8 days in jail, until I am able to notify Moustache. And then his furor. But above all the humiliation of it.

The German bids the men out. The woman in grey hangs a curtain over the panes of our compartment, then starts searching my neighbor, "pawing" her all over, fumbling, looking in her shoes, examining her hair, emptying her suitcase … finding nothing. My turn has come. I look for inspiration. Let's try my luck. As soon as she runs her hand along my ribs, I give a squeak.

"You are tickling me."

"Ach. But it is not possible."

She fumbles in my sleeves. I start wriggling. She passes her hand down my back. I begin to giggle. She looks at me incredulously and smiles. But when she touches the nape of my neck to make sure I have nothing hidden in my hair, I go off into a fit of irrepressibly laughter, folding myself in two. My hilarity is catching. The other passenger is roaring with laughter and our searcher is not able to resist; she joins us, forced to sit down and wipe her eyes. Someone knocks at the door; it is the officer.

"What's happening to you?" he inquires displeased.

"I am coming. I am coming," Says the German woman, ashamed; and without taking time to examine my shoes or open my suitcase, she unhooks her curtain.

"You terrible ticklish." She tells me reproachfully going away.

I've never felt less inclined to laugh.

Vichy. I go straight to the "Hotel du Parc." At the reception office I am preceded by Marcel Bucard. The usher who takes my name and the object of my visit is in a bad mood. In spite of that, I don't have to wait too long. I am well aware that in Vichy the offices are set up in hotel bedrooms. Nevertheless, the sight of files emerging from a wash basin and of a ... bidet transformed into an umbrella-stand, all that in the office of a "Chief of Cabinet," flabbergasts me. Squeezed-in between these two products of our civilization, I notice a writing table, and behind that table a man who darts at me a furious glance.

"And you, what do you want?"

"I should like to see Mr. Laval's Chief of Staff."

"That's me. What else?"

"Mr. Guillaume has telephoned to you on my behalf."

"Guillaume? Guillaume? What Guillaume? I don't know any Guillaume."

"Mr. Guillaume from the Hotel Matignon."

"Matignon.... Ah. Yes, this one. Well, what does he want?"

"He telephoned you last Wednesday."

"No Guillaume has telephoned to me."

"But he did—in my presence. Is there someone else here who has the same name as you?"

"No. But all this is of no interest to me. Proceed. What do you want?"

I explain him my case as shortly and as clearly I can.

"A visa. A visa. For whom does he take me, your Guillaume? Do you think I have nothing else to do but issue visas? Do you think I have that much time to waste?" And to give more weight to his words, he lifts up violently a pile of records from the washstand, scattering the contents and slamming the empty covers in front of him. "Enquire at the passports service. Enquire elsewhere, anywhere. I don't care. I have no time to waste."

Once more I find myself on the landing, restraining a great desire to laugh. Let us see the "Passports Service." No one seems to know where it is. "A passport? What for? Aren't you content in France?" people ask me. I go from office to office; from hotel to hotel; from ministry to ministry. And then, suddenly, when I least expect it, "it's here." A door opens and I find myself in the presence of an old white-bearded gentleman, who gets up to greet me. "Please take a seat. What can I do for you?"

I am so stupefied that mechanically I murmur: "I am looking for the service of passports."

"It is here. You've found it."

I say a little stupidly: "I'd like to have a visa."

He smiles. "Almost everybody in France desires the same thing as you."

"Yes, but in my case, I have been granted one already. I should like merely to renew it." And I tell him my story. He listens attentively.

"Unfortunately," he says when I have finished speaking, "we no longer have the right to deliver visas in Vichy. Moreover, we've nothing to give them with. The first thing the Germans did when they occupied this zone was to seize all our seals, stamps, etc."

"But then where can I get it renewed?"

"In Vichy nowhere. Believe me. I have no interest whatsoever to discourage you. But at present we are powerless."

"So it's useless to try?"

Sadly he shakes his head, his white beard sweeping his black waistcoat, shiny at the edges. I go back to the station. A train leaves at 11 o'clock. This time, I don't leave to random to secure a seat. I go up to a group of idle porters.

"Who wants to earn 50 francs?" I ask them and without waiting for an answer—which I know in advance—I explain: "I'll come when they bring in the train: just before 10 p.m. The one who gets me a seat, will receive 50 frs." At 10 o'clock, I walk into the station. The porters rush to me. The first one to reach me seizes my suitcase, the others go back, dragging their feet.

"This way," says the man, leading me to the platform. The station is deserted but for a few travelers of both sexes, sprawled on their luggage or dozing on the benches. They lift half a lid to see us pass, pull in their necks deeper into their collars and slumber back into sleep. The quay is scarcely light because of the black-out.

"Where are we going?" I ask.

"Just follow me," answers the porter without further explanation. We meet the station-master.

"Hey. You, over there." My guide goes up to him and starts whispering. I notice that he slips something into his hand. "All right," says the other retracing his steps. We proceed, one behind another. The platform ends and we continue along the rail, the station-master ahead, showing the way with his flashlight. Some 50 meters further, on a siding, I can discern the black outline of two railway cars. The station-master stops in front of the first one, takes a key from his pocket and opens the door. The foot-board is so high—it is almost level with my shoulder and they are obliged to haul me up.

"Well. Hell's fire. What does this mean? Where do you think you are?" growls the station-master sweeping the beam of his flashlight over sleeping, huddled-up figures. But he must be used to it, for having grumbled to his heart's content, he lets the people stay where they are and goes away. I pay the promised 50 francs to the porter and settle down. It is dark and darkness makes the cold more penetrating. I have two hours and three quarters to wait before we leave.

―∞―

March 2nd 43

"I hope you are going to tell me a good result?" says Guillaume at the end of the wire.

"What a bore, that colleague of yours." I can't help but saying.

"I beg your pardon?"

"I said that your colleague is not obliging."

"You don't say so."

"I do. Can you spare me a few moments ... tomorrow for instance?"

"Why, of course. I shall be at the office the whole morning."

Having finished with Guillaume, I 'phone Kliemann.

"Back already?" he exclaims surprised.

"Yes. And it is nill."

"Do you mean no result?"

"Exactly."

"When can you come over?"

"Tomorrow morning, I have an appointment with Guillaume. I'll see you after that."

March 3rd

I have finished telling Guillaume about my unsuccessful trip to Vichy. He seems extremely annoyed. "I do not understand how my colleague could say that I didn't ring him up. You witnessed my telephoning him."

"Maybe, this gentleman has no memory. It doesn't really matter. The main fact is that Vichy no longer possesses the stamps to put on the visas. So now, what do you suggest?"

"If you give me until tomorrow morning, first of all to get the situation straight and then to think out some solution, we might renew your visa here, in Paris."

"Very well, I'll come back before lunch."

Kliemann is pacing up and down the drawing-room, his hands behind his back. The window is ajar and a light draught stirs the yellow brocaded curtains. "What do you think about it?" he inquires at last lifting up his head and halting in front of me.

"Frankly, since the free zone does no longer exist, I do not see what difference it makes whether I renew my visa in Paris or in Vichy. One way or another, I'll have to explain it somehow to the British ... supposing I ever do reach England. But then I'll have a lot to explain. Do you think we shall be able to concoct some plausible reasons to offer them?"

"Of course we will. As soon as you have all your papers, we'll work out with minute details your plan of action."

If only Moustache knew how indifferent I am to the likelihood of his alibi for me. But I have to pretend to worry: I have even to make believe that I am scared, hesitant at the last moment. "So tomorrow, when I see Guillaume, if he offers to have everything fixed in Paris, I must accept? Is that the idea?"

Kliemann comes up to me and sits down beside me. "Would you be losing you self-assurance?" he asks taking my hand. "Are you getting scared? You mustn't. I have confidence in your success because you always seem so sure of yourself. You must not doubt. You MUST succeed."

I shrug my shoulders. "I do not doubt. But all this has been dragging on for so long. It's like an episodic novel; one has forgotten the beginning before one has reached the end. One gets bored. I am fed up. Maybe you cannot understand. I have undertaken something with enthusiasm. But, as time goes and nothing happens except waiting, waiting without end, I am losing interest—that's all."

"You mustn't. We are nearing our aim. Have a little more patience, now that you have waited so long."

I smile. Funny; we have the same aim … for different purposes.

March 4th

Guillaume receives me without having kept me waiting. It looks as if he wanted to make up for the bad impression produced by his colleague from Vichy. "I have spoken of you to the Chef de Cabinet of the Prefect de Police. He told me it is fairly easy to renew your visa … providing you can get a German authorization. I told him, I'd talk it over with you and that, if you could obtain it, you'd go to see him personally. Do you think you could get one?"

"What kind of authorization?"

"I don't know exactly. I believe you must show a zone pass and a non-opposition to your leaving France."

"I think that I could obtain these papers through the girl-friend who introduced me to Mr. Genty. She knows a lot of people."

"In that case, there remains for you but to go and see M. Lepinard at the "Prefecture de Police." Ask for the Cabinet de Prefect. His Chief of Staff is acquainted with your business and will tell exactly the papers you will need. Do you want me to notify him of your coming?"

"Please. Ask him if he can receive me this afternoon."

A few minutes after that, Guillaume has Lepinard on the 'phone.

"Will 3 o'clock do?" he asks me.

"Perfectly."

"So that is settled, cher Monsieur," he continues in the 'phone. "Mlle S. will be at your office at 3 o'clock."

I imagined it would be more difficult to get admission to the Cabinet of the Prefet. I imagined I'd have to produce documents, passes, and what not. Nothing of the kind. An agent-on guard—inquires where I am going. I answer: "To Monsieur Lepinard," and he waves me through.

Lepinard is a young man, neither long nor short. Nor stout; neither obsequious nor rude. It is a man who has enough good-looks not to be ugly … and not enough to be handsome. A man without particulars, as a passport would say. I unroll my explanations in mechanical sentences, from too much repetition.

"All right," says Lepinard when I have finished. "To renew your visa is nothing. But what you need is: first, a non-opposition form; secondly, a pass for the ex-free zone. When you have these two papers, we shall constitute a record for you and give you a new visa."

It looks as if today at last I had made a step forward. I stroll home along the quays. I adore this part of Paris; the Ile-Saints-Louis, the Vert-Galant, the book-dealers, and the Seine bordered by plane-trees. The hurrying water; the water that has always run, that will still run when I shall have left Paris. I look at it with particular fondness, realizing suddenly that I won't see it for a long time. Slowly I take consciousness of this Paris, which surrounds me, realizing suddenly that for two years I have been going through life blindfolded to everything but the aim I have imposed myself, a distant, uncertain aim-unaware of the existence around me.

II. Paris, 1942–1943

March 6th

It is unbelievable the amount of time I waste trying to reach Kliemann. I have been trying for two days without result. I pity those who are really working for him: his agents abroad who rely upon him to receive regularly instructions or money. This afternoon, we were to meet at 3 o'clock. At half past six, I am still waiting. He arrives at last and seems surprised to see me.

"Had you forgotten me?"

"Had you to come?"

"Of course. You had fixed an appointment by Yvonne, and it was to be at 3 o'clock."

"It's possible. I am so overworked."

I relate my interview with Lepinard.

"Good. Good. Very good," he approves. "These papers are but a trifle: I'll get them for you. As soon as they are ready, Yvonne will let you know."

March 10th

In Russia, the Germans counter-attack and advance in the Kharkov and the Donetz-basin sectors. I rectify the red-headed pins on my wall-map and feel depressed.

March 12th

I 'phoned several times to Yvonne, but she says that Moustache has nothing for me.

Rennes and Rouen have been violently bombarded. A new anecdote is circulating on Rommel: "What is the difference between Rommel and a clock?—A clock makes a tictac and advances whereas Rommel makes tactic … and retreats."

—⋙—

March 15th

"Go to the Passierscheinstelle N91 of the Avenue des Champs-Elysees," Moustache instructs me. It's in the building where the newspaper "Le Jour" used to be; the entrance is at the corner of the Rue Quentin Bauchart. I think it was a bank. You'll show this paper and you will say you wish to see the officer whose name I've written on it. He will have been notified and will give you the non-opposition slip."

"Don't forget to warn him."

"What are you insinuating?"

"Simply that you are absentminded."

He does not know whether I am earnest or joking. He decided to laugh it off.

March 16th

The officer I am to see is absent, so I must come back tomorrow.

—⋙—

March 17th 43

I have more luck today. After having kept me waiting half an hour, the German receives me. He shows me to a chair, takes one himself and sits facing me, looking at his crossed legs in their fine leather boots. I am conscious of my own shabby, crackled shoes. Although he can't see the big holes on their soles, I still hide my feet as far as I can under my chair. The officer examines me smiling.

"You are going to work for us. That's very good. If all French people realized we are their friends, the war would be over long ago."

I smile, but don't respond.

"Please, show me your passport."

I hand it to him. He notes the number, my name, my address, then gives me a paper bearing a stamp.

"Go to the first floor, to the wicket which I've indicated here. They will attend to you."

He gets up as I do so, clicks his heels and opens the door for me.

"Thank you," I say.

He bows his head, re-clicks his heels.

On the first floor, the German civilian at the wicket takes my paper without giving me a glance and pushes towards me a slip with the date: March 24th on it.

"Come again," he barks.

March 24th 43

Today I say to myself, I'll get that non-opposition paper. Moustache must have my pass—the rest will be a cinch. At the entrance of the Rue Quentin Bauchart, I have to show my slip to be admitted. I go directly to the wicket and confidently hand the slip. The clerk examines it, throws me a glance over his spectacles, takes out a sheet of paper from a file and pushes it towards me. I read my name, the object of my application: non-opposition to departure to Spain, and across the whole page, stamped in purple ink: REFUSED. I look at the paper, I look at the employee, who has returned to his writing, and I do not understand.

"Why refused?" I ask.

He lifts his head, gives me a contemptuous look and answers with his strong German accent:

"Because."

Unconsciously, I turn over and over the sheet of paper between my fingers as if hoping to find an answer on the other side. It's useless to discuss it. I descend to the ground-floor and ask to see the officer but he is away. I shrug my shoulder and go away. I 'phone Kliemann at the hotel Lutetia, not really expecting to reach him, but I am wrong for he is there.

"Well?" he queries.

"Refused," I say, and I start to laugh.

"Refused? What do you mean refused? And why are you laughing?"

"Can't you see how funny it is; your own people messing up your game. Don't you think there's enough to roll with laughter?"

"No. Not at all. It is inadmissible. I want to see you immediately. Can you go to Yvonne's place? I'll take the car and be there in 15 minutes."

I arrive to the Villa Boileau almost simultaneously with Kliemann. He joins me in the yellow drawing-room. "Did I understand you well? You said 'refused?'" he asks without any preamble. Instead of answering, I give him the slip of paper.

"That's a bit thick." He shouts losing his temper, and in his wrath, he starts cursing the culprits in German. Up and down the room he paces—like a caged wild beast—picking up things and shifting them from place to place. At last he slams his fist in his hand. "I'll go there. I shall go there myself. I'll tell them what I think of the way that they work. They'll see. I'll show them. And you'll come with me. We'll go tomorrow morning. You are free?"

"Yes."

"Then be at the "Select" at the corner of the rue de Berri at 10 o'clock."

"I shall be there."

March 25th

11:06—Kliemann's car pulls up along the kerb and stops with a jerk. The Major alights, takes his leather portfolio, which never leaves him, bangs the door of the car and hurries towards me. I see at once that his wrath has not cooled off.

"Good morning. Come along," he stammers, in a breath.

We cross the Champs-Elysees and enter the "Jour" building. A sentry stops us. Kliemann produces a pass but probably not the right one for the stubborn soldier refuses to let us in. Moustache flies into a rage, gets red in the face. The soldier stands "at attention," but continues to block the door. Moustache orders him to go and notify his superior. The sentry apologizes, but does not move. An officer steps out of the lift. Kliemann goes up to him shows him his pass. The officer clicks his heels and stands to attention. He addresses a few severe words to the soldier, who turns crimson, clicks his heels and stiffens still more. Kliemann thanks the officer, who re-clicks his heels and salutes again. We can at last proceed to the lift and go up to the 3rd floor.

Kliemann leaves me in an empty office, while he goes into the next room. Things don't seem to turn out too well and I hear thundering voices: Moustache's, doing all the shouting. I therefore assume, he's got the situation in hand. He comes back a quarter of an hour later.

"I think they have understood, this time," he says fiercely.

We take the lift and go down. At the entrance, the sentry gives us such a click of heels that it stands him a few inches in the air. Outside, Moustache explains: "The idiots. They have, in there, two services supposed to work jointly. One of them had your passport; the other was to deliver the authorization. But the first forgot to pass on your records to the second. That is why the second one refused the permit. I kicked up an awful row, and I don't think it will happen again."

We enter the building around the corner, which used to be the annex of the bank of the Societe Generale, and Moustache asks to see the officer I have already met. We are immediately shown in. The officer clicks his heels and pulls himself up so much to stand "at attention," that his back arches like a bow, and I have doubts whether he'll be able to keep his balance. Then, he rushes to get us seats. He himself remains standing. Addressing him crossly, Moustache tells him what has happened, and the other apologizes. He takes my passport and walks out.

Returning, he tells me: "Pray excuse us, Mademoiselle. If you come back on the 29th, your paper will be ready."

In the street, Moustache rubs his hands. "You see how easy it was. All that was needed was to scream."

March 26th

In Russia, the German counter-offensive seems to have been stopped. In North Africa, the British have broken through the Mareth line. Berlin has been under two terrible bombings.

Winter has come to an end without having been too cold. But the rationing has not improved. My principal food consists of macaroni as I have a special diet card, which entitles me (instead of my meat and cheese rations) to ½ a pint milk daily, 250 gr. (about 8 oz.) of macaronis monthly, 12 lbs. of potatoes, and 750 gr. of sugar. The noodles, when cooked, become sticky and lumpy. They are of such a grey colour that you want to shut your eyes to eat them. Babs does not like them either: but, as it is all we have, we eat them every day.

March 29th

I look at the long strip of paper which is the German "non-opposition" to my departure. I look at it incredulously. "Are you sure it's all I need?" I ask the officer who has just given it to me. "Are you sure I don't need a photo, finger prints or another stamp?"

"You need absolutely nothing else."

It seems incredible that I should have it at last.

March 31st

I show the paper to Moustache. "Have you got to my pass?" I ask him.

"No, because you don't need one. They have been cancelled."

"Is that so? All right. Then I'll just have to go and see Lepinard about my visa."

April 1st 43

"You haven't got your pass," remarks Lepinard when I give him my passport and the certificate of "non-opposition."

"The passes are abolished as you well know."

"It doesn't matter; our orders say: 'when making an application for a visa, the interested party must produce the TWO documents.' Therefore, you must bring us a pass."

"But if they don't exist. Where can I get one?"

"I don't know. But, as long as we have no information as to the contrary, we must request one from you."

There is nothing more to do. I am about to leave him when suddenly a thought hits me and I stop: "It's not a joke you are playing on me? Today is the 1st of April—'All-Fools'—Day.'"

"No, no, it's not a joke."

"Auteuil 65-06? Is it you Annick?"

"Yes, Mademoiselle."

"Is Mr. Moustache there?"

"No, Mr. Moustache is not in. But he has asked several times if you had rung up. He told me to ask you to ring him up at Littre."

"Thank you, Annick. I'll do it immediately."

Five minutes later, I have Moustache on the 'phone.

"Well, have you got it?" he inquires.

"No. I need that 'orange-coloured paper.'"

"What orange par…. Oh. I see. But I have told you that they are cancelled."

"That's what I've told them. But they still insist."

"It's quite ridiculous. Come to see me tomorrow at 9 a.m. We can't decide this by telephone."

April 2nd

"What's the story now?" asks Moustache, meeting me in the hall.

I tell him about my interview with Lepinard.

"What idiots," he exclaims throwing up his hands. "I'll see that they get new instructions. But in the meantime, it will be as quick to give you a pass. Let me see," he says fumbling in his pockets, "I think I have a few blank ones left. Of course, it'll be of no value, as they are abolished. My secretary will fill it in and I shall sign it myself. I'll have it stamped to satisfy your Epinard."

"LÉPINARD," I correct him.

"Your l'Epinard—that's bad French," he remarks. "Come and fetch it tomorrow. It'll be ready."

Saturday, April 3rd

Lépinard is not there but, possibly, I can see him on Monday.

Sunday, April 4th

I have had lunch at Mummy's. It is just past 2 o'clock when we hear a strange sound. As if tanks were rolling along the Avenue de Clichy. Hardly have I made this comparison, when the ACK-ACK goes off in the distance. We all rush to the window. The planes are too high to be seen, but the blue of the sky is polka-dotted with white puffs of smoke. It must be flying Fortresses. They are probably on their way to bomb South Germany or North Italy. At this very minute, the sirens start howling. It's dismal. Babs lifts his paw and imitates them. The alarm lasts half an hour. On returning from the cinema late in the afternoon, I am stupefied to hear that the planes we have heard earlier have bombed Billancourt, completely destroying the Renault factories. Several bombs have been dropped on the Longchamp race-track, causing many casualties.

April 6th

Lépinard puts my passport, pass and non-opposition paper in a pale-green folder. On it, he writes my name and under it the words: "exit-visa." Then he places it on top of a pile of other folders. "All right. Now, if you telephone me towards the end of next week, I shall tell you how matters stand."

April 11th

Have sent a word to V.M., who has come to fetch me, and we go out for a walk. I have got an idea. I don't know what it is worth. V.M. is a career officer. At present, he is inactive as we have no Army. He was in the Topographical Service. I made his acquaintance in Syria. I am as certain of his loyalty, probity and patriotism as of his discretion. My idea is the following: to get V.M. enlisted by Kliemann and have him sent to Algiers, which he knows already. I think, I can tempt the Major by describing V.M. as a hater of the British, a first-class topographer and a soldier. I have already a plan worked out: V.M. is anxious to fight against the British, but he could be much more useful to the German S.R. if he pretended to pass over to the Dissidence and went to join the French Army in North Africa. He could send to the Germans: fortification plans, troop movements, information, and so on. I am sure that Kliemann will be highly interested in such possibilities.

But what about V. M.? Will he accept? Or rather, will he know how to assume and play such a part? He hates the Germans—he loathes them. He is of a proud and obstinate character … and too quick tempered. But he is shy. I can't picture him very well in the role of a rabid N.A.Z.I. The slightest mistake, which would expose him, would at the same time give me away. Am I to risk losing a position patiently acquired in the course of two and a half years—for a questionable success? It is crazy, no doubt. But it's tempting. Tempting to sap the German spy-system, to infiltrate it with counter-spies, tempting to be alone and un-armed … and to try nevertheless.

Stop. I say to myself. This is conceit. But the scheme remains. Such are my thought as I stroll along with V. M. in the deserted alleys of the Bois de Boulogne. Last autumn's dead leaves, which have not been swept away, rustle under our feet. But the bushes are getting green. The day is mild. In a pale sky, clouds are floating without obstructing the sun. I ask V. M. what he intends doing. What are his plans for the future? He tells me he would like to go to England and join de Gaulle's army.

"You might," I say, making up my mind, "be more useful here than in England."

"What do you mean?" he inquires, puzzled.

"I do not know exactly," I say. "I haven't quite decided yet. But I'd like to see you next week or perhaps in ten days, I might have something for you by then."

"All right," he agrees without asking any questions.

―⚬―

April 16th

Have 'phoned Lépinard. He asks me to come and see him on Tuesday.

Lately we've had up to three alarms a night. In the Mediterranean, the British have intercepted a convoy between Tunisia and Sicily, destroying 74 transport planes. In Russia, the situation is the same.

―⚬―

April 16th 43[6]

"You'll be satisfied at last, Mademoiselle. I have good news for you," says Lépinard this morning. "Your record is downstairs at the passport section. All you need is to go down and pick up your visa. Tell them I am sending you. They have their instructions. There only remains for me to wish you: 'Good luck.'"

I thank him warmly. He sees me to the door but, before opening it, he asks: "When are you leaving?"

"As soon as I get my Spanish visa."

"You are going to Portugal?"

"Yes."

"And after that?"

I look at him suppressing a smile, but do not answer.

He smiles too. "I know," he says, "there is 'the aunt.'" This motive you've given us has been officially accepted. But, between you and me ... now, that your visa has been granted...?"

"What would you say if I were to tell you my final aim was England?"

"I should say, I envy you and that you are lucky. But as you've told me nothing, I won't say anything to you either." He turns the knob and opens the door. "Good luck to you." He repeats shaking hands.

The man who receives me downstairs must have been born in the Prefecture. He seems to be part of the walls, of the furniture, of the whole scenery. In his every movement, I recognize the gesture of stamping papers. The curve of his hollow chest follows the outline of his desk, and his spine has been modeled by the back of his arm-chair. His countenance is as conventional as the formula of a visa he delivers. Even the way he waves his hand to indicate a seat is what one would expect from him. I sit down. He places in front of him a folder: my record. He questions without smiling: "Do you need any currency?"

"Yes."

"Do you wish a return-visa?"

"No."

"I am sorry. We cannot deliver a one-way visa. You are supposed to return; of course, you cannot do it—once you are over there, but that's none of our business."

"All right. I agree. Give me a return visa."

"Today is Tuesday. It'll be ready in a week."

"Thank you," I say getting up.

He bows stiffly and, without waiting for me to be gone, concentrates on some new decree.

April 22nd

The weather is grey and cold. The buds must regret having sprouted. The asphault of the pavements is dark but no longer shiny for the rain has stopped. The wind is blowing. I accompany V. M. as far as the Trocadero. He came to share my daily macaroni, and we spent part of the afternoon chatting. I haven't yet disclosed my scheme, and he has made no allusion to my promise of last time.

I am not sure how to start. We advance along the Avenue Paul Doumer. At last I make up my mind. "I told you the other day that you could be useful remaining here," I begin. "Today I am going to tell you HOW. Do not ask any questions. Think it over for a few days. Next time I see you, you'll tell me what you think of it and whether you accept. I am going to explain to you how I intend proceeding."

"I am listening," says V. M.

"I should like you to enroll in the German Secret Service."

V. M. turns sharply round and looks me straight in the face: "You want me to work for the Germans? YOU?"

"Don't interrupt me. You'll understand. If the Germans enroll you, it is almost certain they'll take advantage of two trumps they'll see in you: the first, that you are a French officer. The second—your knowledge of the Topographic Service or the Army. You can be of no use to them in France. But you can be invaluable in North Africa or in England ... that is: from their point of view. Now, think to what extent you can help the Allies, keeping them informed of what interests the Germans ... giving them a possibility to let the Germans know, or believe, exactly what they wish them to know, allowing them to deceive the

Boche at leisure. Don't answer now. Think it over. Ask yourself: will you have the strength to do it? Will you know how to do it? Face the risks and the dangers it involves. You'll give me your answer next time. Should that answer be NO, I'll ask you to forget that I ever spoke to you about it."

We have reached the Iena metro underground-station. "Good bye," I say. "Let me know when you've reached a decision."

"Thank you," he says. "Thanks for your trust and also for having thought of me. You'll hear from me next week."

April 23rd

"Today," says Grün when I arrive for my lesson, "I am going to show you how to take apart and put together a radio."

"Why? What's happening?"

"You are leaving soon."

It seems that Grün looks at me with different eyes. I have become somebody "real" since he knows I'm to "enter in function."

Manipulating a screw-driver, I start to unscrew everything that can be unscrewed, and am at a loss when I have to screw the parts back again. "Don't hurry and don't lose courage," Grün consoles me. "We are going to do it every day until you have learned."

April 26th

A pneumatic from V. M. He is coming tomorrow at 2.

April 27th

"Are you sure that it is all?" I ask the clerk-girl who hands me my passport.

"Yes, of course. Do you want anything else?"

I shake my head. Suddenly it seems too simple. I look at my visa, reading every line: "The titular of the ration-card N2018." So my ration-card is N2018. I didn't know it. (Without this visa, I would have never known it.). "Valid for 3 months." "The crossing of the frontier must take place before the 27/6/43." Etc., etc.

Before returning home, I 'phone Moustache at the "Lutetia." "I've got it!" I exclaim triumphantly when I hear him.

"Good. Now hold on to it; don't lose your passport."

With a true military accuracy, V. M. arrives at 2 o'clock. "I have thought it over…" he begins.

"All right," I interrupt him, "but not here. Let us go out."

We talk of one thing and another until we find ourselves in a deserted alley of the Bois de Boulogne, far and out of ear-shot. Babs frolics in the newly grown grass.

"Well?" I inquire.

"May I ask a question before I give my answer?"

"Go ahead."

"What risks would my parents run if I accept? You see: I have no right to expose them."

"They would run the risks you would expose them to. Their security would depend on your prudence and discretion. I can give you no guarantee to that."

We walk on in silence. I guess the struggle V. M. is going through. I've been through it myself. I understand him. But he has to decide alone. He must face and accept the whole responsibility for the future. I cannot help him. Finally, he looks up. A last wavering.

"I accept," he says.

I do not answer. We walk on in silence. I don't want to press him. It's too important. "Are you sure of yourself?"

"Yes, I am."

"Do you think that you will be good enough an actor to act the part?"

He reflects.

I insist: "Our victory, our success depend on that. You have to become pro-German. At the risk of shocking your friends. At the risk of alienating everybody's sympathy. You must make them believe you are Germanophile. You will be under observation, your words and deeds will be reported. Do you feel capable of facing that?"

"Yes," says V. M.

"Do you want more time to think it over?"

"No," says V. M.

I put out my hand: "Agreed."

"May I ask a few questions now?"

"Yes."

"I have agreed to enter the German Secret-Service to help the Allies. I have accepted the risks, the responsibilities and the consequences. What I should like to know is: how am I to get into the German spy-system? Who is going to introduce me?"

"I."

"You?" V. M. looks at me incredulously. "How will you manage it?"

"I am one of them."

He stares at me, speechless.

"I am a member of the German espionage for 2 and a half years," I continue. "You have to hate a lot to have that much patience. In two months' time I'll have left France, on my way to England. Before leaving, I am going to introduce you to the 'Boss.' I want him to enlist you. After that you'll have to fly with your own wings. I'll fix up a purely incidental interview. Remember that you know nothing about me. It's better for both of us."

April 28th 43

Having waited at the Spanish Consulate of the Boulevard Malesherbes for about an hour, my turn comes at last. I show my passport and explain that the authorization to deliver me a visa is in Lyons. I ask them to have it transferred to Paris. The Spaniard writes down all the required references and tells me to come back in about ten days.

May 3rd 43

The first thing that strikes me on entering the room where I take my lessons is the absence of the portable radio which usually is ready for me to use. Instead I notice some checked paper, black and red pencils, an eraser and a French novel: "Monmartre" by Pierre Frondale.

"What is the game today?" I ask examining this queer assortment.

"We are going to start with ciphering," answers Grün.

"It's about time we did."

We sit down side-by-side. Grün takes from the cupboard several yellow sheets of typewritten paper pinned together. He puts them on the table, unfolds them and spreads them out. They are written in German. At the top, in big red printed letters, it says "SECRET" and, in the corner, in pencil, my name: "LILY."

Grün reads attentively and then turns to me: "Have you ever done any ciphering?"

"Never."

"Very well. In a ciphered message, you have:

1. The indicative or call sign.
2. The message.
3. The key to the message.

The key to the messages serves to DECODE the message; it is to be found in the text of the message, at some place determinate previously.

"For coding your messages, you will make use of this book: MONMARTRE, by P. Frondale. During the EVEN months, you will use the pages: 210 to 240. During the ODD months, the pages: 100 to 131. For your call sign, you will take the THREE first consonants of the 6 first lines of the page corresponding to the day of the month in which you are transmitting. Our call sign will be the last 3 consonants (reversed) of the same SIX lines. Each line corresponds to a FREQUENCY: the 1st line to the 1st frequency; the 4th line to the 4th frequency, etc. Therefore, your indicative will CHANGE with each frequency. You only use the lines which have a minimum of 25 letters. You skip the others. Have you understood so far?"

"Yes."

Grün looks at me with doubt. "Here is the book. What would your indicative be—in 3rd frequency—for today?"

"Today is the 3rd of May." I open the book at page 103, skip the second line, which has but 7 letters, take up the 4th, and say: "C.H.S."

"Good," says Grün. "Now OUR indicative on the 4th of June in the 5th frequency?"

I look up page 214 and find: "D.R.F."

"You have understood, I see. So we'll proceed and start with ciphering. To cipher your message, you take one of the 99 first pages—no matter which—but don't use the lines 'in italic.' Let us suppose, you have the following sentence to cipher: Ai recu telegramme 15.2. Madrid. Lettre suit. Solange.[7] You have to find the 'square.' You allow average of 10 letters for each word and of 20 letters for proper nouns—which must always be repeated twice. You extract the square root of the total sum and thus obtain the side of your square."

"I don't quite catch."

"You'll understand immediately. Take the checked paper that is in front of you. By the way, always use checked paper. Write your sentence at the top. That's right. Now, count: 10 letters per word, 20 for the names, make the total. And another thing: the numbers must be decomposed. You won't write 15 as 'fifteen,' but as 'one five.' 100 will not be 'hundred' but 'one zero zero.' Your 15 will count as two words."

I plunge into mathematics. "I find 120. The nearest square is 10."

"Good. Now, draw a square which will measure 10 checks width, by 10 checks high."

"It's done."

"This here is your 'grille.' Now, you choose a page out of the 99 first pages, suppose the 89th page. From it you pick out a line—let us say, the 5th. Do you get it? You mark these figures at the top of your sheet next to your message: 89—the page, 5—the line, 10—

II. Paris, 1942–1943

the side of your square. The figure 89510 will be your key. I shall explain to you later how to cipher it and where it must be placed. For the present, we'll just write it at the top of the page and leave it at that.

"The 5th line of page 89 begins with the words: 'il eut envie de la quitter.'[8] Skip the line just about your square and, on the next one, write the 10 first letters of the sentence one letter in each square. You have: I L E U T E N V I E. Number each letter according to its place, first in the alphabet, and then in the word.

"You get: I L E U T E N V I E
4 6 1 9 8 2 7 10 5 3

"Now forget the letters and apply yourself to the numbers only. You take the first line and draw a vertical bar after the square, under the 1. On the second line you make a vertical bar after the square corresponding to the 2. And so on for each of the 10 lines. After that, you join the lower point of the vertical bar of the 1st line with the top of the vertical bar on the 2nd line. The lower point of the vertical bar on the 2nd line with the top of the bar on the 3rd line, and so on, until your square is divided in two unequal parts. Do you follow me?"

"Go on."

"You first use the left side, from top downwards: line after line, from left to right. When you have filled in the left part, you proceed in the same way with the right side. Now, you take the number of the page you have chosen for your coding—that is: 89. It is always preferable to take a high figure as it goes quicker. You then blind alternately every 8th, then 9th square, first of the left side, then on the right side of the big square. These blackened squares are—blinds."

"Now, you take your red pencil and mark a letter of your choice (avoiding, however, W and Y. I'll tell you why later.). Any letter will do. You place these dummy-letters after each 'blind square.' You also mark three fancy-letters in the first 3 squares. All these camouflage letters. Now, your 'grille' is ready to receive the message you want to send. Have you grasped that far?"

"Yes."

"Then I am going to tell you how a message is written down.

1. All your messages must be numbered and it is the first thing you inscribe: the number of your message, 1 or 2, or 3, or 9.

2. All the figures and proper names are placed between two Ys; they stand for inverted commas. For instance: 2—will be inscribed: Y two Y. A "decomposed" figure like 15 "one five," will not have a Y between the 1 and the 5. You will write it down as: Y one five Y.

"In the present case, you have February 15th or 15.2. You will write it thus: Y one five Y two Y. Is that clear?"

"Yes."

3. A period is indicated as WW. This is why I told you not to use Y's or W's as camouflage letters.

4. As you already know, the proper nouns, (except your own signature which will be known to us) are repeated twice, so as to avoid any possible error.

"And lastly:

5. When your message is inscribed 'in clear' into the empty sub-squares, you cross out the surplus spaces remaining below to the right.

"Now, write your message."

I write it down.

"Good. Now, you pick up the letters—including the dummy letters, in groups of 5, from top downwards,—starting with the column placed under the 1, then the 2, the 3 etc. Is that clear?"

"Yes. It is rather easy, providing one doesn't get mixed up."

"Now, there remains the key; that is the number 89510. It has to be ciphered too. To do it, you use the same page as the one from which you chose your call sign. Let us suppose your message is dated March 28th. Therefore, it'll be 128. You take the last line (of more than 25 letters) from which you copy the first 10 letters on even days, and the last 10 letters backwards on odd days.

Here we have:

S O T T E A L O R S
7 4 9 0 1 1 3 5 6 6 8

"We number them as for the sub-squares. Beneath—we write down the whole alphabet: the first 10

A B C D E F G H I J
T S R Q P O N M L K
U   V W X Y Z

letters from left to right. The following 10 letters from right to left. And the last 6 letters—from left to right, under the lowest figures. We have thus corresponding to each number two or three letters. Now, to obtain the key, we replace the numbers by letters, and get:

8 9 5 1 0
J R M O Q

or:

K C Z X D

"To finish, I must show you WHERE to place the KEY, so that we should know where to look for it. On even days, the KEY-groups: J R M O Q and K C Z X D will be the 4th and 9th groups in your message. On odd days, the KEY-groups will be the 3rd and 10th. You must *remember* this. The slightest error in the disposition of the KEY-groups would render your message undecipherable."

"You might as well say that everything has to be remembered."

"Yes. As for the rest of the message, you know how it's composed. It begins as usual with K A, a dash, the number of letters, etc. Never forget to check the number of letters in your square. Now, I am going to leave you to finish this message alone."

Ten minutes later, I have obtained the following result:

KA—92

UNRRT	AINDA	UTOWI	JRMOQ	NCULE
ULAWA	YALEY	AYDYE	KCZXD	WISED
IWOUI	PGMDM	RUXTR	MWDGI	YCTTR
EIQYE	AATUD	OWEMS	EN-AR-SK	SK

"Good," says Grün, on returning. "I'll verify it this afternoon. In the meantime, I'd like you to cipher two messages of your choice and bring them with you tomorrow. Now it's time for lunch."

—⁂—

MAY 4TH 43

I've spent yesterday afternoon and evening composing messages and ciphering them. It's fun. This morning I bring them to Grün.

"You are going to work alone today," he tells me. "Set the radio, look up in your book for their call sign; find the station (they'll use the 3rd frequency), take the message. Decipher it. I'll be back by then."

I begin to find it less amusing. I take the wrong page, then the wrong line. At last I get it: C.L.L. I write down the other call signs in case they should change their frequency. I find the station. From now on it goes smoothly. I take two messages: one of 109 letters and the other 127. The radio operator says GB—SK. SK. I answer S K and try to get the last "dot." I don't generally succeed.

So here I am with my two messages. I am not quite sure how to begin. I scratch my head. Grün did not explain to me yesterday what to do. I suppose, one has just to start from the end and proceed backwards. I pick up the shortest and extract from it the two key-groups. I decipher them with the help of the book and this gives me the indication for the side of the square. I draw my square. and stop. What now? I wish Grün were here. But I go on the best I can. The door opens and Grün comes in.

"Why, you have started decoding? But I haven't explained you how to do it."

"I thought you wanted me to find out myself."

"All right. Go on."

"I am stuck."

Grün looks over my shoulder:

"You didn't count your squares."

"How stupid of me. Of course. I finished at last, and my message makes no sense."

Grün shrugs his shoulders: "You ought to pay a little more attention; you have not removed your dummy letters."

I feel deeply mortified.

MAY 7TH

The Spanish Consulate has received an answer from their Consulate in Lyons and raises no objection to delivering me a visa. It seems unbelievable. I have all my papers. I can go. Along the Boulevard Malesherbes, the chestnut-trees are green some in blossoms. The air smells of spring, the weather mild. People have exchanged their winter overcoats for last year's tailor suits, slightly out of fashion and smelling of naphtaline.[9] I feel like singing.

"Hello, Annick? Is Moustache in?"

"Yes. Hold on, I'll get him."

"Good morning," says the Major's voice. "I wanted precisely to see you. You've done well to ring me up."

"I've got all my papers," I say.

"All?"

"Yes, all."

"What are you doing for lunch?"

"Some m a c a r o n i."

"No. What I mean is, are you free?"

"Yes."

"Then join me at the 'Maisonnette,' rue de Passy, at half past one. Does that suit you?"

"O.K."

Mme Boris lifts the curtain separating the kitchen from the restaurant, and catches sight of me. "Alone?" she exclaims coming up to my table. "So Yvonne has left?"

I had no idea Yvonne intended to go anywhere, but I pretend that I know. "I haven't seen her for some time; I've been very busy." I say, not answering directly her question.

"Isn't she lucky?" says Mme Boris with a sigh, pushing back a lock of black hair, hanging over her left eye.

"Yes," I say, "she certainly is lucky," wondering what this luck may be.

"Have you been there?" inquires Mme Boris.

I shake my head. "And you?" I ask in turn.

"Neither have I," sighs Mme Boris, "but I have always wanted to visit Madrid."

I very nearly exclaim: What? Yvonne is in Spain?—but stop in time.

The door opens and Moustache comes in. "Here comes the Major," I say.

Mme Boris turns round and rushes towards him with out-stretched hands. "Dear, dear "Monsieur le Major," it's such a long time since I've seen you. I hope you are well?"

"Yes," says Moustache abruptly. "We want to have some lunch." He dismisses Mme Boris with a wave of the hand and turns towards me: "So it is true? You've got all your visas?"

Discreetly I slip my passport over to him. He opens it, gives it a quick glance and returns it to me swiftly. "Hide it. I'll take a better look at home. I spoke with Grün; he tells me you are ready. How do you feel?"

"I think that I can make now my own way."

"How is the ciphering? Do you still think it difficult?"

"No, I have got used to it. But you did put if off to the last moment."

"Vogel did not want…"

"What didn't Vogel want?"

"That you should be taught ciphering earlier. I think he doesn't trust you, our friend l'Oiseau."[10]

"Why?"

"That's just it. He has not been able to give me any reason for his mistrust. I told him to mind his own business. We even had quite a row. He knows that he is indispensible for the construction of our radios and thinks he can do anything. I can't stand him."

"Have you decided anything about my departure?"

"You mean, fixed a date?"

"Yes."

"I have let it be known yesterday that you were ready. I am waiting for orders to instruct you with the kind of work you'll have to do. This will last a fortnight perhaps. After that, you can get your ticket."

"You are not going to let my visa become overdue again?"

"No, don't worry."

"Because I warn you that I'll resign if you do."

"No. No. You needn't worry." Moustache has asked for the bill. While waiting, he says: "Do you happen to know any ex-radio-operators from the Navy or Army?"

"No. Not to my knowledge. It might be that among my military friends there are radio-operators, but I'm not aware of it. Why?"

"We might need them. In case we should evacuate France. It is always better to be ready beforehand. We'd like to have people ready, to leave behind."

"I see. But must they be radio-operators necessarily? Can't you train them? With a good training, six months should be enough."

"We haven't enough time or instructors to do it."

"No time? What do you mean? You do not think that you'll have to leave France that soon?"

"It can happen any time now." He shrugs his shoulders: "Those who don't believe it are blind." He looks at me wonderingly: "I do not know why I am telling you that. I ought not to talk like that. In any case, should you have anyone in mind, be sure to let me know."

Kliemann has paid the bill. We go out into the rue de Passy. He has his car. "May I give you a lift?"

"If you like. I am going to the Madeleine."

We follow the quays, having cut through the Trocadero gardens. Maybe this is my chance. I say: "The other day I thought of you when I met one of my friends."

"Why?" asks Moustache.

"He is an officer in the regular Army and actually released and without work. He was telling me that, if only the L.V.F. were fighting against the British, he would join it immediately."

Kliemann has slowed down the car. He turns his face to me: "In what unit was he?"

I smile: "No, he wasn't in the Radio work unfortunately. He was only in the 'Topo.'"

"The TOPO?"

"Yes, the Topographical Service—they draw maps. That is of no interest to you."

The car has stopped. We are on the Quai de Tokio, not far from the Concorde.

"Have you a moment to spare?" asks Moustache.

"I'm in no hurry."

He lights a cigarette and draws deeply. "This officer," he questions, "is he in Paris right now?"

"Yes."

"What kind of personality?"

"Very reserved, rather silent, careful and conscientious, stubborn, hates the British, good worker. He is shy with women."

"No babbler—hates the British—is shy with women ... + officer, + topographical service," recapitulates Kliemann. "He does interest me," he says, looking up. "Do you think he would work for us?"

"I don't know. Do you want me to ask him?"

"No. It is too risky. I don't want you to get compromised."

"Maybe we could simulate an accidental interview, without telling him anything."

"Perhaps. I'll think it over."

Place de la Madeleine, I leave Kliemann. The first step is done.

May 12th

Daily I code messages which I transmit during the lessons. I take others and decipher them. This afternoon, I meet V. M., who is impatient to begin. I tell him of the conversation I had with Kliemann.

"So you think I am shy?" asks V. M.

"Terribly shy. That's why I fear an interview between you and the 'Major.' I am afraid he might think that you are not adventurous enough to be successful. The first impression is of great importance in such an interview. I know that you are not shy when at work. But he will judge you from your appearance. Do you think you could manage to control your shyness? Just that once."

V. M. does not seem to think I am talking seriously. "I assure you, I am not as shy as that."

"Well, we'll see. I don't want to push the Major. He might become suspicious. Let him take the initiative."

V. M. has gone. I wonder if he'll succeed? Can he act bold enough, be enterprising and energetic. Will he know how to pretend he hates the British? Is he good enough an actor for such a part? For the first time, I realize that it is not sufficient to have plenty of good will, that something else is needed—I don't know WHAT. My will to succeed can be of no help to V. M. He must use his own will-power—all of it. I have the impression that he hesitates. If he hesitates, he won't succeed. If he hesitates, it's useless even to try.

May 17th

I wonder why Yvonne has gone to Spain. Moustache hasn't breathed a word to me about it.

May 18th

A pneumatic in Annick's handwriting begs me to 'phone "Mr. Moustache" this morning.

"Ach. Fraulein Lily. Ja. Ja. Herr Major is expecting your call. I pass him to you."

Moustache's voice on the 'phone, sounds like sharp raps of a wooden mallet. Probably because he is not very sure of his French and talks in short, hacked sentences. "Good morning. Want to see you. This afternoon. Are you free?"

"As free as air."

"Beg your pardon? I didn't understand."

"I was only saying that I am free."

"Very well. Be at Pam-Pam's, place de l'Opera, at 3."

"I'll be there."

3 o'clock, at Pam-Pam's. There are not too many people, but there are enough. I find an empty seat and hoist myself in front of the counter. I order a glass of grape-juice. People around are standing in groups. Mostly men, business-men, who have left their offices for a few minutes, to meet a friend, a colleague, a customer. I am almost the only woman. As I have nothing to do, I examine in the mirror the groups who have their backs to me, the nape of the waiter, who fills the glasses and pockets the money.

My neighbor, a lonely elderly man, has attracted my attention, because he has kept his hat on his head. He is turning his glass between long narrow fingers, staring in front of him. I wonder what ailment is nagging at him to account for that miserable look? Money worries? A love-affair? Or a cancer, slowly but surely killing him? But his problems are not mine, and I soon forget him and begin to get impatient. It is now 5 minutes past 3:30. From time to time, I glance at the door, which lets in newcomers, none of whom are Major Kliemann. "If he does not turn up in 5 minutes, I'll go," I decide.

The waiter seems to find that I occupy too much room for the price of a simple grape-juice. My neighbor—the man with the sad face—takes out a gold watch from his fob-pocket and looks at it persistently—as if expecting to see it reverse. I experience a certain satisfaction in not to be the only one to wait. Just then, looking up, I discern Moustache's face in the mirror, framed between our two faces: the stranger's and mine.

"Good afternoon," he says. "Have you already got acquainted?"

I look at him inquiringly and notice that the sad man with the hat has slightly turned towards me and is smiling.

"No," I reply.

Moustache introduces us and the man lifts his hat.

"Herr Graf—Mademoiselle Lilly."

Herr Graf's smile broadens, displaying long, equine teeth, yellow with nicotine, and two gold ones. He has pale eyes, very blue, and graying hair.

"Shall we go out?" asks the Major.

We make way through the crowd and direct our steps towards the Avenue de l'Opera. The terrace of the Café de la Paix is crowded with German uniforms. The "Boche" relish the sight of "das gay Paris," of which "they" are the rulers, of this Paris on which they have planted their swastika, and which they think to have subdued. They do not know that there are hundreds, thousands of French people like myself—men and women—who loath them, who elbow them, who work for their destruction. I get nearer to Graf and Kliemann; these two are my prey.

We walk along the Avenue de l'Opera. There are not so many people here as on the Place de l'Opera. Moustache explains: "Herr Graf is going to teach you different things you must know before you go. And to begin with—sympathetic[11] writing. You will meet him every morning in the place that I'll show you immediately. We are going there."

I have an inkling that it's to Yvonne's office, but as I have no idea whether Moustache knows about my visits there, I don't say anything. Instead of that, I ask him: "What about Grün? Am I to continue going there in the mornings?"

"You have finished with Grün. He told me you were ready."

"Good."

We have reached the N29. Moustache stops short. "It's here. Note the address. You'll have to come here every day."

The lift takes us to the 5th floor. It doesn't go any higher, and we have to climb one story more. Kliemann takes a key out of his pocket and opens the door on the right. I know the place; it's nothing new to me. We follow Moustache to the second room, which looks out on the Avenue de l'Opera. He puts down his leather portfolio on the desk; so does Graf, who this time, takes off his hat.

"You said, a moment ago, that I had to learn sympathetic writing. I have been taught one system when I was in Berlin. Here, in Paris, Yvonne showed me another one. Is it still something different?"

"Yes entirely. But first of all fix an hour with Herr Graf for your lessons. I should like you to begin already tomorrow."

Graf takes out a note-book from his pocket and consults it attentively. "What about tomorrow morning at 9 o'clock?"

"All right."

"I shall write you down for every day, from nine till noon. Does that suit you?"

"It does."

"That'll be all for today," says Moustache. "Herr Graf will keep me informed. But I should like to see you from time to time. Ring me up at the office."

The two men pick up their brief-cases. Graf throws over his arm the rain-coat he had taken off, and we go out. Each one of us goes in a different direction.

MAY 19TH

I hurry along. It is 10 minutes past nine by the Place de l'Opera's clock. I am somewhat out of breath, when I ring the bell twice. Steps resound immediately, as if Graf was waiting behind the door. "You are late," he remarks before even greeting me.

I am taken aback.

As if to correct the rudeness of his remark, he adds: "Gentlemen are waiting for you. They are specialists in secret writing. They are very busy and have little time to spare."

"Excuse me," I say, entering. "I haven't been accustomed to strict exactitude by Major Kliemann."

Two bald heads bow simultaneously and two ironical smiles hover about narrow lips. "We know," the two of them admit at the same time, indicating a vacant chair facing them.

I sit down. The stouter of them, the more glabrous one, is going to do all the explaining. The other one won't say a word, and I don't know really why he is there. Graf settles somewhat aside and will only take part in the conversation when his translating will be needed, as the fat German does not speak French. No introductions have been made; I don't know their names.

"I understand if you are already familiar with sympathetic writing in general, but I shall proceed as if you were not, and start by giving you the essential notion applied to any kind of writings done in sympathetic ink, namely: absolute cleanliness. You must have clean hands, the paper must be clean. Finger prints can smear your letters, render a message illegible. Grease spots, however slight, can prevent the sympathetic ink from adhering. There again, your message would be undecipherable.

"The system I am going to show you is extremely simple. Here are pellets. This is the shape in which you'll get them; they take up very little room and are easy to conceal. If need be, you can swallow them; they are harmless. To use them, you dissolve one and dip in the liquid drop a small wooden stick, which you handle like a pencil. The stick must have a sharp point, but not too sharp as it might scratch the paper. You can sharpen a match or a manicure stick, or use a tooth-pick. But always verify carefully the point.

"To dissolve the pill, the most convenient way is to take an ordinary steel pen—a new one—and insert it back to front into the penholder. You put the pill on it and hold the pen over a candle or a cigarette-lighter. Be careful not to raise it too high above the flame for you would get soot in and it would be noticeable in your secret writing. When your pill is completely dissolved, you dip quickly into the drop of liquid the sharp point you have prepared, taking it out immediately and turning it round in the air to let it dry evenly. As soon as it is dry, you bring back the pen over the flame, repeating the procedure. You must not keep the point in the liquid—only dip it in and take it out—otherwise the first layer would melt. You go on until all the liquid in the pen is solidified around your point. You have thus obtained a hard, small, oval ball at the end of a stick. This you will use to write your message. I am going to make you a demonstration; then you'll try yourself."

I watch him manipulate the pen, the lighter, sharpen a match. When he has gone through the whole rigmarole, he hands me a match terminated by a tiny ball of a yellowish orange colour, size slightly over a pin-head.

"You try now."

It seemed easy enough when he was doing it. The result I achieve is quite different. My ball is hunch-backed on one side and a colouring, which could not be mistaken for anything but black. My instructor's countenance is impassible. He hands me over a sheet of paper.

"Try to write lightly. Don't press."

I trace a few letters—hardly touching the paper. They are by no means INVISIBLE, but of a pale-grey tint. Next, the hump of the ball breaks and the rest of it scatters on the sheet.

"It's no good," I decide.

"It's no good," agrees the German. "To begin with, you were holding your pen much too high above the flame and you have caught some smoke into your liquid. Then, you did not hold your match straight enough after having dipped it into the liquid, and you did not turn it quickly enough. And finally, when you dipped it again, you did it too slowly and without turning it. The part, which was solid, melted on one side, destroying the unity of the successive layers. Here is the result," he adds, pointing at the fragments on the sheet of paper. Begin all over again."

I do it five times before he is satisfied.

"And remember one thing: never try to make use of a pellet, which has become black. Throw it away and take another. The risk of being discovered is too great and one pellet is not worth it. Now," he continues, "we are going to see about the writing. You always write in printed characters. Your messages must always be written on the 1st page, then the 3rd, the 5th, and so on. Never on the wrong side of the sheet. You always write ACROSS your cover letter, starting from the left corner down. In other words, the left margin of your cover letter is to be the 1st horizontal line of your message written in sympathetic ink. You start by writing your cover letter, taking care as I've told you already, to have clean hands and an immaculate paper.

"Before starting your secret message, you place your paper on a slab of glass. For that purpose, you can take a mirror, the glass of a photo-stand, a glass-top tray. On your letter you put a sheet of paper which will be for two purposes. In the first place, it will guide your lines as you write, for having reached the end of your page, you move the sheet of paper lower down. And secondly, it will protect your letters from too many fingerprints. And last, leave sufficient space between your letters, also between your words and lines—to avoid the risk of having them one on top the other. It is better to take up more space than too little. I'd like you to try a few writing exercises."

He takes a bit of glass out of his portfolio and gives it to me. "Use this."

I pick up the match I had prepared a moment ago, and follow his instructions. When I have finished, he takes my sheet of paper, examines it closely, then looks at it against the light. He shakes his head in disapproval.

"Not good. Look for yourself: certain strokes are shiny. Do it over again."

I make two other samples.

"This looks better," he says. "Of course, I can't say anything definite before I have had it developed and seen the result. I'll take it with me. If it's good, I'll let you know through Mr. Graf. If it's bad, I'll come to give you another lesson." He gathers up his belongings, puts on his dark-grey overcoat, his matching felt hat, gives Graf a shake-hand, bows stiffly to me and, followed by his dumb colleague, walks out.

Graf takes out his note-book. "I think it will be better to fix our next appointment at 9:30 tomorrow," he says smiling. "Ladies don't like to get up early."

May 20th

"The proofs of your writing are good," announces Graf this morning. "The gentlemen are not coming back. They only send you a message, asking you to simplify the structure of your letters."

"All right. What do we do now?"

"Are you acquainted with different types of planes and do you know how to identify them?"

"Not in the least."

"That is what you are going to learn: plane recognition."

Graf has prepared pencils and some paper. The lesson begins. "We don't intend teaching you to recognize the various models yourself. This would be too long and demands much practice. What you must learn to do is to give us such a description that from it we can unmistakably identify the plane. At the same time, the description has to be as concise as possible. There is a technique of doing it.

"The characteristics of a plane are: the engine, the wings, and the stabilizer. Furthermore, in a grounded plane, you have the position of the wings and the rudder. The fuselage is more difficult to describe. Only few are characteristic, resembling a tadpole, or a square chest … etc. To help you understand, I have brought you this recognition pictorial manual."

I note the different denominations of the wings: straight, tapered, elliptical, curved, sweptback, swept forward, etc., etc.; their different positions: high, mid, low, gull, inverted gull, etc. I learn the difference between a radial and in-line engine. Never had I suspected so many different types of planes. Never had I even paid any attention to the shape of the wings. At half past twelve, I have a long list of planes, classified according to the shape of their wings, and the number of their engines, and feel as if I had landed on an unknown planet where everything is new to me.

―⚜―

May 21st

My list of planes gets longer every day. I can recognize a "Spitfire" a "Typhoon," a "Masters," a "Martlet," a "Mustang," a "Thunderbolt," a "Marauder," a "Mosquito," a "Lysander," a "Lightning," a "Dakota," a "Boston," a "Lancaster," a "Manchester," a "Fortress," a "Liberator," an "Aira Cobra," as well as the two hydroplanes: "Catalina" and "Sunderland." I know their flying silhouette and recognize them from the description Graf makes of them.

I don't recognize them so well when I see them in profile and I don't recognize them at all when I see them facing me, which proves that I know the shapes of the wings, of the engines, of elevating planes and the number of engines, but don't know the outline of the fuselage and the shape of the _____ and not at all the position of the wings and of the engines. In profile I know a few, whose silhouette I wouldn't recognize.

Graf makes me do endless descriptive exercises. Sometimes I am describing and sometimes it is he. "Be sure not to forget to mention the way the wings are attached; it is most important."

"Describe a "Spitfire."

"Describe a "Halifax."

"What shape are the wings of a Dakota?"

"And of a Boston?"

I go on describing—sometimes right, sometimes wrong. At last Graf closes his book and pushes back his chair. "That will do for today. Try to know them by tomorrow."

When I come out in the street, in broad day-light, I have the impression that my head is so stuffed with figures and names that it's ready to burst. Yet Graf assured me I wouldn't have to know all the aeroplanes by heart. I'll have to try and memorize the various profiles. It does seem useless. Or do the Germans think that I shall be allowed to pick daisies on the airodromes of England?

May 22nd

We are through with aviation, and start with the Navy today. Graf brings forward a whole lot of photos and shows me how to recognize a man-of-war from a transport ship or a tanker, a destroyer from an anti-torpedo boat, a sub-marine from an aircraft carrier.

"The tonnage is always of interest to us," he says, "but it would be impossible for you to determine it at sight. You could only get to know it by chatting with people in the ports: sailors, dockworkers, etc. If you find yourself in a shipping agency, you can overhear interesting conversations. The origin, destination and cargo of a ship are of the greatest importance. Also if it is a convoy: of how many ships? The duration of the crossing? Never fear that a detail might be useless. What to you may seem without interest can be added to facts obtained from other sources, of capital importance. You must get accustomed not to judge for yourself, but to transmit even that which you do not understand."

"Now, as we have some time left," he continues, "we can study the ranks and insignias in the British and American Armies. You must know with whom you are talking. The importance of information may vary according to the rank of the informer. Whether he is a colonel or a corporal. When you transmit us your information, specify their source, say for instance: 'Spoken with captain of the Xth Armoured Division,' or 'Have got particulars from mechanic of the Xth Air-borne Division.' Thus we shall know immediately the value of your information. To go back to the marks, unfortunately, I haven't been able to get any drawings. Therefore, I have to describe them and you'll write them down."

I take a sheet of paper and under Graf's dictation note a whole list.

"You are going to learn that for Monday," says Graf, consulting his watch. "Now it is time for lunch."

May 24th

"Have you learned?" asks Graf, arriving at the same time as I.

"Yes, so well that I no longer know if it's a lieutenant who has 2 engines 'in line' on the shoulder, or if a 'Boston' has 2 'pips.'"

"Anyhow, you are sure of the number two—in one case as well as in the other. That's already something."

"What are we going to do today?"

"We are going to continue. As we have begun with the British Army, we'll finish with it. You know the insignias. Now, I'll teach you what colours represent what arms. The British soldiers wear the badge of their arms on their sleeve: between the elbow and the shoulder."

I start to write. It isn't very long. When Graf has finished, he takes the pencil from my hand. "I'll draw a schema of the formation of the British Army so that you should know what is meant by: army, division, company, battalion, regiment, etc." He makes a rough sketch. "You can keep it and study it. Now we'll start with the American Army. It is very easy. The Americans are like big children who are fond of 'images.' In their Army, the different arms are represented by insignias worn on the collar, reproducing exactly what they represent. In other words, the artillery has two crossed canons, the infantry—two crossed guns; the cavalry—2 crossed swords."

"That's wrong: it ought to be 2 horses."

"It was probably too complicated to do. The engineers have a fortress; the parachutists—a parachute, and so on. I won't even dictate it to you; you can't make a mistake when you see them."

"Do they also wear their rank written on the shoulder? Would a lieutenant have 'Lt,' a captain 'cpt,' a major 'mj,' a colonel 'col,' and a general 'gen?' That would be ideal."

"Not quite that simple, but you shall see. To begin with, the Americans put silver above gold. Of two insignias, made of different metals, the silver one will be higher than the gold one. And here you have a short story to help you remember the American ranks. Imagine a ladder: the lowest step is of gold: one gold bar = 'Add/Lt.' The next step is of silver: one silver bar = '1st Lt.' You go up higher: two silver bars = 'Captain.' Still rising, you reach the first leaves of the tree: one gold leaf = 'Major.' One silver leaf = 'Lt/ Col.' Above the tree, a bird flying = 'Colonel,' and above the bird, in the sky, there are stars: 'General' with one star; two stars, 3, 4, 5, stars. Easy enough, isn't it?"

"There mustn't be an army easier to make out."

Graf looks at the time and proceeds: "We have 15 minutes left. I am going to tell you a few words about the military vehicles. In the army, a car, a truck, a tank can have lots of numbers, inscriptions, signs. We are only interested in one thing: the mark, sign or figure on the left front wing or side, and the left rear wing or side. Remember that for you the left front mud-guard will be to your right, as to look at a vehicle you have to face it, whereas, looking at the rear, you stand in the same direction as it does. It is the shield on the LEFT wing of all military vehicles that interests us. It is easy to see and easy to notice even at a distance. Your descriptions will enable us to identify the units to which these vehicles belong and furthermore locate these units, as well as be aware of their movements. Therefore, always look and not any markings on the left wing and forget about the right one. That'll be all for today."

—⚬—

MAY 25TH

Though I shall never need Graf's teaching, I conscientiously study the notes I take during my lessons, for I presume I'll have to go through a severe examination before they let me loose. This morning, Graf gives me a lecture upon what he calls the "strategic geography of England." He has spread out a few maps. One is a railroad map, another shows the industrial regions of Great Britain. Others are local maps. Graf explains what economic regions are of "military" importance, and what makes them so. Then, he points out to me the railroad junctions, which command them, indicative their vulnerable spots. He outlines the areas where troops are concentrated, like Salisbury-Plain; the centres of war industries; the ports of arrival of convoys. He talks about the camouflage, the defence and the guarding of war factories. He demonstrates the effects on certain remote regions, resulting from bombing of railway junctions, highway crossings, destruction of bridges, of viaducts. The lesson comes to an end. I'll go home, take a map, a geography of England, and try to memorize that useless junk.

—⚬—

May 26th

"This morning, for a change, we are going to do some descriptive work," announces Graf with a smile displaying long, yellow teeth. "Your brains must be over-stuffed with names to remember. This'll be a rest. I am going to explain you how to describe and situate an aerodrome. Suppose that you have discovered an airfield. To 'situate' it, you have to give the names of the two nearest towns, on both sides of the airport, specifying: 'it is on the road from X to Y (meaning you follow that road in this same direction)—parallel or perpendicular to this road (this will give us the orientation of the ground). 'Begins at the mile X and ends at mile Y' (which will give us its approximate size). Most of the roads in England have milestones indicating the 'mileage,' just as in France you have the 'borne kilometrique.'[12] However, they may have been removed or you may find yourself on a newly built road with no milestones; in that case, you indicate your means of locomotion. If you are in a car, it's quite simple as you have a meter-counter that gives you the distance. If you are on foot, or on a bicycle, you will be obliged to chronometer the distance. You will mark the time it takes you to walk from the locality to the airport, from the beginning of the airport to its end, and from there to the next locality. The same, if you are on a bike. Try to keep up a regular speed. Describing the airport, you will mention the shape of the runway, its orientation in regard to the road, its constructions (cement, asphalt, metallic sheets, turf). Then the disposition of the sheds (always metallic sheets, turf). Then the disposition of the sheds (always in regard to the road) and their number. Generally, it's easy enough to see the difference between sheds and workshops or other buildings, which may be on the premises. Nevertheless, you can also mention these. And the area surrounding of the airport. Mention if there is a mountain, or river, on one of the sides; if the airstrip is encircled by barbed wire or a fence. Find out if it is watched by patrols, or guarded by dogs. It can so happen that the aviation-ground is in the neighbourhood where you live. If you can establish a post of observation without being been (from a height for instance), you'll be able to know the intensity of the traffic and the type of planes that come down and leave. You might even identify the grounded planes."

Having finished his explanations, Graf shows me photos of airports, and I have to describe them to him. The lesson continues until one o'clock.

—⚒—

May 27th

Nothing new this morning. We recapitulate. The lesson doesn't last very long.

—⚒—

May 28th

These lessons bust me. Maybe I've crammed too many things into my head lately, or simply that my head is too small. But between the formulas of ciphering and the characteristics of airplanes, the main points in the description of airports, the formations of the Allied Armies, the distinction of ranks and arms, the strategic point in England—names, figures, lines, colours—everything seems to get confused, blurred, subdivided then multiplied like in a giant kaleidoscope incessantly changing and punctuating all this like a swarm of flies—the dots and dashes of the Morse.

Graf informs me that Moustache wants to see me and rings him up. There will be no lesson tomorrow.

"Ach. At last." echos Kliemann's voice at the end of the line. "Why haven't you called me before?"

"I had nothing to tell you."

"I must see you. By the way, where do you live?"

"In Passy."

"Wait a moment. Yes, I have your address. Will you be in tomorrow before noon? Can I see you at your flat? Yvonne is away just now and I do not go to the house."

"You can come to my place. At what time will it be?"

"Eleven o'clock."

"All right."

—⚜—

May 29th

At twelve, no one has come. At half past twelve, I am still waiting.

"The hell with him," I say to Babs. "You want to go out and so do I. Let us go."

I find an old woman under a porch; she is selling lettuces at 15 francs a piece. I buy one. We go down to the Muette for Babs to run. I am back at a quarter past one and find a note from Moustache: "I'll come again. Kyll." What does he mean? That I am to wait the whole afternoon? He could have fixed an hour.

"Let's have lunch, Babs." Babs is not very interested at the prospect of the meal. He suspects it'll be again noodles, or macaroni, or else spaghetti, whatever shape or name might be. Nevertheless, politely he wags his tail. "Yes, old chap, noodles and salad. I know you don't like salad."

My meal is finished. It did not take longer to eat than to cook. There is a knock at the door.

"Already you!" I exclaim, opening it to Kliemann.

"Yes," says Moustache. "I have had lunch at the Maisonnette." He stops on the threshold: "You've got a nice place."

I look around me with surprise. It's true, it is nice. The yellow walls are of a warm shade enhanced by the bright muslin curtains. Bookshelves everywhere. A Persian chiseled ewer; an old tile brought back from Aleppo; a low divan heaped with cushions from Turkey, Syria, Greece; a small, round white and blue china table from India. And on the floor, a large earthenware vase full of fragrant white peonies, on which plays a ray of sunshine. I've collected every object: everyone has its story, its meaning.

"It is nice," repeats Moustache, advancing in the middle of the room. He examines one after the other my paintings on the walls, a few tapestries; he is interested by a Kurd cutlass with a horn handle and a silver sheath. Finally, he stops in front of a small wooden cupboard, which I have painted white and decorated in Breton-pottery-style. "Amusing," he says. Then, coming to the sofa, he sits down and looks at me. "I don't understand. You have all this," he says indicating the room. "You write, you paint, you have a charming home, you like pretty things—(I am sure that you love your books)—and yet you are ready to leave all that ... not even for money: What for then?"

"Have you ever hated?" I ask slowly. "If not, you cannot understand. Do not ask why. I have no explanations to give you. Anyhow, you probably wouldn't believe me, so what's the use? Simply, if it puzzles you too much not to know WHY I do all that—ask yourself how far can hatred lead?"

Kliemann looks at me in silence, gently tapping his right palm on the knuckles of his other hand. At last, he shrugs his shoulders. "Let us admit it. But that's not why I've come to see you. It's about your friend—that officer."

"Oh, yes. What about him?"

"I'd like to meet him."

"You want to meet him, yet you do not wish me to speak to him. How do you propose to do?"

"That is what I wanted to discuss with you. Have you any idea?"

I think a moment. "Listen. He believes that I am pro British—as this is what I have pretended to be since I'm working for you. Nevertheless, he didn't hide from me that he hates the British nor did I hide from him my intention of going to England. But we are old friends and consider that we are free to have our own opinions. I can tell him that I made your acquaintance through a friend and you helped me to get my papers and permit to go away. As he confessed to be without a job and in financial difficulties, I could tell him that you are in search of a cartographer and could perhaps employ him. I'll introduce him to you. You will fix him an interview. And when you are alone with him, you'll put down your cards, pretending you didn't wish to talk in my presence, as I know nothing about you, am soon leaving to go to the bedside of a sick aunt in Portugal, but I've spoken to you about him and that, according to what I said you deduced his sympathies were on your side and he was disposed to work for you. Suggest to him absolute discretion in regard to me. He'll thus have the impression that I was far from suspecting your real personality."

"I think you've got something there," murmurs the Major deep in thought. "Are you quite sure that this captain doesn't suspect anything?"

"Absolutely sure."

"Very well. Let's try your scheme. When can you arrange a meeting?"

"I can send him a pneumatic today, asking him when he could come. But in case he fixes a date, can you manage to be there in time?"

"I don't want to rush him by fixing a day myself. First of all, I don't know when he is free; and furthermore, too great an eagerness might surprise him."

"That's right."

"Ask him to come, and let me know as soon as you've settled a day. Ring me up at the office. I'm there all the time."

As soon as Moustache has left, I write a word to van M. "When can you come?" I needn't say more. He will understand. I go out to mail my letter.

May 31st 43

This morning the lesson is about the coastal defence of Great Britain; the organization of the "home-guard"; about the various information I have to send regarding the changes in the rationing in the U.K.; about the fluctuation of the public opinion and morale of the nation.

"If you happen to be in a town or city during a bombing, try to find out what objectives were hit."

"Only in case strategic points are touched?"

"No, anything that is hit, for you cannot know what we were aiming at. So, even if nothing strategic has been destroyed, your indications will inform us of the precision of our bombing, the exactness of our maps, as well as of our information." To finish, Graf explains to me the wording of the messages, pointing out what is essential and all that is superfluous. "Next lesson," he tells me, "will probably be the last one. We have now covered the whole program."

At home, I find a pneumatic from V. M.: "Will you be at home Tuesday at 2?" It says. I go out again to telephone from the corner bistro.

"Splendid," says the Major when I tell him of the interview. I have fixed it at 3 o'clock to have time for a word with van M before he sees Kliemann. "We'll proceed as agreed," the Major concludes.

June 1st 43

Graf greets me with empty hands.

"We can do nothing today. I haven't received the instructions. I hope to get them tomorrow."

V. M. is punctual at 2 o'clock. He seems nervous and not too sure of himself. In a few words, I tell him the facts. "Be sure to remember this," I caution him. "YOU DON'T KNOW ANYTHING ABOUT MY WORK and I know NOTHING OF WHAT KLIEMANN IS DOING. Nor are you supposed to know his real profession: I HAVEN'T TOLD YOU ANYTHING. Agreed?"

"I see. When he reveals it to me, I'll be nonplussed?"

"That's right. You can even ask him, with APPREHENSION, whether I suspect anything, as if you didn't want me to know what you were about to do. And please, de l'AUDACE— beaucoup d'AUDACE."[13]

"I'll do my best."

Kliemann arrives at a quarter past four. The suspense of waiting has set V. M.'s nerves on edge. I observe him with awe. The introductions are over. Moustache sits down on the divan. V. M. takes the Morocco arm-chair, and I draw a low stool between the two. Kliemann looks quite at ease. However, the way he thrusts his handkerchief into his front-pocket and pulls it out again shows me that he is nervous. I am afraid to look at V. M.

"Our friend here," starts the Major referring to me, "tells me you have been working in the Geographical Service. Would you be interested to do some map-work for us?"

V. M. says he would. Kliemann then questions him about his studies, his army life, the countries he's been to. V. M. manages it quite well, and I begin to hope again. After 25 minutes, Moustache consults his watch and gets up. "I'll take your name and your address," he says. "I should like to talk some more with you about that work we intend to give you. Could you meet me at the 'Weber,' rue Royale?"

They take a date for the end of the week. When Moustache has left us and we've seen him from the window get into his car, V. M. turns to me and asks: "What's your impression?"

"I have none. This was just a contact. Everything will depend from your next interview."

V. M. isn't satisfied.

"What's wrong?" I ask him.

"I don't know. It was all so rapid. He didn't seem interested in the least."

"I've warned you. He doesn't want you to know that I am 'in the plot' and won't tell you anything so long as I am there. I'll call him up tomorrow to see what he thinks of you and will let you know."

June 2nd

Graf has two very thin sheets of paper unfolded in front of him on the table. They are typewritten and have the usual "Geheim"[14] in red ink at the heading. Below there are numbered paragraphs. I take a clean sheet and look for a pencil in the depths of my bag.

"No, put that away," says Graf. "You won't write what I'll tell you. You'll have to remember it by heart. These are the instructions for your work in England." Slowly he reads, translating the text, commenting on each paragraph. Most of the instructions are generalities which I already know: the description of all airfields (excepting the official airports), of all troop movements, especially of the Americans, etc. Others are more specific: "The whole area of Salisbury Plain is of the greatest importance. Try to get information about the combat gases and whether the British intend using them? And if so: HOW? (in form of bombs? in sprays? etc., etc.). The British have Ack Ack rockets. They can be seen in the centre of London, in the eastern part of Hyde-Park. Get their description, their number. Aeroplanes are to be fitted with rockets. What types of planes are to be used for this purpose? At what stage are the experiments? A telephone-cable is established between England and the U.S.A. Its terminal is at LAND'S END in Cornwall. Notify us of any work that would be undertaken in that field: installment of any new lines, etc. Is the use of dogs to guard the airports generalized? Are the airports provided with ammunition depots? Can you repeat to me all that is expected of you?" Graf asks, when he has finished reading the two pages.

I recapitulate the essential points, trying to forget nothing. Herr Graf folds carefully the papers, puts them back into his pocket, gets up and bows ceremoniously to me. "My role in regard to you is finished," he says. "If you succeed in accomplishing the confidential mission you are entrusted with by the III-d Reich, I shall be proud to have contributed to it in a certain measure. There is nothing more for me to do than offer you my wishes of success. On leaving you, I shall report to Major Kliemann and tell him that you are quite ready to start in your functions."

It sounds like it was my anniversary. I grin a smile of satisfaction and emotion and thank Herr Graf for all the trouble he has taken to impart to me the finishing touch which makes the perfect spy. We part forever. On reaching home, I take a pad, some lemon powder, guarant seed "natural" which I bought at the "Printemps," and a new pen. I don't know if it'll work, but I'm going to try. I dissolve a bit of power and use it as I would some ink. I cut off the 13th page from the end of the block-note and write down everything Graf told me this morning.

June 3rd

I ring up Moustache. "I am informed," he says. "Graf has told me about you. He is very satisfied. I'll see you next week: let's say Monday at Yvonne's, at three o'clock. In the meantime, I'll start preparing your departure."

"Don't forget that I must have left France before the 27th of June."

"No, no. I do not forget. You'll go before that."

"Another question: what do you think of that friend I introduced to you?"

"I don't know," hesitates Kliemann, " terribly shy. I'll see about it later."

JUNE 7TH

Yvonne is back, delighted with her trip.

"What the dickens did you go to Madrid for?" I ask.

"To show a collection of dresses from 'Heim, Jeunes Filles.'"

"A REAL collection?"

"Yes, a real collection. I know what you think, but it wasn't that. I was to go to Lisbon, but we couldn't get the Portuguese visa. I had asked for it through a friend, but when at last the authorization came, the Spanish visa was nearly over-due, and we had to return."

"WE?"

"I was with a woman-friend, who is an employee at Heim's: Mme Marty-Chanclos."

"How did you spend the time?"

"Wonderfully. We stopped at the Ritz. We went out a lot: receptions, parties. Madrid is very gay. What a difference from Paris. People dress for the evening. You'll see. It's wonderful. By-the-way, how are things with you?"

"I'm ready to go. But, between us, let me tell you that since you've been away, I've had difficulty in joining both ends."

"You haven't been paid?"

"No, he owes me April and May. When the cashier leaves, the cashbox closes."

"Here he comes. I'll see that he leaves me the money for you."

The garden gate bangs. The gravel of the alley grates, the entrance door opens then closes. Steps go to the drawing-room then retreat to the staircase.

"Hullo," calls out Moustache.

"Hullo," we answer simultaneously.

"Where are you?" the Major asks.

"Come up," I say, leaning over the banister.

"Already here!" exclaims Moustache lifting his head.

"You're kidding. It's 22 minutes past four."

"It's not possible," he protests coming up the stairs.

He joins us in Yvonne's room, in the midst of a picturesque disorder of crepe de Chine underwear scattered all over the blue silk upholstered furniture. He looks around him with an indulgent and slightly amused air. "Let's go into the bureau," he says a moment later. "We'll be better there than in the drawing-room."

The bureau is on the first floor. It is situated on the side of the house and overlooks the backyard of a boarding-school. It is dark. Moustache puts down within reach his inseparable leather dispatch-case, and settles near the writing table.

"So you are ready," he says, rubbing his hands. "Let us see. There are certain things, I must make sure of." He takes out a small address book and consults its pages. "There it is. I have here the names of your diverse relatives and friends. There is your aunt the nun, then your aunt in Madeira, your Polish cousin, your English cousin and your friends near Bristol. Very well. To whom have you written?"

"To my aunt in Madeira and to my Polish cousin, who is in London."

"Have you had any answers?"

"You've seen the answer from Madeira, as you have yourself supplied the telegram that my uncle had refused to send me. From my Polish cousin, I had no answer."

Moustache takes notes. "In Madrid," Kliemann proceeds, "you won't attempt anything in order to go to England. You'll just write to your cousin in Cambridge to ask her to back up your demand of a visa. After that, you'll apply for a Portuguese visa. You'll get it without any difficulty if your aunt, the nun, helps you. It is only when you are in Lisbon that you'll go to the British. You'll explain them that you have been able to leave France thanks to a telegram from your aunt. You'll tell them of your wish not to return under the German occupation but to go instead to England and serve the Allied cause by any means in your power. Try, however, not to get stuck in a factory for 24 hours a day. Is that clear?"

"Perfectly clear."

"From now on, that will be your 'tale.' You have fled France. Don't forget it. How? With the help of a friend of yours, who has influential relations, you were able to buy the documents. It's being done. It's very expensive, but quite possible. You must live your part; impersonate the character you have assumed." And he repeats: "Escaped from France." Moustache stops and looks at me.

I repeat slowly: "I am a refugee. I've abandoned everything. Baffling the Boche, I have fled under their very nose and have reached Spain. I am free—FREE at last. And I take off to England, offering to serve the Allies in every way I can until the blessed day when France too will be free."

"Good. Very good. Very, very good," approves the Major. "You looked quite REAL saying that. You ought to go on the stage."

I look at him without answering. But it IS true, you fat blockhead. Can't you see it is, you Schweinskopf?[15] I want to tell him. Instead, I start laughing. "Maybe, that's what is awaiting me after the war: the stage. Unless ANOTHER KIND OF PLATFORM claims me before the end."

"You mean?"

"I believe they hang spies in England, don't they?"

Kliemann hits the table with his fist. "I forbid you. I forbid you to think such things." And then, lowering his voice: "You mustn't ... you must not go with such ideas at the back of your mind. It would interfere with your work."

"On the contrary. You see: I am immune. But don't worry—I was only joking."

Moustache looks at me doubtfully, then proceeds: "Amongst these addresses I have, I think I can cross out the one in Madeira. The Rev. Mother C. can be of use. Supposing we were not able to send you money to England, I could always find someone to take it to her, saying that your mother is sending it to you and, not knowing your address, begs Mother C. to forward it to you. In the meantime, you'd have written to your aunt and given her your address. If, when she sends you money, the British inquire as to its provenance, they'll find out that it comes from a respectable nun. What do you think of that?"

"It seems an excellent scheme."

"Once in England, try to go as often as possible to visit your friends in Bristol. It's one of the most interesting sectors. Avonmouth[16]: the post of arrival of convoys from America. Troops, war-material, supplies, everything comes through there. Now, let us see the nearest future: MADRID. I'll give you addresses in the ex-free zone, where you can write to me. Your letters will be forwarded from there. For you are probably aware of this absurdity: the whole of France is occupied, the demarcation line has been abolished, yet you can correspond with Spain from the ex-free zone ... but not from the so-called OCCUPIED zone. Have you any friends in the South of France? Or in some other country to whom you could write from Spain and, later on, from England letters that would be forwarded to me?"

I try to think. "Sweden?"

"Capital."

"I've got some friends there: but I'd have to let them know beforehand and I can't do it because of the censure."

"I'll get the letter through censure. Just write them."

"Very well. What do you want me to tell them? I mean: what address and what name do you wish me to give them to forward the letters?"

"Give Annick LE QUEAN's name. I'll have them intercepted."

"I'll have to think what I'll tell my friends. I know. I'll tell them simply that if they receive letters for a certain ANNICK LE QUEAN, they are from her fiancé, and I shall ask them to send them on to: 2, Villa Boileau, Paris 16e. This leaves me free to choose a name and I can look one up in the London phone directory."

"That's perfect. Write the letter as soon as possible and give it me. I'll do the rest. We'll reserve this for England. Have you got someone else you can write to from Spain?"

"I can write to someone I "slightly" know at La Ciotat. But I know him well enough to ask him to forward my letters. Must they also be sent to the name of Annick?"

"Yes."

"It will also be the 'bluff of the fiancé.' Here is the address = Mr. H. M., Avenue Fernand Gassion. La Ciotat, Bouches-du-Rhone."

Moustache writes down the name. "Now," he says, "here is something for you. As soon as you arrive in Madrid, ring up LUIS MIRET—Navarez 50, phone number: 51.242, and give him your address. Your name will be 'CANUTO.' Remember, 'C A N U T O.' Of course, you must never telephone from your hotel. Go to some café or to the post-office. Luis Miret is but an intermediary. It is to avoid any direct connection with our Secret Service. Every time you'll have to see one of our people, or want to let us know something important, which cannot wait to be sent by letter, you'll notify Miret, who will put you in contact. He has been warned and is expecting you. But don't forget that for him you are 'CANUTO.'"

"Then here is another address which I want to test, but of which I am not sure: Miguel OTTONDO. He's a smuggler. He does it for money; he is bought by us. If someone pays him more, he'll let us down. Of course, he thinks that he is passing private correspondence. Therefore, there is no reason for anyone to 'buy him over.' You'll put your letters in a double envelope. He'll stamp the second one from France. As soon as you get to Madrid, you'll write me in secret ink, using both addresses: I want to see how it works and which is the quickest. It's possible that the letters won't arrive at all or that they'll be detained so long by censorship that we'll have to find some other means of corresponding. Just in case, I'll give you another address, but which you can only use from Spain as it is in Germany. Here it is: Herr E. Killburg—Ferleinstr. 4, Frankfurt a/M. This channel is the quickest and most reliable, but I also want the others. And while I am at it, I may as well give you the address of our agent in Lisbon with whom you'll get in touch as soon as you arrive to Portugal. It is: Rudolf Morgener, Rua Antonio Augusto de Aguiar, 9, 3rd floor, on the left. This is all in the way of addresses.

"Now you must choose a name for yourself, which you'll use as signature to your letters and messages. Choose one for me too, and then forget that I am called Major Kliemann. Baptize me, something not too common, to avoid confusion."

"Have you a calendar?" He hands me over his memorandum-book. I point with my finger at random: "Octave," I announce.

"Octave? Octave? Octave. It sounds good. It's not common. You will remember it?"

"Yes."

"So that's settled. From now on, I am Octave. And you?"

"I should like to be 'SOLANGE.'"

"All right. Good morning, Solange."

"Good evening, Octave. You are late, Octave, as usual. It is nearly 8 p.m., and I am going to tell you goodbye, Octave."

"Already? I must see you again. When? Tomorrow: impossible. Shall we say the day after tomorrow?"

"All right."

"Then here, in the morning."

"Very well. And before I go, a last question. What is the result of your interview with V. M.?"

"He didn't show up."

"No? It's not possible. I've never known him to miss an appointment or to be late. Come on: confess—at what time did you arrive?"

"We had agreed to meet at 5 o'clock, and I was a little late because I had been detained. It must have been 5:30. Don't smile. Upon my honour it's true. And I looked for him everywhere: on the terrace, inside, even upstairs, for as you know, the bar is on the first floor at the Café de le Paix, and I thought...."

"At the Café de le Paix?"

"Yes, of course. Why?"

"But you were to meet at the Weber."

"At the Weber? Do you think so?"

"I am positively sure."

"You may be right. This would explain I didn't find him."

"What are you going to do now?"

"I'll write to him. I've got his address."

I leave Kliemann and go home. Stuck under my door, I find a note from V. M.: "I came twice but you were out. I'll come again after dinner." I have hardly finished reading the note, when there is a knock at the door. It is V. M.

"I know, I know," I say before he has time to open his mouth. "Major Kliemann didn't turn up. I've seen him a moment ago. He pretends to have waited for you at the Café de la Paix. Maybe he has; maybe he hasn't. He is absent-minded enough to do such a thing. He told me he was going to write you."

"And you think he'll do it?"

"Perhaps. If he doesn't lose your address in the meantime. You know what we'll do. You cannot write him, as I'm not authorized to give you his address, but I can give you the number of his office phone. You will wait eight days and, if by then you haven't heard from him, you'll ring him up. It is: LIT. 45-10 or 44-10. But don't show too much eagerness. I'll see Kliemann the day after tomorrow. I'll tell him you called me, were very annoyed to have missed him, and thought it was your fault. I'll also tell him that I gave you his telephone number, but pretended not to know his address. Will that do? But above all, don't show you know I saw him in between. You are not supposed to know that I have anything to do with Kliemann."

At this moment, I have another visitor—Solange de G. Solange de G. is the sister of one of my school friends. I often see her. During the collapse of France, Solange distinguished herself by her valiant conduct. She was awarded the Legion d'Honneur. I thought one time of letting her work with me. She has guts. She would have done well. Unfortunately, a few months ago, she fell ill with cephalo-spinal meningitis. She has recovered since, but her memory is bad. It'll be all right in time. Only for my sort of work it is too dangerous to "forget," even for a few minutes. One can't note anything. And Solange has to write down everything. "I am even obliged to look up your address in my note-book every time I come to see you," she tells me.

It's probably my fate to remain alone. I should have liked to work with Solange.

"Do you still intend leaving," she asks, throwing her bag and hat on the divan.

"Yes."

"You are lucky. If only you could take me with you."

I make a helpless gesture.

"I know," she says. "I keep on trying. Do you think you'll still be here next weekend?"

"I don't know. What date will it be?"

"The 12th, I believe: Whitsuntide."

"I suppose I'll still be here. Why?"

"I'm going to spend the weekend with some friends in the country. Come with me."

"It's impossible. I can't leave Paris. Just before going away I have heaps of things to do."

"Then join me on Saturday. Just Saturday and Sunday," pleads Solange. "On Monday morning, we'll return together. You can't refuse. Anyhow, I've already told my friends you were coming."

"Solange! You have not done that?"

"Sure! I have! And they are expecting you."

V. M. goes, and soon after Solange leaves too. Babs jumps on the divan, creeps up to me, puts his shaggy head on my knees and looks at me. His honest eyes seem to be saying: "I am here! You are not alone!" His warm contact makes me realize suddenly that what overwhelms me is loneliness, not only of the empty room, but of the whole sleeping town around me, of the whole world. The loneliness of the task and of the silence I have imposed upon myself. I envy desperately those who fight in groups, who receive orders to obey and carry out. I envy those who are not alone.

June 9th 43

This time, Moustache is there, waiting for me. "I have an idea," he announces as soon as he has closed the door of the bureau. "I want to hear what you think of it. The Intelligence Service has agents everywhere. It's almost certain that if we mark your name in our 'BLACK BOOK'—if we set the police in search of you, if we notify all the border posts, sending them your description and your photo (all that after you'll have left France, of course)—if we do all that, the Intelligence Service is sure to get wind of it. They might even try to verify your identity through someone they have in Paris. One can never tell. In view of this, I'll have the GESTAPO question your 'concierge' and search your flat. You know how quickly gossip spreads. The whole quarter will know that the Gestapo is after you. It'll be perfect. I might even have your parents arrested."

"Isn't that going a bit too far? Under the pretence of preserving my reputation, don't go and shoot my whole family!"

"Don't let your imagination run away with you. We'll merely put on an act. Your parents will be released immediately. But they will talk about it—everyone will know. That's precisely what we want."

"What makes you think that the British will check on me all the way back to Paris?

I'll be no more or no less than a 'refugee.' I can't imagine them wasting their time and agents, checking on the whereabouts of all those coming from France!"

"Don't forget that everybody doesn't leave France with a passport and legally, and when they do, it's not to go to England!"

"That's true. There may be something in what you say. It would have simplified matters if you had let me cross the border with a "passeur,"[17] as I had suggested. To begin with, we wouldn't have lost all that time getting the visas."

"We would have lost much more time had you landed in the Spanish concentration camp of Pamplona. No, you see, when we have a good agent, we don't like to run the risk of losing him. Concerning your future work, you must understand that it is more important for us to have an agent in England, even if he remains idle, than to have him send us regular information if it is to expose him. It may sound paradoxical to you, but when you have to choose between your personal security and the possibility of obtaining information, however important, our Services would gain nothing by getting that one piece of capital information if it cost them an agent in England.

"Remember that caution comes first. Now, I'll give you some money and you can go and get your ticket. In the meantime, I'll have received the money which you are to get for your stay in Spain. The rest will be given to you in Madrid or Lisbon. I'll bring it myself for, of course, I'll see you before you leave definitely for England. I don't think it wise to take too much with you. It's not safe to carry in on your person and still less to leave it in the hotel. Do you agree with me?"

"Absolutely."

"I don't know yet what currency I'll give you. French francs have no value, and the Spanish banks don't exchange the sterling pounds and the dollars. Nor can you bring pesetas into Spain. I know it because I've made several trips to Portugal and Spain and have met with the same difficulties each time. There only remain the Swedish Kronen, the Swiss francs and the Portuguese escudos. These currencies have a firm exchange rate. I'll find out which is the most easily found on the Paris "black market" and get it. For you'll have to pretend you bought it on the black market and not say you have exchanged it at the bank. You'd need too much pull to be authorized to get foreign currency. This would render you suspicious to the British.

"To take your money out of France you'll have a special permit, but it won't be marked on your passport. You'll pretend to have smuggled it. The German frontier authorities will be informed. You'll have nothing to fear. I think we've covered everything for today. Ring me up on Tuesday."

June 11th

I'd like Mummy and Daddy to leave Paris. They could go to Algiers to my sister. But they say that if they went, it would seem suspicious to the Germans. So they are going to stay. From now on, existence will be a nightmare, knowing that the slightest imprudence, the least false step will endanger their lives. I'll be out of reach for the Germans, but they… Yet they are going to remain, and I am going to leave.

I went to see Pat. "Pat" is the Reverend Father O., a friend of the family. I told him everything. Then, I asked him, in case of emergency, to help my parents to hide. I'll find some way to let him know if I feel that the Germans suspect something. Pat has promised. He did not ask many questions. He only asked if I wanted him to notify the British of my arrival. I said no. I prefer to do it myself.

It almost seems incredible that I am REALLY to go. There is one thing that worries me: I didn't tell Kliemann about my trip to Algiers. At first I didn't do it thinking he'd reproach me for spending my time and this money for personal motives. So I kept quiet. Afterwards, I decided it wasn't very wise to keep my journey secret, especially having been in Algiers a fortnight previous to the Allied invasion. I waited for an opportunity to mention it casually, but none turned up. So I remained silent. After that, I had waited too long; it would have seemed queer. That's how I stand. Maybe they know about it. Maybe they wait to see if I'll confess it. Maybe they want to see what I'll do. But I have waited too long. It's too late. There is nothing I can do now. It's possible I shan't go after all. It's possible they'll have me arrested on the train. And for such a stupid thing. I'll wait and see.

June 12th

The railway station where I alight is the second after Gournay. I knew the road to Gournay. I've been there more than once last year, to get some food—when nothing could be found in Paris. At the end of the platform, I see the fair head of Solange. She too has seen me and waves her hand. The distance to the house is short. The place isn't "occupied" having been classified as "historical monument." It is a lovely chateau in the Louis XVth style, surrounded by a vast park. Solange takes me up to the room we are to share, and I hasten to change my clothes.

"Besides Francinette and her husband, whom you've just met, you'll see her sister, her father and a friend of theirs, Jacques Roberti. You'll find him wonderful or hateful; it depends. He finds himself wonderful!"

In the course of the afternoon, Solange, Roberti and I find ourselves alone in the drawing-room. "So you are going to leave us," asks Roberti, looking at me through half-closed eyes, an ironical smile playing around his mouth and his hands comically crossed on his stomach.

"Yes, Mona Lisa. If that's O.K. with you."

He opens his eyes and un-crosses his hands. "Fancy! You can even be nasty."

"You haven't got that monopoly, although I bet you were scheming something with that Mona Lisa attitude."

"No," he says, giving up joking. "I was only thinking that if you go to Madrid, I could give you the address of some friends of mine. Remind me of it before you go."

"Thank you. Is he a Spaniard?"

"No, an American: Colonel Stevens. He was military attaché when I made his acquaintance. Now he is at the Madrid U.S.A. Embassy. I am not sure what his present job is. At any rate, he and his wife are charming people. Go to see him. He will surely be able to help you."

This is a trump I certainly did not reckon upon.

June 14th

"Pleased with your weekend?" Solange asks me in the train, which takes us back to Paris.

"Delighted! Most charming people, including Mona Lisa!"

"You know, I think you offended him, calling him that!"

"I don't think so. Haven't you notice that he's got sense of humour?"

II. Paris, 1942–1943

"Are you going to see that American friend of his?"
"Yes, I'll go and see him. I most decidedly will go."

June 16th

Major Kliemann arrives only 3 hours and 27 minutes late. But he hadn't forgotten that we had a date. "I haven't got your money yet, but it's not important. There is another question we must discuss. By what means will you smuggle into England the necessary funds? You can't possibly arrive there with a lot of money; you'd never be able to justify its provenance. At the same time, we have given you enough dough to hold you at least six months, possibly a year, for there might be no opportunity to send you some for a long time, and we don't want such an occurrence to handicap your work."

I feel inclined to smile, knowing Moustache's slackness in his payments here in Paris, where he has no obstacles to overthrow. I can imagine what it'll be when I am over the other side of the Channel! "You could give it to me in form of jewels," I suggest. "It does not take much room. I'll be able to sell them, losing money in the process, of course; and if I am asked about their origin, I'll pretend to have them from my grandmother."

"I think you've got something there. Do you mind if the jewels are not modern?"

"It's better that they shouldn't be. Also have them evaluated at their real value, not at the price they cost here today. See if you can find out the price of stones and of gold in England."

"I'll do my best."

June 17th

My last days of Paris, of France. My last days of "occupation." Feverishly, I pack up and tidy what I leave behind. I go through all the papers, and destroy some of them. There remains this diary. The day before I leave, I'll bury it in the cellar. I have prepared a tin box, which will serve the purpose. I'll put in it my copy-books. I'll dig a hole under the place where the coal was usually kept and where there only remains coal dust. I'll put the tin box at the bottom of the hole and pour some cement over it. How foolish to have kept a diary.

June 18th

"You can book your seat. Everything is ready," announces Moustache over the phone. "When do you want to leave?"

"On Tuesday, the 22nd."

"As you wish. When does the train go?"

"At 6 p.m., I believe."

"Very well. Come and see me in the morning and I'll give you what I have got for you."

I have an almost physical impression of "turning over a page." Something new is going to start. I cling desperately to all and everything that surrounds me. I look, listen, inhale—as if I could take something of Paris with me.

June 19th

Here ends my diary written during the German occupation. On Tuesday—Wednesday at the latest—I shall have left Paris, left France to go towards the unknown. Am I right? Am I wrong? Only the future will tell. I trust my lucky stars. Someone told me once: "Do not turn round. Do not regret. Have faith."

Whatever happens, I regret nothing, and if some day I turn to look back, it'll be from beyond this abyss: to measure its depth. If I must die, I accept death, for I have not undertaken this work blind to its risks. I have waited; I have waited too long this departure to experience any joy. All perception has died in me. I don't feel anything.

June 21st

I have a reserved seat for the 22nd. It's tomorrow. Tomorrow seems terribly near.

June 22nd 43

He will have waited until the last minute to give me the money, the good Kliemann! And, of course, he isn't even there, when I arrive at the Villa Boileau this morning. Am I anxious? Am I impatient, as the moment of the departure approaches? Am I afraid? Am I doubtful of myself, of my final success? The minutes drag on slowly. I have plenty of time to ask myself these questions, while "Moustache" doesn't come.

No, I'm not anxious. And if I'm impatient, it is only of the time I'm wasting here; for the rest, I have waited too long. It has come too late for me to experience any joy, any enthusiasm or any triumph. It has come too late for me to feel anything at all. As for being afraid, for doubting, I would like to see myself face to face in reality, but no matter how I try, I continue, as in a semi-sleep, to live a dream. No, I am not afraid. There is no place for doubt. Failure is not possible.

Later on, when I read again these lines, they will probably appear to me fantastic, presumptuous. But then, later on, to what will amount this long, dull enervating sometimes hopeless waiting—this waiting that has been going on for two years? To uninteresting pages one will skip to reach quicker the main subject. But I, I had to live them, those two long years: seven hundred thirty days; 17,230 hours, 1,036,800 minutes; 62,208,000 seconds, without being able to skip a single one, without the tiniest being shared to me! I have made these calculations to help spend the time. I know so well the living-room in which I am waiting, that it offers nothing new to my inspection.

The garden gate squeaks, the path gravel rolls and skids under approaching steps. The front door opens, then the living-room's. "Hello!" says "Moustache." "You're already here?"

"Yes, for one hour and forty five minutes." And I add: "I thought it's today I was leaving."

The Major seems surprised. His thick eyebrows go up questioningly: "But of course! Have you changed your mind?"

"Not I. But you are causing me to waste precious time, and I'm not ready yet."

"Don't worry; it'll take but a minute to settle everything. Let's go upstairs."

On the first floor he ushers me into the small dark bureau, where we have previously discussed the final plans. He takes out of his leather briefcase a fat envelope. "I shall give it to you in escudos: 20,000. This is just to start with. You'll be able to get on the spot—whether in Madrid or in Lisbon—all the money you will need. The reason for which I chose escudos is that it is the currency that has the highest rate in Spain, and the only one that'll be changed officially. As I have told you, the French franc has no value; no bank will accept it. On the black market you get 5 pesetas for 100 francs! There remains the Swiss franc and the Swedish crown. I have preferred the Portuguese escudo. I hope you agree with me?"

"It is quite all right."

"Then, here is also £10 note just in case. When we'll meet in Spain, you'll receive some jewels. I'll have more time to look for some in the meanwhile. This way, the money angle is settled. Now, this is your authorization to take some currency out of France. In this way, you won't have anything marked on your passport. But I advise you to declare this money on the other side of the border; otherwise you won't be able to change it in a bank. Another thing: the German authorities in Hendaye[18] are notified. When you get out of the train, make it so that you are the last among the passengers. Stay behind. When you present your passport to the control, I have given out the order that they omit to stamp it. In that way, there will be nothing German to show how you passed the border."

"Why do you want to do that?"

"Well, I just thought that you'll always be able to justify your exit visa by saying that you got it through special favor, or through an acquaintance, or by paying for it. But in all three cases, by some Frenchman, whereas a German stamp would throw suspicion on you."

"But how on earth do you want me to explain my passing the border?"

"I have thought of it. You'll say you got off the train at Hendaye. Between Hendaye and Irun, which is the Spanish border town, there is a river and a long bridge. So you can tell everything had been arranged for you, and a "passeur" was awaiting you at the station. He was to recognize you by your little dog—as you insist on taking Babs along. You followed the man; he took you along in a horse cart; then you had to walk. He got you over the river in a boat. On the other bank, he handed you over to a Spaniard who accompanied you safely to the railway station of Irun. There you took the train and proceeded to Madrid."

I shake my head without conviction. "Why should I be doing all this, when my papers are in order and I have all the required visas?"

"Because these are 'favor' papers, and at the last moment you had some doubts about them and got scared you'd get pinched at the German control."

"It wouldn't be 'at the last minute,' if I said that the 'passeur' had been all organized and awaited me. This generally takes time."

"Well, then say you didn't trust the one who 'organized' your exit, and feared an ambush."

"I wouldn't have gone through all the rigmarole necessary to obtain a visa, if I weren't sure the latter was legal."

"Why argue, when everything is already fixed!"

"I don't like it. It's clumsy; it's sewn with white thread. But as you place me in front of an accomplished fact, there is nothing left to me but to accept."

"Have you faith in me? You know well enough I wouldn't do anything to handicap you?"

"All right. But do you know the time? It is 13:35. My train is at 18. I haven't finished packing and I don't even know what kind of transportation I'll find to take me to the station."

"I'll drive you home, pick up your suitcases and have Richard take them to the station. He'll be awaiting you on the platform. I would have liked to see you off, but I suppose Madam your Mother will be there, and it is better she doesn't see me."

"Moustache" drives me to rue Jean Bologne, and I give him the two suitcases that are already packed. He leaves and, shortly, I hear the starter of his car. One last time I glance around the room. Inanimate things, you that have a soul, good bye.

Mummy, Daddy and Babs are impatiently awaiting me at the rue Sauffroy. Nothing but a few more hours left. I pack up my last suitcase. I am ready. We look at each other. I am going to leave. They are staying. I would like to find something to say, but what can one say when one knows that, perhaps, one will not meet again? When one knows that Life is no longer a game, when one is not sure that there will be such a thing as "tomorrows." One doesn't say anything; one remains silent—and the minutes pass. One is together. Soon one won't be. As long as one is together, one repeats to oneself: one is together, as if to make sure of it—for later on—and one remains silent. The minutes go.

"It is time," I say.

"It is time," repeats Mummy.

"Yes, it's time," says Daddy.

Babs doesn't say anything. He is already waiting in front of the door.

Afterwards the morbid spell is broken by the rush in the metro, the crowd, the transfers. We arrive to the Austerlitz station with three quarters of an hour of advance. I look for Richard, but see him nowhere. We walk up and down the platform without much speaking. From time to time, Mummy insists: "Look after yourself. Be careful."—"Write as often as you can." I agree with a nod and squeeze tenderly her arm she has slipped under mine. "You'll let me know as soon as you have arrived?" asks Mummy.

"Yes, don't worry."

Five more minutes before the train leaves, and still no Richard to be seen. Funny how the thought of missing my train doesn't upset me. Two minutes before the departure, I climb into the car, take my suitcase from the compartment and bring it back onto the platform. Babs, who doesn't understand what is happening, is getting nervous. At last the doors are closed. Babs pulls desperately on his leash and tries to jump on the running board. I watch the train start, pick up speed. At this precise moment, at the end of the platform, Richard appears dragging my suitcases. Calmly, I advance towards him and showing him the red back light of the train, diminishing and disappearing in the distance: "Too late," I say.

He drops my suitcases. "Where on earth were you?" he asks, wiping the sweat from his forehead.

"It's exactly what I was going to ask you. Where were you? The Major told me that I would find you on the platform half an hour before the train left."

"And to me, he said to wait for you at the entrance of the station. I've been standing there for an hour."

I shrug my shoulders. "I should have foreseen it. Never mind, I'll start all over tomorrow."

"What will the Major say?"

"Aren't you interested to know what I am going to tell him? Never have I met someone so careless."

Twenty four hours of respite! Back at home, I telephone immediately "Moustache." Richard hasn't had time to warn him.

"You!" exclaims Kliemann. "I thought your train was leaving at six o'clock."

In a few words I tell him what happened and add: "I have thought of something which I want to talk over with you. Can I see you tomorrow morning?"

"All right. When and where?"

"At 10 a.m. at Pam-Pam, rue Royale. And when I say 10, I don't mean 10:30. I won't wait."

"I'll be there."

June 23rd 1943

Kliemann arrives nearly on time: only 18 minutes late. "What's wrong?" he inquires wearily.

"It's this stamp business. It will never do!"

"Why? I thought the question was settled."

"The more I think it over, the more hazardous it seems to me. Suppose for one moment that somebody has seen me in the train? Suppose the British should gain such an incredible fact at the border post of Irun? There isn't such a quantity of travelers nowadays that it should not be possible. They even probably have lists of names of all the people who cross the border by train. That'll be the end of me. Believe me. It'll be a thousand times easier for me to explain the presence on my passport of the German border control stamps than to account for its absence."

"Moustache" ponders with knitted brows. "As you wish," he agrees at last. "If you feel it easier to explain one way rather than the other, we'll do as you want. I'll have the instructions cabled immediately to our border control at Hendaye. Are you satisfied?"

"Thanks."

This time I'm leaving. Nothing happens to hold me back at the last moment. Leaning out of the window of my first class compartment, I wave a handkerchief at Mummy standing on the platform. Babs sniffs with satisfaction at the wind. I watch the dear form diminish, Mummy become smaller and smaller. Then a curve hides her. It's finished.

I pull up the window, make a place for Babs and pick up a book. But I don't feel like reading. I don't even feel like thinking. I look at the landscape going by: fields, woods, houses, more fields, more woods. It's France. I'm leaving France, to try to help those who want to see her free.

I examine my bare hands spread out on my knees. Alone and unarmed. What can I do? Fields, woods, fields, woods. Dusk in nearing. I can do a lot. I hold a key which will open a door, a door through which the British will have a way into the German fortress. Maybe, it's but a tiny key. Maybe, it's but a tiny door. But all the same, it's a gap. And there are thousands of others like me, each of whom opens a little gap. We're doing the work of worms, a work without glory. But when everything will be over, we'll have the right to tell ourselves: "We didn't remain with folded arms."

I must have fallen to sleep. Someone is shaking me by the shoulder. I wake up with a start. A man in civilian clothes, his hat on the head, is standing in the doorway, looking at me with cold eyes. "Papers!" he orders.

My neighbor, who woke me up, whispers: "Hurry, it's the Gestapo!"

I hand over my passport to the man. He examines it, glancing at me now and then. "Your name?" he snaps. I tell him. "First name?" I tell him again. Then he asks me my date and place of birth, etc., etc. And at last: "Your father's name?"

"Serge."

"His surname?"

I bristle up. "What are you trying to insinuate: that I'm not his daughter?" He stares at me without answering, then chucks my passport into my lap.

"Better don't come back," he grumbles.

"I'll come back if I want to," I answer very crossly, and in spite of the cautioning my neighbor is giving me with his elbow. The man of the Gestapo throws me a last look and slams the door of our compartment. "What manners!" I exclaim, furious. "To wake people in the middle of the night to ask them if they are their father's children!"

"Hush!" whisper simultaneously all my fellow travelers. "You don't know what you're risking! He might come back and force you to alight. They have all the rights."

I shrug my shoulders and don't answer. Babs growls and snuggles against me. I get back to my corner and go to sleep.

III

Madrid, 1943

Jun 24th 1943

The train is crossing the Basque country. The houses are low, painted yellow, with arches and orange tile roofs. The sunshine envelops everything. In between the houses, the cypress and eucalyptus trees, I catch a glimpse of the turquoise blueness, fringed with foam, of the Atlantic.

I'm alone with Babs in our compartment. The other passengers must have left during the night. I go out into the passage and discover that the remainder of the car is empty. Not many travelers, nowadays! The train advances slowly. Through the window, I see forts and concrete blockhouses, guarded by German soldiers. The train slows down still more, and we enter the station of Hendaye.

In spite of myself, I have a vague feeling of apprehension. For I have with me a book that is cut and which is stuffed with letters I intend to smuggle into Spain. I call the porter and, following my luggage, go to the German control. Some fifteen passengers are already there. I'm the last one in line, as "Moustache" has advised me to do. I have to wait quite a while. Carelessly, I leave my book on the customs table and go back to my place in the line. When it's my turn, I hand over my papers. The German officer consults a list, stamps my passport, keeps my papers and sends me to the customs. A fat German soldier opens my suitcases, empties their contents, shakes everything, looks inside my photo camera and umbrella, then gathers everything in a heap, barks: "Es geht!"[1] and loses all further interest in me.

A German woman, who has silently observed the operation, signals me to follow her. She leads me into a sort of closet and orders me to undress. I obey without protesting. She feels and shakes all my clothes one by one, carefully examines the soles of my shoes, and then gets hold of my handbag. Having found nothing, she looks in Babs' ears and passes her hand under his stomach, which has the result of making him growl. All that is done silently, with a seeming indifference and boredom. The search is over. The woman says: "You can dress," and leaves me alone.

I'm ready. I open the door and go out. Just then I see a soldier coming towards me with big strides, his face very red. "They're going to arrest me," I think to myself. No. He salutes me, clicks his heels and says: "Bitte, Fraulein, kommen Sie mit mer."[2]

I follow him and he takes me into an office. In the next room, I hear a hurried shuffling of chairs. The search woman appears, crimson and confused, murmuring as she slips past by me: "I apologize: I didn't know!" and disappears. The officer who follows her seems to have sprung out of the threshold. With a sign of the hand, he waves the soldier away and, turning towards me a terribly upset face, says in French, but with a strong German accent: "I'm so terribly, terribly sorry! I don't know how to apologize! We have only this minute received the telegram concerning you."

"It's quite all right," I assure him. "I'm not mad."

"Ach! But it's awful! What a reception! And to whom? To you!"

I calm him as best I can. My passport is lying on his table. He hands it over to me. "You must have been very anxious when you saw your passport being stamped. But I want to reassure you right away. First we had orders not to stamp your passport. Then we received a counter-order to stamp it. So you see, it's not an error."

I tell him I knew it and wasn't at all worried. He seems relieved. I pick up my passport and get up. He looks at me with an undisguised admiration and repeats, bent in two: "My compliments, Mademoiselle, my compliments and all my congratulations. And good journey to you! I deeply regret not being able to accompany you to the train, but it wouldn't be wise."

I walk out of his office. The customs room is empty of passengers, but the eyes of all the German officials fix me with curiosity. The same porter as previously is waiting to carry my suitcases. On my way, I pick up my book, which no one has noticed, and go to the platform where a local train is waiting. The other passengers have already taken their seats. I find myself a place, then lean out of the window. Suddenly I notice the German customs official, who seems to be looking for someone, hoisting himself on tiptoes and peeping through the windows. Seeing me, his face lights up and he dashes towards me. He salutes me, then, taking off his cap, he says very rapidly in German: "I wanted to apologize.... To tell you how very sorry I am... But I hadn't been notified ... so I couldn't guess!"

I smile and answer nobly: "You did your duty."

"Yes," he concedes. "It was my duty. It isn't much, but it's my duty all the same! But you! You! It's really a big duty!" I bite my lips not to burst out laughing. "I wish you lots, lots of success," he finishes confidentially, "and good journey!" I go back to my compartment. Apart from that, the secret has been well kept!

At the Spanish customs of Irun, nothing happens. I pretend to take out the 20,000 escudos from the lining of my suitcase, which provokes an amused smile on the lips of the constable and the customs officials, but no comments. All this acting is unnecessary; nevertheless, I go through with it, decided as I am to play thoroughly my role of German spy. I have more than an hour before the train for San Sebastian leaves. I have time to lunch at the station restaurant.

I have often wondered what impression one would get to enter a normal restaurant, to see normal people eating normally! And there I am! The diners around me seem to eat without paying much attention to their food, without goggling at the neighbour's plate, without watching enviously what the waiter carries to the other tables. I sense that I'm not normal, for I examine with a kind of stupor the dishes laid out on the tables and feel my mouth water. It's nothing but fish, steaks, roasts. I don't even know if I'm hungry! But it's the fact of seeing all these casually assembled foods as if it were the most natural thing. And suddenly I see a fruit dish loaded with oranges and bananas. The waiter expects my order. I indicate the fruits. He doesn't seem to understand. He seems to think that I ought to begin with something else. I get impatient. "I want oranges and bananas," I say.

He shrugs his shoulders and goes to get the fruit dish which he puts before me. He waits a few minutes longer, shrugs again his shoulders and goes away without paying me any further notice. I take an orange and roll it between my palms. Then I put it to my nostrils and smell it. The scent is cold, bitter, sweet and penetrating. At last I make up my mind to peal it, sniffing it from time to time, trying to make the pleasure last, putting off the moment to taste it. Lifting my eyes, I notice that some of the guests look at me with curiosity over their newspapers. I don't mind. I eat an orange, then a banana; and another orange. And I'd like to eat a second banana, but cannot. I'm full!

The train arrives at San Sebastian at 3 p.m. High mountains surround the town on three sides. Everything is full of light and sunshine and seems to "laugh!" Yes. Yes, people laugh! On the platform, a group of porters are roaring with laughter. In the waiting room, women laugh noisily, bursting out loudly. I suddenly realize that this also is missing in France: laughing. That for the last three years, one doesn't laugh anymore in France. And when I hear this joyous laughter, something painful comes over me, and I have no wish to laugh.

As the Madrid train doesn't leave before 11 p.m., I take a room at the station and go for a rest. "I'm in Spain," I say to myself, and it doesn't seem true! What I have been waiting for two and a half years has now happened! And it doesn't sound true. I've had the best of the Germans! I will now be able to help defeat them! No, no, it doesn't seem true. I must be dreaming. I will wake up in my room with yellow muslin curtains; tomorrow I'll go to have my Morse lesson with Grün—and I shall keep on waiting—waiting indefinitely for departure which will probably never take place.

The express rolls in the night, breaking through the darkness which it strews with sparks. Tomorrow I'll be in Madrid. And then—the unknown.

June 25th 1943

I land at a station burning with sunshine. Dust seems to be part of the air. The crowd hustling on the platform, in the waiting room, appears to be covered with rags. Everything looks poor, and hot, and noisy. I don't know even where I will go; I haven't got the address of a hotel. I follow the porter who carries my suitcases towards the exit. Outside, in the dazzling light, I blink my eyes. In front of the station, about twenty hotel porters are waiting to get hold of the new arrivals. They rush at me and surround me. Mechanically, I read the hotel names on their more or less dirty caps with cracked or slit visors. I choose one at random: California, without any particular reason, but that it must be a fine country, California!

My luggage is hoisted onto a shattered bus, already full of people, and we start. I should have preferred to take a taxi, but nobody seems to ask for my wishes. I am disembarked as automatically as I have been embarked. My luggage is disappearing in the entrance and, scared to lose them, I hurry behind. On the prospectus which has been thrust into my hand a few moments before, the Hotel California is represented as a huge six-story building. I recognize the house on the photo, but the Hotel California occupies a single floor of it.

I have succeeded in joining my suitcases in the elevator and we land together on the third floor. There is no one behind the desk at the reception. The porter, after having carelessly discharged my luggage on the floor and mopped his face and nape with a filthy handkerchief, starts to scream at the top of his voice. "He! Boss. He! A cus-tomer!"

A door opens letting in a whiff of kitchen smell, and a fat man, in short sleeves and loose suspenders, appears on the threshold. "Ha, Senorita! Que tal?" He stops. His round and jolly face inspects me; then a merry laugh shakes his double chin, extends to his shoulders, spreads out over his enormous stomach, goes down along his short legs to his flat feet, until all his opulent form is shaking. "Una estrangera! Una estrangera!"[3]

I don't see any reason for his mirth. "I'd like a room," I tell him.

"French?"

"A French room?"

"No. You. You are French?"

"Oh! Yes. Yes, I'm French."

"Where do you come from?"

"From Paris."

"From Paris! Santa Madre de Dio![4] From Paris! Across the mountains?"

"Do you have a room, yes or no?"

"Oh! A room," he says, a little disappointed. "Wait." He looks at the hotel book. "There will be one free at 3 o'clock. In the meantime, if you wish to rest, I'll put you in a double room."

I'm able to change and to have a wash. Then I ask for a pack of envelopes, get all the letters out of my book, seal and address them, then return to the office to ask some stamps. There are a few people in the hall. I don't pay much attention to them. I wait for my stamps.

From the adjoining dining-room come scraps of conversation, in French, Dutch, Polish and something I presume to be Luxembourgian. Outside the heat is stifling. I go down with Babs to post my letters. I enter a "parfumeria" to get a cake of soap. It seems so light and smells so nicely. Real soap! It's almost incredible to think that for three years one washes, in France, with a "compound of kaolin and goodness knows what, which leaves the hands as black as they were, in addition, to a whitish deposit.

On my way back, I see in the window of a brasserie a roll of small hors d'oeuvre plates. Some of them contain salted almonds, others fish with mayonnaise, roasted hazel-nuts, an assortment of slices of sausage, of pink shrimps. Shrimps! I haven't seen any since the war! I go in, order a beer and shrimps. The waiter pushes towards me a saucer with eight large "bouquets." They look firm and well cooked. The carapace is shiny, hard and transparent. Three years since I saw some! I eat one, another, a third one and begin a fourth, but cannot get through it. It suddenly seems to me my stomach has shrunk. I can hardly swallow anything.

I go back to the hotel, have a bath with a profusion of soap, for the delight of seeing it lather! About 6:00 I go down, walk into a café, enter a telephone booth and dial 51242. At the third summons,[5] a woman's voice answers.

"Monsieur Miret, please," I say.

"Comme?" returns the voice.

I don't speak Spanish. Nevertheless I try: "Senor Miret."

The woman seems to have understood. The voice replies something that must mean: "Wait," or "Hold the line," or "One moment." I hear the shallow sound of the receiver being put down. A silence. I wait. At the other end steps are approaching, someone takes up the receiver, and a man's voice says: "Hello?"

"Senor Miret?"

"Si! Estoy yo. Quen habla?"[6]

"Here 'Canuto,'" I say, without understanding what he tells me. "Canuto!"

"Si! Si! Muy bien! Address? Address? Telephone?"[7]

"Moustache" could at least have chosen someone with whom I could talk! I tell Miret the name of the hotel and the telephone number. He says, "Muy bien," which I understand, something more which I don't understand; then "Adios," which I understand very well as I hang up.

The main thing is done. I have warned [them] of my arrival. I can now go home and to bed. In the hall of my hotel I make the acquaintance of another Belgian pair. The man's arm is in plaster; he had a fall when crossing the Pyreneans. The Polish doctor invites me to his table. We are finishing dinner when the proprietor comes for me: "Someone to see you."

"Me?"

"Yes, I suppose so. He gave a description of you and said you arrived this morning. It's a young man. He gave another name—Canuto—but I presume it's you he wants to see."

"It's a nickname my friends give me," I say, smiling. And I think to myself: "What a fool!" A young man is actually awaiting me in what is supposed to be the drawing-room. I hesitate. He comes towards me: "Miss Canuto?"

"Yes."

"My friend Miret told me you had arrived. I have come to inquire if you didn't need anything."

"Thank you. I've got all I need. It was just to let my friends know that I was alive and where I could be found." And I add in a lower tone: "Don't come again—and don't call me Canuto."

"Ah! Excuse me."

"Good bye. I'll let you know if I want to meet you in town."

He goes. "In fact," I wonder, "how easily it could have been a trap! Canuto—Miret, and the address have been said on the telephone. What do I know about the man to whom I've just spoken?" Madrid appears to me suddenly as a place full of ambushes, intrigues, a place where all are plotting, betraying, bribing and selling themselves. What so far appeared to me as extraordinarily easy, now seems to be full of difficulties. Without returning to the dining-room, I go up to my room and go to bed. It's long before I can go to sleep. The Gran Via, which passes under my windows, is noisy, and the traffic doesn't seem to subside during the night. The heat is stifling.

JUNE 26TH

Nevertheless I have slept soundly being tired. Babs must have caught flees, as I have been stung. I begin the day by writing letters: to my cousin in Cambridge; to my Bristol friends; to Mummy, which I will send "via La Ciotat." Then I begin to ponder about the best course to take. I decide that the first thing to do is to write to Pep, in Algiers, asking him for his advice. He might tell me whom to see. Because I haven't the least intention of going from consulate to Embassies telling my "little story." I want to know exactly where to go to. If Pep cannot help me, the second step will be to call upon Jacques Roberti's friends.

So I write a letter to Pep. But at the post office I am told there are no postal communications with Algeria. I return to the hotel, write a second letter to Mere Catherine and ask her to forward the one addressed to Pep. Mere Catherine lives in Portugal; and from Portugal one can correspond with Algiers. I return to the post office. This time they take my letter.

Sunday June 27th 1943

The Museum of the Prado opens at 8:30 a.m. I am early and walk without aim in the neighbouring streets. It is very hot. For the three days I've been in Madrid, I haven't undertaken anything, haven't decided anything. I feel rather unsettled. I try not to think about what I'm going to do and wait for answers to my letters. Should there be nothing but the Prado in Spain, Spain would be worth while visiting. I spend a whole morning among the Goyas and Grecos, forgetting all worries, preoccupations and uncertainties. I believe that to understand a painter, one has to see him in his birth country. I don't know yet if I like El Greco; he surprises me and makes me shy. I plan to return to the Prado every morning.

To-night at dinner I have seen again the Belgian Jew with the smallpoxed face. We have chatted after the meal. "If you have letters to be sent rapidly to England, I know someone who could have them sent by the diplomatic bag," he proposes.

"An Englishman?"

"No, a Belgian. Someone very highly placed who works with the British and the American."

I thank him and tell him that I will have something to send tomorrow or the day after. I have already written to my cousin Bessie but I decide to send her another letter with full details. I don't know anything about this Belgian but I say to myself that, should he work for the Germans, these letters will show that I try to go over to England and explain how I left France, all this according to what we had decided. If my letter comes into the hand of the British (of which I have not the slightest doubt, if the fellow tries to pass it through the mail), I hope to draw their attention, perhaps to be summoned by them in order to give some explanations and get in this way in contact with the right people. My reasoning might be wrong; nevertheless, I want to try it.

I have been awakened during the night by Babs' frantic jumps. I have put on the light and found my bed covered with bugs. I'm looking for another hotel.

I do what, I presume, every "good dissident" Frenchman arriving from France to Spain would do. I present myself to Monsieur Durand at the rua San Bernardo. "San Bernardo," as it is usually called, bears the official name of French Red Cross but is in reality the consulate of Free France. San Bernardo works in close touch with the British and American Embassies. It's at San Bernardo where one enrolls for the de Gaulle army, makes the necessary steps for the liberation of French prisoners from the Spanish concentration camps. San Bernardo gives subsidies to those escaped from France, pays their hotel bills and helps them with their clothes. San Bernardo makes investigations and keeps index cards.

The waiting rooms of San Bernardo are crowded with Frenchmen whose heads have been shaved clean during their detention. By the length of their hair one can approximately say how long they have been out of Miranda or Pampa Luna. A few women but mostly men. They all wear Basque caps and black bathing shoes, because these are included in the equipment San Bernardo gives them.

Among them I'm a little conspicuous: I don't have the shabby look of those who have passed the Pyreneans on foot. I am stared at. I hear whispering. Everyone is suspicious of everybody. I have asked to see Monsieur Durand, because I have been told it was Monsieur Durand one was to see, Monsieur Durand being the chief after the "Colonel." After waiting for half an hour, I am received by Monsieur Durand in a very large room with several other desks with secretaries, files, filing-cabinets and everything one expects in a perfect organization. M. Durand's desk is a little larger than the others. His arm chair also is a little higher, a little wider. I couldn't have known otherwise that M. Durand was M. Durand.

He's a man who is young, has auburn hair, doesn't look sleepy, isn't rough and doesn't make you feel as if you were a fly on his soup. He smiles at me and shows me a chair. I give him my passport, tell him how I have come, that I want to go to England, and ask him what I am to do. He looks at my visas, seems to find everything very natural, isn't in the least surprised, doesn't ask me anything but the address of my hotel and advises me to go directly to the British consulate, giving me its address.

I find myself in the street, entirely satisfied with my interview, because it has lasted but three quarters of an hour and that, in short, I've got the address of the British consulate, which will save me a search in the telephone book.

—m—

Tuesday, June 29th

I have given to the Belgian a letter for my cousin in Cambridge and have at the same time decided to act contrary to Kliemann's instruction, i.e. to begin my "official" steps in Madrid. The fact is that to go to the British consulate with a legal aim and in an open way will facilitate my meeting the English when I shall have to see them with different objects.

First thing to do: warn Kliemann of my decision. I shut myself up in my hotel room, get my pills, pen and lighter, take down the mirror over the wash-stand and set at the task of writing him two letters. The first one is a love letter from a would-be fiancé of Annick's, which I write pulling out my tongue and trying not to think about the bugs, the existence of which I have just remembered. As it's a letter which will to go through the censure, a letter in which I cannot say anything more important than words of love, I have to be content with one page, which is about all I can squeeze out of my imagination today. I prepare an envelope and address it to Mr. H. M., 3 Boulevard Fernand Gassion, La Ciotat (Bouches de Rhone) France.

For the second I imagine the writer as a girl of fifteen—a little country girl; she writes to her "auntie," awkward sentences, a clumsy handwriting, of which I carefully draw up the slightly trembling lines; questions and answers without any punctuation; full of familiar and a little ridiculous diminutives. The general meaning of the letter is: "One eats well; one is in a fine hotel; there are oranges and bananas; I've got shoes with leather soles, etc., etc." I'm pleased with my achievement. I sign: "Your little Jeanette." I shall keep the personage of Jeanette for other letters sent by the same way—Miguel Ottonde, the guide.

Having finished my two texts in clear, I dissolve one of the pills, agglutinate it on a tooth-pick and compose my message in secret ink across the two pages. It says: "Have arrived safely Stop Miret warned stop Contacted your agent stop on account of present circumstances have decided beginning steps in Madrid stop Will keep you informed. Signed Solange." I seal both letters, put one under double envelope and go out to post them. That's done!

Then I go to the French Vichy Embassy and ask for Monsieur Corre. He is on leave and will not be back before a week. I go back to my hotel, find the United States Embassy in the telephone book and ring it up. When I'm through, I ask for Colonel Stevens.

"Who are you?" inquires a voice.

"A friend of Jacques Roberti's whom he knows well. I come from France."

"One moment, please," says the voice. I hear muttering after which the voice resumes: "He isn't here. You'll find him at 31 Almagro."

"Thank you," I say and hang up.

—m—

Wednesday, June 30th

I find no difficulty in finding the Boulevard Amagro and the number 31. I ask for Colonel Stevens. I'm asked to fill in a form and to wait in the entrance. The walls are decorated with posters representing American planes. I recognize almost all of them and, mechanically, start to make their description as Graf taught me to do. Other people are waiting. At last it's my turn.

A very tall man with grey hair asks me to go in and introduces himself: "Colonel Stevens." I hand him Jacques Roberti's card. He turns it over, but there is nothing written on it. I tell him I've seen Jacques a short time ago, that he sends his best regards, etc. Colonel Stevens seems to wait for something more but, as it's all, he asks me a few questions about France, about how I left Paris. He looks surprised. His eyebrows are lifted high on his forehead which he wrinkles, but he doesn't say anything. He also asks me if I didn't notice anything interesting along the Pyrenean border. He stills examines Jacques's card. He certainly asks himself why Jacques has sent me to him. At last, as I am taking leave, he says: "You don't need anything? Is there anything I can do for you?"

"Thank you. Nothing for the present. Later, perhaps. I don't know."

He seems to be wondering. I leave him. I'll wait for a few more days, and if in a week's time I have received no answers, I'll speak to him.

I return to the Prado. Before going home for dinner, I sit down at the terrace of a café. I hesitate what to order. Next to me, a fat and much painted woman eats an ice with whipped cream (that won't improve her figure!). A man who must have returned to childhood—some long time ago!—drinks a large glass of milk through a straw. I think of our people who are deprived of all this—not enough milk for the children, not enough bread for the old ones—enough of nothing for the rest. And again I am overwhelmed with bitterness. Here, in this country of sunshine and laughter, everything hurts me, shocks me: the sounds of an orchestra coming from a café, the abundance of fruit in the shops, the profusion of wares in the show-windows—and above all the general carelessness. I try to be fair, to tell myself that they also have had their civil war and that we didn't stop laughing while they suffered and killed each other. Everyone in turn! But this thought doesn't comfort me.

I order a lemon squash and regret it immediately, because I remember that, in Paris, a lemon cost 75 francs on the black market. I thought I would be happy to be in a free country, a country where one doesn't at every moment fear an air raid, where one doesn't hear the sirens, where there is no curfew, and where the heavy step of patrols doesn't resound at every hour of the night. What an irony! One has only to look at these faces of Belgians, Frenchmen, Dutchmen, Poles, at these frightened glances, these bitter mouths, these mistrustful looks of being accustomed to be watched, to live guardedly, hunted, uncertain of the morrow. My fate has been a better one than theirs, but defeat, invasion, occupation have marked us in the same way, have equally bruised us, and the contact of normal life is a shock more than a joy, hurts more than it does good.

I pass my hand over Babs' rough hair. He sits very still on a chair near me and looks at me with his amber eyes, the corners of his mouth seeming to lift in a smile. He pulls out a long pink tongue; it's hot. I smile at him and feel less lonely.

—⚏—

July 2nd 1943

Returned to "Monsieur Durand" to ask him the address of a hotel, having so far had no luck in my search. The hotels in Madrid are full of refugees, and I have no wish to live at the Ritz or at the Palace. So far I haven't been bothered. My papers are in order and nobody seems to have the slightest interest in me. Monsieur Durand (How I love this name! It's such a change after the Monsieur Pierre, Monsieur Paul, Monsieur Andre!) Mr. Durand, as I was saying, receives me cordially, asks me amiably about the progress of my walks and gives me an address: Pension Argentina, Jose Antonio 62. I run, I fly there. I am told there will be a room to-night, and the landlady assures me there are no bugs. She shows me the room which I like, and I reserve it: 30 pesetas a day for the full board.

From there I go to the British consulate. I'm shown to the passport section. I say I want to go to England. A fair young girl gives me a form to be filled in. I do it—both sides. There is nothing very complicated about it. The blonde young girl tells me I'll be advised, and I leave.

Tonight I move. Babs is happy. I am happy. Everything is for the best.

July 15th

Back at the boarding-house, I ring up my former hotel to ask if there is any mail. They have nothing. Good. There is nothing left for me then to go to Stevens tomorrow. Since I have decided doing it, I feel better. I was worried by it! I telephone to the Boulevard Almagro and fix an appointment.

I then tear off my writing pad the two sheets of paper on which I have written in lemon juice the German instructions. I hope they are the right ones, as one cannot see anything. I fold them and put them into an envelope, and seal it after having added two of the five remaining pills. Everything is ready now for tomorrow.

July 16th

I was long going to sleep last night. I have thought over and over again about what I would say. I have prepared sentences, which none seemed to be right. I have tried to imagine this interview, and there was always something wrong! Then I went to sleep and had foolish dreams.

Now, wide awake, ready a long time in advance, I await the moment to go out. I still don't know how I will begin. I don't want to think about it. The distance to the Boulevard Almagro seems too short. I confess: I am nervous. In the entrance the furniture is the same, and on the walls are the same posters representing the same planes. The people who are waiting are different. I tell myself that it's today Mummy's birthday and try to imagine what she is doing.

The door of the left office opens and makes me start. Colonel Stevens appears and beckons to someone to enter. Then he sees me, comes over and says: "I am very busy today. Couldn't you see my wife? She'll attend to you."

I shake my head: "No," I say. "It's you I want to see."

He seems annoyed by my insistence. "What is it about?"

"Military information."

"Ah! Good. Can you wait for half an hour?"

I agree. He returns for me after twenty minutes. Having shown me a chair, he resumes his seat in the armchair behind his desk, picks up a paper knife and looks at me. He doesn't say "Well?" or "What is it?" or "I listen…" He says none of the little sentences which help one to begin. He doesn't say anything. I also look at him. Then I say: "I am sent by the Germans."

It hasn't been as difficult as I expected. Stevens nods ever so slightly, as if it were quite natural, and I continue: "I have received the mission to go to England. When I will have obtained my visa, I will receive a camouflaged transmission radio. I must also meet, either in Madrid, or in Lisbon, my chief, Major Kliemann. Until then, I am to inform him of my activities by messages in secret ink, or through one of their agents." I open the envelope I have brought with me: "Here are the first instructions I have received. They are written with lemon juice. And here are the pills which serve for the secret writing."

"Does Roberti know about it?"

"No. I don't know him, I told you. I have met him at my friends a few days before I left."

Stevens looks at the two pink pills and at the sheets of white paper, pondering. He lifts slowly his eyes, looks at me searchingly, and lowers them again on the sheets. At last he lifts his head and asks: "What organization do you belong to?"

"None."

It doesn't seem to surprise him. "Who is your chief?"

"I haven't any—unless you consider Kliemann."

"No. But who has introduced you to the Germans?"

"Nobody. I did it myself." In a few words, the least possible, I tell him about my first meeting with Dassel and how, by and by, I have come to Kliemann. When one overlooks the two and a half years of waiting, it appears very simple: a child's game. When I have finished, Stevens drops the paper knife, leans back in his armchair and asks: "You came to see me two weeks ago. Why didn't you speak then?"

"I have written to one of my friends in Algiers. He knows about what I am doing. I asked for his advice, because I didn't know to whom I could apply here. I waited for his answer—but I didn't get it."

"And how do you know I was the one to apply to?"

"I don't know it. I simply think you could tell me what I am to do."

"Good. I'm sorry you have waited so long. Nevertheless, let us see what we must do. According to your mission, your work concerns more the British than ourselves. I will inform them and you will hear from them, probably tomorrow. By the way, where do you live?"

"At the Pension Argentina, Avenue Jose Antonia. There is a telephone but I don't remember the number."

"They'll find it. Now something else: the telephones are not reliable. How can they tell you they want to see you and fix an appointment without provoking any suspicion should anyone overhear you?"

"I have made an application for a visa at the British Consulate. It is quite official; there is nothing secret about it. If I am called from the passport department and told there is information missing on my form, I can very easily return there to fill in the blank, don't you think so?"

"O.K. You can then expect to get a telephone call concerning your visa."

I get up. "Thank you."

When Colonel Stevens stands up, he seems to unfold himself. He is very tall. He doesn't smile easily. "Good luck," he says, accompanying me to the door.

We find ourselves in the street again, Babs and I. Babs is happy—not as happy as I am! What was it I was so afraid of, after all? I believe I expected Stevens to burst out laughing when I told him: "I am sent by the Germans."

III. Madrid, 1943

July 17th

I'm waiting for my telephone call. It comes at 10:30. "Benton, here," says a man's voice in English. "Benton, from the passport department of the British Consulate. You have made an application for a visa, giving as reference a cousin who lives in England. We would like to have some complementary information. Could you come round this morning?"

"All right. I will be there in an hour." I ring off and return to my room. Babs jumps on an armchair, takes his collar from the table and brings it me. "You're never wrong, you! You always guess when we're going out!" He stamps his stiff paws and looks expressively at the door.

"Mr. Benton," I tell the guard at the door. He pushes a slip towards me to fill in.

"The object?" he says, seeing I have left a blank line.

"I have an appointment."

"Oh! All right. Kindly wait in the next room."

In the waiting room I pick up an English magazine and mechanically turn the leaves over. The same blonde young girl as last time throws an indifferent glance at me above the partition that divides the room and resumes her typing. The door opens and the office boy beckons to me. I cross the entrance behind him and follow him through a passage. At the end, to the left, he pushes a door and holds it open for me. A man rises as I enter. He comes towards me, hand outstretched, and introduces himself: "Benton."

Then he shows me to a chair with a cracking wicker back. He is young, tall, slim, auburn, has a narrow, long head, a straight brow with hair beginning to get thin foreboding a precocious baldness. He is a typical sample of "the Englishman as one draws him." He moves a bundle of papers on his desk, and his fingers are long and dry, with well apparent articulations. Then he turns towards me, and his eyes show dark brown. He refers to his notes: "If what I have understood is correct," he begins, "one of your friends, Mr. Roberti, has introduced you as an information agent for the Germans, who made you go through a course of radio training, after which Vichy has sent you to Madrid."

I smile: "No you didn't understand at all! Mr. Roberti has nothing to do with the question. He is a friend of Colonel Stevens and there his participation ends. Neither has Vichy anything to do in the story. But maybe in would be simpler if I told you everything from the beginning."

"I believe it would be better. I'll take notes."

For the second time I begin my story, but giving fuller details today. Benton makes a summary of it, writes down notes, and several times asks me to repeat things. The time passes. The Consulate must be closed; it's Saturday. At last he gathers the scattered leafs. "It's better that you shouldn't remain any longer. I would like to see you again on Monday." And he adds: "It naturally interests me enormously. We shall be obliged to control your savings.[8] If they are exact, I can tell you that you have done very good work. For the moment: be careful." Benton ponders, "O.K. But I should like you not to communicate with the Germans anymore without letting me know beforehand. It would be better."

"All right."

He accompanies me to the stairs. The offices are closed and the hall empty. He bends down and pats Babs on the back. "He's nice," says Benton.

"Yes," I reply. "He's my mascot; he never leaves me."

Monday, July 19th

"I want a few precisions,"[9] says Benton this morning, looking over the notes he took Saturday. "Firstly, I would like to know the contents of the letters you have written to your cousin in Cambridge."

"I have tried to ask her to warn your Services. I thought you would find the means to contact me and direct my work. We might have done more. Unfortunately, I only used the ordinary post to write her. I couldn't therefore explain everything very clearly. I told her I had been invited by the owners of the place where we had spent a summer together. The only summer we ever spent together was during a voyage in Czech-Slovakia, and the new owners of Czech-Slovakia are the Germans. I thought she would understand.

"I told her the new owners had offered me an interesting job; that personally, I didn't want it, but that it might be useful to 'her people.' If Bessie understood the Germans had offered me a very interesting job, she would guess that by 'her people' I didn't mean her family. I ended by telling her that, owing to the disturbances caused by the war, I didn't know how to join her people, I asked her to inform them of my request and that they should contact me.

"As far as I can remember, I have sent three letters. One through an address someone had given me: one of these addresses where you have to use a double envelope and a 5 franc note. Another one through a friend going to Vichy and who was to post it in the free zone. I sent off the third one myself from Marseille. I never got any answer. I don't know if these letters ever reached their destination."

"This will be checked. And, before I forget, what is to be done with the two white sheets of paper you gave me? I forget to ask you about it last time."

"Iron them. It's lemon juice."

"Iron them?"

"Yes, with a hot iron."

"Ah. All right. Then I would like to know what you have written Killburg[10] since you arrived in Madrid." I tell him. "What do you intend doing now?"

"If I had to decide about the next step, I would telephone Miret and meet the German agent. I would hand him a letter, in clear, for Kliemann, or Killburg if you prefer. In this letter I would show myself slightly distracted. I would say that, having started the formalities in order to obtain my visa, I foresee a close interrogation, and there are missing links in my story: the name of the person who introduced me to the Hotel Matignon and how I made his acquaintance. In other words: two names instead of those of Yvonne Delidaise and Genty. Because Kliemann will never be willing that I should mention these. I would insist on the urgency of my letter and will convey to the German that I might be questioned by your Services at any time, in which case I won't be able to give any explanation.

"And I'll tell you why I would do all this: first to cover myself. It is possible I might be watched, shadowed, although I didn't notice anything, in which case they would notice my frequent visits to your Consulate. I would stop their suspicions by being the first one to speak about coming here and saying why. Also to rouse Kliemann, oblige him to answer, to establish a contact, and see how rapidly he reacts. And last, being distracted, panicky, would be logical in my case."

Benton smiles. "Not bad. Have you ever before worked in this profession?"

"No, but don't forget I have been acting in a play for the last two and a half years."

"I think your plan good, but it must have the approval of my chief. I therefore will ask you to do nothing until tomorrow. Ring me up before noon. Ask me if we have sent the telegram to your cousin, or not. According to my answer, i.e. if I say yes or no, you will know if you must act, or wait. If there were anything to change about your plan of action, I would tell you your text isn't clear, and you would return to see me. But I don't believe it will be necessary. Don't call upon me before having obtained a result, or at least unless you have something very urgent to tell me. On our side, we will proceed with the verifications."

―⚹―

JULY 20TH

"Yes, your cable has been sent," I hear Benton's voice on the line.

"Thank you, sir." I ring off. Then from the same telephone booth, I dial another number: 51.242. With the help of a dictionary, I have prepared a sentence: "Want to see your friend tomorrow at 11. At the Café Lys." It doesn't sound very grammatical, but who bothers about grammar! A man's voice answer almost immediately. I ask for Monsieur Miret. It's he. I say "Canuto," then, very carefully, I repeat my little sentence. It's surprising. He has understood.

He says: "Muy bien, muy bien: manana a las onze, a Lys."[11] It sounds almost French.

I go home and write "Moustache" a letter on four pages. I explain to him that I have made the decision to begin the formalities for my British visa in Madrid, because it's the usual thing to do, and the most logical way of proceeding. That I have already been summoned twice: the first time to give details about my nursing studies. (In my application I expressed a wish to do nursing work in England.) And the second time to explain my journey in Syria. "One has the impression," I write to Kliemann, "that my bicycle trip puzzles them very much, and they seem to attach a great importance to the year I spent in Beyrouth." Then I ask him urgently to send me a name I can give instead of Genty's, and some tale to explain how I made his acquaintance. Also to tell me the rate of the escudos on the black market in Paris, as I am supposed to have gotten them in this way. I insist repeatedly on the urgency of the reply I expect from Kliemann. I appear positively distracted! I sign: Solange.

―⚹―

JULY 21ST

I arrive much in advance at the "Lys," because I have nothing to do and not time enough to go to the Prado before my appointment. I often come here when I have nothing to do. The "Lys" is situated towards the end of the Gran Via. There is only one range of tables on the terrace and one sits on very comfortable settees. I like to watch people pass, a lemon squash in front of me, and a saucer full of salted almonds on the table. People walk past like manikins and are most heteroclite. Many foreigners. One can immediately recognize the Germans by their stiffness. They have got used to the uniform and still seem to wear it. A few Englishmen pass also; their stiffness is due to the British phlegm. It's a different stiffness and seems to say: "never show your feelings." The Frenchmen passing on and off are not stiff; they walk, dragging their feet, wear espadrilles, and turn from side to side their heads covered with Basque berets. They are "at liberty," without money and without work. So they have nothing else to do: walking without aim, looking at the show windows and staring at people.

The Americans wear too wide brimmed hats—reminds one of cowboys. American women have feathers on their hats. Spanish "society" women never walk; they drive in cars and are nearly always overdressed. They seem to have a preference for black, velvet and satin; lots of showy jewels, real or sham. But those one sees most are women of lower classes, poorly, very poorly dressed. Almost the whole of the Spanish population, men and women, wear espadrilles. It is probably because a pair of shoes costs 80 pesetas and that Julia, the maid of the Pension Argentina, who works from 7 in the morning until midnight, only earns 60 pesetas a month. Poverty among the people seems to be extreme. Groups of urchins, of four to eight years, in rags and tatters, barefoot, follow you in the streets, begging. They stop before the café terraces and if they meet your gaze and you don't drive them away, they hold out their hand and say: "Senora, give me an almond."

But this morning I'm not on the terrace and no little beggar asks me anything. I've chosen for my appointment a secluded corner. There are few people about. Absent-mindedly, I push the slice of lemon down to the bottom of the glass with a straw, and try to keep it there. As soon as I let it go, it returns to the surface. The sugar forms under the water an opaque mass which doesn't seem to melt. I sum up the events of these last days. I have the impression of having connected both ends, and having made a strong knot between them: the English side, the German side. They fit. If I don't blunder, if I do nothing imprudent, if Kliemann's people discover nothing, then I will have realized my programme, I will have executed, one by one, all the details of the plan so carefully established three years ago! I wonder if Bessie has received at least one of my three letters. Benton said it would be checked. I'm not worried about that having a clear conscience.

"Good morning, Miss Solange."

"Hello! Good morning. I didn't hear you coming."

Miret's friend sits down next to me. "You were absorbed by your lemon juice. How about going somewhere else? I know many people coming to this café. I would prefer that we should not be seen together."

"Let us go elsewhere. I don't mind. I had chosen the "Lys" because I don't know Madrid, don't speak Spanish, and find it difficult to talk with Monsieur Miret."

"I understand." He calls the waiter, pays for my lemon squash and we go out. Dressed in a brown suit, a light-coloured shirt, bare-headed, he has lost the "gloomy" appearance he had on our first meeting, when a loose rain-coat and a grey felt hat hiding the upper part of his face would have obliged a new born baby to look round in its cot! "My car is round the corner in the next street."

We get in. I note the type and the registration number. Before me, a brass plate bears the name and address of the owner: I read: "H. von Buch." The rest is indistinct. My companion takes me to a fashionable bar, completely deserted, in the _____. The tables are low. One sits in deep leather armchairs. It is dark. I have to give up my perpetual lemon or orange juice; the spot requires spirits. I order a port. "There," I say, holding forth the letter written yesterday. "It must be forwarded, as quickly as possible, to Major Klie-mann. How many days will it to get an answer? It's very urgent."

"Your letter will leave tomorrow by the diplomatic bag, which means that the Major will have it the day after tomorrow. If he replies immediately, he will be able to send off his letter on the next day and it should be here in four days counting from tomorrow. Let us say five days."

"It's too much. What can be done to gain time?"

"Send a message by radio."

"No, it would be too long to explain. It's better he should get my letter with all the details. But you could ask him to cable his answer."

"All right, it will be done. Shall we meet here again in two days?"

"Very well. At 6 o'clock?"

"That's perfect."

I decide it will be better not to wait for two days to give the description, the number of the car and the name of its owner to Benton. I therefore return to the British Consulate immediately after lunch.

"What is the news?" asks Benton introducing [bringing] me into his office.

"Just this," and I pass on the information.

"Von Buch?" he says. "Hmm. Do you believe it was he?"

"I didn't say that. It's the name which was on the car. It may not have been his."

"It's very possible. Try to learn more about this guy and let me know as soon as you have something."

July 22nd 1943

The Pension Argentina has five rooms to let. Three have a view on the street; the two others are just nooks. Apart a young French dancer who came with an opera group from Monaco, or Monte Carlo, a year ago, the rest of the lodgers change constantly. The large room next to mine has been successively occupied by a German attaché, then by two Frenchmen, now by Belgians: mother and daughter. In one of the "nooks" lives an elderly Frenchwoman returning to France after having come from Algiers. She has taken the [appearance] of an old peevish asthmatic. In the "nook" opposite, a blonde young Frenchwoman, Madame Cooper, cries and sighs, and shows me every day the waist of her skirt becoming looser and looser. She awaits her husband who is still at Miranda. "The claquette dancer" as I have nicknamed the "perpetual lodger," who is out of work, has resolved the lodging and payment problem by becoming the patronne's boy friend. This one also has found a way to lose nothing on the price of her room, to keep her beau and to help him. She knows Mr. Durand. The Red Cross pays for the room, pays for the last year a small allocation to the workless dancer, and everybody is satisfied.

I have asked the "perpetual lodger," "Have you no wish to join the de Gaulle army? You are young, healthy."

"And not a fool!" he completes for me. "Why should I poke myself in this bear-garden when I can live here peacefully?" Perhaps he's wise.

The landlady is a well eyed brunette. She owns 39, forgetting the rest, which must have been long! She sometimes come to see me, sits down in an armchair, against the light and starts to tittle-tattle about the other lodgers. I listen in silence, because I don't know very well how to put people out. When she leaves my room, I know she will go elsewhere telling the same things about me. If one adds to it an abominable and insufficient food (the maid told me our meals amounted to 3 pesetas 30 per day and per person), served in the rooms because there is no dining-room, one can have rough idea of the Pension Argentina.

Since two days, I have Spanish lessons. The hair of my professor is jet-black and carefully smoothed with brillantine. He is thin and dry, with a swarthy, olive-tinted face, a large mouth adorned with long teeth, and he wears glasses set in imitation tortoiseshell. He is a republican and hates the actual form of government. He teaches me grammar and in the evening, when I'm alone, I read a Spanish novel. I don't understand much, but go on stubbornly. I want to know enough Spanish to understand Miret on the telephone! My teacher comes every day for one hour.

July 23rd

The German isn't there yet. It's not quite 6 o'clock. I take out my Spanish book and continue the novel. Every now and then I lose the thread of the story, because I'm reading without a dictionary and don't understand three quarters of the words; the last quarter I guess, and even that mostly wrong. I lift the eyes just as the door is opening. Today he is in grey. He walks directly towards my table, sits down opposite me and says: "Still nothing."

July 24th

"Again nothing," he says, arriving.

This time I seem really upset. "It's absolutely necessary that you should send immediately a radio message asking for an answer. I am summoned to the Consulate on Monday. What shall I answer if I'm questioned? I'll be lost!"

"I'll have the message sent immediately, and will meet you here again tomorrow at 11 o'clock."

July 25th 1943

"Here is the answer," says the German agent as I pull back a chair and sit down. "I haven't brought with me the original text because it was in German. This is the translation."

I take the sheet of paper scribbled in pencil and read: "You have been introduced to the Matignon by a certain Monsieur Perault whose address you ignore and whom you haven't seen anymore. He was introduced to you in a café by Madame Boris. Good luck. Octave." Madame Boris! I think to myself. The Madame Boris of the "Maisonnette," where "Moustache" always used to take his meals.

"Are you satisfied?" asks the German.

"Quite! I won't need to trouble anymore every time I go to see the British. May I keep the sheet of paper to memorize the names? I'll destroy it afterwards."

"Don't lose it!"

I seem relaxed and we remain a while chatting. I don't know in which respect my interlocutor tells me his name: Fingado. "That's not a German name," I remark.

"No. My family comes from Italy. It immigrated to Germany in the time of Luther and adhered to the new doctrine. Since then my ancestors have lived in Germany up to my father who, after his marriage, came to establish himself in Barcelona. I have been brought up in Spain. I only returned to Germany at the advent of the Führer. I joined the Party. In '39, I wanted to enlist in the army but was ordered to remain here. You see, I speak the language perfectly well and can pass for a Spaniard. So they thought, there, that I would be able to render greater services in Madrid."

"Is your first name at least German?"

"If you want: Gerard. But I am called, Spaniard-wise, Gerardo."

"In fact, Gerardo Fingado isn't very German!"

The cable he has transmitted to me seems to have given him confidence. He speaks to me about his childhood, the Nazi Party, of which he is proud to be a member. Before I leave, he gives me his telephone number in case there should be anything urgent. Miret will be absent during a few days. "It'll be my Mother who will answer. Ask for Senor Gerardo. She will be advised and will let me know."

From there I go for lunch to the "Pewca de mar." I feel entitled to a good meal!

MONDAY

"Something new?" asks Benton, pushing towards me always the same groaning wicker armchair.

"Yes." I hold out to him Kliemann's answer to my letter.

"Perault? Do you know this man?"

"No."

"Have you ever heard this name?"

"No, except as the author of fairy tales."

"And this Madame Boris?"

"I know her. She is the owner of a Russian restaurant: La Maisonnette, rue de Passy, in Paris."

"Good. In any case they don't interest us. If Major Killburg has given their names, it means he doesn't intend employing these people. I'll keep this paper. I'll have it analyzed. One never knows. It might give something. Besides there is the handwriting. Do you happen to know how the letter was sent?"

"Yes, by the diplomatic bag; and the answer has been cabled. I've something more for you. The name of the German is not von Buch. He is called Gerardo Fingedo, and here is his telephone number."

"This is perfect. I knew it wouldn't be von Buch; the description didn't correspond. This is likely. By the way, the information we had concerning you is satisfactory. You are all right. I'm entitled to tell you that you can be of considerably aid to us, that, up to now, you have very well managed your work, and that we shall be happy if you agree to work with us."

I feel that I blush stupidly, so much have I longed for this moment! And I can only say: "Thank you. That is what I have wished most."

"So you will be able to get your visa whenever you wish," pursues Benton. "But I think it would be advisable, for likelihood's sake, to extend the delay. I must confess, besides, that [I've] had the authorization to deliver it to you arrived for some time past. London had already advised us when you first came to me with your revelations. They perhaps knew something about you there. Or else, your departure from France seemed to them suspicious and they might have wanted to get hold of you. In any case, the authorization was here on the 10th! I'm glad on your account that you didn't wait to be in Lisbon to speak. The delay wouldn't have been in your favour. And now, what do you intend doing?"

"I thought I might write to Kliemann, inform him of the satisfactory development of my proceedings. Tell him I'm given good hope concerning my visa. Ask him to get ready to come and meet me. This will certainly take him very long, as much as I know about him. After which I might perhaps start to see about my Portuguese visa?"

"Yes, I believe this is a good idea. I would like you not to lose touch with the Fingado. You could perhaps meet some others of their agents. How are you, financially? Do you need money?"

"No. So far, I have enough."

"Nevertheless, ask for some. It will be a pretense to see them again. They expect you to ask for some."

"All right."

"Keep me informed if you have something."

On the point of leaving, I sit down again. "Mr. Benton, I have another request. I have worked for you. I will continue to work for you. I don't ask for any payment in exchange, just a favour. I want to keep Babs with me."

"There is the quarantine."

"That's exactly what makes it a favour: avoid the quarantine. Babs has been vaccinated. I've got his anti-rabic certificate. There is therefore no danger. It's the only reward I ask, but I insist on it."

"All right. I'll see what I can do. I presume it will be easy."

July 29th

Micosia, in Sicily, is taken. Almost the whole of the Spanish lesson is taken by discussing politics with my professor and to rejoice about the Allies' successes.

July 30th 1943

I send "Moustache" two short messages in secret ink, one through Miguel Ottondo, the other one by La Ciotat. Antoine Corre is back at the Vichy Embassy. He welcomes me cordially and says he'll be happy to take care of all my letters to Mummy.

August 3rd 1943

The Russian have taken back Orel and Belgorod, and the British Catalina, in Sicily. Everything seems to go on so well, that I wonder if I'll have time to get to England before the end of the hostilities.

Yesterday, I have telephoned directly to Fingado, and this afternoon I meet him at the "Aquarium." I hand him a letter, written in clear, for "Moustache" in which I explain him that I still have some escudos left, but that I wouldn't like to exchange them all, as it would be entered on my passport, and that it will make it more difficult for me to explain the origin of the notes I'll take over to England. In other words, I ask him for money. I inform Fingado of what I am writing about.

"Do you want us to advance it to you immediately? The Major's answer will take some time, and when we get it and know exactly how much we must give you, we'll simply deduct from it what you will have received."

I am on the point of refusing, when I remember in time Benton's advice, and accept.

"How much do you want? Will 3,000 be enough for the moment?"

"Largely."

He points out to me the café near the Prado and recommends that I take Babs with me. "It won't probably be I who will be there, as it is likely that I'll take the Barcelona train tonight. But the one who will come in my place will recognize you by your little dog."

After parting from Fingado, I go for a stroll in the Retiro Gardens. Evening is setting in, tinting in gold the dust suspended in the air. Babs frolics, barking after the children. I walk on, think that, when the question comes to money, I become absolutely stupid. I cannot even pretend to be interested in it. It's painful to me to ask for some. I find it impossible to discuss conditions. I'm always inclined to refuse, to say I have all I need. I would like to be able to name a figure with assurance, to exact without retort the fixed sum. I should like to be greedy for gain—or at least to be able to pretend it. Just now, it would have been so much better if, instead of answering: "Largely," I had said: "You make me laugh! Why, it would hardly last me three days. I want 15,000." He would have given them to me and would have thought, with envy and respect: "That's somebody!" Whereas now, he must be saying to himself, not without scorn: "Really, she is satisfied with little." But what does it matter, after all! It's long time my indifference in money matter makes them shrug their shoulders and has catalogued me as a "crank to be exploited."

August 4th 1943

Behind the queens,[12] the tables are empty, except one, occupied by a man with grey hair, dressed in grey. As he doesn't make any sign of recognition on seeing me, I sit down a few tables further, open a book and begin reading.

"Mademoiselle Solange?"

I lift my eyes. The unknown man in grey is before me.

"Our friend Gerardo couldn't come. I'm here in his place."

"I know. He has warned me."

The German pulls a chair nearer and sits down. He speaks in a "velvety" way, without the usual Germanic accent. His way of speaking made me think of a cat's gait, choosing the spots where he puts his paws and advancing them then delicately, precautiously. Having told the waiter to bring his glass over, he says: "You understand Spanish?" Just to say something.

"No, I'm studying it."

He waits for the waiter to have regained the bulwark formed by the bar, to put on the table an envelope. His elbow pushes it imperceptibly toward me. "Take it without it being noticed," he says, "and slip it into your bag. It's money."

I do as he tells me without looking at what is in the envelope. I know I don't need to verify; it will always be right.

"Sign," says the man in grey, passing me, between the pages of a notebook, a paper on which is written in German: "Received August 4th 3,000 pesetas." I sign: Solange.

We remain, chatting, for a quarter of an hour. He asks me how I spend my time in Madrid. I tell him I go every morning to the Prado. I notice he has a fairly good artistic culture. He is interested in painting and advises me to visit Toledo "if you like el Greco."

Before we part, I tell him: "I don't know when I will need to see you again, you or your friend. It might be in a few days, in which case I will telephone. Otherwise, let us agree to meet here in a week? I shall in my case have a letter for Paris to give you." We fix an hour, and I go.

August 5th

At the Portuguese Consulate I am told I cannot apply for a Portuguese visa before having the British one. The Portuguese want to be sure it will be a transit and I won't remain on their hands!

August 6th

Return to see Benton, who hands me a paper certifying that the British visa will be granted to me. He presumes that should be enough to allow me to make an application. He questions me about the man in grey, but I can tell him very little. "I don't know his name, and he had no car. I saw him walk away. Have you had an answer concerning Babs?"

"Not yet."

"Mr. Benton, be sure to tell them I won't go without Babs. If my work is important, it is worth the exemption I request. If it isn't worth as much, then it isn't worthwhile for me to go to England. You might think me ridiculous. You think: 'To make such a fuss about a dog!' For you, it's but a dog. For me, it's more than a million Pounds. It's Babs! Tell that to your London people."

"All right," says Benton, smiling. "I don't think that they will refuse it you. You've well earned it."

August 7th 1943

This time, the Portuguese Consulate accepts my application for a visa. I give two photographs, which I have had taken this morning, with Babs on my lap.

"A visa for the little dog also?" asks the Portuguese employee, smiling.

"Or course!"

One has to wait ten days for the answer. I find it long!

August 11th

I meet the man in grey at the same place as last time. I hand him a letter for "Moustache," but cannot discover anything new about him. In my letter, I explain to Kliemann all I've done, how far I have gone with formalities, and enjoin him to be ready to come to meet me, either at Madrid or Lisbon.

"An answer has come concerning you money. We have received the order to give you anything you ask!" He looks at me without concealing his admiration. Kliemann is a good psychologist: he knows I won't take advantage of this full power; he knows this mark of confidence will made a good impression upon their Services at the Embassy; he presumes I'll be flattered. Yes, I am pleased, but not on account of the money: because he is satisfied with the manner in which I have managed, and that he doesn't suspect anything—that is the important point.

"How much do you wish?"

I ponder: "Five Thousand."

"That is all?"

"Yes. I would be apt to spend too much if I had more—and that might make me conspicuous."

"I haven't got the money with me. I expected the sum to be much more important."

We fix an appointment for tomorrow at the Calla de Alcala, near the Plaza de la Independencia, in the dark bar with the large armchairs.

August 12th

In a corner, a couple of lovers, hidden in the dark. A man alone in another armchair. My German in grey isn't there. As I hesitate about what table to choose, the solitary customer rises, bows and shows me the armchair next to him. I don't know him, but that is nothing to surprise me. "Mademoiselle Solange," says the stranger, "our friend has been delayed at the last moment, and I am here on his behalf." Then, bending: "Hello Babs!" he says. Babs sniffs at him, surprised, then looks at me as if saying: "Is it an acquaintance? I don't remember him."

My present interlocutor is of a different standing from the others. His bearing is easy, unconstrained. He seems to be a man of the world. He asks me how I spend my time and if I like Madrid. I feel that sport and dancing interest him more than the museums. He's a man of about 35, with thinning hair, grey eyes and a typically German face, crossed by a scar. As much as I can see, he is tall and has a sportsman's broad shoulders. He talks to me of swimming.

"Are there swimming pools in Madrid?"

"Yes, there are a few. "El lago" is a public swimming pool. I am member of a club who owns a fine one." He shows me his member card, and I see: "Hans von Buch." So the car was his! As he didn't introduce himself, I don't quite see the point of his showing me his card. By mistake, or that I should know his name?

It is only as I am leaving that, picking up my gloves from the table, he hands me an envelope at the same time. Then he says aloud, for indiscreet ears which might overhear him, as he puts a sheet of paper before me and unscrews his pen: "I would be happy if you could put down your address for me."

It's a receipt for 5,000 Pesetas. I sign.

August 17th

The days pass slowly, all more or less alike, all likewise hot. I cannot even leave Madrid, as an unexpected event can happen any time. The best moment, the only steadfast point in these passing hours, are my Spanish lessons. I like to study. To feel that, by degrees, a veil is lifted and something so far unknown becomes familiar. I have experienced the same pleasure when learning Morse, or being taught by Herr Graff. It was something new. I can already easily read Spanish and begin to understand when people are talking. It reminds me of the time, when, as a little girl, I learned to swim.

The Portuguese Consulate has no answer yet about my visa, but the employee thinks it won't take long now.

I have changed the time of my lessons: from 5 to 6. It allows me to go to the swimming pool—not von Buch's one, the other, "El lago"— and to remain there from 11a.m. to 4 p.m. It's the best time. People are having lunch and there is hardly anyone. The rest of the time it's crowded. One drawback only: dogs are not admitted! So, in the morning, I begin by going to the Manzanarez, to allow Babs to have his bath. He loves the water.

At the Portuguese Consulate, still nothing for me. The employee seems surprised. As a rule it doesn't take so long.

August 23rd 1943

The Russians take Kharkov back, but, to me, nothing new happens.

August 24th

"There is something for you," I am told this morning at the Portuguese Consulate. The employee searches through his files: "There. I regret, but Lisbon has refused your visa."

"Refused? Why?"

"I don't know. The Ministry never gives a reason."

"But it wasn't an entry visa: just a transit."

"I know."

"Is it unrevokable? Can I make a second application?"

"You can make one, but I don't think it would be any good."

"Tell me, between ourselves, do you think it could be because I got a passport to leave France?"

The Portuguese shakes his head. "I don't think so. It's more likely to be your native country. You were born in Russia. We are very mistrustful of Russians, because one never quite knows which side they belong to."

"But I've spent my whole life in France! I've been brought up there; I have a French passport."

"You could nevertheless work for the Soviets."

I leave the Consulate. There is nothing that can be done. I look up Benton. On the way there, I think over what the Portuguese told me. How very confused everything is, and how very complicated! I expected to be told that, owing to my birth, Lisbon would suspect me of collaboration with the Germans. And they suspect me of working with the Russians! Yet the Portuguese are pro–Allied. They ought to be pro–Soviets. It appears, it's not so. At that point, I reach Benton and tell him of my vexations.

"I expected it a bit," he says. "The Portuguese are terribly scared of communism. It would be easy for us to get you this visa, but I am afraid it would be known. We mustn't appear too anxious to get you over to England. I believe we will prefer to give you a transit visa via Gibraltar. I'll give you an answer tomorrow, and we shall decide upon the next course."

August 25th

"Yes, my chief is of the opinion to give you a visa for Gibraltar. Now, can you have Kliemann come to Madrid?"

"Yes."

"How will you manage that?"

I take some time before answering. I think of the best way. "Here is what I suggest. I'm going to ring up Miret and ask to see urgently von Buch, or Fingado, or the other fellow in grey. I'll hand him a thoroughly "desperate" letter to Kliemann, whom I will advise that the Portuguese Visa has been refused to me; that I will hand in another application at the British consulate to go via Gibraltar, but that I put off doing it to give him time to arrive. He must come immediately, as we will have no other chance to meet, Lisbon being eliminated. Besides the letter, I will insist that the Embassy should send him a radio message: 'Come urgently.' He won't be here before two weeks—he wouldn't be Kliemann otherwise.

Two days after the first letter, I will send him another one. I'll tell him in it I cannot put off much longer applying for my visa, and will ask when he expects to be able to be here.

"I don't very much count upon an answer. I'll wait for four more days. Then I will tell him, I couldn't delay any more applying for my visa without raising the suspicions of the British. Have been at the British Consulate, have explained the Portuguese refusal, and my request of a visa via Gibraltar has been granted. I had been informed that the ratification from London would take eight to ten days. And I will have a second S.O.S. radio sent, urging him to come. Kliemann will believe I am losing my wits!"

"You don't think he'll find you lose them too much?"

"No. But he'll be anxious to reassure me."

"All right. We'll adopt your plan."

"Something else. Could you have sent to me from London, signed by the name of my cousin, a cable saying: "Have done all necessary obtain visa. Love. Bessie". That will help make them swallow the pill!"

Benton starts laughing: "All right. I see you turn his trick on him."

I am quite surprised to find it so easy explaining to Miret what I want. I fix an appointment with his friend (whichever it is) "at the same place as last time," tomorrow morning at 11.

"Ahora habla Usted espanol," remarks Miret. "Esta muy bien!"[13]

I return to the boarding-house and compose a detailed letter for "Moustache." How well I have learned to lie!

—⁂—

August 26th

It is von Buch who is awaiting me. I take a very distressed air; ask him to send off a message; speak too rapidly; am obliged to begin again.

"What's happening to you?" asks von Buch with concern. "Nothing unpleasant, I hope?"

"No, not yet. But I'm so terribly scared lest the Major should not be here in time, and according all probabilities, I will be obliged to leave via Gibraltar."

"That is, indeed, very serious. But don't be alarmed. We'll send him a message which will make him arrive immediately! So you are leaving? Do you know, it's marvelous! What a success!"

"Wait. I'm not gone yet."

Back home, I lie down on the settee and close my eyes. I begin to feel the nervous strain. This double game, these alternative calls, directly from the ones to the others, this perpetual change of personality, without the slightest respite to become myself again, tire me and wear me out. The slightest noise makes me start. There are times when, in the presence of von Buch, I feel a sudden terror to confuse him with Benton, to allow him to read my thoughts. If he were a clairvoyant or a hypnotizer? It's stupid! I drive these foolish thought away. But they prove to me that my normal balance in unsettled. I get up, take my bathing suit and go for a swim.

The three letters to "Moustache" have gone "according to the pre-established plans," each one denoting a rising anxiety. Each time, it was von Buch who came to the appointment. He tries to calm me, and I pretend to be on the edge of my nerves. I didn't return to see Benton. I want to have some result. In the meanwhile, Taganrog has been taken back by the Russians and over 40,000 Germans have been killed there. The Allies have landed in Italy.

—⁂—

September 9th 1943

I spend my time between swimming, Spanish lessons and spaced meetings with von Buch. Still no sign from "Moustache." What can he be doing? This morning came the cable signed "Bessie," but I know it isn't from her!

September 11th 1943

This morning, the maid Julia came to tell me the "young lady with the little dog" was asked for on the telephone. I guessed it must be someone from the German gang. On the line I recognize von Buch's voice. He says: "It's Miret's friend." I said: "I know." He said: "Will you come and have a cup of tea as last time?" I have accepted. It means: same place, same hour.

I meet him at 5 o'clock. No sooner have we sat down, than he proclaims: "We've had a message from the Major. He is coming."

I give a sigh of relief. "At last! When?"

"He doesn't say."

"Ah!" I am disappointed. For if he doesn't give a date, it can be as well in a week, as in two, or a month. It means strictly nothing. Von Buch promises to inform me if he has anything new, and I leave him.

September 17th 1943

It's amazing how, seen from here, these Allied victories appear less important! No doubt, because one doesn't feel the war around one, under one, over one's head, because one isn't any more in the midst of it, in the very action.

September 19th 1943[14]

I have a telephone call. Something tells me it will be von Buch. And, in fact, it's his voice I hear through the receiver, a jolly voice. "How are you?"

"Fine. Thank you."

"Well, he is here, our dear friend. He wants to see you. Will 2 o'clock suit you?"

"Sure!" And I hang up. "Moustache" is here!

Is it possible that everything happens as it seems: so simply, so very simply! Everything in broad day-light, without any mystery! The British know when I go to the Germans; the Germans know when I go to the British; nobody is suspicious; confidence reigns. Is it going to last? Am I so strong, are they blunderers? I have carefully prepared everything for a long time: answers to all possible questions; explanations to all ambiguous situations! I am ready—ready since two years. But I expected struggle, difficulties, opposition, and I don't meet any! Trust, and everything developing as I had wished but had not dared to hope! And here I am, telling myself: It's too simple to be true. It's an ambush. It isn't possible! Well, very soon, I'll know.

In the darkest corner, in the deepest armchair, it's not von Buch I find—it's "the man in grey." I ease myself on the brown velvet seat of the sofa next to him and say: "Do you know what I have discovered? I love el Greco!"

"I was sure you would, eventually," replies the German. "But it's seldom one starts by that. El Greco doesn't reveal himself easily, and you have to persevere to understand him." Then leaning towards me, he whispers: "We have to wait for the others."

I nod an acknowledgement. Babs, not liking it under the table, climbs on the seat and stretches out full length. Suddenly he pricks up his ears, gives a yelp of pleasure and, bouncing over the low table, dashes to the door. I look up and see "Moustache" accompanied by von Buch. Babs has recognized "Moustache" and whirls and jumps round him. Babs loves "Moustache" and "Moustache" loves Babs. I see Kliemann stop, bend down and take Babs in his arms, and Babs lick his face while he continues to waggle tail and body. I look at them and think: "This is something true. This instant taken alone, apart from the ones preceding it, and the ones following it, is genuine, real, free from falseness. A man and a dog, who don't lie to each other during this short instant, are themselves, independent from the rest of the world."

Kliemann lifts his head and smiles at me. And already I know he is no longer the same one that was tugging Babs a minute ago! The two men come to us. "Moustache" squeezes my hand. Von Buch says: "Don't let's remain here."

Someone pays the bill—I don't know who. I pick up Babs's leash, go round the table, approach "Moustache" and slip my arm under his. "Well?" I ask.

He smiles widely and says with a friendly hug: "You have been wonderful!"

It fills me with deep joy. And I can see myself, three years ago, on a lonely beach, with just a sentry pacing far away. And behind me an olive grove. And above me the mounts of Libabon. And in front of me the sea, and beyond the Future ... and a Dream. This Dream. I have lived it. It's the Present. "Yes," I admit very low, "I have succeeded!"

The "Man in grey" bows to us and discreetly retires. Kliemann, von Buch and I get into the latter's car. "For how long are you here?" I ask Moustache once the car has started.

"I am going back on the 20th."

"Already."

"Unfortunately. But it still gives us three days."

"Not tomorrow morning. I've been summoned to the British consulate; they said I may get my visa next week—perhaps Monday. I would have liked you to be here."

"It'll be wonderful if you get it. I'll see what I can do about staying a bit longer."

I try to guess where von Buch is taking us, but am completely lost. After having followed the Alcala, in the direction of the Gran Via, he has turned to the right on the Plaza de Castello, has taken the Paseo de Calvo Sotale, a large avenue bordered with trees. We have passed in front of something that looks like a stadium. Another turn to the right. After that I lose all sense of orientation. I am sure but of one thing, and that is I never came to this part of Madrid. I try to memorize the names of the streets, but it's practically impossible to watch out for the street signs, to read the names, to remember them, and at the same time to speak with "Moustache," answer his questions, and appear natural.

"What are you looking for?" he asks me once.

"Nothing," I say. "I just thought I had recognized a Belgian, but I was mistaken." Nevertheless, I decide to give up street-reading. "But we are in the country!" I exclaim after a while. "Are we leaving Madrid?"

"No. We have nearly arrived." Saying so, von Buch turns off the avenue, crosses a tramway track and stops in front of a high iron gate. Getting out, he unlocks it and pushes it open. It creaks. Von Buch gets back in the car and we move on. Beyond the gate a steep slope runs up between thick bushes. We come out in the back yard of a villa. A man and a woman, who were sitting in wicker chairs near the threshold, greet us and retire. Probably the housekeeper and his wife. Von Buch leads us into a big living-room with large bay-windows overlooking, through the trees, the avenue by which we have arrived. He leaves us alone. "Moustache" pulls out two armchairs facing each other, and we sit down.

"First of all, I want to hear in detail everything that happened since you arrived to Madrid," says the Major. I start telling him. While I speak, his gaze doesn't leave my eyes. When I come to the narrative of my first visit to the British consulate, he says: "I thought you had been given orders?"

I don't answer immediately. Then I say: "I am going to tell you an anecdote: The Germans have the reputation of always strictly following instructions; they go to the right if an arrow points that way, halt if a sign says "Stop," etc., etc. One day, a Frenchman and a German (it was before the war) were mountain climbing together. They were advancing along a glacier. Suddenly, the Frenchman stopped crying out: "Be careful. There is a precipice in front of you!" The German shrugged his shoulders: "No signs says it," he observed. And he continued advancing, fell in the precipice and killed himself." I look up at "Moustache" to see how he has appreciated my story. He is waiting. "Ought I have done like the German?"

He smiles: "What can I say after your initiative was crowned by success?"

I continue to relate, and it is long, for I spare him no detail. I end by showing him the telegram supposedly from my cousin.

"That's very good," he says. Then he starts laughing: "Do you remember the faked telegram with your aunt's signature I had sent to you? Yes, all that is very funny! "What I want to know now," says Kliemann changing subject, "is why the Portuguese refused the transit. Do they suspect anything?"

"They gave no reason. The employee only told me he thought it was because of my Russian birth."

Kliemann meditates. "I could, of course, get you a visa. We have someone is Lisbon. But I'd rather not go through that channel."

"You don't need to, as I have applied for a transit via Gibraltar."

"And if you don't get it, after all?"

"I don't think so," I say smoothing out the telegram on my knees. "I don't think so. But if it did happen, it would be always time to try your system."

"Moustache" agrees. "Yes, I suppose so."

When I have finished telling him everything, and he has asked all the questions he wanted, he fumbles in his briefcase and brings out a fat envelope. "This is the money. You ought to have enough in there for six months. How much have you still got?"

"Eight thousand escudos."

"Good. If I give you forty or forty-one thousand more, will you be able to explain (in case you have to do it) from where you got them? Perhaps from your Portuguese aunt?"

"Yes. It's feasible."

"Then that's settled. In addition to this money, I've also got these two things for you. (He hands me a solitaire.) "Two carats," he says, "set in platinum. I bought it second hand: 90,000 francs. I don't expect you to get as much for it in England, but even less, it'll be money." The other item is a small old fashioned brooch in the shape of a branch on which five little diamonds represent flowers. "It's not very pretty," remarks "Moustache," "but I took it for the diamonds. It has cost me 12,000 francs."

I put away money, ring and brooch in my bag. The Major passes me a receipt for the money and the jewels (with their description) and I sign. It must be late, for the sun has gone down and it's getting dark. I hear a car changing gears to climb the slope. Five minutes later, von Buch comes in.

"Tonight I am dining at our Embassy," says Kliemann. "I wasn't able to refuse the invitation. I am terribly sorry: I would have rather taken you out somewhere. Maybe tomorrow."

As we leave the room, I notice a wall telephone near the door. Unfortunately, it is too dark for me to see the number marked on the dial.

Von Buch takes us downtown and drops me off at the Plaza de Castello, opposite the post office. We agree to meet tomorrow at twelve, at the Plaza Colon, after my visit to the British consulate. I haven't been able to pick up one single indication that would help me to locate the place where they took me. It makes me furious!

September 18th

10 a.m. I arrive to the British Consulate. Without telling me to wait, the office boy introduces me directly to Benton's office.

"It's some time I haven't seen you! Any news?"

"Yes. Kliemann is in Madrid since yesterday."

"Hey! That's fine! Let's hear about it." He seems anxious to know the details. I tell him about yesterday afternoon, describe the villa, and try to situate it as best I can. "I haven't been able to see the telephone number, but I'll try again today, for we are returning there at 12 p.m."

Benton covers a few pages with notes. "How long is he going to stay?"

"I don't know. He intended leaving on the 20th, but I believe he'll remain longer. He hasn't made up his mind yet."

"Even if he does stay longer, I would like to see you in the meanwhile. Do you think you could manage it? Perhaps the day after tomorrow. But not here. Come to the apartment of my secretary, Miss Molly. If you have to give Kliemann some explanation, tell him she has invited you for tea. I'll be expecting you at 4 p.m. I'll also ask you not to bring with you Babs: one notices you too much with him. So don't forget: the 20th at 4p.m.," he reminds me, escorting me to the door.

I am in time at the Plaza Colon, but von Buch's car is to be seen nowhere. It's not surprising. Kliemann being in it, it's bound to be late! I wait. Passing by women examine curiously Babs, because dogs are scarce in Madrid. Many turn round and stare back for a long while. The younger ones point their finger at Babs and laugh: "Un perrito con una barbadilla! Ha! Ha! Ha!" (A little dog with a beard!) But the old ones are scared; they gather their long skirt round them and step aside as they go by.

At last, at 12:40, I sight von Buch's car, followed by another one. He stops only long enough for me to get in, and starts off immediately. "What is it?" I ask, indicating the car behind us.

"Our 'technicians,'" answers the Major.

We take the same way as yesterday. Here is the Stadium. We turn to the right, then more turnings, and I lose track of the direction. At last I recognize the avenue. I watch the houses and notice yesterday's villa. Now I'm going to pick up the number. The gate is open, but there is no number on it! Both cars, one behind the other, climb up the slope and park in the yard. The place seems deserted. No one is in sight. The guardians have disappeared. Two men alight from the second car. The five of us go into the house. Something is different from yesterday: a table has been brought in, and chairs place round it.

"Gentlemen," says Kliemann, "pray, be seated." He brings me to a chair and sits next to me. I say to myself, it reminds me of a Court. What if they were going to tell me: "We have proofs that you are double crossing us!"—What then? What would I do?—Nothing! There'd be nothing I could do.

"We have decided," starts "Moustache," "to use as means of corresponding with you, the micro-photography. These gentlemen are experts in the matter, and they are going to explain to you under which form the micro-photo presents itself and how to use it. I'll do the translating."

The oldest of the two Germans gives me a detailed lecture. He tells me that they have, at the Embassy, very powerful and perfected apparatus to reduce the photograph of a printed sheet of paper, to the size of a dot, and even much smaller. To read such a micro-photo, one has to fix it on a glass slide and look at it through a microscope. Under naked eye, laid on a piece of white paper, such a micro-photo has the appearance of a black point. The micro-photos are to be sent to me, stuck in a place of the punctuation full stops in short, personal, type-written letters. The German takes a few slides out of a small case he has brought with him. At first sight, they appear blank. He then sets up a microscope, focuses it and tells me to approach. I bend over and look. I have before the eyes—in small size, but very neat—a whole printed page. I can read every word, every letter.

"It's amazing!" I say. The German takes out the slide and hands it to me. I examine it carefully. "I can't see anything," I tell him.

He takes it out of my hands, looks at it a moment in the light, then indicates to the left corner: "Here," he says. Only then, do I notice something so imperceptible that it would never have attracted my attention otherwise. "You'll never have any as minute," he tells me. "It's not necessary. This is what we'll have for you." And he shows me another slide that seems to have a fly speck. "Now, try to find it under the microscope."

I try. It's about as easy as to locate a palm tree in the middle of the Sahara. Eventually I spot it—but it takes me time. Then the German explains to me how to unglue the micro-photo and how to fix it on the slide without spoiling it. All that hasn't taken very long, and after an hour, the experts retire, leaving "Moustache" and me alone. "All this is very nice, but you don't expect me to take a microscope with me, I hope?"

"No. That's just what we must talk over together: the possibility for you to obtain a microscope in England. If you are going to work in a hospital, as you intended to, it ought not to be difficult."

"You think so? One doesn't borrow a microscope as one borrows ten francs!"

"You can—you'll see how—I have thought of that too. As soon as you arrive in London, you are going to pretend to be interested in microbes. You'll buy a book that has been recently published: "Microbe Hunters" by Paul de Kruif. You'll speak about it in your surroundings, even at the risk of boring everyone. You'll make it out to be a craze. Then, one day, you'll ask an intern to lend you his microscope to examine something that you read about. I don't think he'd refuse."

I find "Moustache's" idea childish and depending on too many "hics" to be realizable. But as I won't have to use it, what the hell! And I agree. "It sounds quite possible," I say. "But have you changed your intention that I take a radio along?"

"Yes, for the present. Your achievement in penetrating into Great Britain is so unexpected that I don't want to risk compromising this success by loading you with a radio. We have a Portuguese who travels as diplomatic courier. He'll take it over to you."

"Isn't it dangerous? You'll have to enlighten him, at least partially. You'll have to give him my name, my address."

III. Madrid, 1943

"Have no fear. He'll give the phonograph to an authentic Englishman, who'll be asked to transmit it to his girlfriend, who in turn will take it to someone else. One day, you'll get a word: "Go to X to pick up your parcel." It'll be perhaps an Art gallery, a junk dealer, or a record shop—I couldn't tell you for sure. But one thing is certain: before arriving to that destination, it will have gone through so many hands that it'll be untraceable. In the meanwhile, you'll correspond with us mainly in sympathetic ink. Here is an address where you'll write: Miss Sabina Romans. 15 Calle Lesseps, Barcelona. It's a student. You have met her in Madrid; you'll write her in that sense."

"I get it. But to come back to the radio, you think I'll know how to use that 'phonograph?' It will be very different from the transmitter I have learned on."

"You shall receive the complete detailed instructions and a diagram of the apparatus, the way to work it and to transform it—if you had to. All these indications will be microphotographed, and you'll find them inside the gramophone. So we have to agree on the place where we are going to conceal it, so that you know where to find it. If you don't know where to look, you wouldn't discover it, even with the most powerful magnifying glass. I have thought of a place. You know the little screw that holds the needle? If you unscrew it completely, you'll see its extremity is cut and flat. The surface is large enough to glue on it four, five, and even six micro-photos. It's easy for you to find, easy to take out, also easy to remove. What do you think of it?"

"It sounds all right."

"So it's agreed: on the screw. Will you remember?"

"Yes."

"When you arrive in London, the first thing to do is try to get a radio. The best would be a Halicrafter. These are American radios. It ought not to be difficult, with all the Americans that are actually in England. Now, here is a change in the instructions you were given in Paris. It is a simplification. We'll have only two call signs which will always be the same:

X R F on 8650 meters wave length.

M L O on 5100 meters wave length.

Do you want to change the days of transmission?"

"No."

"Then we'll be calling you as we have agreed on Mondays, Tuesdays, and Saturdays, at 12 and midnight G.M.T. In the daytime we'll come on 8650 m.; so you'll automatically listen for X.R.F. At night it'll be on 5100 m. with M.L.O. as call sign. All right?"

"Righto."

"We won't start calling you before three weeks after your presumed arrival to London, and will keep on calling without sending any messages, until you let us know that you hear us. But you, as soon as you get there, let us know it by letter. And for God's sake be careful. Don't rush anything. Take your time. If you see it is difficult to get a radio, forget about it. If you think you are being watched, don't write. Wait two months, three months, four months if necessary, before starting anything. Don't ever risk."

During the conversation, we have been changing places. From time to time, "Moustache" gets up and paces across the room. Now it's I that stand looking out of the window. What do I hope to see? On the other side of the road are fields. Nothing is there. Suddenly, I hear the rumbling of a tram. That's what I was waiting for: the tramway. It's coming, yellow and decrepit, and nearly empty. But that's not what I am after. I see what I wanted. It's the N 25. Now I'll be able to find my way. There still remains the telephone on the wall, near the door, but that corner is rather dark, and the phone is hung rather low. It is impossible to do anything right now.

A car drives into the court and the next moment von Buch opens the door. "Are you through? It's 6 p.m. You must be famished!"

"Let's go and have supper," says Moustache. "I'm keeping you. You have no engagement, have you?"

I say I haven't and we get ready to leave. As we reach the door that von Buch is holding open, I get hold of my handbag upside down and spill all its contents on the floor. "Gosh! I am clumsy!" I exclaim, while the Major and von Buch hurry to gather my compact, the lipstick that has rolled under a chair, a comb and a few scattered papers. I bend down to pick up my hanky and, doing so, read the number marked on the telephone dial. It hasn't been so difficult after all. I gather the last two bits of information as we leave the villa. I note that the neighbouring house is in construction. Only half of the walls are finished; red brick walls and around them bricks are piled up in heaps. On the other side of the villa, the house that precedes it and is separated from it by two or three vacant lots and has the number 64. For today, that's all.

Von Buch takes us to a dingy looking restaurant near the Puerta del Sol. He leads us behind the dining room to a series of private booths with opaque glass partitions that remind one of telephone booths. "Here you won't be disturbed," says von Buch taking leave from us.

A table, four chairs, and hardly enough room to sneak in between! A waiter comes to take the orders. "Moustache" studies the menu. "A chateaubriand?" he asks me.

"Fine."

"Three chateaubriands," says Moustache to the waiter, "one of which very rare, and a portion of cream carrots."

I look at him in amazement. Is he ordering two portions for himself? And carrots with that? Pouah! Kliemann reads disapproval on my face. "He doesn't like carrots?" he asks, alarmed.

"Who?"

"Babs! I thought he'd like red meat with cream carrots."

I burst out laughing, but I am touched. "And I thought you were ordering it for yourself!"

While we are waiting for the meal to be brought in, we drink aperitifs. All of a sudden, I notice how much he has aged, shrunk since our last meeting in Paris. He turns the stem of his glass between his fingers and fixes thoughtfully the space in front of him. He lets out a sigh.

"Anything wrong?" I ask.

He glances at me, shrugs his shoulders. "Bah!" he says. I examine him. He swallows his Armagnac at a gulp, with an impatient gesture. He repeats: "Bah!"

"Yvonne?" I ask. I don't know why I said that—a simple coincidence.

Kliemann is startled; he stares at me. "How do you know?" he asks. It's my turn to shrug. I don't answer. "Yes," he admits in a low voice; and he buries his head in his hands.

I say: "Jealous?"

He looks up. He looks pitiful. He says: "You must think me ridiculous? Maybe I am. Or maybe I'm mad? She is young, pretty, gay and witty. And I … look at me! A married man of forty-six!" He stops talking because the waiter is bringing in the food. He proceeds as soon as the door has closed. "Am I boring you?"

III. Madrid, 1943

"Not at all," I protest.

"Then let me speak. It does me good." I listen to him, for even if I didn't, I would still hear him. His story doesn't interest me, doesn't concern me. But it relieves him, so I let him talk. He tells me how he met Yvonne, soon after his arrival in Paris.

"Her brother Richard had done a little work for us before the surrender of Paris; that's how I was brought to visit him! Yvonne was there. She was a little "Midinette" in some "maison de confection."[15] I believe she was out of work at the time. She hadn't a penny. She made herself dresses. I don't think she had enough to eat. Just then I fell ill. I knew no one in Paris. Richard took me to his flat; Yvonne looked after me. This was to be the beginning."

"Moustache" cannot stop anymore. He filled and emptied his glass five times. I would like to go home. I tell Kliemann that if we stay any longer, we'll attract the attention to ourselves, for we are at table for three hours. He says, "All right, we are going" and begins to get ready ... and forgets. Even after the bill has been paid and I am standing near the door, he continues to talk, and another half hour elapses. So I take him by the arm and oblige him to get up. In the street, the noise, the crowd, the lights sober him up. He says: "Let's walk."

We follow in circle avenues and the streets, coming back on our steps. It doesn't matter, because "Moustache" isn't looking where he goes. He is still talking. At midnight, I say: "I am tired. I'd like to go home."

"Please! Not already! Don't leave me alone!" he begs. He looks like a scared child. "Come, we are going to sit down," he adds, dragging me towards the terrace of a café. For a while he remains silent. Then he leans over to me. "Lily, help me!" he says.

"Help you? How?"

"Yvonne spent the month of May in Madrid. She came here with that woman who is her bad genius, this Madame Marty Chauclos. They stopped at the Ritz. After her return to Paris, Yvonne was no longer the same; something must have happened while she was here! I want to know what."

"But what do you want me to do?"

"I'd like you to go to the Ritz, to question the chamber maid, the porter, the lift boy—who do I know? Someone must know something!"

"Listen." I tell him, seeing his ideas aren't very clear. "What are you asking me risks ruining completely my trip to England. If I start to inquire about a person who came from France and went back, it cannot fail to attract attention to me. I'll be traced immediately!"

"Ach!" says the Major. "You refuse! You were my last hope! I was certain you would help me!"

"I shall help you," I promise him. "But we must think out something else. First of all, you must enlighten me a little more, so that I should know in what I am getting involved. After that, we'll search for a solution and will combine a plan of action."

"So you don't refuse to help me?" exclaims Kliemann, reassured.

"No. But now I want to go home. I am sleepy."

"Just a moment more!" pleads the Major.

But around us, in the café, the lights have been extinguished one by one, and the somnolent waiter wipes insistently the table next to ours. He watches for a sign from "Moustache" and comes rushing when he sees him take out his bill fold. Once more we find ourselves in the street. "What's the time?" I ask him, for I have no watch.

Kliemann consults his. "3:30 a.m.," he says. The streets are practically deserted. "I'll have to look for an open bar," sighs Moustache.

"What for?"

"I don't feel like sleeping. I don't feel like going back to my hotel. I am afraid of loneliness."

"Nuts!" I say, losing patience. "You are going home. And you are going to sleep. And tomorrow we'll see what can be done. But you've had enough drinking for tonight. I want you to promise me to go straight home."

"I promise," he groans reluctantly. We plan to rendezvous at 10 a.m. at Lys's.

"In case I should miss you, in which hotel have you stopped?"

"At the Palace."

"Under your own name?"

"Yes. Kliemann."

We part. In the silence of the sleeping town, a nearby clock strikes four as I drop on my bed, completely exhausted.

September 19th 1943

I am slightly late for my rendezvous, but it's of no importance, because Moustache isn't there anyhow. At 11 a.m. still no one. At 12 a.m. I return to my boarding house. At 1 p.m. the telephone rings. It's Kliemann. At the other end of the line, his voice has a distant and muffled sound. "You must excuse me," he says. "I wasn't feeling good. I had to lie down. But I'll come now, if you don't mind returning to the same place."

I tell him to hurry and that I am hungry. But I think to myself, he's been drinking again! A quarter of an hour later, we arrive practically at the same time. "Moustache" has a cut above the eye and a bruise on the forehead. "Who hit you?"

He makes a vague gesture: "I lost consciousness and fell. Let's go and have lunch."

I take him to a restaurant in the Calle del Desengano, parallel to the Gran Via. The food is good and it isn't as lugubrious as von Buch's glazed place.

"I have thought over what you told me yesterday," says Kliemann as soon as we have sat down. "Your objections were right. You mustn't risk compromising yourself for my sake. On the other hand, I have decided to act differently. I'll do it through an investigation agency."

"Not knowing what it's all about, it's difficult for me to advise you, or even give an opinion."

"I might as well tell you the whole story," says Kliemann with a deep sigh. Has Yvonne ever mentioned to you a certain Espiritu Santos?"

"No. Never."

"It's a Portuguese—a very wealthy banker. He often came to see Yvonne. A flirt. You know how Portuguese are! Yvonne amused him; she is jolly and witty. But he has a very beautiful wife—and very jealous too. What does Yvonne mean to him? Nothing! He can find lots like her! But I am afraid that Yvonne got caught at her proper game. I suspect her of having met him here. It was nothing for him to come from Lisbon to Madrid. He always stops at the Ritz. I want to know if he was there at the same time as Yvonne."

"What gave you these ideas?"

Kliemann lowers his head in his head in his hands. "She isn't the same since she came back," he whispers without lifting the eyes.

"What do you mean: not the same? Doesn't she want to see you? Did she tell you she loves you no more? Did she let you understand there was someone else?"

"No. None of all that. She continues to be nice, and thoughtful, and sweet. But I often feel her impatient. She treats me like a sick man, or like a brother, and it's not what I want, not what it was!"

"And you. How do you treat her? Do you torment her with your suspiciousness? Do you pursue her with your jealousy? Do you harass her with mistrustful questions?" Kliemann doesn't answer. He is staring in front of him with a stubborn, tired gaze. "And you are surprised," I exclaim, "to feel her impatient! You are surprised she treats you like a sick man? But I, in her place, would have thrown the whole furniture at your head! I, in her place, would have forbidden you my door! If you want my opinion, Yvonne is an angel of patience!"

Kliemann sits up and snaps at me with rage: "Why do you defend her? I ask you to help me and you take her side!"

"It's you I am defending against yourself! You who are making a fool of yourself. You who are inventing the nonexistent to sustain your jealousy. You are sick, morbid man torturing himself! You start on nothing, on a hypothesis, and you make yourself miserable. And you render Yvonne's life infernal!"

"But I love her! Don't you understand? I have dreamed to free myself, so as to marry her, have a home, a wife, children. It's that dream she is destroying, and I haven't got the courage to give it up." He is crushed. Fortunately, a palm tree hides partially our table. In what a new mess am I getting involved! "Listen," he says looking up. "Tomorrow I'll know if she has betrayed me with that damned Santos. I'll know it, if I have to turn over sky and earth. And if she has deceived me, if she has met him here, then ... then...."

"Then what?"

"Then, there is only one thing for me to do—ask my transfer to the Russian front!" he finishes with a sob.

"And it would be idiotic!" I put in. "You forget we have a task ahead of us. That we have undertaken something we must achieve. That is so much more important than your personal affairs or mine. That we are on the point of succeeding ... for we are succeeding! Think of those two long years of training, of the plans we have elaborated, discussed, carried out together. One day, you told me: "We shall win, you and I!" That day has come. You have no right to let me down. Not now; not when I am going to find myself in England. You cannot abandon two years' work, destroy two years' efforts. You can't."

He looks at me in amazement. "Lily, from where did I get you?'

I laugh. "Have you forgotten? Through Felix Dassel."

"Dassel? Yes, it's true. You know him well?"

"Yes. Do you?"

"No. The first time I met him, it was about the case of the kidnapping of that Russian General Miller."

"General Miller?" I repeat incredulously, and then I add: "He was my uncle."

"Your uncle?" Kliemann looks at me, astounded. "I didn't know!" he says.

"You didn't? I thought I had told you."

He meditates. Then, making up his mind, he leans forward: "I'll tell you how it happened," he says. "I never saw clearly Dassel's part in the affair. When Paris was taken, our Secret Services were naturally the first ones to enter the city. We had just only taken possession of our Headquarters, when I received an order from Berlin, enjoining me to put myself at the disposal of a certain Dassel, who was on his way to Paris, and to carry out his orders. A few hours later, he was there. He told me to take some men and to come with him to the Palais de Justice. When we arrived there, he had the place surrounded. Then we went to the Archives. He had all the employees lined up and asked to have all the papers of the Miller case brought to him. I can still see myself yelling to the terrified guards, with my two words of broken French: "All … instantly … if not: KAPUT!" They went to get them, and Dassel escorted them. He took everything there was—and there was a lot! Amongst other things, there was a thick book with a strange wooden cover. He told me it was a Bible. He left for Berlin the same evening, but it wasn't I who accompanied him. I have not seen him since."

Kliemann becomes silent. I reflect. His revelation stirs a world of thought and memories in me. I dearly loved my uncle! I remember that in 1934, finding myself in Berlin during a bicycle tour across Europe, Dassel had asked me for a letter of introduction to General Miller, saying he intended to visit Paris. Later on, as I questioned my uncle about the impression made on him by Dassel, he only shrugged his shoulders in reply. I can still see the scribbled note my uncle left before he disappeared, that note mentioning he had an appointment with "an attaché from the limitrophe countries (meaning the Baltic countries) Strohman and a Mr. Werner.… Both speaking Russian well." My uncle suspected a trap. He wasn't mistaken. This same note was in Dassel's possession when he handed it to me in Berlin, in January 1941, telling me with a strange look: "I want you to return it to the General's wife. She has a right to it."

Dassel is Balt, and he does speak Russian! Then I remember another fact, further back, during the trip I took to Berlin right after my uncle's kidnapping, in November 1937. I was making an investigation of my own. I had gone straight to Dassel. I still hear the irony in his voice as he was saying: "Strohman! How didn't your uncle see through it at once? "Strohman" means: straw man, stooge, in German!" After that he had handed me over to the Gestapo, who wanted to hear all about the inquiry. They told me they wanted to help me find my uncle. I was very young. I believed them. They questioned me for two whole days. After that an inspector drove me to the station, without having allowed me to see Dassel again. While we were pacing the platform waiting for the train, he asked me: "Why on earth did you go to Dassel's in the first place?"

I said: "Because he is the only one I know in Berlin."

He hesitated. Then he said: "He is the last person you ought to have seen. You understand: the last. Anyone but him!"

"Why?" I asked.

He shook his head. "Because!" he answered. But it's all he would tell me.

Dassel is Balt. Dassel speaks Russian. Dassel is the last one I ought to have trusted. Dassel is the one who came to take away all the documents concerning my uncle's disappearance. Dassel presented me with Plevitzkaya's Bible. Dassel wanted me to return General Miller's last note to my aunt. Dassel sneered: "Strohman!" Strohman is a dummy. Strohman … Dassel … Strohman … Dassel, DASSEL … Dassel?

"What's the matter?" asks Kliemann, frightened.

"It's my head! It's splitting. I suppose I didn't get enough sleep last night."

"Will you help me all the same?"

"Help you? With what?"

"Will you accompany me to a private detective? I don't speak Spanish; you'll have to do the talking."

"Yes, of course, I'll go with you. But I hope you realize the baseness of what you intend to do?"

"I've come so far," he says, lifting his shoulders in discouragement. "I'm going back to my hotel to ask the porter for the address of an agency. Are you coming?"

While Kliemann has gone in, I walk up and down, not far from his hotel, still pondering what he has told me. What role did Dassel play in the kidnapping of General Miller? Have all the investigations carried out six years ago gone on a false trail? Have the Soviets had no part in it? Could it have been the deed of the Germans? But for what purpose? With what aim? To put the blame on the Soviets? To stir the French public opinion against communism, against Soviet Russia? This was the year 1937; the war was near. Oh hell! What do I know! It is head-breaking! Everything is possible, yet everything is incredible. Will the truth ever be known?

I sight Kliemann, hurrying along. "I have two addresses," he says with satisfaction.

One of them is near where I live, Calle de Preciados. We decide to start by there. It's a populous street. The house must be inhabited by modest employees, judging by its severe and homely appearance, by its wooden staircase, large and dark, with landings in between each floor; by its stillness. The door at which we ring has no brass plate, no indication. An old woman opens it to us. I tell her the name. She has a vague smile.

"He is very busy," she says, "but if you'll step into the waiting room, I'll let him know there is someone to see him."

She pushes ajar the door into a dark room, where an artificial palm tree seems to cling with its too green and dusty leaves—which look like long fingers—to the net curtains hanging in front of the closed blinds. The air is stuffy. The old fashioned divan, the two rigid, uncomfortable looking armchairs and the three chairs have dirty slip covers. From a round table, the discoloured fringe of a mechanically embroidered square droops sadly.

"This woman," I say to "Moustache," "must be the mother of your sleuth, and I bet my little finger he isn't doing anything just now, but keeps us waiting to impress us."

"You think so?" says Kliemann with indifference.

At this precise moment the door opens and the old woman bids us in. A man gets up from behind a narrow table and bows to us ceremoniously. Behind us, the woman has brought in one of the covered chairs from the waiting room. The place, the man, the whole business disgusts me. There is something slimy about the whole thing. We sit down, and I explain to the detective in a few short words what is expected of him. He notes the names of Yvonne, the Ritz, Espiritu Santos, the dates, etc.

"All right," he says. "The investigations will be carried out with utmost discretion. We are a trustworthy agency. Would you now give me your name and address?"

"It's not necessary," I say. "I'll come myself for the answer. When?"

"In eight days."

I give the translation to "Moustache."

"No," says the latter. "I want it tomorrow."

"This gentleman," I translate to the detective, "is leaving Madrid tomorrow at 1 p.m. He must know the results before then."

"But it's utterly impossible!" whines the man throwing up his arms. "Realize. I must go on the spot, question the servants, discover where this lady frequented, interrogate in turn these people. And tomorrow is Sunday!"

"All that is unnecessary," I say. "The only things we are interested in are: Was Mr. Espiritu Santos in Madrid in May? Did he stop at the Ritz? Did Mademoiselle Delidaise and he meet? Period!"

"But even that takes time! Give me Monsieur's address and I guarantee you that he'll get the answer in a sealed inconspicuous envelope."

"It's not possible," I tell him. "This gentleman is going back to France, and there is no postal communication with France."

"Ah," mumbles the little man in black, and he pulls on his short moustache, as if he hopes to extract out of it an idea.

I realize I didn't give him much time to make his inquiry. "If you have until Monday evening, would that be sufficient?"

He thinks it over: "Simply to discover whether this lady met the Senor Espiritu Santos?" he asks.

"Yes, just that."

"I think I could have an answer for you by 5 p.m. on Monday."

"Then let's have it that way. I'll come for it, as I'm only leaving by the midnight train."

"It will cost you 200 pesetas, and you'll only pay when you have the result."

In the street we walk in silence. "You disgust me!" I say to "Moustache." He doesn't answer.

We enter into a big restaurant. The dining room is brightly illuminated, with a profusion of mirrors, waiters in dinner jackets, very high class. Kliemann orders a sumptuous meal, and starts it with three cognacs, followed by red and white wine and champagne. But I am in a bad mood and remain silent.

"Why do I disgust you, Lily?" asks the Major, as if I had said it just now and not half an hour ago.

"Because you pretend to love Yvonne, yet you accuse her of deceiving you; because you lower yourself spying upon her. You'll go back to Paris, and you'll smile at her, and you'll kiss her, while all the time you'll be remembering the abject little dick, whom you will have paid to repeat servant's gossip about the woman you say you love! You call that clean? Answer!"

"I want to know the truth," says Kliemann in a thick voice.

We are at table nearly two hours. I've had all I could stand of that moaning. "Proofs! Always proofs! You say you love Yvonne, but you won't trust her. But me, you trust me!" I blurt, exasperated. "What proof have you that I don't betray you? What proof have you that I am not working for the British? What proof have you that I am not lying to you? What proofs have you got, tell me, Major Kliemann?"

Leaning on the table with his head in his hands, Kliemann at first doesn't move. "He is completely drunk," I say to myself. But slowly his fingers part and I notice his eye fixing on me. He is looking at me. And by and by, his vacant gaze becomes lucid—terribly lucid and cold. He is sobered up. He doesn't say a thing. His features stiffen into a head mask. We confront each other, like two fighters looking for their vulnerable point. "I went too far," I say to myself, but I cannot take back my words. With both hands, Kliemann is griping the edge of the table, pulling the table-cloth. He leans still more towards me.

"If I knew you were betraying us," he says through his teeth, "I'd shoot you right here—now!" His eyes are nothing but narrow slits under thick knitted brows. "But no," he adds slowly, "you won't betray us—never—because your parents have remained in Paris!" His eyes open, wide. "In P.A.R.I.S!" he repeats.

This time, it's my turn to lean forward rising from my chair. "So you hold it, YOUR PROOF!" My hand goes up, then falls limp at my side. "I don't know what stops me from slapping you," I say in a low voice, sitting back again.

But the tension has lessened. Kliemann hangs down the head, shameful. Then he looks up, holds out his hand over the table, with a penitent smile: "Forgive me," he says. "I am so enervated."

"Forget it."

September 20th

We have an appointment at the Prado. That way I don't mind if "Moustache" is late. He arrives at 11 a.m. and finds me in front of the Goyas. "I am invited for tea," I warn him at once. "I didn't want to refuse, because it's one of the secretaries from the British consulate."

"What about the result of the investigation? You promised to go for it," asks Kliemann anxiously.

"But that is tomorrow," I say.

"Oh! Of course." He seems reassured. During lunch, he says: "I forgot to tell you. The day after you left Paris, we sent some of our guys from the Gestapo to your studio, as we had agreed."

"Ah, yes? What happened?"

"They questioned the 'concierge,' but she knew nothing. She said you had gone to the country, to visit a friend. They asked her for your parents' address, but she didn't know it. She pretended not even to know you had parents!"

"Good concierge!" I think to myself.

"After that," continues Kliemann, "your parents were taken to the Gestapo HQ and interrogated. Their version was that you had gone to look after a sick aunt in Portugal and that you had obtained your passport from the Prefecture de Police. When they were asked about your intention of going over to England, they seemed very surprised and denied knowing it. They were let free the same day. Anyway, they are far from suspecting that you have any connection with our Secret Services! By the way, do you know that you nearly did get arrested for good a few days before you left?"

"Is that so? How? And why?"

"Because your father confided to one of his friends that you were getting ready to leave for England. And it so happened that this friend of his was an informer of ours. He immediately notified the Gestapo. Luckily, practically all the reports go through my hands. This particular one fell under my eye, and I was able to explain what it was about! But it was a near escape!"

"I guess it's my lucky star."

Punctually at 4 p.m. Miss Molly brings me into her small sitting room where Benton is waiting already. I give him an account yesterday afternoon and this morning. I tell him about Major Kliemann's affaire d'amour and about our visit to the private detective. "He is really badly affected!" I say. "It makes him lose all sense of caution. For two days we can be seen everywhere together, and he realizes so little what he is doing, that he's gone as far as to ask me to make a personal inquiry at the Ritz! I dread to think what he would be capable of, if he learned that Yvonne has indeed deceived him! He speaks of asking for his transfer to the Russian Front!"

"That must by no means happen!" declares Benton. "Now that we know all about Kliemann, and can have an eye on him, we want to keep him. Can you manage to go to that investigation agency before he gets there?"

"It's easy enough. I am the one who is going to pick up the result."

"In that case, you MUST obtain from that man a favourable answer! Whatever the truth should be, he must say that Yvonne was faithful. You understand? You can buy these types of people. Pay him. You have carte blanche! But the answer must be: NO BETRAYAL."

"All right."

"Wait a minute." Benton goes out and returns with a dossier that he goes over. "Here we are: Delidaise. Yvonne, 26 years … accompanied by Mary Chanclos … Ritz … room … date…." He continues to read, turning over the page. "No," he says at last: "I don't see anything about an Espiritu Santos. But anyhow, in case there was anything, Kliemann must ignore it."

"I get it. Now, just another thing: could I have my visa? I'd like him to see it before he leaves."

"As you wish. Come for it tomorrow morning. I'll have it ready."

Monday, September 21st

"Here you are," says Benton handing me my passport with the British visa via Gibraltar. "And don't forget this evening," he reminds me, "that Kliemann must be reassured about Yvonne."

"I will not forget."

5:45 p.m. I arrive to the agency. It is the man himself who opens the door. He has got his hat on, ready to go out, or coming in. I was waiting for you," he says. "Here is the result of my investigations. I'll read it to you." He gives me Yvonne's age, the dates of her arrival and departure, the number of the room she shared with her friend Madame Marty Chanclos, indicates that both were often seen at the hotel's bar, changed dresses many times, etc., etc. … details which are of no interest to me. At last he comes to the facts: Espiritu Santos wasn't either at the Ritz, or in Madrid last May.

I tell the man to seal the envelope, slip it in my bag and lay on the table 200 pesetas. I had brought with me 2,000 extra ones, in case I should need them. I don't. I rejoin Kliemann at the bar of the Lys. I find him prostrate in front of a cognac. He stares at me with blank eyes. I take out the envelope with the tip of my fingers and drop it before him. "Catch! Here is that filth!"

"Filth! Why?" he asks turning over and over the envelope that bears no external indication. "What is inside?" he adds without opening the envelope.

"There is inside that you are an idiot," I tell him with contempt.

He raises his eyebrows, looks at me, then tears open the envelope. Having glanced at the paper, he hands it back to me: "It's written in Spanish I can't read."

I take the sheet, make out with difficulty the fine scribbling, then translate it for him.

"Is that exact?" he asks.

"What do you mean? Do you want the waiter to translate it for you, if you don't believe me?"

Kliemann doesn't answer immediately. "What I mean is," he says at last, "is that the truth? Haven't you paid that man to write what's on that paper?"

"Major Kliemann," I say, losing patience, "let me tell you I don't care a hang about your affaires d'amour. They are not worth a penny to me! In a few days, I'll be in England and you in Paris. I shall probably never see you again. So what is it to me, whether Yvonne deceives you or not?"

"Don't be cross!" he says, smiling at last. "I have been so unhappy that I can hardly realize it is over. I would like," he adds timidly, "to order some champagne to celebrate!"

"I prefer that!" I say laughing. "Let's drink champagne!"

It is only then that I bring out my passport and show it to him. He examines it carefully, then lifts his eyes and looks at me, nodding. He smiles. Then suddenly he exclaims: "It's FORMIDABLE! You seem to succeed in everything! Lily, you are my mascot! Because, for me too, it is a beautiful success! I, Major Kliemann, have trained an agent and have managed to send her to Great Britain!"

Later on, in the street, on our way to the restaurant, I stop at the edge of the pavement, and point to the gutter. "Why are you showing it to me?" he asks, not understanding.

"For you to throw in there that dirty scrap of paper. That's where it belongs."

And as he hesitates: "Do you intend offering it to Yvonne with a bunch of roses? I'm sure she'd be flattered!" That decides him. He takes the letter out of his billfold, tears it into little pieces and throws them in the sewer. "And now, try to forget if you can," I say.

September 22nd

We spend the morning shopping. I help "Moustache" choose underwear and presents for Yvonne. Today he is beaming! That's a guy who is done for, from a professional stand point. He has the two defects that are the most dangerous in espionage: he drinks and he is in love. He suddenly remembers that I have asked him on different occasions for the time.

"Haven't you got a watch?" I tell him that I haven't. "Let's go and buy one right now."And without hesitation, he offers me an "Omega" costing 1,350 pesetas.

"Moustache," who is going to take back some presents for my parents, comes to the "Pension Argentia" to fetch the parcel. "I'll add an album of sketches," I tell him.

"May I see them before you put it in?"

"Sure!"

I hand him the album and he goes through it. He stops at a drawing I did of Babs. "Couldn't I have this one?" he asks. "It would be a souvenir of Babs and you and of these five days spent in Madrid during which you helped me so much; and also of the success that awaits our work. Will you let me have it?" I tear out the page and give it to him. "Write something underneath, won't you?"

"You know, I can't put very much and certainly not my name. It would be too compromising!" I consider a moment. Then I write: "To Octave, in remembrance of Solange."

"Thank you," he says, slipping the drawing between two documents in his leather briefcase.

We don't have lunch together, because Kliemann has to take leave at the German Embassy. But we agree to meet at "Fuyma."

The Major arrives at Fuyma with half an hour's delay and looks terribly upset. "Lily, are you sure you gave me the drawing?"

"Why yes! What is the matter?"

"It has disappeared!"

I smile: "Had it been a Greco, a Goya, or a Rubens, I would understand. But a sketch of Babs. Why would one take it?"

"That is just what I don't understand! I had put it at the top of my suitcase, with some other papers when I came back from you, and had locked it up. An hour ago, I returned to my hotel. I needed something from my suitcase. I opened it. It seemed to me the loose papers weren't the way I had left them. I went through them. Your drawing was missing! I looked everywhere, sorted one by one all my papers, unpacked and repacked all my things, verified the contents of my briefcase; the sketch is to be found nowhere!"

"Didn't you tell me your suitcase was locked?"

"I did. But this is the kind of cheap lock anyone can pick. I beg you; go back to your boarding house and see if, by any chance, I didn't leave it there."

"You just said you had put it in your suitcase? Surely, you know what you did?"

"I know! I know! But maybe I dreamed it. I don't seem to know anymore where I stand! This affair about Yvonne has completely knocked me off my balance. Please, go!" he begs with a distressed look.

I return to the "Pension Argentina" only to tranquillize him, for I am sure of the result in advance. I find nothing. "No." I say, back at Fuyma's. "It isn't there."

He takes hold of his head, burying his fingers in his hair, balancing his body from right to left, from left to right, very lightly: "Why? Why? I don't understand. What does it mean?" Suddenly, he sits up: "What was it you had written under the drawing?"

"To Octave, in remembrance of Solange." It would mean strictly nothing to a third person! You can have met a "Solonge" who has asked you to take back that little souvenir to an "Octave." So what? It proves nothing!"

"No, it doesn't prove a thing. Still I don't understand."

"Stop worrying. Even supposing your things were searched and that drawing was taken (someone might have thought he was holding a clue), it won't give away anything. It compromises no one! So do relax!"

"I suppose you are right."

—⁂—

September 23rd 1943

The time of parting has come. Major Kliemann gives me his last recommendations, tells me to remain in contact with von Buch, through Miret, until I leave Spain, and to keep him informed about the ultimate proceedings. "Ask him for all the money you need—and don't hesitate." I take a few steps with him in the street. He hails a taxi, gets in. Leaning out of the window, he makes me a last friendly sign. Standing at the edge of the pavement, I watch the cab turn on the Plaza del Callao and disappear along the Gran Via.

"He has left. He hasn't discovered anything," I say to myself with relief. And now: to England.

—⁂—

September 24th 1943

I go to the "Seguridad," Plaza del Sol, to get an exit visa. The employee examines my passport. "We don't deliver any visas through La Linea," he tells me.

"Then how am I to go to Gibraltar?"

"Through Portugal."

"It is because I wasn't able to get a Portuguese transit visa that I am going to England by Gibraltar."

"I regret," repeats the employee stubbornly, "but I cannot deliver you a visa for La Linea." And he pushes closed the glass pane of the wicket.

I deliberate about the best thing to do and decide to go and see Mr. R. at the Ministerio

Asuntos Estranjeros. I had a word of introduction for him from his cousin whom I met in Paris and had visited him first thing after I came to Madrid. Mr. R. had greeted me very amiably, but when he had seen my passport with its German visa, he had shown regret at not being able to help me and had advised me to go straight to the British. I probably seemed most suspicious to him!

The Ministry of Foreign Affairs is only a few streets from the Puerta del Sol, on the Plaza Santa Cruz. Mr. R. receives me without having me wait and shows much more eagerness when he sees the British visa. He gives me a word for Senor Diegez of the Seguridad, whom he tells me, will straighten out everything.

Without losing any time, I go to the N 1 Calle Esparteros, climb a large very dirty wooden staircase to the second floor, ask to see the Senor in question and am introduced at once. I explain him my difficulties.

"The fact is," Senor Diegez tells me, "that La Linea is a closed frontier. To give you an exit visa by La Linea, we would have to make an exception. We cannot make an exception for a private individual, but we could do it on the demand of your Embassy. See if you can get the French Embassy to write us a letter asking us to authorize your passage by La Linea."

"Senor," I say, "how do you want the Vichy Government Embassy to patronize my trip to England? You know yourself it is impossible!"

"It's true," he admits, scratching his nape. "Annoying. I don't see any other way!"

"And if I had the demand made by the British?"

He considers it: "Well! Bring me a letter from the British consulate, and I'll see what I can do."

So I go directly to Benton, to whom I relate the result of the investigation about Yvonne, "Moustache's" two last days in Madrid, and finish by this last incident at the Seguridad.

"Are you sure the Major Killburg (Kliemann) left completely reassured and that he has renounced the Russian Front?"

"Quite sure."

"Good. What concerns your Spanish exit visa, you will get a letter from us, but I must first see under what form we'll give it to you. It's a delicate matter. It would be a document that would remain in the hands of the Spanish. In other words, the Germans could have knowledge of it. We must act carefully not to 'burn' you. Come to see me tomorrow."

September 25th

I look over the type written sheet of paper with consular heading that Benton has just handed me.

"We didn't want to write more than that in this letter," says Benton. This is what we would have given anyone. It can't make you look suspect." The letter is addressed by the Passport Control Service of the British Consulate to the Passport Section of the Spanish Security, asking them to facilitate my passage by La Linea.

I return to the Calle Esparteros and give it to Diegez who tells me to go on Tuesday directly to Seguridad, Puerta del Sol. "In the meanwhile the Service of Visas will have been given orders."

Tonight, the B.B.C. announces the recapture of Smolensk by the Russians.

September 28th

"No," the employee from behind his wicket tells me, "we haven't received any instructions at the Securidad to deliver an exit visa for La Linea to you. Come back tomorrow."

October 1st 1943

The 5th U.S. Army has captured Naples. In Naples I stayed at the Grand Hotel. How beautiful the bay dominated by the Vesuvius, with its white plume of smoke, was. It was spring. In the streets young Napolitans sold gardenias. I visited Pompey, Capri and the Blue Grotto. I climbed the Vesuvius. Now, one is fighting there. To the ruins of Pompey, other ruins will be added, still greater, for men can be more destructive than a volcano.

October 3rd

Sunday—I can't leave Spain without having visited Toledo. Early this morning I take the train and a few hours later I find myself in El Greco's town of election. I don't regret that I came, and I would have never forgiven myself had I missed it. I wish I could come back. Unfortunately, I have booked my sleeping car for tomorrow night, and I do expect to have obtained my exit visa by tomorrow morning. I'll come back later—after the war, in peace time—if there ever comes a Peace.

October 4th 1943

The French have taken Bastia. How fast the hearts must beat in France and hope revive!

Every day, I go to the Seguridad and every day I am told "Manana."[16] Today I got mad and said: "You are like the Arabs! The only difference is that they say: 'Bookra.'" They were not pleased. They don't like to be compared to Arabs!

At the Calle Esparteros, Senor Diegez, surprised, tells me that he doesn't understand how it is possible; he has given the necessary orders; and my dossier has been sent to the Seguridad a week ago! I tell him that, trusting his word that I'd have my visa in three days, I have booked already twice a sleeper and had to cancel it both times. Diegez assures me that manana (tomorrow) for sure I'll have it.

October 5th

The employee lifts the window of his wicket and throws me an exasperated and furious look. "Why do you insist?" he asks. "We haven't anything for you. I have told you repeatedly; you cannot go by La Linea!"

But this time I get really cross and demand to see his chief. I make so much noise that he finally fetches a man who takes me to another room. He listens to my explanations, and when he learns that Senor Diegez is handling my case and that I have been at the Calle Esparteros, he rings a bell and gives orders to a policeman. "He is going to accompany you to the Filing Section, and the clerk there will look for your dossier in front of you."

Two hours later, having been in a dozen offices and seen four or five different persons, I find myself sitting in front of a table going through piles of folders containing dossiers.

A young employee takes them out of their compartments along the walls and hands them over to me.

"No!" I say. "You are giving me the ones for the year 1939."

He apologizes: "You have seen all the ones for 1943."

"All right," I say. "Take me back to the Senor I-don't-know-what, the one I saw a while ago." I have to cross endless passages, unaired rooms, go up and down stairs. At last, we arrive at the destination, and the clerk leaves me.

"Ah! It's you!" says the same man.

"Yes, Sir, it is me," I say trying to keep calm. "I have just gone through all the dossiers; mine is not amongst them. Eight days ago, the Senor Diegez had it carried by courier from the Calle Esparteros. Even if the courier had stopped at every show window on his way, it wouldn't have taken him more than fifteen minutes. That's how far it is! Yet my dossier isn't here. So it has disappeared between the Calle Esparteros and the Puerta del Sol: a distance of 100 yards! There was a letter from the British Consulate to the Spanish Seguridad in that dossier. You have till tomorrow to find it. I'll return tomorrow for the last time. If tomorrow you haven't got it, the day after tomorrow the British Embassy will address a letter to your Foreign Ministry to notify them that the Seguridad has lost the letter that the British Consulate has sent it and to demand an explanation. That's all."

And without listening to his protestations, I go out, slamming the door. I know very well that I am not entitled to make these threats. I also know perfectly well that the British Embassy won't write any letter to the Ministry of Foreign Affairs. I am just chancing my luck. It'll work, or it won't. I'll know tomorrow.

October 6th 1943

"I have your dossier," says the employee as soon as he sees me. And he adds with a large smile: "You see there was no need to despair."

Ten minutes later, I come out of the Seguridad having obtained an exit visa through La Linea. My first move is to go to the railroad agency to book my sleeper. But then I discover I can't even buy my ticket having no pesetas left! I telephone Miret. "I want to see your friend at 3 p.m. I need money," I tell him.

"He'll be there and you'll have what you want."

I must act fast having little time left. Next I go to see Benton. "I am leaving this evening. Have you arranged for Babs?"

"I haven't been able to have him avoid the quarantine in Gibraltar. The regulations there are very strict. But it'll only be a few days. I thought you wouldn't mind. Once there, our people have been notified, and they will see to Babs' transportation to U.K. and his exemption from quarantine."

"Is it sure?"

"Absolutely."

Would it be possible that he is lying to me? "Mr. Benton, don't try to make me go if I can't keep Babs."

"Don't you trust us?"

"Yes. There isn't much choice."

"I'll notify them of the time of your arrival. You'll have nothing to worry about."

The "Man-in-Grey" is waiting for me. (I'll leave without knowing his name!) He gives me 3,000 pesetas, and we agree that I'll return what I'll have left over to-night at the station.

He takes for me two parcels for Mummy; he will have them sent to Paris by the German diplomatic bag. I have been using simultaneously three diplomatic bags: British, French, and German! I use the Vichy Government bag to send and receive letters from Mummy. Leaving the "Man-in-Grey," I go to pick up my ticket and from there to the French Embassy.

"I've come to say good bye," I tell Corre. I know he isn't pro-Vichy, not collaborator. Yet, it's a delicate thing to say, here at the Vichy Government Embassy: "I am going to England." Still I have to do it. And I add: "I am leaving for England."

Corre smiles. "Good," he says.

"I want to ask you a favor."

"What?"

"The letters you will receive for me from Mummy, could you forward them c/o Mr. Benton, at the British Consulate?"

"Certainly. I'll even send them by messenger."

"I wouldn't want you to get in trouble because of me."

"Don't worry. You'll have your letters."

The train has started. Farewell Madrid! Goodbye sunny and miserable Spain, where so many are hungry, so many are afraid, so many go bare feet! Babs is looking out of the window, turning now and then his head to see if I am still there. Babs is happy because he wasn't left behind, because I've taken him with me. How simple is the happiness of a dog.

IV

Gibraltar, 1943

OCTOBER 8TH 1943

"Hello! What a surprise!"

My compartment's door is ajar, and in it stands a young Englishman. I have forgotten his name. I only met him once at the "Pension Argentina" where he was visiting a French comrade, and ex co-prisoner from Miranda, or Pamplona, a certain Monsieur Paul! But in these times of uncertainty, where one makes friends in an hour and loses them in a day, it is nearly incredible to meet someone a second time! "Come in! What are you doing here?" I say, rejoicing at the encounter.

"I am going to Gibraltar, on my way to England. And you?"

"I too."

We chat about lots of things. The fact of being almost at our destination gives us a feeling of security. The reciprocal mistrust disappears. He tells me how he was wounded at Dunkirk, hidden and cared for by peasants; how, after great difficulties, he was able to escape to Switzerland, but once there, unable to get to England. He was obliged to come back to France, hide again. He was denounced, but managed to run away. At last, he got over the Pyreneans, but it was only to fall in the hands of the Spanish and be imprisoned in a concentration camp.

"It is a lucky thing," he says, "that our Embassy doesn't let us mould too long! We are here a small group going to Gibraltar. There is a Frenchman amongst us. If you wait, I'll go and fetch him."

He brings back with him a young Jew, and also an Englishman from the Embassy in charge of their group. At lunch time, as there is no dining car, they bring to my compartment some corned beef, bread, cheese, fruit, chocolate and a thermos bottle of tea.

"You know that the train doesn't go as far as Gibraltar! Where are you getting out? Is someone meeting you?" asks the Englishman.

"I believe Algeciras. No, no one is waiting for me. I suppose I'll find a cab," I say to answer all his questions.

"In that case, get out with us at San Roque. A bus is coming to pick us up."

"You think I can? I am not part of your group."

"It doesn't matter," says the leader. "There'll be enough place for you."

When the train stops, benevolent hands get hold of my luggage, and I find myself on the platform of a small railway station where we are the only passengers to alight. An old dirty and decrepit bus is parked a few feet away. A civilian has approached our group. He is counting the newcomers, consulting a list he holds in his hand. When he arrives to the end, he knits his brows and counts us over a second time. His surprised gaze stops on me. He advances.

"I am not on the list," I say, "because I am not part of the group. But as I am also going to Gibraltar, the group leader told me to join them."

"Oh! Of course. It is quite all right! You are English?"

"No: French." (I show him my passport.)

"My name is Lucas—Captain Lucas," he says, introducing himself.

We all pile into the bus, Lucas fixes the door with a piece of string, and we start. At La Linea, slight formalities at the British consulate: our documents are superficially verified, and what pesetas we have are changed at the official rate into British currency. Half an hour later, we get back in the bus and drive under a dark vault. At the other side, we stop in front of a heavy iron gate. A customs officer and a policeman threw a glance inside our vehicle. I have to get out and have my passport checked. Lucas has a collective paper for all the other passengers. Everything is in order. Two guards push open the gates, and we enter the no man's land. Five hundred feet further a similar gate lets us through and closes behind us. We are in Gibraltar. The bus stops. We all get out and I see the first British uniforms!

Only then do I fully realize that I have attained my aim! I look around me, having to restrain myself not to smile at all the soldiers. How could they know what they represent for me, for us—who were over there, in defeated, occupied countries, putting all our hope in them who were free and continued the fight. How could they guess that I have dreamed of the moment when I would see the first Allies—and that it is now, and that it is they? How could they suspect that the mere fact of being here is a victory for me? For them, we are nothing but refugees, and they see so many arriving every day.

I lift my eyes and see, towering over our heads, the Rock of Gibraltar. It leaves you breathless; it is so huge, so solid, so terribly proud! "Impregnable!" is the word that comes to the lips.

"You'll have to go through the customs," says Lucas's voice at my side.

"Yes, of course," I say, startled.

The sergeant who opens my suitcases is an old red-haired Scotchman. "I wouldn't want to disturb anything," he says, lifting as best he can my clothes with his clumsy big hands. "You have nothing to declare, have you?" And when I tell him that I haven't, he closes them with relief.

At the Passport Control I give up mine. I am asked if I have any other papers; I must leave all written material. I give them my address book, but keep my diary and Mummy's letters. Lucas comes near me. He looks annoyed. "They say," he tells me, pointing with his chin towards the customs, "that you cannot take your little dog with you; there is the quarantine."

"I know. What am I to do?"

"Wait a minute." He crosses the road and disappears in the barracks on the opposite side. He comes back after five minutes, accompanied by a lieutenant. "This is the C.O. of the post. He'll keep your dog for you until tomorrow; then we'll see what there will be to do."

I examine the officer; he looks a good guy. I pick up Babs and press him in my arms. He gives me a lick of his warm rough tongue on the cheek. The difficult moment has arrived. But Benton has promised it would be only for a few days.

"Don't worry," the Lieutenant reassures me. "I'll take good care of him. I've left a little dog I loved very much at home."

I put Babs in his arms. He starts patting him. But Babs looks at me with a desperate anxiety. I take him back. "Let me hold him a few more minutes," I plead, "until it's time to go." As soon as I put down Babs, he forgets his anxiousness and begins to sniff busily the neighbourhood.

"As I have received no instructions concerning you," says Captain Lucas, "and as it is too late tonight to do anything, I am going to get you a room at the Grand Hotel, and tomorrow morning I'll take you to the French Committee."

"The thing is," I say, hesitating, "I mustn't go to the French."

"Ah?" Lucas is surprised. "And to whom must you go?"

I look at him in indecision. "I don't know," I admit.

He pushes his grey felt to the back of his head and scratches perplexedly his nape. "That's very annoying," he remarks.

Feeling I owe him some sort of explanation, I say: "When I left Madrid, Mr. Benton, from your consulate, assured me that he would notify the proper authorities of my arrival and that I needn't worry about anything."

"Did he tell you who "the proper authorities" would be?"

"No."

"Well, I better begin by taking you to the hotel. Then I'll see what I can find out. It oughtn't to be difficult."

I call Babs, attach his leash and hand it to the lieutenant who is waiting. Babs, who has noticed my movements, looks at me with surprised eyes. But when he sees me walk towards the military car, of which Lucas is holding open the door for me, he starts to struggle wildly and to bark. I can't make up my mind to leave him! I run back to him, snatch him up and whisper in his ear: "Be a good boy, Babs. I'll come back. I'll come the first thing tomorrow morning." I put him down and get quickly in the car, without turning around. As the car starts, I hear a piercing desperate howl.

Captain Lucas presses my hand. "Don't be sad," he consoles me. "In five minutes Babs will have forgotten; they'll spoil him at the post." I smile because he has said "Babs" without having asked me Babs' name.

There is nothing grand about the Grand Hotel. Over in France, in a provincial town, it would be considered a third rate hotel. But Gibraltar mustn't have that many hotels! This one is situated on Main Street. To reach it, the car must make its way through a dense crowd of soldiers, sailors, army men of all nationalities, coming from all the points of the globe. The room I am given is far from luxurious. A brass bed, a pine-wood cupboard, a table and a chair compose the entire furniture.

I go down to the restaurant. The dining room is filled with officers: British, Australians, but no Americans. It's extraordinary to see all these uniforms after having lived three years amongst Germans. I sense a feeling of relaxation, of security. I am being carried along by the events, by my destiny, and I let myself go, persuaded that everything will finish well.

GIBRALTAR, OCTOBER 9TH

A military band gets me out of my bed and to the window. I lean out and see the musicians going by, the big drummer with his leopard skin walking ahead of them. It is the first time I hear and see a British military band. The panther skin surprises me and fills me with admiration. Outside it is going to be a beautiful day. The sky is deep blue. I stretch out with delight. I feel happy. It is funny; it seems such a long time—such ages, since I have been able to say to myself: "I am happy."

It is early yet. Lucas won't come for me before 10 a.m. I dress in a wink, swallow rapidly a cup of tea downstairs in the restaurant, pushing away the others ingredients of a large English breakfast. Out in the street, I try to orientate myself. I find my way without any difficulty. Passing under a fortified vault, I leave the town. It is only about two miles. I cross the airfield. I can see him already from there, my Babs. His ears are pointing; he is alert, while pacing up and down with the officer who is holding him on the leash. He stops now and then and looks round him. Forgetting all dignity, I start to run. He has seen me; he yaps frantically and bounces in the air. "Babs!" I cry.

The lieutenant lets go the leash and my "wiry one" comes dashing along. I take him in my arms and he starts licking my hands, my face, my clothes, everything he can reach, with his pink tongue. I put him down and he jumps and jumps, and jumps around me.

"If you only knew how I've missed you!" I tell him. Babs needs no words to prove me that he missed me too. Unfortunately, I cannot stay long and after twenty minutes, I have to abandon him once more. He gives me a reproachful look, atrociously human.

In the hall of my hotel, I find Lucas waiting for me. He is in uniform today. It changes him to his advantage. "You were out early!" he remarks.

"Yes," I say, confused. "I went to see Babs."

"I was going to suggest taking you to see him before starting with our proceedings. Do you know that I haven't found out anything yet! No one seems to have been notified! No one is expecting you! Are you sure you were not given a name?"

"Absolutely sure."

Captain Lucas tells me a few names of people who might have been warned, but I don't recognize any of them. "There remains only one thing for us to do: visit all the offices that have something to do with aliens." We get into the car and start our round. After two longs hours, we are no more advanced. Coming out from one of the buildings, Lucas says: "I really don't know where else to take you! Wait! I am going to ask this chap," he adds, sighting a civilian coming down the street towards us. "Maybe he will know."

"Hello!" greets the latter, leveling with us.

Lucas explains my case. The civilian scrutinizes me. "Have you a little dog?" he asks.

"Yes."

"Then I am aware." And turning to Lucas says, "Take her to our office. She is expected."

"Well!" says Lucas starting the car. "So that is it! If you had only told me to start with. How could I guess?"

We come to an old house, in the lower part of the town. We go up a creaking wooden staircase. It leads us onto a sort of gallery overlooking a closed yard. "Wait for me a second," says Lucas and he vanishes behind a door. He reappears five minutes later. "Now I am going to leave you here," he says. "Will you have dinner with me tonight, if you have nothing better in mind?" I gladly accept; and he adds: "I'll pick you up at 7 p.m."

I walk into the office from where he came out. A man, still young, gets up from behind a table. There is something queer about him. Maybe it is the set of false teeth that clashes with his age. Or maybe it is his blond stringy hair parted too high for it to be on the side, and not enough to be in the middle—his hair that doesn't look alive, but seems a hemp wig. His clothes are black—very black—and look as if they had just been taken out of a trunk inherited from his father. One expects them to smell of naphthalene.[1] His shoulders are covered with dandruff. Captain Lucas introduces us: "Mr. O'Shaga—Miss Sergueiew." Then taking leave, he retires.

Mr. O'Shaga grins at me with all his too even teeth. "I was expecting you."

I ask: "So Mr. Benton did notify you of my coming?"

"For sure."

"In that case you might have prevented me searching all Gibraltar. It would have been more discreet."

His pale eyes under this discoloured lashes rest upon me as he says, half smiling: "There has been a misunderstanding as to the date of your arrival. How are you settled?"

"It could be worse."

"From now on, you have nothing to worry about. We are in charge of everything: your board, your transportation. You'll be notified as soon as there is room on a plane."

"There is something else. I have a dog. Mr. Benton has promised me you'd arrange his transportation and would see that he is spared the quarantine."

"I know. We'll see to that too. He is called Babs, isn't he?"

"Yes."

"Where is Babs actually?"

"At the guard post, at the entrance of Gibraltar."

"Leave him to me. And now, would you give me a few details about your mission?"

I shake my head. "No. Mr. Benton assured me that I'd have to answer no questions before I got to London."

"As you wish. I was only going to ask you how long it took you to gain the Germans' confidence."

"Two and a half years."

"Gosh! And what gave you the idea to do that work?"

"Probably the same thing that animates all the resistance movements: the hatred of the oppressor, the desire of seeing France freed."

O'Shaga tries a couple more questions, but in the face of the vagueness of my answers, he gives it up.

After lunch, I return to visit Babs and am allowed to take him as far as the aerodome. The taking off and landing of planes makes a great impression on him. It is from the airfield that the Rock of Gibraltar is the most beautiful. It rises like a sugar loaf, with sides so steep and smooth, that its summit seems inaccessible. From downtown one cannot see it very well; one has to stretch the head back too far. It dominates with all its crushing mass the houses clinging to its flanks.

I take Babs back to his guardian and start walking home. The bay is glistening in the sun. The opposite coast fades in a light heat mist. The pale grey of the war vessels blends with the paleness of the water. At 6 p.m. the Main Street begins to be animated. Each time a door opens, fragments of songs and puffs of music escape from the bars. Holding by the waist, sailors are coming up from the port and going into the cafes. The "souvenir" stores are full of buyers. Chinese and Indian junk fabricated for exportation sell well.

I go up to my room to change, and at 7 p.m. sharp, with military precision, the maid comes to tell me that an officer is waiting for me in the hall. Derryck Lucas is all polished up for the occasion. He has booked a table at the Yachting Club. I am in a good mood. Derryck is a very gay companion. He has a face that would dissipate any melancholy: a round face, with a too bushy moustache of which he rolls the ends in two little points. His laughing eyes are black, under thick joining brows, and he roars all the time so good naturedly that it's contagious. Derryck is "Town Commandant." One of his jobs is to locate the newcomers, whether civilian or military.

The blackout is at 11 p.m. in Gibraltar. "If we leave at once," says Derryck at 10.30 p.m., "we have still time to go and say good night to Babs. I bet that is what you are longing for!"

When we arrive at the guard post, I look through the window and see Babs, rolled in a round on a blanket near the stove and sound asleep, his nose under his hind paw. I can't wake him up. He would only be disappointed again. We go away without him having seen us.

October 12th

I have made the acquaintance of an American aviator this afternoon, and he has invited me to dinner at the Rock Hotel. His name is Ken-I-don't-know-what (I didn't catch his second name). I wish I was staying at the Rock instead of my lousy "Grand." Here one has an admirable view of the bay, and the hotel is situated in the midst of a pine tree park.

During the meal I tell Ken about Babs. "Why do you leave him at the Post. He would be much better here, in case they won't allow you to keep him at your hotel."

I explain that there is a quarantine and that the C.O. of the Post won't give me back Babs without special permission. "Let's go and kidnap him," suggests Ken.

The idea appeals to me. We discuss of a plan of action. The final decision is that Ken will drive me in his jeep as far as the aerodrome and leave me there. I'll continue on foot, while he will cross the airfield and will go to the other side of the post. I'll unleash Babs and throw him stones to run after in the direction of where Ken will be standing. It is dark and the path is bordered by bushes. Ken is to catch Babs when he gets within his reach, put him into his jeep and drive away. He'll wait for me at the other side of the airfield.

The lieutenant at the post is surprised at seeing me come so late. Babs bounces with joy. "Only five minutes," I pray. I start throwing stones as far as I can. Babs disappears in the darkness and comes back as soon, proudly dropping the stone at my feet. "This time he won't come back!" I think to myself hopingly. But the light spot gets more precise telling me that Babs is still at liberty. For ten minutes I throw stones with no result. Once I have heard a whining, followed by a growl, and the following instant Babs was back, but without a stone! The next time he brought two!

"You must go home," says a voice at my side. I turn round and see the officer. "You'll miss the curfew and get arrested by a patrol. It is already ten to eleven," he adds. Furious and disconsolate, I put Babs on his leash. "I'll accompany you as far as the other side of the aerodrome to be sure they don't stop you," says the lieutenant. We take Babs with us. On our way the Brit asks: "What were you up to?"

I don't answer. After a short silence, I say: "Let me take away Babs."

"You know very well that if it was only for me, you could have him right now. But I have orders. I am responsible for Babs."

"But if Babs ran away while I am there? It wouldn't be your fault, would it?"

He smiles. "No. We would have to look for him and if we couldn't find him, we'd have to write a report."

"Tomorrow morning I'll come back, very early, and Babs will run away. All right? Please, say yes."

He tosses his head. "It's very irregular, what you ask me to do!"

"Please," I beg. "Please, don't refuse."

"All right!" he finishes by acceding. We have crossed the airfield. He leaves me and walks back, with Babs pulling on his leash, looking at me.

A little further, Ken is waiting in his jeep. "Well? What happened?" I ask him, getting in.

"I wasn't able to approach that little stinker! Once I got hold of him, but he turned round, bit me and just slipped out of my hands!"

I tell him that the officer consented to close his eyes, so that we could start all over tomorrow morning. Ken promises to come and pick me up at my hotel at 6 a.m.

October 13th

At the agreed time, I am down in the hall. A Gibraltarian servant, more Arab than Spanish, is washing the tiled floor, unhurriedly. It is only just getting light. Times passes. 6.15—6.30—7 a.m. Still no Ken! Now it is quite light. It will be more difficult to take Babs. At a quarter to eight I decide to start alone. The streets in the morning are practically empty. I am about to enter under the fortified vault to leave the town, when a policeman approaches me: "Are you the French lady that has a little dog?"

"I am," I say surprised.

"I was instructed to go and get him with you, and take him to the pound."

I look at him with horror: "To the pound?"

Maybe he guesses something of my thought, for he hurries to add: "You need not be afraid. He will be well taken care of there." We get into an old bus that runs from the town to the Gibraltarian frontier. "How did you know it was I?" I ask the policeman between two jolts.

He laughs: "You are the only civilian woman on the Rock except the Spanish that come to work, and those are easily recognizable."

I am wondering if it is the C.O. of the Patrol Post who has warned of my fruitless attempt of last night. I can't believe it. It would be too dirty a trick! Babs greets me with his usual jumps. The officer isn't there. We take the same bus that brings us back to town. We have to walk the remaining way. The pound is at the other end of the Rock. We pass in front of the Rock Hotel and go along the garden. I let Babs loose. "Here we are," says the policeman at last.

We enter a yard that looks like stables. Effectively, there are a couple of horses in their stalls. From a neighbouring yard comes barking. My heart shrinks. "I won't let Babs be put in a cage. For nothing in the world will I allow it," I think to myself.

"We have to wait for the sergeant. He mustn't be far away and won't be long coming," says the policeman. As he finishes speaking, a soldier appears on the threshold of a door. His sleeve bears the three stripes of a sergeant. He salutes us and asks of what help he can be. The policeman explains that he's been ordered to bring him Babs to be kept in Quarantine and asks him to sign a discharge. The sergeant writes his name at the bottom of a sheet of paper, and the policeman, who is in a hurry, leaves us.

The sergeant, a red-haired Irishman with huge hairy hands, a red freckled face and nearly white eye-lashes, crouches down to pat Babs. From the position he is in, he lifts his head and smiles at me. "Come on; stop worrying, Miss. He won't be unhappy. I'll keep him in my room. He can sleep on my bed. The door is never locked: you may come any time you like."

"True? You'll do that?" I say regaining confidence.

"Don't you think I know what you feel like?" he says standing up. "I've had a dog fifteen years, and when he died I was sick with grief. Come here, little one. What's your name?"

"Babs," I say.

"He must be four?"

"Four and a half. He was born in February 1939."

The sergeant is a veterinarian; he loves his work. We chat till midday. I walk back feeling better, reassured about Babs' future. I have left him in the bedroom. The sergeant is going to give him a bath this afternoon. He needs it badly.

Tonight's radio announces the Badoglio has declared war on Germany. What weathercocks these Italians!

October 25th

I am still in Gibraltar. I spend my time the best I can, taking long walks with Babs who is quarantined only in name. I fetch him in the morning and bring him back in the evening. Sometimes I keep him over night. Each time I go into the sergeant's room I leave some chocolate, or cigarettes on his bed; once or twice I have been able to get him some port and some vermouth. Everybody is satisfied. Nearly every evening I am invited out to dinner. I have many friends: Derryck, and one of his friends Ray Grumbar, nick-named "Prince Charming"; Ken and Cliff Lord, and Daddy Long-Legs, who share the same room at the Rock Hotel; Loulou Lioubinski, a Polish lieutenant who knows my cousin Janio.

Since I am here, I have made quite a discovery. I've discovered that the British and the Americans can't stand each other! The British are jealous of the Yanks because these are better paid and can spend more money: "They take all our girls!" complain the English. The Americans envy the British their traditions and think they despise them because they are a young nation. Anyhow, the two never mix. Ken reproaches me for seeing Derryck, and Derryck bears grudge because I go out with Ken.

When Derryck can free himself on Sundays, we go for long strolls. When I say "long," it is a way of speaking, for we can't go any further than round the Rock! Derryck made me visit all sorts of underground passages. The Rock of Gibraltar is like an ant-hill, perforated from side to side by thousands of tunnels transforming it in a gigantic empty shell.

Certain nights the darkness is transpierced by the luminous darts of hundreds of search lights hidden in an incalculable number of openings made in the rocky slants and invisible in day time. The whole Rock bristles up like a monstrous porcupine.

We went with Ken one afternoon to the very top of the Rock, where the summit ends in a crest. In the distance, dimmed by the mist, one could distinguish the African coast. To the left, the Mediterranean was very blue; to the right, the tide coming from the Ocean had a green shade. Driving down, on our way to town, Ken had stopped his jeep to show me the apes in the trees. He told me there is a legend that says that when the last monkey dies on the Rock, the British shall lose Gibraltar. It is why, some years ago, a fresh supply of apes was brought over from North Africa. The weather continues to be fine. When, by chance, the sky does get overcast, a crown of clouds hangs over the summit long after the rest has dissolved or been swept away.

October 29th

I am beginning to find the time long. Benton had told me I wouldn't be staying more than a few days in Gibraltar, and it is already three weeks since I arrived. It is why I return to see O'Shaga.

"I am not forgetting you," he assures me. "If there were only you, you could leave any day. But there is also Babs for whom I haven't been able to arrange anything."

At dinner I tell Ken the difficulties I am having with Babs. "Why don't you send him to London with one of our pilots?" he asks me. "They don't go through any customs or controls. No one would say anything to them. Many of my friends have dogs as mascots."

"You think it would be possible?" I ask hesitatingly.

"But certainly!"

"I wouldn't entrust Babs to anyone."

"Do you want me to fix the whole thing for you? If I find you someone, you'll be able to rest assured he is trustworthy."

"All right. Thanks."

October 30th 1943

"I have good news for you," announces Ken. "Clifford Lord is flying over to London next month. He is willing to take Babs for you. You better go and talk to him yourself."

Cliff is an American A.F. pilot captain. I don't know him very well. Once or twice I've seen him dead drunk. Except for that, he seems O.K.

"I have to be in London between the 10th and the 15th," he tells me. "If you go before me, you can leave Babs with me. I'll take great care of him."

"What if you didn't go to London after all? If some hindrance arises? If you were sent elsewhere? What would become of Babs?"

"I give you my word of honour that I will be in London sometime in November. If, by any chance, (which is quite improbable) I was prevented from flying over there myself, I would see to it that Babs should get over anyway."

And I accept it.

November 1st 1943

I go back to see O'Shaga. I explain the situation. "If it can be done this way, it'll avoid you a lot of bureaucracy and official proceedings. But in case that officer didn't go to London, and Babs was left behind in Gibraltar, may I trust you will get him over to me?"

"You may."

"Is that sure?"

"Quite sure." In spite of that I am hesitant. "You have my word," says O'Shaga in an engaging tone.

O'Shaga, Derryck told me, is an unfrocked priest. He received a dispensation from the Pope for the duration of the war. And I am wondering if this fact renders his word more valid, or if it also dispenses him from keeping it? From promise to promise, how far will it go? Benton in Madrid; O'Shaga here. "All right." I accept at last. "But I may as well warn you now. If I don't get Babs in November, I shall not work."

"You'll get him," he repeats. "Now, if you are decided to leave, be ready. You may have to go any time. I'll try to let you know as long ahead as possible, but it can be only a few hours in advance. If you leave your hotel, tell the porter where you are going, so that I can reach you if need be."

November 2nd 1943

Ken has left yesterday for Italy. Today I have definitely taken Babs out of his supposed quarantine. In future he'll live at the Rock hotel, in Cliff's room. I wanted to give a farewell dinner to my friends. But when the Americans heard that I had invited some British, they didn't turn up, without even bothering to warn me. The British too found a good reason to refuse politely. Sadly, I ate all alone a very good meal.

November 4th 1943

The proprietor of the hotel knocks at my door just as I am getting ready to go out. "There is a telephone message for you," he says. "A gentleman will come to see you at 10 a.m. He asks you to be at home. He didn't give him name."

"Thank you," I say.

It must be O'Shaga. At 10.30 Lioubinski is to come for me. We wanted to go out for a walk and then have lunch together. It doesn't matter; he can wait a minute if O'Shaga hasn't finished. I take a book and go down in the hall. At 10 punctually O'Shaga makes his appearance. He walks like everybody, but I don't know why he gives me the impression of advancing sideways like a crab. Simple optical illusion, I suppose.

"Can we go up a moment? I want to talk to you?" Once we are in my room, he lowers his voice to ask: "You have got some money, haven't you?"

"Yes."

"I would like you to let me have it, as well as all the papers you might still have in your possession. I'll give you a receipt. You'll be probably leaving tonight. Are you ready?"

"Yes. But you are the one who has my passport."

"You won't need it. Here is a paper you will give to the control officer of the airport at your arrival. I have rebaptised you. I found you another name: Dorothy Tremaine. I choose the names according to the persons. How do you like yours?"

"I don't," I tell him. "I don't like the name Dorothy. I have known a Dorothy; she squinted!"

"Ah! That's too bad! Your paper is all typed out. Do you absolutely want me to change it?"

"No, as long as I don't have to carry it the rest of my life, but why this change of personality? You have only given me a name—what about the rest of my identity? If I have to fill in some landing papers?"

"Don't worry; you'll have nothing to fill in, no questions to answer. No one will interrogate you; you won't have to open your mouth from here to London!" I hand him over the money: 49,000 escudos and £10. He signs me a receipt. (I wonder what for!) "Now we can go down."

We return to the hall, empty at this hour. "I'll have an officer from the airport come to pick you up at 10 p.m. You are entitled to 45 lbs. of luggage."

"45 lbs.!" I protest. "But I have much more than that!"

O'Shaga rubs his chin in annoyance. "You'll never be allowed to take it with you on the plane. They are over loaded as it is. But I know what we are going to do. Put in one suitcase all the clothes you won't need immediately, and I'll have it shipped. It may be three months before you get it—but eventually you'll have it." We agree that I'll leave the suitcase with the porter whom I'll also give the key in an envelope (for the customs), and O'Shaga will have it picked up.

Just then arrives Lioubinsky. He seems surprised to find me in O'Shaga's company. He knows him. After O'Shaga has departed, Lioubinsky remarks: "I say! You have some acquaintances!" To which I don't answer. He takes me to lunch in a small restaurant in the Main Street. In the midst of the meal, he suddenly says: "Look who has just come in!"

I turn round and notice a man whom I have never seen before. "Who is he?"

"Mr. Darling, you know!"

"And who is Mr. Darling, pray?"

"Oh! Stop pretending! Your 'boss' of course!"

"My boss? What boss? I have no boss!"

"You haven't?" he says doubtfully. "Well, let's call him O'Shaga's boss if you prefer."

"You run too fast in conclusions," I tell him shrugging. We speak of something else. Back at my hotel, I unpack and start to repack all over my suitcase. Derryck comes to keep me company at this last dinner. "Are you sure that you are leaving tonight?" he asks me.

"Yes, of course. Why?"

"Because I have consulted all the passengers' lists of the departing planes and your name is on none of them. The only woman's name I saw was a Miss Tremaine. I don't know who she is. Never heard of her!"

"Maybe they'll mark me down at the last minute, if there is a spare place," I tell him reassuringly.

"Maybe," he says unconvinced. "But it is strange. I wonder who the Miss Tremaine is? She is called Dorothy. Fancy being called Dorothy!" He tosses his head repeating: "Dorothy!"

His remark vexes me and mentally I curse O'Shaga: "Fancy being called Dorothy!" At 10 p.m., still no one has come for me. Nor at 11 p.m. I wait until 11:15, then deciding it is not for tonight, I go up to my room and to bed.

November 5th 1943

I get up early, notify the porter I'll be at the Rock Hotel, and hurry there. Cliff has already gone. But Babs is in his room. I take him out on the terrace. I look at him ferret around, then come back to me and lay his shaggy head on my knees and gaze at me with his golden eyes. Why do I love my dog so much? Why am I so attached to that small animal who cannot talk and understands me but little? Little? Maybe not. But what I am certain of is that amongst so much deceiving, lies, treasons, mistrust, hatred, loneliness, he is something stable, clean, true. With him I am not alone. To him I need not lie. I love him with the best part of myself.

I go back for lunch to my hotel to see if there is any news. I take Babs with me. A girl in police uniform is awaiting me. "I'd like to talk to you," she says. After she has left, I push over to make room for Babs on the chair beside me.

"You see," I tell him, patting his wired hair, "even here, amongst our Allies, you can trust no one! You meet people, you believe them to be your friends; they smile at you; and behind your back they denounce you!" Babs listens, his head to one side. Then he jumps down, goes to the dining room door and looks back at me with his expressive eyes: "It's time to eat," he seems to say.

While I am at table, the porter comes to tell me a gentleman will see me at 2 p.m. and asks me not to go out. It's O'Shaga, more than ever looking like a conspirator. He backs me up into a dark corner and whispers: "Have you the receipt you signed yesterday?"

"Yes."

"Do you mind giving it to me? I'll make you out another one." I look in my bag and hand it to him. He gives me a paper he had already made. "I thought this would be safer." I look at the receipt; it says the same thing, only instead of "O'Shaga," he has signed "Smith."

I repress a strong envy to shrug my shoulders. "Well. When do I leave?" I ask him.

"Probably tonight. No plane left yesterday, because of the weather. But I think this time I am telling you goodbye for good. Have a good trip, Dorothy Tremaine!"

I take Babs back to the Rock Hotel. Cliff is there. He tells me that the way things look, he'll probably be in London next week. I make him more recommendations about Babs. He asks me to ring him up if I am really leaving tonight. He'll drive me to the airfield. "We'll come and wave hankies, Babs and I!"

10.15 p.m. This time I am going! An officer is waiting for me and helps me out of the jeep. "Miss Tremaine?" he asks.

"Yes, it's I!"

He unloads my luggage. I pick up Babs in my arms. But all this bustling, these people, the lights in the night enervate him. He struggles and I put him down. I hate goodbyes and want to hasten them. I turn to Cliff: "I entrust to you what I care about the most—you know that, don't you? If you think you won't be able to bring him to me, please, say it now. There is still time. I'll take him with me. And over there, I'll find some way out. I don't know what or how, but I shall, I am sure!"

"Stop worrying!" says Cliff. "I've given you my word." He gets back into his jeep and whistles for Babs, who emerges from between people's legs and bounces on the empty seat. Cliff starts the engine. Babs looks at me with surprise, pointing the ears, waiting for me to get in. Cliff puts an arm round him, and the jeep takes off, plunging into the night. For a few seconds, I still distinguish the light spot of my little dog's body in the darkness. Then, nothing more.

I turn away and walk into the waiting room of one of the wooden barracks. I am stunned by the lights, the noise, the crowd. The narrow room is filled with soldiers and officers waiting to leave. The captain who greeted me approaches: "You needn't bother about your luggage; it will be carried into the plane. Just listen to the loud speaker. When your turn comes, your name will be called out. Just follow the rest of the passengers to the plane. Is there anything else I can do for you?"

"Thanks. I have got everything I need."

"Then I wish you a good journey and a happy landing in England!"

I lean against a wooden railing, and over the dark shapes of the grounded planes I look at the black silhouette of the Rock rising in the sky. The imperceptible moon crest, like a nail cutting, doesn't shine, and today no search lights illuminate Gibraltar. I try to realize that tomorrow I shall be in London. But somehow, it doesn't seem true; it remains vague, like a dream.

The loud speaker creeks and cracks, and I listen to it with one ear. "It's funny," I say to myself, "when did I hear that name, Mr. Maine? Sounds familiar." The loud speaker stops, then repeats: "Mr. Maine." A soldier comes to me: "Pardon me," he says: "aren't you Miss Tremaine?"

I am about to say no, then realize that "Mr. Maine" was "Miss Tremaine," curse once more O'Shaga and his mania of giving names, and, confused, hasten to follow the soldier who leads me to the plane. The other passengers have preceded me and are already seated.

V

England, 1943–1944

We take off at midnight. We have been warned that it will be cold, as we have to fly at high altitude. Each one of us has received three blankets and some provisions. I am tired; my brain is benumbed. I don't know what awaits me, and I don't care. I have slept, waking up frequently. It is 3:32 a.m. by my watch. It is cold. I pull up my blankets that have slipped. I try to guess where we are. The windows are blacked out; the electric light is on. The other passengers are asleep or dozing. The engine's noise is deafening. I have the impression of being locked up in a box which a giant would be shaking. Now and then, one of the passengers wakes, verifies his watch, glances around, unscrews his thermos bottle, swallows a tumbler of tea, and tries a better position to continue his sleep.

I would like to read, but the light is insufficient. I must have drowsed off. I open my eyes as the crew members are coming out of the pilot's post. A bleak light outlines the rectangle of the door. It is nearly 4:30 a.m. "They probably have a different time in England," I suppose. Time drags along. Suddenly I have the impression we are going down, and when I least expect it, I feel a jerk, which is the contact with the ground. Everybody starts fidgeting. We must be ahead of our schedule time for I was told it would take about 6 hours. The plane comes to a standstill, and after a time that seems endless, the door slides open and a very pale, very low sun hesitatingly floods the inside of the plane.

"A quarter of an hour's stop," we are informed. "You may come out but don't walk away." Someone says we are in Ireland. An icy wind sweeps the drenched asphalt of the runway, wrinkling the puddles. All around the landscape is monotonously flat. The sun is rising from a glistening sea of pale gold. Clouds are trailing, disheveled, in a washed out sky. Frozen Americans, their coat collars lifted, their noses red, drive at top speed, leaning over the steering wheel of their jeeps. The British, more indifferent to the cold, go about on foot.

"I have nearly arrived!" I say to myself. And I try to look back at the Past to measure the distance covered since that day I decided for the first time not to accept Defeat. I remember Syria, and the plans I did at night, in bed, and how Chimerical they seemed next day. It is so long ago—so much further than three and a half years ago! It was in another life—it was in another world! And I realize that it shall never be the same as "before," for those who will have "lived" this war, they'll be the same.

V. England, 1943–1944

November 6th 1943

We take off soon after and arrive finally at 6:15 a.m. "Where are we?" asks a soldier. "At Bristol," answers another.

"I'll be able, when the formalities are over, to go and spend the night at my friends' who live near here," I say to myself.

It is cold and a kind of melted snow is falling from a low grey sky. We are all, taken into a formalities room where we are given questionnaires to fill out. I examine my sheet of paper with indecision. There is a medical paper for the doctor; I have to note the illnesses I had in the current of this year, the date of my last vaccinations, etc. The second sheet of paper is for a complete identification: age, place and date of birth, nationality, names of father, mother, nanny, and all, and all. I hesitate but a fraction of a second, then shamelessly I write down: Surname: Tremaine.

First name: Dorothy.

Birth date: (My mother's!)

Place of birth: My cousin's address in Cambridge.

Nationality: British.

Passport No: ...I make it up.

And I hand my paper to the corporal who takes it without giving it a look. When everyone has filled in his sheet, the corporal leads us to another barrack where we are told to wait. A soldier brings in some tea and sandwiches. A round stove spreads limited warmth in which we crowd, trying to warm at least one side of our body. After a while, I notice a captain coming out of a room. He points with his chin in my direction and the sergeant he is addressing comes to me and asks me to follow him. He brings me into a narrow office. The captain and another man, a civilian, sitting behind a table, are expecting me.

I get out of my bag O'Shaga's letter addressed "to whom it may concern." It certifies that Miss Tremaine, Dorothy, British subject, is travelling to London on official business. I hand it to the captain. Having read it, he passes it to the civilian, brings me a chair and asks me to sit down.

Mr. Gold (I anticipate calling him by his name) rubs his hands and looks at me with small eyes encased between heavy lids. He is thick-lipped, long broad hook-nosed and has a pair of protruding ears that would make an African elephant jealous! Nature has been less prodigal with his hair—but one can't have everything. He leans towards the officer, putting a fat hand in front of his mouth and says in a whisper that must be heard in the corridor: "I am going to ask her a few questions?"

"If you wish," answers the officer unenthusiastically.

"Miss Sergueiew?" asks Mr. Gold engagingly. I don't react. "Your name is Miss Sergueiew, isn't it?" he insists.

"Is that what the letter says?" I ask him indicating O'Shaga's paper.

"Hum ... well ... I proceed."

"First of all, who are you to be asking me all these questions?" I say.

"You are right. I didn't introduce myself. I represent the Home Office. The captain, he represents the War Office. So you see, you are quite safe to talk."

"And may I ask how many more 'Offices' you have in Great Britain? You could gather all their representatives for me to make a speech!"

He leans again and whispers in the captain's ear: "I am going to question her on her relations with the Germans." The officer only shrugs his shoulders. Backing slightly away, he rubs his ear. Mr. Gold addresses me again: "I believe you got in touch with the Germans?"

"Ah! Yes?" I say with an air only mildly surprised.

"What can you tell me about it?" he continues without losing courage.

"Nothing!" I say. "You seem to know more than I do."

Mr. Gold is beginning to get nervous: "According our information, you would be sent on a mission by the Germans." I remain silent. "Well? What have you to answer?"

"You've stated a fact. It wasn't a question."

"Let's have it, yes or no, are you sent by the Germans?"

"Why the Germans?"

"How: why?"

"Yes, why the Germans rather than the Japs or the Italians?"

Furious, Mr. Gold stretches towards the captain and blows in his face: "I can't get anything out of her."

"Drop it," advises the latter from the corner of his mouth, and taking out a handkerchief he wipes his face. Mr. Gold makes a last try: "So you refuse to tell us anything?"

"I could never tell you in five minutes as many astounding things as you have just stated. I wouldn't even try!"

The captain turns away his head to hide a smile. Mr. Gold bends a sulky nose to examine the sheet of paper I have filled in. He lifts his eyes on me: "Anyhow, you didn't spare yourself years! Generally ladies prefer to make themselves younger."

"Alcohol!" I say.

"What do you mean—alcohol?"

"I am preserved in alcohol. I drink. It preserves in certain cases."

He shrugs his shoulders.

"How much money have you got with you?" he asks with a sigh.

"Two pennies and half a peseta."

"You can keep them," he declares generously. "That'll be all."

"Thank you," I say rising.

"And allow me to congratulate you for your discretion!" The officer accompanies me into the passage. "I apologize for this little incident. I wasn't able to prevent it. But you needn't worry; it won't go any further. Now I'll take you to customs. Then we'll give you someone to accompany you to London."

"Oh! You needn't bother. I am used to finding my way."

"It is no bother," he replies slightly embarrassed. "It's a custom."

"Ah," I say disappointed. "I hoped to spend the night at my friends' who live at Wraxall, 8 miles from here."

"I am terribly sorry but it's impossible. You're expected in London."

In the customs hall my luggage is thoroughly searched. Apologizing, the customs officer gathers all the papers he finds in my suitcase: brown paper wrapping presents bought in Gibraltar; tissue paper from around a hat; newspapers I have stuffed in my shoes to prevent them from getting crushed. He smoothes it all out, folds it carefully, adds to it the book "Montmartre" and says: "I am obliged to confiscate all that."

"Do."

My clothes are not examined, nor my handbag in which I have Mummy's letters. Ten minutes later, a woman in the blue police uniform comes to fetch me. She is tall and fat, without grace or sex, and a homely face that one imagines difficultly expressing any emotion. She must wear a 12 shoe size. Under the black uniform hat, her dull hair is pulled back into a meager chignon. A stray lock is hanging in front of her ear. In her hands she is holding a large brown envelope with official heading, and bearing my name—my real name, not Dorothy Tremaine.

A taxi is waiting before the door and takes us to Bristol's railway station. I notice all the neighbourhood has badly suffered from bombing. Some parts are completely wiped out. My guard has bought third-class tickets. The train is crowded. We go through carriage after carriage without finding a seat. I am about to offer to take first-class tickets and I'll pay the difference, when I remember that I have no money with me.

Eventually we are able to sit down. Opposite to me a man is reading a newspaper. The large headlines of the front page announce the recapture of Kiev by the Russians. I am overwhelmed with joy. Glancing around me, I am surprised to see but dull, tired faces that express nothing.

"Look," I tell the policewoman. "Kiev is liberated!"

"Yes," says she with indifference.

I try to imagine myself unfolding this newspaper in the compartment of a train in France: everybody's enthusiasm and emotion; people all talking at once; making hypothesis for the future; calculating the rapidity of the Russian advance; evoking the capture of Kiev two years ago; seeing in it the obvious proof of the German defeat, hoping an imminent liberation; and then that feeling of fraternity drawing together strangers, causing hearts to beat in unison.

The train starts to move. No one speaks. Each passenger has a paper, or a book, and buries his nose into it. We are crawling. I look out of the window. Here is Bath: a mass of ruins. The heat, the rocking of the carriage, the monotonous toc, toc, toc of the cross sections under the wheels of the train, but mostly the fatigue of a sleepless night in plane and of the formalities that preceded and followed it, overcome me rapidly and I fall asleep, sliding slightly to one side. It is nearly night when I wake up. The train is slowing down.

"We are nearly there," says my guard. I sit up. I don't understand where I am. "This is London," the policewoman informs me. It is true. I am in England!

The train stops, and we get out into a big scarcely lit station: Paddington. My companion takes out my suitcase, without losing sight of me. Then, she seems to look for someone. "We must wait," she says. Suddenly she starts to wave her arm and shortly a man approaches us. "Come," she says.

The man picks up my suitcase. We all go to a car parked a few feet away. The driver seems to know our destination, for the policewoman has given him no address. The car edges into the traffic and speeds through crowded streets. Night has fallen. A few search lights lazily sweep the sky with their luminous shafts. We leave the centre of the town for more deserted streets. At one time it even seems to me we are out of London and are driving in the country. But it only must be the suburbs. At last, the car stops in front of a two-story house surrounded by a wall, and we get out.

The policewoman rings at the wooden door in the wall. A bell sounds somewhere inside the house. It seems to me I hear a key turn a couple of times in a lock. A door opens. I discern clicking. Steps approach the gate. An eye must be observing us through an opening. The lock squeaks; a heavy bolt is lifted. The door opens. In the rectangle of light coming from the house, I see a man wearing a vizored cap, similar to what museum guards wear, and holding in his hand a bunch of keys on a big ring. He moves aside to let us in, and the policewoman and I go up the three steps of the porch.

"Where are we?" I ask, pulling her by the sleeve.

"Don't be impatient," she answers. "You shall see."

"Will I find a room here?" I inquire, wishing more than anything for a bed to stretch out and go to sleep.

"You'll have everything you need."

The man with the keys comes in behind us. He gives three turns to the lock, pulls two huge bolts, checks the door, then goes away. A woman comes towards us. She has grey hair and a kindly face. She shows us into an office. My guardian gives her the big brown envelope, asks her to sign a discharge, then turning to me, she says, without a smile: "Good bye and good luck!"

Then she is gone. I look at the woman in grey. I feel very lonely, very lost, like a bit of straw tossed by the waves! She smiles at me. "I am Mrs. Maud," she says. She has a sweet voice that reassures me.

"Where am I?" I ask.

"Amongst friends. You'll stay here until you are interrogated. I'll do everything I can so that it shouldn't seem too long. You have nothing more to fear. You have come to the end of your voyage. Now you must relax and rest. In a few days you'll be free to go where you please."

I smile back at her. After months she is the first really human being I have met. I know that, for me, it is not yet finished, that I am not at the end of my voyage, that there still remains a long way to go, that the hour of relaxation has not yet come. Nevertheless, it is good to hear her say the contrary.

"I have a paper with a few questions you have to fill in," she adds, "but I suppose you've had enough of all that for today? It can wait till tomorrow."

"No, let's get it over now."

She takes a printed form out of a drawer, and brings an inkstand and a pen. I read the questions and hesitate, the pen in mid-air. Surname—first name... What am I to write? My own or Dorothy Tremaine? As if she read my thoughts, Mrs. Maud says: "It matters no longer; you can now give your real name. All the women who come here have fake names. But this is only a police record. You needn't be afraid."

"Are there many other women?"

"Fourteen at present. You'll see them in a moment."

I give her back the form I've filled in.

"Take out of your suitcase everything you'll need for the night. The regulations don't allow you to keep your luggage. It'll be stored in the trunk room, and you can ask to go there every day from 10 to 12 a.m. Now, I am going to show you which will be your bed," she adds, when I have finished sorting my things.

I follow her along a large passage, where it is very cold. She opens a door, and I find myself in a dormitory with six cots. The bedspreads, as well as the curtains pulled across the window, are royal blue. A chair at the foot of each cot and a chest of drawers with a mirror, a few jars of cream and combs, compose the entire furniture.

"This will be your bed," says Mrs. Maud, pointing to the one nearest the door. "Now I'll show you where the bathroom is. Dinner is in half an hour," she warns before leaving me.

Once I am ready, I go out in the corridor in search of the dining room and find myself nose to nose with a blond young woman whose appearance seems familiar.

"You are French?" she asks point blank. "So am I!" she adds without waiting for my answer. "Do you know where you are?"

"Where?"

"In prison!" She observes me, her head slightly to one side. I don't answer. "Is that all the effect it makes you?" She seems disappointed.

"I am looking for the dining room," I tell her. "I am hungry."

She shrugs her shoulders. "It's this way. Follow me." As she walks in front, I suddenly remember where I've seen her grey tailor suit, her over shoulder bag.

I ask: "You were in Gibraltar?"

"Yes."

"At the Grand Hotel?"

"Yes."

"That's where I saw you (but always from behind). I was at the Grand Hotel too."

Mrs. Maud joins us in the passage. "I see you are already acquainted. Come, I'll introduce you to the other girls."

As we approach the dining room, the noise of voices grows louder but stops as we enter the room. All the eyes are fixed on me. Mrs. Maud tells them my name, then points out to me each occupant of the two long tables. I have the surprise of finding Francine, the little Belgian girl from the Pension Argentina.

"And this is Miss Brown," finishes Mrs. Maud indicating an elderly woman who is helping to pass the dishes. The latter gets hold of both my hands and assures me warmly: "You'll see how happy you will be with us!"

I take place between Nelly de V, my first acquaintance, and a Breton with close cut hair and big black fierce eyes. In front of me I have Francine, and next to her a Czech whose orange mop of hair is rolled into curling pins. I am too tired to eat or talk. I have but one thought: sleep.

After dinner I ask Mrs. Maud when she thinks I'll be interrogated. "Tomorrow?"

"Oh! No. Tomorrow is Sunday. Only earthquakes happen regardless of Sunday!"

"It is ten days I am here," remarks bitterly Nelly, "and I haven't been interrogated yet!"

It is not encouraging, but tonight it leaves me indifferent. "I am in England," I say to myself. "The third chapter of my adventure is finished. Tomorrow I start a new one."

November 7th

It takes me some time to realize where I am, when I wake up. The curtains are drawn. It is quite dark. I discern a smell of tobacco smoke. Yesterday's events come back to me. I turn to the side where someone is smoking and whisper: "Good morning."

"Good morning," answers a voice which I recognize as belonging to the Breton.

Breakfast gathers us round the same tables. We are allowed to have as much bread and porridge as we want. The margarine is different from what we have in France; ours is white and tastes of candle; this one is yellow, salted and doesn't differ much from butter. I feel good this morning. As we leave the table, we meet Mrs. Maud coming out of her office.

"I have just had a telephone call concerning you, Lily. You'll be interrogated today at 11 a.m." Everyone gazes at me in amazement, and Mrs. Maud doesn't seem less surprised.

"I thought," says Nelly, "there never was any interrogation on Sundays?"

"This is the first time!" asserts Mrs. Maud.

"Have you any idea why they make an exception for you?" asks Nelly a little later.

"Not the least! Maybe because they have nothing to do today." I very much doubt Nelly accepts my explanation. She simply remarks: "I've been here for ten days. They might have started with me!"

At 11 a.m. Mrs. Maud comes to fetch me in the drawing room where I am trying to put together a zigzag puzzle which has some pieces missing. "You are going up to the first landing and there you'll see. It's the second door to the right. They are waiting for you. You can go alone."

Suddenly, my good mood disappears and I feel the old combative spirit rise within me. I am well decided not to go on telling my story to anyone who chooses to be curious. There has been O'Shaga, and then Gold who have tried to make me spill it. Now I'll only talk in front of the ones who are going to handle the case. "But how am I to know who the right ones are?" I wonder, climbing up the wooden stairs that creak under each step. "Wait and see," I say to myself.

A door is open, and I enter into a sparsely furnished room. The first thing that attracts my attention is two pairs of legs: the man's because he wears khaki socks with civilian trousers and shoes; the woman's because they are twisted one around the other like a corkscrew. Their owner is sitting on the edge of a chair, her arms folded, chin resting on a closed fist. She glances at me through slightly slanted greenish eyes; her gaze is not friendly. Her brown hair is soberly brushed up and fixed without art, and her features are icy. "She would be easy to hate," I reflect.

The man with the khaki socks is young—maybe twenty-five years old—with regular, slightly insipid features which one forgets as soon as one doesn't see them. He has elaborate symmetrical waves in his black hair. I've taken in all these details from the threshold where I have stopped. No one utters a word.

I am the first to break the silence: "And you, who are you?' I ask addressing both of them.

Obviously, my question isn't what they expected, for they look at each other, startled, and the woman says: "Who do you think we are?"

I don't want to think. I don't want to guess. I want to know. I ask: "Do you know Benton?"

"Yes," says the man.

"Because if I am going to answer questions I want to make sure it goes in the right ear and that I don't have to start all over again the next day."

"You may rest assured nothing of the sort will happen. Now, if you'd sit down." I take place on a sofa, facing them.

"Will you tell us everything from the beginning?" says the man. "It'll be simpler than asking you questions."

I start speaking. It takes me far back, when I left Paris to walk to Poland, thinking it would help me to conquer my freedom, confirm my independence. I tell them of my arrival in Berlin, my meeting with Dassel. Now and then, the man interrupts me, asking clarification, some details. He notes them on a pad. It seems as if we had only started when Mrs. Maud calls us for lunch.

"Will you come back at 1:30 p.m. so that we can proceed?" says the man.

At table, everybody looks at me with curiosity. "What did they tell you?" "Who is questioning you?" "How many are they?" Nearly all of them have already been interrogated, but most of them have been questioned, it appears, by uniformed officers from Scotland Yard. When I tell them that, for me, it was a man and a woman, it provokes an uproar of questions and exclamations.

"What can it mean?" "Why such a difference?" "And besides, on a Sunday!" They sense some mystery! They look at me with envy, a slight jealousy, some admiration and plenty of suspicion.

"I really don't know why!" I say. "They ask very ordinary questions."

The fact that my questioning isn't over surprises them too. In most cases, an hour and a half is sufficient! The afternoon ends without us having entered the main subject: my actual work. We have only reached the numeration of the times I have met Dassel during the years 1935, 1936, and 1937, of the reason for which I travelled to Germany, of the newspapers for which I wrote, of the interviews with Goering, etc., etc....

Mrs. Maud brings in some tea and cakes. At 5:30 p.m. they let me go.

"We'll continue tomorrow at 9 a.m.," says the man.

November 8th 1943

The interrogation continues with an interruption for lunch and ten minutes at tea time. No detail is passed. It reminds me very much of the questioning to which I was submitted by the Gestapo three years ago.

November 9th 1943

I am beginning to be tired. It may seem nothing to speak from 9 a.m. to 5 p.m., but when one considers the brain effort necessary to remember all the dates, the names, the places, to situate each detail, to remember all the encounters, all the rendezvous in their chronological order. There is nothing astonishing that by the evening I should be worn out. My bed neighbor, the Breton who smokes at night, gives me a pill. "This will help you," she assures me.

November 10th 1943

Today, I am just a nervous wreck. During the interrogation, because the young man asks me an insidious question on a certain date, I get so cross, that things threaten to take a bad turn. At lunch, I notice that my hand shakes, and I have some trouble lifting the food to my mouth. I feel an iron circle about my temples.

"Do you want another pill?" asks the Breton, full of concern.

"What are they supposed to do, your pills?" I ask suspiciously.

"Why? Haven't they helped yesterday? They are a very good stimulant."

Now I understand why I had a sleepless night, why my heart is beating wildly, why I was so nervous and irritable. I needed something to calm me down, and she gave me a stimulant!

November 11th 1943

I have nearly reached the end of my tale. The words come out automatically as I recapitulate the past months: my arrival to Madrid, Kliemann's visit, my meeting with Fingado and von Buch. I am surprised myself at the simple development of all these events. I hear my own explanations with amazement. I am not wondering whether they believe me, this man and this woman who are listening to me. By and by, I forget their presence, evoking, aloud and for no one in particular, the slightest details that took place before I came here. And once more I remember the bygone time when I dreamed all that in Beyrouth. Having come to the end of my story, I stop talking.

The man turns to the woman: "Can you think of anything else you'd like to ask her?"

"No," she answers. "I think we've got it all."

"I have still something I must give you," I say.

"What is it?"

"The pills for the secret writing and the jewels."

"How!" she exclaims in surprise. "You've got the pills?"

"Yes. They are in my suitcase."

"Weren't you searched?"

"I was, but they were in a too obvious place, so they were not found."

She accompanies me to the luggage room and has my suitcase brought into the office. I hand her a glass tube containing two files, wooden sticks for the nails and hair pins. "It's in there," I tell her.

"I don't see anything," she says having shaken it.

"Because you are looking for a pill! Here it is," I tell her, taking one of the small manicure sticks and showing it to her. "It's on the end of it." And I add: "When it is possible, a glass container is the best hiding place! The customs officer hardly gave it a glance, while he thoroughly searched the inside of my umbrella and of my camera!" Then I give her the broach and taking the ring off my finger, hand it to her. "Now I am quit. I've given you everything."

"Good," she says. "That'll be all for today." And smiling for the first time: "You must be fed up! But I should think that you feel better, now that you have told us everything?"

"It depends. If what I have been working for during three years is of any value."

She observes me with attention, then says: "Can you have any doubt? But about that we'll talk tomorrow. I'll be back at 11 a.m. Try to sleep a long time; you need it. By the way, are you satisfied with your room?"

"I am in a dormitory."

"Shall I tell them to give you a room? It's easy."

"No, thanks. It's OK as it is."

Mrs. Maud is out this evening. We are in the custody of "Eye of Moscow," an old hag whom nobody loves and who spies upon us through the keyholes and from behind the doors. An authentic jailer, this one!

Nelly has the blues and has spent the day in her room, crying. Poor Nelly, she can't get over the way she is being treated in England. She who had been assured that she deserved to have a red carpet spread out under her feet! And after that, to find herself here, at "Nights-in-Jail." (6 Nightingale Lane). Francine too has a red nose. The Breton is gloomier than ever, and the Czech is on the verge of hysterics. Things are bad in the ladies prison!

"Let's pull a fast one on 'Eye of Moscow,'" I tell them. "I have just noticed that one can easily get of our window, and the fence separating the front yard from the neighbour's lot doesn't look too solid. I'll go and notify 'Eye of Moscow' that I am going to take a walk. Then you'll entertain her while I'll slip out into the street. I'll come back by the front door and will ring. It'll make a hell of an uproar!"

"You'll get in trouble," protests someone.

"The hell with it! We need some diversion. One rots here!"

At that precise moment the door opens and "Eye of Moscow" pokes in her head. She grins. "What are you doing, children?"

"I was just saying, Ma'am, that I felt like going to the movies."

"Good idea! Don't come back too late."

"I won't. And for you to know, when I come back, I'll ring five times."

"O.K. I'll be waiting for your bell." She retires.

"Now," I say, "let's go and warn the jailer."

"You don't really intend to go out in the street?" asks Nelly in the passage.

"Sure!"

Our jailer has a small room near the entrance. At our noisy approach, he pushes back his spectacles, lays down his newspaper and asks: "What's the trouble, ladies?"

"I have just come to tell you, I'm going out and warn you that when you hear five rings, it'll be me."

He readjusts his glasses and gives me an underbrow look. "Have a good time," he grumbles, picking up his paper. On my way out, I pinch his warden's helmet.

"Now all of you go to the living room, but let someone come and close the window after me."

It's dark outside, but the night isn't complete. To get out of the window and let myself drop to the ground is a cinch.

"Are you O.K.?" whispers a voice.

"Yes. You can close."

Groping my way, I push through the bushes and reach the wooden fence. I wasn't mistaken; the boards are loose, yet not enough to detach them with the hands. I turn backwards and send them a mighty kick. With a piercing crack, one of the boards gives way. I listen, holding my breath, persuaded that the alarm has been given. But nothing stirs in the house. I slip through the opening, put back the board and start walking towards an open gate I see to my right. I pass a R.A.F. soldier who tells me "Good evening!" and doesn't seem surprised to see me there! I find myself in the street.

How little we realize the value of freedom. Although I know that my temporary detention at Nightingale Lane is more of a staging than anything else; although I know that tomorrow or the day after I shall be free, it seems to me that the air in the street, out of the walls and the barbed wires, is different, more vivid, I breathe ecstatically, expanding my lungs. I tell myself: "I'm free!"

It is warm outside; a slight fog blurs everything out. The street is dimly lit because of the blackout. Rare passersby emerge from the darkness and vanish again. Now the night is complete. "I mustn't stay out too long," I say to myself. "Otherwise they'll imagine goodness knows what!"

I have some difficulty finding the bell on the gate. It's hidden in a groove. I get nervous. But here it is. I put on the warden's helmet I have brought along with me and then ring five times. I hear the clicking of the bolts of the inner door and, as on the day of my arrival, steps cross the yard; only tonight the steps seem more hurried. The gate door opens suddenly. On the threshold, I am standing, very straight under my helmet.

"Hello!" I say.

The guardian looks at me flabbergasted, with round eyes and open mouth.

"…From … from … from … where do you come?" he manages to articulate.

"From the movies of course!" I say, bursting out laughing. And passing in front of him, I dash into the hall.

"Eye of Moscow" is there, standing in the middle of the room, her glasses in one hand, her knitting in the other, and behind her in the dimness my co-prisoners with Nelly in the front row. "Where were you?" mutters "Eye of Moscow," haggard.

"Didn't I tell you? At the movies!"

The jailer has finished locking the door. I return him his helmet. "Thanks!" I say.

"My helmet!" he exclaims. "Where did you get it?"

"I borrowed it from your table."

He is too indignant to answer. We all crowd into the drawing room. "Eye of Moscow" doesn't follow us there.

"You ought to have seen her face when you rang five times!" "She started to count us mentally!" "We've never seen her run so fast as from here to the hall." "She was furious!" "She couldn't believe her ears!"

Anyhow, I've attained one result; everyone is out of the dumps. I myself feel relaxed. Yesterday has been wiped out, and tomorrow doesn't yet exist. For a quarter of an hour we are left in peace. We all gather in our dormitory and continue to laugh and chat. A hard knock at our door cuts short the laughing. All the heads turn round in the same direction while someone says: "Come in!"

They are three to enter: the guardian whose helmet I had taken, the night watchman, who has just arrived and is going to take his place, and of course "Eye of Moscow." The night watchman claims to be the son of a Lord; he has a vermillion nose, stinks of alcohol and wears a bowler hat. He resembles the coachman on old English prints. He is the one to speak: "Which of you, ladies, has taken the liberty to go out in the street?"

"I," I say, stepping forward.

"It is very naughty!" he says sententiously. "How did you go out?"

"It was very easy," I tell him shamefully. "There is a tree with a protruding branch in the garden. I got hold of that branch, swung myself, swung myself ... and hop! I threw myself over the barbed wire."

"Eye of Moscow" is scandalized.

"It's very naughty," repeats the son-of-a-Lord, as the three of them retire in order. Five minutes later we follow them. Judging from the draught of cold air coming from the staircase, the door into the garden must be open. We tiptoe into the ping-pong room where the curtains haven't been drawn; the windows look out onto the garden. We can see the bright spots made by the torches searching the darkness; each tree is being carefully examined. Later on, we can hear voices under our windows. Probably they discover the loose board, for our room is subject to a second incursion; they nail up our window and the one on the landing, but forget the two small side windows.

November 11th

This morning Mrs. Maud greets me with a reproachful look. "You have behaved very badly, Lily."

"Oh! Mrs. Maud, it was only a joke! You're not really cross."

She smiles. "Nevertheless," she adds, "your joke can cause plenty of trouble to the ones who were in charge of you. They were responsible."

"But I had warned them! And I did come back!"

"I know! I know!" says Mrs. Maud. "Now, hurry and run upstairs; you're wanted."

Who would imagine that we are grown up women, escaped from the German occupation, amongst whom many have certainly risked their lives! Who would believe this is a prison under a disguised name? One could think we are school girls up to some mischief and afraid of being punished.

On the first floor I am met by the amused smile of my examiners. "Well, you have some inventions!" says the woman. The ice of the first days has melted; no trace of hostility remains. I confide in those people whom I don't know and feel secure. The man has now become quite amiable. The woman continues to be icy, but I have the impression that it's her usual way. She doesn't look very happy. Maybe she has a difficult life. There isn't much left to do. The man consults his notes and asks for a few more clarifications.

I go down for lunch, and when I come back, the woman is alone, waiting for me in the office. She is sitting at the table and says: "We're going to talk."

Up to now, she has hardly opened her mouth, content at being present, to observe, to be silent. She has become so much part of the background that I have finished by forgetting her presence. What she tells me is more of less the same as what Benton told me already: that I can be extremely useful to them, that the work I am bringing them is of great importance, that they will be happy of my collaboration, that I must realize the gravity of the situation, etc. etc.... The thing on which she insists, and which Benton had omitted, is that by helping the British I will be working for France, for her liberation.

"That's clever!" I say to myself. "But why should she think that I wouldn't want to help England, even if France did not come into the question? Isn't England our Ally? Doesn't she defend the same cause? Isn't she pursuing the same purpose?"

I tell her I am happy that my efforts haven't been vain, that the result (which has required so much patience) has proved useful, that I am happy to be able to serve and proud to work with them. Yes, all this is true; but what I feel is so much beyond that which the words can express. How could I tell this compassionate woman the exhilaration of having attained my aim, the enthusiasm at being no longer useless, at being able to struggle, to fight, I too, against the invader, to be one with those who will liberate France. What would she care, even if she could understand?

"Would you mind very much spending one more night here?" she asks me. "It's a little late to get you out today, for there are some formalities to accomplish."

I assure her that it's all right with me. Before we part, I tell her: "There is another question I'd like to discuss with you: It's about my dog. I have left him in Gibraltar."

"I know," she says. "O'Shaga has written to us about it, and we have answered him it was impossible. He cannot be exempt from the quarantine."

I look at her in amazement: "That's not what he told me! He assured me that he hadn't yet been able to arrange anything and that is why I remained so long in Gibraltar. But he didn't tell me that you had refused!" I cannot realize that it should be true. "So you have refused? This small favour I ask?"

"Yes," she says: "It is contrary to the regulations."

"And to travel under an assumed name?" I say softly.

"It's different," she answers. "It's in the interest of the State."

"And if I refuse to work as long as I don't have my dog? Will the interest of the State require a hitch in the regulations?"

"In this case you would be considered as an enemy of the State."

I look at her in silence. A veil has dimmed my joy. I feel a deep disappointment. "Listen," I say. "I have arranged for Babs to be brought here by an American pilot. I've done it to avoid formalities and all kind of complications—not in order to cheat. But should this means fail, you'll have to get him here for me. O'Shaga has promised to see about it. And I positively refuse to believe that you would stoop to such bargaining. I refuse to believe that, having promised me in Madrid, having promised me at Gibraltar, you British should not keep your promise after having brought me to England! It would be cowardly, and it would be vile! Don't answer me. I hope that Cliff will bring Babs over in a few days and that everything will be settled in this manner. Let me keep my illusions."

She leaves me and I go downstairs to join the others. I try in vain to get back my good temper. I find a change nearly every evening when I return from my examination. The Czech and the Breton girls have left. We are transferred, Francine and I, to a dormitory on the first floor. I know it is the last night I am spending here. Nelly has the dumps and hasn't been out of her room the whole day. She puts in a short appearance after dinner. "Tell me, are they writing your biography?" she asks me.

"Practically," I tell her.

"I suppose you'll soon be leaving us," she remarks with envy.

"I suppose so," I say.

She gives me her aunt's address so that we can get in touch after we've been freed.

Late in the evening a new prisoner arrives, and I have the surprise to recognize Mrs. Joris, the wife of the doctor I met in Madrid. We talk about Spain. It's funny the pleasure a prisoner can get from meeting a familiar face, of being able to say: "Do you remember?" to have common acquaintances to speak of!

November 12th

We have just finished breakfast. I am in the living room, working on the same jig-saw puzzle of which a corner is still missing. Mrs. Maud glances through the door and seeing me pushes it wide open. "Go and get dressed, Lily," she tells me. "You're leaving us."

"You lucky thing!" "Aren't you fortunate?" "And after five days only!" "And we, Mrs. Maud, when are we going to be interrogated?" "Yes, when are we going to leave?" each one wants to know.

Mrs. Maud tries to calm them down. "Your turn will come. Be patient."

I'm sorry for Nelly. She has been here for two weeks! She must be suffering what she considers to be an injustice. I hope she'll get out quick. Upstairs I take up my things, put on my coat and come down. Mrs. Maud is waiting for me at the foot of the stairs.

"I must warn you," she tells me, "that it is strictly forbidden to accept any errands or take letters, or send messages for the detained. I trust you'll comply with the regulations and will refuse to take anything they might hand you."

I tell her she can rely upon me and enter the living-room to say good-bye. Mrs. Joris has prepared a letter for me to take, and when I tell her it is forbidden, she asks me to send a telephone message. I reply that that too is forbidden. She is disappointed, poor thing! When I'm gone. Nelly will go back to her room to cry. Her eyes are already full of tears. I say good-bye to Mrs. Maud. She thinks I'm joking when I assure her that the five days spent at "Nights-in-Jail" will remain a good souvenir. Nevertheless, it's true. In the hall, "Eye-of-Moscow," holding a big envelope in the hand, awaits me a mawkish smile spread out on her face. The jailer throws a vindictive glance; we get into a bus and start off.

Outside, the day is dull. The bare trees appear to be sulking and the houses seem grumpy. After a quarter of an hour's drive, we arrive into a park guarded by soldiers. They must know the car for the sentry lets us through the gate, and we drive up to large buildings which must have been a college before the war. Following "Eye-of-Moscow," I go through a few offices.

"You're going to be photographed," she tells me.

"All right," I accept unnecessarily.

We enter a small studio. A soldier tells me to take off my hat and gives me a board with a big white number on black background to hold in front of me. I'd like to see those photos some day. As it is, I'm not photogenic. On this, I'll probably look like a jail-bird.

From there, "Eye-of-Moscow" takes me into a large room where uniformed men are working behind tables. Near one of them I discover my interrogator. It is towards her that my guardian steers me. A few more forms to fill in, a few more signatures.

"That's all. You are free!" says "Eye-of-Moscow," taking leave of me.

The man behind the desk opens an envelope: "I'm going to give you back your belongings," he says, and he takes out of it the newspapers that were stopping my shoes, the brown paper that was wrapping the presents, the tissue paper that had been round my hat.

"You can have it all!" I tell him laughing. And noticing a wastepaper basket I drop everything into it.

"Now follow me," says the woman who had previously interrogated me.

We follow another way. Apparently, this is the equivalent, for men, of "Nights-in-Jail." But they are much more numerous than we were. Many of them are partially dressed in uniform; others have civilian clothes.

"Hello! How are you?" exclaims a known voice. I turn round and recognize an English boy with whom I travelled from Madrid to Gibraltar. "It is three weeks that I am here!" he tells me with disgust.

"I'm just getting out," I say.

But already my companion is hurrying me away and we find ourselves outside. "By the way, my name is Mary," she tells me suddenly.

The car takes us into an austere and gloomy street, before a house similar to all those around it—a three-storied house of bricks blackened by years and the fog and smoke in London; a house with a plain front without fantasy nor ornaments, as sour as an old spinster coming out of a jaundice. I follow Mary to the first floor. She rings at the door to the right. It is opened by a woman with a round jovial face. She has lavender blue eyes, a small turned up nose and is over forty years of age.

"This is Maritza," introduces Mary, "our cordon bleu." And she adds: "Maritza is Croatian." After that she takes me round the flat. "This is where you will live," she tells me. "Does that agree with you?"

I say yes. The rooms are clean, comfortable, and impersonal like the rooms of a hotel. I say to myself that I shall never want to unpack my suitcases and put away my things in the drawers.

"We are waiting for Colonel Robertson who is coming for lunch," says Mary. "He is your chief."

I accept in advance this new chief, just as I have been accepting all things, people and unexpected events which have been thrown into my life in the past three years—passively. Five minutes later Mary goes to answer the doorbell. I hear some voices in the passage. The door opens and Colonel Robertson walks into the living-room. "So here you are at last," he says with a friendly smile holding out his hand. "And first of all, let me congratulate you for your work. It's a success."

"Thank you."

"How do you feel?"

"Perfectly."

"Now you must relax, forget your fears, banish uncertainty. You are among friends. Nothing more can happen to you."

No 19 Rugby Mansions, the London apartment where Lily first stayed, is located in Kensington (photograph taken by the editor).

I smile without answering. What relaxation can there be when your nearest are in the hands of the enemy? What security, when you know that they will pay for your slightest mistake? And I suddenly remember the look in "Moustache's" eyes when he told me: "You will not betray us—never. Because your parents have remained in Paris—in P-a-r-i-s!"

We sit down to lunch. Robertson approaches his forties, from one side or the other; it's difficult to say which. He has the pleasant looks, the regular features and the dull chestnut hair parted on the side of a wax mannequin in a shop window. His thick red nape indicates a sanguine constitution; he must be bad tempered. He's got ugly thumbs with a short bell-shaped and turned back second phalanx. But he is jolly and asks many questions. He wants to know how I made up my mind to throw myself in this adventure, and why? This "why" always surprises me. Someone who would have lived through the invasion of his country, its occupation by the enemy, wouldn't ask why!

Robertson tells me I'll be working mostly with Mary and asks me to make all the suggestions what will occur to me and continue to direct the work as if I were alone, for I know my correspondents, their methods, what they expect from me, and thus will avoid any possible mistakes. "You understand that through you," he tells me, "we can give them exactly the information we want them to know. This will be most important when the landing takes place, for it will enable us to deceive them and spread confusion. I want you to write the messages with the data supplied by us, to find the pretests, or explanations which would have enabled you to gather the information which you will be transmitting. Most of all, you shall tell us if you consider it incredible that you should have obtained some of the information. This contact that we have through you is far too precious for us to take the risk of losing it."

The meal served by Maritza is gorgeous. It makes you wonder if there are any restrictions in England! Coffee is served in the living room. "There only remains the financial question to be settled," says Colonel Robertson. "How long was the money you received from the Germans supposed to last?"

"Six months."

"We'll take this money from you, as well as the jewels, and shall give you £50 per month. We'll also reimburse your travelling expenses. Do you agree to it?"

I nod in approval, but it surprises me. I don't need any money. I don't want it. What I have done wasn't done in order to get something out of it. The Germans valued me at £250 per month. I could have presumed that the British would have enough self respect not to offer me less. They didn't run any risk. I should have refused.

Robertson leaves us at 2:30 p.m. and Mary tells me to get ready. We'll go to get some papers: authorization to reside, ration cards, etc. My residence is at 19 Rugby Mansion. It's not very central. The day is grey; it isn't cold but damp. We take a bus and get out at Piccadilly. I'm not used to the left hand driving and am nearly overrun a few times. What strikes me in the streets is the "shabby" appearance of the people: worn out overcoats, shiny sleeves, out of fashion clothes having lost their freshness. In the show-windows the dresses are straight, without facings, lapels, collars or belts. Small hems, nothing in the seams. Anything that could pretend to the least luxury has been pitilessly sacrificed; all the articles have uniform colours with a predominance of apple-green. You can see it on Mannequins, on coat-stands and find it again on people passing in the streets. We stop before a show-window full of handbags, and I look with amazement at the exposed models and at the prices. If I were to make them myself, they couldn't be worse, and I have never in my life made hand-bags!

"All the leather workers, men and women, have been mobilized," Mary tells me. "In England, we consider handbags as not being essential, that there are many other things more necessary and that for this reason, women can do without them in war time. Those you see here are made by old ladies, or invalids, with recuperated materials. Besides," she adds, "all our British women are in the Army."

And this is true. As I look around me I don't see anything but uniforms. Provided with a landing card and a temporary ration card, we go home. On the way I stop at a shop to buy a lipstick. "I would like another colour," I say to the shop girl who hands me a tube with something that looks like a piece of exhausted almost black chalk. She looks at me in surprise: "But that is all that's being made! There exists only one colour." And she adds: "You forget there is war." I shrug my shoulders, leave the lipstick and walk out of the shop.

"Why are you so particular?" asks Mary. "Can't you use the things everyone uses? Must you always have something different?" I feel a deep disapproval in her voice. She mustn't like me. What a funny woman this Mary is: cold, reserved, with a mouth which sets easily, long legs and cork-screw stockings! Even her laugh seems to be purely exterior and not come from inside.

We get back home. Maritza has prepared some tea in front of the living-room fireplace.

"I suppose you'll want to go and see your cousin and your Bristol friends?" asks Mary.

"Oh! Yes. May I do it?"

"Naturally. I was going to suggest that you could begin by going to Cambridge. When you're back, we'll plan a program. You probably want to find some sort of a job? You spoke about working at a hospital. We'll see what we can fix up for you on these lines."

"Could I immediately ring up my cousin?"

"Yes. But before that we must settle one thing: what are you going to tell her?"

"The truth, if you don't object to it."

"We would prefer you to tell her nothing. You must realize that the fewer people who know about your activity, the better it will be."

"I understand," I say. "But on the other side, my whole alibi for the Germans is based on this cousin and the importance of her situation. I don't know what means of verification the Germans possess in England, maybe none, maybe very extended ones. In any case, as it is my cousin who is supposed to have let me come, as it is she who is supposedly in the future to obtain all sort of facilities and favours for me, I should like to prevent her from being too astonished in public, about my arrival in England; one never knows what ears can overhear you. Besides, I have an absolute faith in her, in her comprehension, in her total discretion."

"All right," says Mary. "You'll act according to your judgment. We'll leave it to you."

A quarter of an hour later I have Cambridge on the line. When Bessie realizes that it is I who am speaking, she is so absolutely taken by surprise that she can only emit a sort of clucks that belong to no language! "When can you come?" she finally manages to articulate. "Tomorrow? I'll keep you for the weekend. Do come."

I suddenly feel less lost, less alone.

"How would you proceed if you worked on your own account?" asks Mary when I have finished telephoning.

"I would begin by sending a message through Sabina Romans, which would be worded approximately as follows: "Well arrived Stop. Have spent a month in Gibraltar closely watched. Stop. Arrived London November 6th. Stop. Six days' quarantine for verifications.

Stop. Released on 12th. Stop. Am staying with cousin. Stop. Solange." And I would send it from Cambridge.

"Why from Cambridge?"

"Because if 'you' did not exist, I would have naturally gone there."

"O.K. We could draw up the message tomorrow morning, before you go? I have your pills and everything that's necessary here."

November 13th

The camouflage letter is a very short one, written on one page and asking for news of Sabina from whom I haven't heard for a long time and saying that here everyone is well. Mary rings up the War Office and asks them to give her some name and address in Cambridge. I put this address at the top of my letter and sign it. I have changed my handwriting and should I see it after some time, I couldn't recognize it. I word the message across, prepare the envelope, write the sender's name at the back and hand the whole to Mary. She locks it up in her leather attaché case.

I take the train after lunch, and at 3:30 p.m. I am at Bessie's. While we are having tea in front of a log fire, I ask her: "Did you get my letters from France?"

"Yes, two. But I couldn't make out what you wrote me about."

I then explain to her. I tell her the reasons why I am now in England, how I have left France. I confess her all the lies I have told the Germans to have me sent to London, and according which she was a most important personality—an intimate friend of the Queen's! My revelations surprise her. She didn't suspect anything.

"You have passed me a dead hand (Tu m'as passé un coup de main morte)," she remarks. And she adds after a few moments silence: "Why did you get involved in this adventure?"

I look at her in astonishment. "Why? But because there is war. Because France is occupied. Because, for me, it is the only way to fight!"

"You had no business to get me mixed into it! What can you do, you, a woman, against a power such as Germany?"

I consider her with growing stupefaction. "You don't understand," I say. "It isn't I who count. I'm just a tool. But it's those in whose hands I have put myself who will be able to do something. Bessie, do you disapprove of me?"

"To tell you frankly, yes," she says. "I don't see the necessity of it. War will come to an end. It would have happened as well without you."

"But you won't refuse me your aid if I need it?"

"Non," she says after a short hesitation. And she asks: "What kind of an aid could you expect from me?"

"I would just want that if speaking about me you should hint that it's through you that I came to England. So far it's all. If later on I should hang something more on you, I'll let you know."

"O.K.," says Bessie.

I had hoped to find some news of Babs at Cambridge, but there was none. I sent off a cable to Cliff.

November 15th

I am back in London.

"Now," asks Mary, "what about this visit? What exactly did you tell your cousin?"

"I told her that I worked with you and have given her a brief summary of the truth, without any particulars. Mary, I would like you to go and see her."

"Why? Is anything wrong?"

"No. But Bessie doesn't seem to take it all very seriously, or rather she doesn't see its usefulness. Maybe if you or someone from the War Office talked to her and explained to her that it's not a whim, nor an adventure on my part, she would believe you."

"All right," says Mary, "we'll talk to her."

November 16th

This morning Mary isn't alone. Two men accompany her. I couldn't catch the name of one of them. The second one, "Ronnie," is a boy of about twenty-five, small, with a pale face, a big nose and hair of a pretty blond colour, but much too long in the back (the "artist" kind such as was worn in bygone days). Ronnie must be a radio expert, for he questions me thoroughly on the type of radios the Germans used for my instruction. He shows me series of photos of receiver-transmitters asking me to show him the one most resembling the radio employed by me. There is one absolutely identical in a small portative leather case. After the two men have left, Mary and I discuss of the best way of organizing my life.

"I don't know," says Mary, "if an occupation in a hospital will be very practical, not 'officially' at any rate, as you would not be able in your letters to Emile be able to pretend you move much about. (Mary calls Kliemann "Emile.") And it is very possible, even most probable, that the kind of information you would have to transmit them couldn't be obtained on the spot. If you absolutely insist upon working as a nurse, we'll have to invent some other version for Emile's benefit."

We don't decide anything definitively except that I will first go to my friends in Bristol and that the few next letters will be written from there. Mary will ring me up in advance, and I shall meet her in Bristol.

November 18th

The surroundings of Paddington station have been badly damaged by the bombs. London has had much to suffer from the bombardments. Mary brings me to my train. I cannot exactly situate her—jailer or nursery governess? I don't know either if she hates me, despises me, envies me or admires me. On the whole this has very little importance! I'm happy to leave London. I hate this yellow fog, which creeps in through the window chinks and clouds the end of the passages; tarnishes the silver and the mirrors; I like neither my street nor my house, nor my apartment, as unpleasant as a mother-in-law. The only ones for whom I have sympathy are Maritza, our Croatian—whom I have nickname Petelincek (little cock) and to whom I speak Serbian or German—and the barrage balloons, good natured and clumsy, looking like baby elephants, overhanging London at the end of their cables. I like to see them come down at feeding time (for a new supply of gas) and go up again, enlivened.

Mary, a friend of hers, Louise, and I have lunched at a restaurant, "Kempinski." The food wasn't bad, and I was impressed when I learned that the maximum price the restaurant was allowed to charge amounted to 5 shillings per meal. The very smart places have the possibility of making up on wine and extras if one wants them. I think it's very good; it prevents black market. One doesn't need coupons in the restaurants.

Mary finds a seat for me in the train. "I'll see you in a week," she tells me before leaving me. I'm travelling first class, as there is no second class in England: only first and third! I go out at Flax Boston. A taxi awaits me. Ten minutes later I am at Wraxall with my friends. Her name is also Mary. I have known her since I was eight—that means I have nearly always known her. It is seven years since I have seen her. How little is needed to pierce the hard carapace life forces on you—how little is required to make the mask disappear, to be oneself again: a friendly voice, a little affection, a little tenderness. One has hardened oneself by sheer mistrust, lies. One tells oneself that never, never again would one be able to trust. One has to be strong, because one is alone, because one has to be. But at the moment you're not alone any more, at the moment you're not obliged to fight, to pretend, to be hard, the moment friendly faces surround you, smile at you, all this armour melts as snow in the sunshine. And you can trust again.

That's what I feel in finding her again. The first time I am relaxing, for many years! We have such a lot to tell each other. Very simply, I tell her what I have done since the beginning of the war and how it has brought me here. I didn't ask the other Mary—the War Office Mary—for authorization to divulge my secret to "my Mary." Why should I have done it? I know that I can tell anything to Mary—but I want to leave her out of all this.

"I knew you would do something like that!" she tells me. She is neither surprised nor critical. She finds it quite natural.

—⁂—

WRAXALL

For three days that I am here, I feel alive again. We have been paying a few calls, "my" Mary and I. The fact that I come from France makes me appear as a curious animal. "What do the Germans look like?" I am asked. "Is it true that when they enter a shop or restaurant, everyone is obliged to go out?" And when I say that, no, they don't horsewhip you in the streets, everyone looks surprised. "So it isn't as terrible as that," I am told. It is difficult to make people feel something they have never experienced, they can't even suspect, cannot imagine; the horror of occupation, the loss of liberty, the daily humiliation of being defeated; and the mean degrading fight for one's living; the cunning, the cheating one has to use to escape hunger. How can one explain hunger to someone who has never been hungry? They nod, say: "It must be awful!" but they do not feel how awful it is. I am questioned about the rationing, and when I have enumerated our French monthly rations, my English friends ask me incredulously: "Yes but then, on what does one live?"

"One manages somehow," I tell them.

"How?"

"With the black market! And the ones who have no money exchange whatever they can: a tie for some butter; shoes for some meat." The mentioning of the black market causes a silence. I feel a vague disapproval. Yesterday my friend told me: "You oughtn't to speak about the black market. It's very badly considered here!"

"But I am not talking of the ones who are using the black market to make money. I refer to those who are obliged to buy their food at terrific prices not to die of hunger!"

"All the same," she insists skeptically.

No, they don't understand. I feel they are very far from me. An abyss separates us. I shock them. They hurt me. Besides, since I am in England, everything seems to offend me. I have arrived so full of ardour. I expected to find them full of the same enthusiasm, of the same Faith, of the same fighting spirit. I was faced by calm people, positive, cold, stubborn. They are sure of victory. They fight methodically, staidly, without risks nor glamour, sure as they are that time is working for them. Maybe there lays their strength—but I feel very far from them.

This morning Mary (mine) tells me: "What you want in France is organization and above all discipline. If your rationing system were organized as it is here, and everyone was complying with regulations, the black market wouldn't exist. It doesn't exist in England."

I must be particularly enervated this morning, and it is more than I can stand. I push back my chair with violence and get up. "It's easy to criticize when one has everything! Look at that: plenty of bread, butter, eggs, bacon, marmalade, milk and coffee. And you give porridge to your goats and bread soaked in milk to your ducks! But in France one is short of bread for old people, people don't get any milk, and there is no porridge for the kids. They are starving there. STARVING, do you understand?" I leave the dining room and take refuge upstairs. "It isn't their fault," I say to myself. "One cannot understand what one hasn't experienced."

December 1st 1943

This afternoon, while Mary and I were paying a call at Bristol, I was suddenly seized by shivering and trembling. As soon as I was home I went to bed, but I continued to shiver with cold. Although I don't feel well, I insisted upon getting up. A telephone call summons me to the Flax Borton police post. I am there at 11 a.m. A plain clothed inspector issues me into an office, shuts the door carefully and tells me: "I have been ordered to take you tomorrow after lunch to Bristol. It must be done with discretion, not to waken your friends' suspicion. Can you invent a pretext to meet me on the road, just outside Wraxall, at 2 o'clock?"

"Certainly, it's easy. I'll say I'm going out for a walk. How long will it take?"

"Two and half hours, perhaps three."

I find it difficult to ride the bike back home. I'm giddy and very nearly fall. Once at home, I warn Mary that tomorrow I'll have to go to Bristol. She seems upset and displeased.

"You're not fit to get up. You ought to be in bed." And she adds: "Can't you tell them to come here? You might as well work at home."

"I shall ask, but I don't know if they'll accept."

"If they do, I would only want them to notify Teddy (her husband). I haven't told him anything, but I think it's only fair that he should know what is happening in his house. If I were to tell him, it wouldn't be sufficient. For I know you, but he doesn't, and after all, there is a war on! If anything should happen, the first thing "these people" would do, would be to accuse him of having sheltered and tolerated under his roof goings on of which he knew nothing."

"I understand," I say. "I'll talk to 'them' about it."

I've spent an awful night, alternatively shivering and sweating. This morning I wake up feeling terribly stiff. A fine vertical rain dims out the landscape, making the asphalt of the road shine. A black car is stopped round the curb, its engine idling. The inspector pushes the door open, and I get in next to him. We drive the eight miles separating Wraxall from Bristol in silence. I don't know the town. He stops the car in front of a villa. Behind the house in the garden, wooden barracks have been temporarily erected. It's cold inside. I'm frozen. The inspector goes straight to a door and opens it. Mary, of the War Office, is there. She awaits me. She tells the policeman that she'll bring me back. He needn't wait. He goes.

"How are you?" asks Mary.

"O.K.," I say, lying.

"Good," she says. "We're going to word a message." She gives me, in English, the information I have to transmit. She shows me an insignia and tells me to describe it. It is a tricoloured isosceles triangle resting on its base, yellow at the top, blue on the left, red on the right, having in its center, overstitched in black, two wheels, a sort of gun shield, the whole surrounded by a chain. Over this schematized drawing, a red lightning bolt, and in the yellow upper part, the number six. Today's message simply says that I have just arrived at my Bristol friends; that I have seen in town a large number of soldiers bearing the described insignia and relate a conversation I overheard between two officers who spoke about their immediate transfer, and their units, to a given town.

In the middle of the wording, I am taken with such violent shivers that I'm obliged to stop. My teeth chatter, and the characters dance before my eyes; the sheet of paper alternatively gets nearer and further. Then everything becomes confused and hazy.

"I mustn't! I mustn't," I say to myself. "It will pass. It's better already." I hear Mary's voice as from a far distance:

"What's the matter with you? Aren't you feeling well?"

I press my eyelids tight together; then I open my eyes again. All objects are back at their usual places and distances. There only remains a confused ringing in the ears. "I believe it's the grippe,"[1] I say with an attempt to smile.

"Shall we stop? We can send off the message another day, if you're tired."

"No, let us finish."

Never would I have believed that it could be so difficult to control one's fingers, to separate the letters, to separate the lines. One has to hold with an extreme delicacy the little sticks which are used for secret writing. The least pressure leaves a shiny mark on the paper, like a line drawn with the nail. As I cannot see what I write, I must be sure to remember every traced letter, carefully the place where every line begins so as not to suppose anything. All of a sudden I feel an awful blank in my head and I don't know—absolutely not what was the last word I wrote. I look at Mary in despair. "I don't know where I am."

"Have you written 'officer?'"

"I don't know."

"In any case you have begun this sentence. Don't get nervous. If the two preceding words are missing, it's of no importance; and if you repeat 'officer' twice, this has no importance either. Just continue with 'officer.'"

I don't know how I get through it. Anyhow two letters are written. One will go through Sabina Romans; the other, by Sweden, is addressed to Annick Le Queau and bears the return address of a certain Maurice Le Feuvre from London.

"You must take care of yourself," says Mary. "You cannot be ill. You haven't got the right to be ill."

"I'll do something about it." I'm so tired. I feel so heavy, that I would like to lie down on the earth, lower than the earth not to feel the weight of my body. "Couldn't we work at my friends?" I say. "It would be so much simpler."

"At your friends?' But what would they think if they saw me come constantly?"

"You would tell them I work for the War Office. They are discretion personified; they wouldn't ask anything."

"I'll speak to Colonel Robertson about it. We'll see what he will decide."

A military car brings me back to Wraxall. I have decided to re-baptize the Mary of the War Office and to call her "Mariya." It is too complicated to have two Marys.

The doctor has been this morning. He examined me and found that I had the grippe. He said I had to be very careful as there was actually a grippe epidemic in England. He ordered several medicines (which I don't intend to take) and me to stay in bed as long as I had a temperature. I don't feel ill: just tired, terribly tired. It isn't only physically, but also mentally. I am disappointed! If one should ask me "why," it would be impossible for me to say. About nothing in particular, and about everything as a whole. The enthusiasm, which animated me when I arrived in England, has disappeared. I feel far away from the war, notwithstanding my work which continues. The calm of the English, their passive acceptation of the events, their hasteless certainty of victory, have brought me to a sort of torpor.

And then I miss Babs! From my bed I can see a green meadow rising in a mellow slope and crowned by a cluster of trees. The grass is very green under the falling rain. How Babs would love to romp through it. When Babs is here, we'll have walks, the two of us, in these woods, and he will chase squirrels and rabbits without ever catching them. When Babs is here. When will he be there? To my cable sent from Cambridge Cliff Lord has answered that Babs was well, without any indication of the date of his arrival in London. Could he have lied to me? Didn't he intend to come? Was his word of honour of no value whatsoever? I wrote to him yesterday asking for clarification.

How tired I am! My back, my shoulder blades are so painful! This morning I have no temperature. I got up. But I can hardly stand up; I feel drained of all strength. Nearly every evening my temperature rises. I don't feel like doing anything. I doze. Mariya has telephoned. Mary didn't want to let me get up. Nevertheless, I went to the telephone. Mariya wanted to know if I would be able to meet her in Bristol. I told her I didn't feel well. She said I needn't bother; she would ring me up again.

My diary becomes more and more irregular. I don't even know what the dates are. And besides, what could I enter? That the days are dragging on; that it's raining outside; that I continue to have relapses and spend most of my time in bed. Another telephone call from Mariya: "Everything is arranged," she tells me. "Someone will go to see your friends on our behalf and then, if they are willing, I'll come to work with you at their place."

At noon Mary comes to my room, closes the door and whispers: "Teddy has just had a telephone call from the Bristol Security to tell him Major Lane would come to see him at 3 o'clock. He is very much intrigued and wonders what it might be. It's on your behalf, isn't it?"

"Yes, I suppose so, according to what Mariya said this morning."

At 3 o'clock, I hear a car stop at the gate, the sand grate in the walk and the ring of the bell. The door is opened almost immediately. Then I hear voices in the entrance and I know that Teddy is leading the visitor into the living room.

I am in bed today. My temperature has risen to 103, which seems to be high.

Half an hour later, the entrance door is opened again, and I can hear Teddy escorting Major Lane to his car. In a few minutes he knocks at my door and enters my room. "Well! Well!" says Teddy looking at me with surprised admiration. "Who could have thought that! It seems you're quite somebody!"

I begin to laugh: "What did Major Lane tell you?"

"So, you knew?"

"Yes," I say. "I was told this morning."

"Ah! What he told me? Oh! He told me you were above all suspicions; that the War Office trusted you completely; that you are doing a most important work; and that he asked me to allow you to pursue it here. I naturally said yes. He added that Miss. M. S. was well known to them; that you could be quite easy on her account, as well as in respect of every person she might bring with her. It's Miss M. S. who will be coming here to work with you. Do you know her already?"

"Yes," I say.

Teddy looks at me, nodding. "All the same! All the same!" he repeats. And he adds: "It's fine, what you have done there! I don't know what it is, but I guess it's fine."

"Thank you, Teddy."

At this moment, Mary enters the room. She smiles to me, and I feel suddenly a soft warmth invade me. My friends' trust touches me. I feel that Teddy is burning to know; but I know also that he will ask no questions. "Tell him," I say to Mary. "I'm too tired to do it."

We have worked downstairs in the dining room. Mariya arrived at noon. She had lunch with us; then we worded a message. Taken separately, the information I transmit doesn't seem to make much sense: bits of conversations mentioning rank and unit; trains supposedly seen in stations; information obtained by chance during a conversation in a railroad carriage. But it's probable that the Germans will draw deductions and conclusions out of them. It's probable that the Intelligence Service has a definite and coherent plan of action and that the information they send has a connection between them that escapes me and which I don't try to guess.

A telephone call from Mariya: "Your suitcase is there. What have you got inside? I have the impression that it has been searched. What did you have inside?"

"Frocks, underwear, gloves, a new hand bag, a blanket, a pillow, and iron and some other things."

"You'll have a look at it. It's nearly empty. We'll naturally pay you for the things that were stolen."

It's nearly a fortnight now that this grippe drags on. I cannot remain any longer a burden on my friends who have no servants and for whom the presence of an invalid means extra work. So this morning I have taken the decision to return to London. Mary didn't want to hear anything about it, but I persuaded her that it was urgent for my work. She gave in on this reason. I telephoned to Mariya that I wanted to go back.

"When?" she asked.

"Today. This evening!" I said.

"But there is someone in the flat, and it's a little short notice to dislodge him."

"Who is it?"

"Larry Marshall." Larry Marshall is the "official" owner of 19 Rugby Mansions.

I ask: "Does he use both bedrooms?"

"No, but...."

"But?"

"What I want to say is, would you mind spending the night alone in a flat with a young man?"

I burst out laughing: "Mariya, You're an angel! You're uneasy about a spy's reputation! Don't worry; I can protect myself!"

"All right," says Mary. "If you don't mind, I see no objection to it. I'll warn Maritza and Larry."

That's why I'm on the London train, curled up in my corner, a blanket over my knees. Mary has brought me to Bristol, put me in my compartment, has put a hot water bottle on my knees. "Take care of yourself," she bids me when leaving.

We pass slowly Bath, Swindon, Reading, and the day fades away. The journey seems endless. The passengers are silent and read. As soon as it becomes dark, the blackout curtains are drawn. I feel oppressed as if we were rolling in a tunnel. Outside the train brushes past the night as if it was consistent and if the passage granted the train were too narrow.

And then, all of a sudden, it's London. I collect my luggage, step out onto the platform. I realize with horror that the ground is unstable under my feet and am obliged to lean against a pillar. I wait for a taxi, but after four or five cars taking passengers, there are none coming any more.

"I must take the bus," I say to myself, and I start to look for the exit. But I'm lost in this Paddington station. From time to time a shiver comes down my spine, and my temples are caught as if it were in a vice. "I'm ill," I say again, and I think: "I must hurry or else I won't be able to get home." I cannot find the exit anywhere. People are waiting on benches; some of them are asleep. I should like to do the same. Suddenly I find myself on the platform where I left the train. It's empty now. "I'll wait for a taxi," I say to myself mechanically. I still carry my hot water bottle, now completely cold and which I forgot to empty.

Sometimes, it's as if I began to dream all awake: confused dreams without much sense in them. I don't even turn round at the approach of steps. "Can I help you?" says a gruff voice. I raise my head and see a bobby.

"I'm waiting for a taxi," I tell the policeman.

"A taxi? There won't be any coming now; there are no trains due. Where do you want to go?"

"To Rugby Mansions."

"Rugby Mansions? Don't know. Where is it?"

"I don't know," I reply. "Somewhere near Olympia, I believe."

"You're not from here?"

"No, I'm French."

"French?" he repeats, surprised. "Well, take the underground. It'll put you quite near your place."

The thought of getting involved in the underground's labyrinth fills me with such dismay that I cannot refrain from to entreating: "Oh no, I pray you, I would prefer to take the bus. I know the 96."

"The 96? But it passes Piccadilly! It's not here!"

I realize that I'm mixing up Piccadilly and Paddington, that I have a fever, that if I don't get home immediately, I won't have the strength to keep up. The policeman shows me where to go. I walk up a stairway with great difficulty, get into a train that stops. I'm afraid to miss my station. Finally I get out in Hammersmith. I find myself in a street thick with fog and pitch dark. I have the impression I'll never find my way, that I'm definitely lost. It's then that I hear the sound of an engine. I feel my way towards the sound. I nearly bump into a stopped taxi. My legs give way and I drop onto the foot-board. The dizziness doesn't persist.

"Please," I say, "bring me home."

I dimly saw the outline of a head bending over me through the door and a voice asks: "Who spoke?"

"I. On the foot-board. I'm not well." I'm so scared he should refuse me.

"Well! Get in," says the driver. "Where do you live?"

"In Rugby Mansions."

Fortunately, he knows where it is. "It's quite near," he says.

Five minutes later, Maritza opens the door. Her face brightens when she sees me. "I was so scared!" she tells me. "You should have been here an hour and a half ago! Mr. Marshall is in the living room."

I go to have a chat with Larry whom I don't know yet, but I feel the fever rising and I don't know very well what I'm saying. Neither do I recognize my laugh. But since I'm back, I have a feeling of security. I'll be better tomorrow.

December 19th

Mariya comes for lunch. I got up late. Everything seems unreal today, as if I were not myself, but someone else were taking my part. Mariya has brought with her my suitcase, and I can ascertain the disaster. The locks have been forced. Inside there only remains paper, a bathing suit, an old blouse and two unmatched shoes. When I imagine the thief's countenance on discovering that there is one shoe missing out of each pair, I'm seized with such frenzy of laughter, that even the theft's disaster appears insignificant. Mariya asks me to give her a list of what is missing and tells me that I'll be reimbursed at the actual price of the objects and shall receive the corresponding amount of coupons. It's not of much interest, as everything I'll be able to buy now will be awful. And all my frocks had been made for me! So much the worse; there is a war on!

After the meal we proceed to the living room where Maritza lit the fireplace. I sit on the floor quite near the fire. I'm hot in front but cold in the back. Mariya says: "We'll be able to work tomorrow morning."

I say, without any connection to what she was speaking about: "Funny, I expected to be put in prison."

"In prison? Lily, what are you talking about?"

"Yes," I say, pursuing my thought. "When I had told you everything, given the code, the cipher, and all the information, I expected you to lock me up and do the work yourselves."

"Why?"

"Isn't it your usual way of proceeding?"

Mariya looks offended. "I don't know why you should judge us like that. In any case, if you expected such a treatment, why did you bring us your work?"

"I didn't do it for you. I did it against Germany, against the "Boches" and for France. Only you see, Mariya, I now sometimes doubt if it will benefit France. I have often the impression that England alone will benefit from it."

"Your reasoning is false," says Mariya. "Even if you pretend that we don't fight to liberate France, you well know that the German defeat will liberate her! Then!"

"That's why I'm continuing." A silence follows. "Mariya," I say after a moment. "It's certain now that Cliff Lord won't bring Babs here. Then, could you let him come?"

"No, I have already told you so."

"Do you mean to say that you refuse to keep the promise made to me by Benton and confirmed by O'Shaga?"

"We can't help it if they have promised you something contrary to the regulations."

"In this case I'm discharged of the promise I made to them."

"What promise?"

"To work with you. From now on you can get on alone."

Mariya looks at me, unbelieving. "You refuse to work?"

"Yes."

"Do you realize that you will be considered our enemy?"

"I'm not at all interested in how the War Office who fails to keep his promises should consider me." I feel that Mariya makes a violent effort to control herself. I don't look at her when speaking. I look at the flame which licks the large blocks of anthracite. I feel calm, almost indifferent, as if I were speaking from far away—as if I were speaking by telephone—and say: "You see, I believed this work was important."

"It is!" asserts Mariya. "We have said and repeated it, and you know it."

"No, it isn't," I continue slowly. "When I believed it, I was ready to risk the life of my parents who have stayed as hostages, because we all accepted the risks which would help us to liberate France. You probably don't realize it, but when I work these messages, where I transmit blindly information which I don't understand, each time I ask myself: 'Is this one going to give me away?' 'Is it after this one that they'll see that I betray them?' And all the time I know the price I shall have to pay if the Germans discover what I am. But now you prove to me that the work I'm doing isn't worth anything—or so little! Then, really, continue it without me. You have everything. And I am so tired!"

"But it's stupid! You know we need you! You can well suspect that could we do without you, we would have done so! I cannot do more than assure you that the services you render are of capital importance!"

"Nevertheless they are not worth a dog."

"You act like a spoiled child! You want something and you're set on obtaining it. Well, you won't have that!"

I don't reply. I look at the flames unceasingly licking the hot coals. I would like to sleep and not think. How far is the confidence which filled me when I arrived here! Gone. Vanished. A mere remembrance which I can hardly explain.

"You still refuse to work?" I nod affirmatively. "Do you know that we have the means to force you?"

I slowly turn back: "Oh! No," I say. "Oh! No. Before I came here, before I left France, I considered various possibilities: death for me and mine; torture; blackmailing. I have accepted everything. It has no hold on me. You couldn't employ me by force, because you wouldn't be any longer sure of me. And you know it." Now I look at Mariya. She is furious.

"You're ill!" she says, rising. "You'll reason differently when you have thought things over. I'll send you Dr. Page tomorrow morning." And without taking leave, she walks out banging the door.

December 20th

"Well? What's wrong?" says Dr. Page entering the living room.

Dr. Page is young, tall and thin, slightly bent forward, with a face so pale that I always want to tell him that he doesn't look well. He calls up in my mind the picture of a dead fish swimming with his belly upwards. When he smiles, his smile is brief as a sunray between two winter clouds. I feel a sort of affection towards Dr. Page, because he rouses in me the wish to tease him and always puts me in good temper.

This morning, without giving me time to answer, he sticks a thermometer in my mouth and gets hold of my wrist. I see his eyebrows go up and his forehead wrinkle. He examines the thermometer, throws me a glance and remarks without commentaries; "You should be in bed! "You've got the flu, and a strong one. You mustn't joke with it."

"How long will it last?"

"It depends; it can last six weeks, as well as one."

"It's over two weeks that I have it."

"And you don't take care of yourself! Now go to bed. I'll be coming back to see you in a few days."

December 21st 1943

I got up for lunch and went to bed again before dinner. In three days, it's Christmas. As the day approaches, I feel a little more alone, a little more lost in this London where I don't know anyone, where I'm not allowed to see Frenchmen, not even allowed to ring up my cousin Janio, or Nelly because I mustn't give my address to anyone! I'm not even ill—just weary—crushingly weary.

December 24th 1943

I don't have the strength to get up. Outside it's dark as if it were going to snow. I think of Mummy, Daddy, home, and by and by I forget where I am. Reality is suddenly ushered upon me under the features of Maritza who brings in my breakfast tray. But I'm not hungry and she has to take it back, a little disappointed, without my having touched anything.

Is it today? Is it yesterday, or tomorrow? I wake up from a chaos of nightmares. The room is dark, except for the red light coming from the electric heater. I dreamed that Babs had fallen under a tram's snow-plough and that the tram had started going. I could not get Babs from under the snow-plough, but I told myself that if he ran before the tram to the next stop, I could release him then. "Run, Babs! Run!" I encouraged him running at his side, and Babs ran. But the tram's speed increased, and I saw the moment when I wouldn't be able to keep up pace, when I would remain behind, and Babs would want to join me and would be run over. And I ran as fast as I could, out of breath, until I suddenly stumbled and, with a cry of terror, woke up. Suffocating, with my heart beating furiously and my sweat drenched hair sticking to my head, my pajamas soaking wet, it takes me a long time to get to sleep again.

The closing door starts me from my sleep. A dim daylight outlines the window. My bedside lamp is burning throwing light on the breakfast tray. The smell of coffee makes me nauseous. An indescribable weariness crushes me down. I can hardly move round.

"Maybe Ken will arrive with Babs today," I say to myself. And immediately it becomes a certainty. "Why Ken?" I think. "It's Cliff Lord who has Babs." Names get confused in my brain. For a long time my hearing is strained towards the front doorbell. "Bessie will telephone that Babs is with her." This thought, hardly formulated, becomes exclusive. I await the telephone ring until the tension becomes so acute that it reaches actual physical pain. "Why should he be at Bessie's?" I suddenly tell myself. "Cliff knows my address here. It's here that he will bring him. Maybe he'll be here for lunch. He's sure to be here for lunch.

Maritza enters to see if I want anything. I ask her to add a cover at lunch. She looks at me in surprise. "Miss Mary is coming?" she asks.

"No," I say, "but Babs will be brought to me.

"You won't get up!" says Maritza disapprovingly.

"But of course, I'll get up! It's Christmas today." And I try to sit up, but fall back, exhausted, upon my pillows. When I open my eyes again, the breakfast tray has been changed to the lunch tray, and Maritza is there, looking at me in silence. "Has anyone telephoned?" I ask feebly.

"No," says Maritza.

"Ah!" I turn my head away from the tray and close my eyes. "He hasn't come," I say to myself. And I begin to listen to the passing cars. If one stops in our street, my whole attention is bent upon catching every sound: a banging door, footsteps on the asphalt. Then it's expectance for the door bell to ring. Seconds are passing. I can count them by the painful beatings at my temples.

"No, he isn't here!" And again I begin to wait, to listen, to hope. The window's rectangular outline becomes fainter, disappears. Again, I'm in the dark, with wide open eyes, waiting for the miracle that does not come!

The door is opened carefully allowing a ray of light to enter the room. Maritza's voice murmurs: "Miss Lily? Are you asleep?"

"No," I say.

"Do you want to have dinner?"

"Dinner? Is it time already? No, thank you, I'm not hungry."

The day is at an end without Babs being here. It was Christmas today: Christmas 1943. Like a balloon getting slowly emptied, becoming smaller, shrinks together, until nothing is left, so my hope is dying. Everything becomes blurred, vague, the corners of the room seem to approach, to fold across, an invincible weight of my own body. I'm not oppressed by it. I simply sink down, deeply, still more deeply, always deeper.

I must have slept. It is night. I feel better. I hasten to go to sleep again. Very softly, slowly, I begin to sink into a black well. Its walls are wadded. It's warm inside. I sail along without effort. I sink lower, lower still. Here is silence, peace, calm. No noise reaches here. My brain is empty of any thoughts. May it last. May it last forever. Everything becomes confused. There is nothing more.

It's broad daylight. My bedside lamp is on. Smell of coffee. The pictures disappear nearly as quickly as they appear, and again I drift like a corpse between two currents. I would like to sink, to get where there is nothing. Dark walls surround me, rise around me, and again I begin to slip into darkness, feeling and indescribable well being. Little by little I dissolve, am transformed in air, in darkness, in a sensation that evaporates.

I am a bubble rising to the surface, first slowly, then more and more rapidly. The air is cold, the walls hard, darkness is dispelled. The bubble I am reaches the surface and bursts. I open my eyes. The room is dim. My face is bathed with sweat, and my nightgown sticks to my skin. I'm cold. Maritza comes and helps me into other pajamas. I am anxious to be left alone. I am feeling well now. I want to get sailing again.

Time doesn't exist. Neither does space. I go on sailing. I sink in the abyss where everything is wadded, everything is deadened, where reigns oblivion. I cuddle up in the dark. I strip off my shape, I become disembodied. I am nothing. When I return to the surface, I'm not a bubble any more bursting at the contact of air. I'm lighter than the air. I rise higher. I'm gliding across the room, hit the ceiling. I'm light, light… A thought of no importance occurs to me: "I'm very ill," followed by another: "I'm going to die." This is of no consequence. It's all right. "I'm happy," I say to myself closing my eyes.

Nothing hurts me. I don't wish anything. I'm lost in an infinite blissfulness which surrounds me by its thick veil. My eyes are open. I look at the ceiling, but no thought, no sensation of the exterior world reaches as yet my brain. My ears are deaf to all noise. My eyes blind to all impression. The ceiling, the pink light from the lamp-shade, the moving shadows suggest no image to my mind. To remain thus forever!

By and by, my gaze follows the shape of the shadow on the ceiling. By and by, my hearing discerns a presence, and words of which the meaning still escapes me. I haven't got the strength to turn the head, but lowering my eyes, I notice a hand and part of a skirt against my bed. Maritza leans over me. "You're not feeling well?" she asks.

I have difficulty forming the words. I have difficulty making the effort to speak aloud. My will power seems to have left me. All I manage to articulate is: "I'm all right, thank you."

"I have called the doctor," she says.

I don't answer. Suddenly, I'm very tired. It bored me to talk, to listen. I want to be alone. I close my eyes. When I open them again, the room is empty. I go to sleep. A sudden feeling of cold awakes me. It's the hand of Dr. Page on my wrist. He examines me without saying much. I don't even hear him leave because I fall asleep. Then it's Mariya who is there. She is saying something: "Can you hear me?" she asks.

"What were you saying?"

"Dr. Page would like you to go to the hospital. You cannot be looked after properly here. Will you do it?"

"Yes," I accept with indifference.

It's night again, night outdoors and night in my brain. A few clearings here and there, a spark of consciousness during which I say to myself: "I must be very ill for Mariya to have come! She didn't even look cross anymore." "Maritza," I say to the maid who has come in to draw the curtains, "how many days have I been lying here?"

"Four days, Miss Lily."

Mariya has rung up and asked Maritza to tell me to be ready tomorrow morning. She's going to fetch me to take me to the hospital.

I have great difficulty dressing; the walls seem to dance round me and the floor to move. But most of all, an overpowering want to sleep threatens to get the best of me at any moment. I'm not ready when Mariya arrives. She helps me to finish dressing. The taxi shakes me up terribly. I'm glad when at last we arrive at St. Mary's Hospital. A nurse takes me into a corner yellow and green room. Mariya again helps to put me to bed. Then she goes away saying that she will come back tomorrow.

After that there are some nurses, some blood tests, blood pressure, temperature. I haven't got enough blankets and shiver. They bring in two extra ones and a hot water bottle, and I go to sleep. I don't know what day it is. I had a visit from Dr. Page. He said he wanted me to be X-rayed. I don't care. Mariya came too. I think so—unless it was yesterday. I sleep the whole time. They wake me up to tell me that I'm going to be taken down to be X-rayed. I go to sleep on the chariot and wake up downstairs. A nurse comes near me.

"I will take two or three direct radios before Dr. Hanfield Jones, who will give you I.V., arrives," she says. "Breathe deeply. Keep your breath in. (I hear the click of the cliché). You can breathe again." This is repeated three times. "And if you want something, just call me. I'll be in the laboratory." The nurse collects the three plates and disappears in the dark room.

I have light dreams of flower covered meadows, of breeze in the branches. I am running, and there are moments when my feet don't touch the ground. And I go on moving across space with long soft strides. Suddenly everything becomes mixed up as the figures of a kaleidoscope and I see an unknown face bending over me.

"You were asleep?" says a surprised voice. "You must be very sleepy to sleep on something this hard." And he adds: "I'm Dr. Hanfield Jones."

"How are you, Doctor?" I say, trying to sound amiable.

"I'm going to give you an injection in the arm," continues the doctor, "but before that I want to have a look at the X-rays that have just been made." And he joins the nurse in the dark room.

A few minutes later, the opening door brings me out of the torpor in which I was already sinking. The doctor is standing on the threshold. He is looking at me. His white hair gives a compassionate expression to his face, which at this moment shows a deep sadness. He comes up to me, takes my hand and, patting it gently, says: "My poor child, an injection is no longer necessary."

"Good," I say, although it leaves me quite indifferent.

"No," says the doctor, shaking sadly his head, "it is not good. For what renders it unnecessary is what I have seen on the X-rays. You have stones in both kidneys." A silence follows. My eyes are closed. He must think I haven't understood. He asks: "Have you heard what I've told you?"

"Yes, Doctor, stones in both kidneys."

"A very large number of very large stones."

"Well," I say, "at least now we know. It's always that." And I add after a silence: "What do you suggest, Doctor?"

He continues to pat my hand, absentmindedly. "There isn't much choice. You'll have to have a blood test and as soon as I get the result, if it is feasible, you'll have to be operated on." As he finished the sentence, his gaze avoids my eyes. He thinks that I don't know, that I don't understand.

"What kind of operation, Doctor?"

"The left kidney will have to come out as quickly as possible."

"You want me to live with only one bad kidney?"

"The other one will have to be operated too. Later."

"You believe in miracles, Doctor?" I say, smiling.

"I'll come to see you in your room," he says, getting up.

I return to my bed, and half an hour later, Dr. Hanfield Jones comes in as he had promised.

"Doctor," I say, "I'm quite alone here. I have no parents, no friends to whom you can confide the truth, taking them outside the door. I'm alone. You have to tell me the truth. What chances have I got?"

"How can I answer without knowing the result of your blood test?"

"You can, at least approximate. Tell me how long I can live as I am?"

"Without the operation? Impossible!"

"How long? How many months? Or must I say: how many weeks?"

"I can't answer these questions. It depends on too many things."

"Doctor," I say slowly, "I won't have an operation."

He looks at me disbelievingly. "I don't think you realize."

"That I'm going to die? I do. You have said it. I cannot live thus. Do you think I don't understand? I know what awaits me: uremia.[2] I can describe it to you. You see: I know! I also know that if you take out one kidney, and leave me with only one badly damaged, it will but postpone the issue and in the meanwhile will make an invalid out of me. I love life, Doctor. I love life with all its hardness, its unexpectedness. I want to live, not vegetate.

I want all or nothing, and 'nothing' doesn't frighten me." I have braced myself up while speaking. I fall back, exhausted. It does seem that "Nothing" is my lot.

Dr. Hanfield Jones is furious about my stubbornness. "It's stupid!" he says. "You won't live six months like this."

"Six months," I say. "Six months is a long time! One can do a lot in six months."

"Think it over," he says shrugging his shoulders. "You might come to a saner disposition of mind. I'll come back to see you."

I slide backwards, softly, and sink again in the blissfulness from which I have been roused. Dr. Page comes to visit me. Then it's Mariya. I tell Mariya, just for the sake of saying something: "It seems I won't live."

"Nonsense," she says.

It makes me smile. I love the way Mariya says "Nonsense." She does it with so much conviction. Somebody is shaking me. I open my eyes. "Happy New Year!" says the nurse. It must be another day. Where am I? Of course—at the hospital. And I have been told that I would die. But it's another year. Already. It is as if I had gained a whole year since yesterday.

What a queer idea to wish it "happy" to me. How 'Happy?'" But it was Christmas yesterday. It's not possible. I push away the tray the nurse brings me. "How long have I been here?"

"Four days."

I don't sleep. I follow the flight of seagulls before my window. I listen to their piercing voices. I think of nothing. There's a knock at the door. Mariya comes in. "I'm bringing someone to see you," she says.

Colonel Robertson is with her. He brings me a bunch of jonquils and daffodils which Mariya carries. "Well! What have you been saying?" He is good humoured and playful, as one always is with people seriously ill. Why does he think it necessary to be superficial? I quite sympathize with him; he doesn't know what to say. I try to put him at his ease. I ask for the latest news, in a general way, and about that war. "Let's see," says Robertson. "The Sharnhorst has been definitely sunk off the Coast of Norway, and the Russians have taken back Korosten and Jitomir."

"That's fine," I say. "And how about the landing? When will you start the fight?"

He smiles: "But we are fighting up to the last Russian!"

"The Russians are prolific," I say. "You'll never get to the last of them. I should like to see the end of the war," I say turning my face away towards the window and following absent-mindedly the monotonous circling of the gulls.

"You'll see it if you undergo the operation," states Robertson. I shake my head. "Why don't you want the operation?"

"There are too few chances! And I don't want to die here—not on an operating table—nor in England. I don't want to be buried in a drenched soil. If I died now, my soul would get lost in the fog." And I begin to laugh: "I have no time to die."

Robertson gives me a quick glance. "No time? You have nothing more to do. We'll have to interrupt working in your actual state."

"Why? I'm not dead yet."

"You believe you'll be able to go on working?"

"Yes." And I add: "Will you let me have Babs?"

"I'm afraid it's impossible," says Robertson laughing. I don't have the strength renew the discussion and Robertson changes himself the topic. "What will you do after the war?"

"I'll publish a book. I'll speak about you."

He laughs in a rather embarrassed way. "Do you think I'll like that?"

"I doubt it," I say, smiling. "My aim won't be to please you."

"Do you believe that it'll be easy to land in France?" he asks, changing the subject.

"If the German defenses haven't been reinforced since I left, yes. They hold France much more by bluff than by anything else."

"The danger doesn't come from the Germans anymore," says Robertson. "They're vanquished in advance; it's just a question of time."

"But the Russians?"

"Yes, the Russians!"

"They're very strong," I remark.

"Too strong," says Robertson. And he asks: "What do you think of them?"

"That it's too late to fight against flood once the dams have been ruptured!"

"Hm," says Robertson. "We had to choose between two evils; I don't know whether we have chosen the minor one."

"Do you fear the Russians?" I ask.

"We do," he admits. Fortunately, Robertson hasn't got too much time and must leave. The days go by. I continue to sleep.

—⚬—

January 3rd 1944

This morning I wake up when the nurse comes to take my temperature. It looks as if there is sun outside. I have a funny sensation in the pit of my stomach. "I'm hungry," I say.

The nurse looks at me in amazement. "What did you say?"

I repeat: "I'm hungry."

She leaves the room in a hurry and comes back with the matron. "What am I told?" asks the latter. "That you're hungry?"

"Yes," I say, surprised in turn. "Is there anything wrong in being hungry?"

"No, on the contrary! Wonderful!"

I eat everything they bring me on a tray. I could eat twice as much. Nurses come to see me, look at me with wonder, then smile. I pick up a book and start to read. But I notice the hand that is holding it, and I can hardly believe it's my own. It is strangely pale and transparent, with depressions designing the contour of each bone. "It's my hand," I think. "And I'm alive. But soon I won't be any more. And this same hand that I can move will become still and cold. It has already the appearance of a dead hand."

And for the first time I realize there is change in my life: no future! A blank wall barring the way which is the end. No, it's not frightening; it's strange. "You have six months to live." Nothing but six months, and so many things to do! Will I have the time? The time to finish my work; the time to finish my book; the time to settle everything. Does it mean I'm going to work? In spite of my decision? Yes. Nothing matters now. It doesn't matter that the War Office or the Intelligence Service have lied to me, have exploited me; it doesn't matter what I think, or what I feel in the short time that's left to me. The only thing that matters is the war that goes on and that must be won.

Mary has come from Bristol to see me. She refuses to believe what she is told. She has sent a telegram to Cliff to ask him to send Babs. The days go by, and slowly I revive. My strength is coming back. Tomorrow I'm going home. Nelly came to see me.

—⚬—

January 6th 1944

Once again, I'm in the flat at Rugby Mansions. Once again, Maritza looks after me and spoils me. It's fun to be alive! This afternoon, Mary rings up from Bristol; she has received a telegraphic answer from Cliff. He says that Babs is well, that he is in Algiers with my sister. I was so anxious regarding to Babs all this time that I have the impression of a heavy weight being taken off my mind. And like an idiot, I start to cry with joy.

Mariya comes and we send a message to "Moustache" to explain my long silence. I have asked Mariya to bring me photos of the preceding letters, so that I could repeat one of the writings and use the same return address. It is funny to see those samples of my own writing which I would not recognize myself.

In the afternoon Ronnie brings me a small radio which I'm going to take with me to Bristol to be able to listen on the days when the Germans are supposed to call me. It's a Skyrider Hallicrafter, exactly what "Moustache" told me to get.

Tomorrow I go back to Bristol, where Mariya will come every week.

Bessie paid me a visit this afternoon. I've only seen her once since I arrived, and I was happy that she came.

Wraxall

Teddy came to meet me at the station. Mary was waiting for me at home. Wonderful sensation to find oneself again amongst friends. The day's exceptionally warm for the beginning of January. In the distance, the green squares of the pastures and the brown squares of the fields are blurred out by the golden mist of the evening. The sky's pure, with just a few tiny fluffy clouds that the declining sun lights up from below.

Smokes rise here and there, spreading out in white sheets which fuse with the mist. A great peace envelops the English countryside, so neat with its hedges dividing the landscape into regular pattern. I'm lying on the terrace in front of the house on a chaise lounge propped up by pillows and tucked in blankets. I look at the horizon behind which the sun will soon disappear. I'm breathing. I'm alive. I'm saying to myself that life is really worth it, that I have never before realized its value. Mary observes me anxiously. I give a squeeze to her hand and smile at her. "I'm happy!" I tell her. I would like to reassure her. To tell her it's nothing. Mary has lost her father on Christmas Eve, and now she observes me with distress. I understand what she feels. It's so much easier to be the one that goes than the one that remains. I'm conscious of my egoism, because others worry for me, others suffer, while to me, it's indifference.

I wanted to take a walk, but I have discovered that I must first learn again how to walk! Mariya comes, and we compose a new message. I wonder why "they" can't write their messages themselves. To tell to "My dear, dear Sabina" that "all the family is well," that "Daisy has now grown into a big girl," and that "Brigitte has just got engaged," and to sign this message in a disguised handwriting with a name picked out of the telephone book. Anyone would do as well as me. Anyone could write out the message in secret ink and block characters. I'm not indispensable. My part is finished, if there is nothing else to do.

January 12th

"Mary," I say, "this telegram Cliff has sent."
"Yes. What about it?"

"Does it seem O.K. to you?"

Mary looks at me in astonishment. "What do you mean?"

"I don't know myself. I wonder if it's the truth. Why should he have left Babs in Algiers? If only I could have my Babs here, I have the impression everything would turn well."

"I think it's shameful the way 'they' have acted towards you. To promise, to lure you over here, and then not to hold one's promise."

"It's very difficult not to take advantage of one's strength when one is the stronger!"

"All the same, it's disgusting!" Mary, as most Englishmen (unfortunately with the exception of those with whom I have to work), is thoroughly honest and doesn't admit any cheating. For her there exist no impediments to the rules of a game. The famous British "fair play" which I trusted myself.

"But why should this American aviator lie to you?" she adds.

"I don't know. Maybe he has become attached to Babs and wants to keep him."

"Listen. Stop worrying. Just write to your sister and you'll know." She is right.

We send another message to "Moustache," this time telling him that his diamond has been valued at only £200. (The War Office has effectively had it expertise.) Therefore, I have thought it more advantageous to exchange it with an American pilot against a radio plus £50. Description of a Halicrafter (Sky Ryder) radio. I warn "Moustache" that from now on I shall be listening to them on the appointed days. I add that on my last visit to Bristol, I have noticed a large number of American soldiers and officers bearing a large black A on their sleeve. I also give the situation of important motorized vehicle depots on the Bristol-Clevedon road.

When the message is finished, Mariya slips my letter in a large envelope which she locks up in a small suitcase which never leaves her. "Have you got an idea how we could induce 'Emile' ('Moustache') to send you a transmitter?" she asks me. "We are very much interested in your having such a radio, because it's probable that very soon one won't be able to correspond by letters, and it's essential for us to have the means to transmit information to the Germans."

"I could tell him I have the impression that there is something in preparation; that if events develop, correspondence by letters will be too slow; that besides I may have to ask him for an urgent advice and that in consequence, I would like him to arrange that the promised radio should be sent over to me."

"The point is," says Mariya, "that if we let him 'arrange' matters, either he won't know how to do it, or else it will take him so long that we will miss precious opportunities. Have you no way to suggest? For instance, could you tell him to hand the post over to someone who would bring it over to you?"

"It's more complicated than all that," I say, "and I would have to present him with a circumstantial, plausible and sufficiently long story. I couldn't just suggest him a 'means of transportation' without any ado. He would be suspicious. If you want, in the next message, we could begin asking for a radio."

"All right," says Mariya, "and in the meanwhile try to think of something."

With the listening helmet applied to my ears, I listen mechanically, shifting slowly the needle around 8650 meters. I listen so, without much hope, three times a week since I have brought home the radio. I never catch anything. But I don't worry much about it, as I know that in London they are listening too. Suddenly I strain my ears: I seem to have heard X. R. F. I return backwards, just in time to catch the last X. R. F., the dash, the number of letters and then K.A. K.A. Distractedly I rush in search of a pencil, cannot find one, run downstairs and into the living room where I snatch one from Mary's desk. That's my luck. I always have everything prepared, and there was no message. And this last time I got tired waiting without ever hearing anything. "They won't call me," I thought and didn't prepare pencil or writing pad! And there they are!

The time to run up again, to readjust the helmet, and they are already repeating the message for the second time. I note three quarters of it. The beginning is missing! I'm terribly excited. At last they have given a sign. I was beginning to get the impression of corresponding with a blank!

I have a telephone call from the War Office that Mariya has left for Bristol, that she will be with me in the beginning of the afternoon. She arrives at 4 o'clock. Her first words are: "Guess what happened!"

"Kliemann has been giving news!"

"Ah!" says Mariya, a little disappointed, "you know already! They have told you at the office?"

"No, but I have taken the message."

"You've heard it! They are deciphering it. May I ring them up?" When she returns from the telephone, she seems very disappointed: "It has no sense whatever! They cannot decipher it. Are you quite sure that you have explained the deciphering in the right way?"

"Quite sure."

"I have brought with me the text of the message and the book in case. Shall we try?"

But after half an hour's useless efforts we are obliged to give it up—impossible to find the key! It's maddening to be there before the puzzle on a sheet of paper and unable to solve it. I believe we are equally annoyed, Mariya and myself!

"Don't bother," I say at last. "The day after tomorrow they'll repeat the message and if they have forgotten something, they will notice it and we might be more lucky then."

As I had foreseen, this morning I take down the same message with a slight alteration. Ten minutes after the end of the broadcasting, Mariya rings me up: "This time we've got it! I'm coming round."

The message Mariya shows me is very short. It simply says: "Information very interesting—letters arrive well—continue." And it ends by this unofficial sentence which is very much like "Moustache" and which makes me burst with laughter: "You're very charming!"

"What does it mean?" asks Mayiya, suspiciously.

"Nothing, but that 'Moustache' thinks me charming!"

"Funny thing to put in a message addressed to an agent!" says Mariya, who doesn't seem quite convinced.

I live in a very quiet way, without any events, in the country, spending half of the day in bed, but regaining strength by and by. Yesterday, an American surgeon who came to see us examined my radiography. He tossed his head. "It appears I have six months to live," I tell him.

"He hasn't been very generous, the one who gave you six months! You can easily live for a year with that!" Six months or a year—what difference does it make, when there is nothing behind?

January 21st 1944

Moussia's letter shakes in my hand. I read and read again the first sentence without being able to realize that it's true. "My poor darling," she writes, "I hate the pain I will give you, but it's better you should know, so as to make no plans for the future. You shall not see your Babs again. He has been run over."

Three weeks ago I have been told that I would die. It didn't matter to me! But not that—not losing Babs. Everything is indifferent to me now. The circle of loneliness has closed around me. I am alone, absolutely alone and full of scorn for those who by their false promises have brought me to it. My long solitary walks remind me of the plans I made for the time Babs would be with me—and these walks are without aim. I try not to think, but I cannot forget. We don't choose the room we give to our affections. And Babs was part of every day.

In the night I dream that I'm searching for him, that I follow his steps, that I find him. I see him from far away, I run, I catch him up in my arms. But it's another dog, every time, a dog looking like him, but with a yellow head. And so, even in my sleep, the most foolish hope gives way to bitter disappointment. I have come to dread the nights. I have temperature again. My sight has become very bad. At ten meters things are dimmed. I don't speak about Babs and forbid my friends to speak about him.

I didn't read the letter to the end. If there are any details, I want to ignore them. But it was written on the 3rd of January. On the 3rd of January Babs was dead, and on the 11th Clifford Lord cabled me that my dog was well. The coward! He didn't even have the courage to tell the truth!

Mariya is there. Mary must have warned her telling her not to speak about it. She doesn't say anything! Nor do I. We write down the message, the one demanding a radio. Then Mariya asks me: "Have you thought of something?"

"Yes, you know Carmen E. in Madrid, of whom I spoke to you? I could suggest to Kliemann to pack the radio in an old suitcase with some worn clothes and have it deposited at Carmen's. I'll tell him that a friend of my cousin Bessie's will go to Madrid on a mission from some ministry; that I have met him and that he is willing to bring me back a suitcase which I have left at a friend's (Carmen), because I had an exceeded of weight when crossing by plane. It's up to you to decide on what date the supposed friend will go to Madrid and the ministry he will represent.

"Then I'll write a second letter to Carmen. I'll tell her I've been obliged to leave a suitcase in Madrid, not being able to take with me on the plane. Unfortunately the person I left it with is obliged to leave for 3 months in the beginning of February, perhaps. A friend of mine will be in Madrid in March (does this month suit you?) and could bring it over to me. I'll ask Carmen if I can have a suitcase brought to her and if she could keep it between the departure of the person who has it presently and the arrival of the friend who will take it. So Kliemann will feel safe. I don't think he will hesitate to avail himself of the opportunity to leave the radio at Carmen's. What do you think about this plan of action?"

Mariya, who has been taking notes, says: "I must see 'the office' about it. At first sight it seems all right to me! I'll ring you up as soon as I have an answer."

How everything has changed for me since I arrived here. In three months, England has deprived me of all the enthusiasm, which three years under the German yoke were not able to stifle. I had worked with passion. I continue with indifference. I admire the British, their tenacity in struggling, their composure, their endurance. But I wouldn't want to be like them. I want to love and hate, feel, vibrate and live. They are cold, non-communicative, non-demonstrative, and impenetrable. I would like to see Mariya laugh, or cry, or scream. I would like to see her face wrinkle or relax—but express something. I have come to consider her as a sort of automaton, not as a human being.

This morning, Mariya has telephoned again. "I'll be coming this afternoon and we'll write two letters as you suggested yesterday."

I'm waiting for her. She'll get out of the car at fifty meters from here and will walk this distance. She pretends that it draws less attention. But already everybody is whispering in the little village of Wraxall about the mysterious "panther woman" whom a military car drops behind the curve! In wind, rain or snow, Mariya arrives dressed in her ocelot-skin coat, carrying her old little suitcase. From my room, I can see the corner of many curtains being lifted in the two houses on the other side of the road, and curious glances following and watching her. Mariya wouldn't be a good spy!

We have written the two letters to "Moustache" and Carmen. We have given as a probable date for the arrival of the so-called friend of Bessie's in Madrid between the 3rd and the 6th of March. This gives "Moustache" over a month to prepare, send off and leave the radio post. I have put down in cipher the name and address of Carmen.

"Do you think it will do?" asks Mariya.

"Why not?" I say shrugging my shoulders. I cannot feel any interest for this work anymore.

I'm working at a new novel which I have called Jean (Fragment of a life). It's diverting and prevents me from thinking. My sight is terribly bad.

February 18th

A telephone call from Mariya. "How do you feel now?"

"Why this solicitude?"

"Would you like to travel?"

"Don't tell me you're concerned with tastes! Where to?"

"To Portugal."

"Aren't the letters sufficient?"

"We cannot wait."

"When?"

"In two, three days. Can you come to London today?"

"No. Tomorrow."

"O.K. Take the eleven o'clock train. I'll be waiting for you at the station."

I put the receiver slowly down. Portugal! That means seeing the Germans again, having to take up again bluffing, lying. I lack energy for it! Shall I still know how to do it? I haven't got the hate anymore I had when I was in Spain. I haven't even the hatred. It has dulled with the contact of these people who fight without hating. The other day we discussed what we would do if a German plane were shot down in flames and its occupants came down in parachutes. Some would go out to capture them with a rifle, others with a pitchfork, the third ones with a cudgel. And someone cried out: "War or no war, I know that I would offer them a cup of tea! It might be forbidden, but what on earth! They are human beings all the same!" And everybody approved. Yes, the war is a fine sport for some people.

I go down to the kitchen where Mary is preparing lunch.

"I go to Portugal," I tell her.

"Ah!" she says, "but will you have the strength?"

"I'll have to. Maybe, if I manage to get into the mood, I'll do it."

Mariya is waiting for me at Paddington station. From far away I can see her ocelot

Above and opposite: **The second apartment that Lily occupied was at 39 Hill Street in the Mayfair district in London. From this apartment, Lily could hear the firing of anti-aircraft guns in Hyde Park (photographs taken by the editor).**

coat. We take a taxi. The address she gives the driver, 39 Hill Street, surprises me. "Where are we going?"

"You'll see." And she adds: "The flat in Rugby Mansions is occupied, so I'm taking you to another place."

The taxi stops before a large "block of flats," the only house in the neighbourhood which hasn't been touched, all the others being demolished and showing empty frames in which pigeons have taken their abode. The lift takes us up to the 8th floor. At the end of the passage, Mariya takes a key out of her bag and opens the door to N 83. It's a tiny little flat, charmingly furnished and with a marvelous panoramic view of the whole town. I can see Big Ben, the Parliament, Westminster Abbey and in the far distance the dome of St. Paul.

"What a nice place!" I cannot help to remark.

"You like it?" says Mariya. "I was sure it would please you. Make yourself comfortable. We'll talk later."

A bedroom, a bathroom, a living room opening onto a diminutive hall, and a tiny recess with an electric stove. That's all. But it's furnished with much taste and the shelves are lined with a quantity of books in gay coloured bindings. It's so much better than Rugby Mansions!

"Now I'll tell you what is the matter," says Mariya. "The War Office would like you to go to Lisbon, to meet Emile, and to bring back the transmitter. Will you do it?"

"Naturally."

"Good. Perhaps we could send him a cable to warn him of your arrival."

I don't reply at once. I consider the question. I try to imagine what "Moustache" will think of this journey to Lisbon. "What reason?" I say at last.

"For the cable?"

"No, for my journey to Portugal."

"Grosso mode.[3] You'll be sent by the M.O.I. (Ministry of Information) where you're supposed to work. Ronnie will come tomorrow to give you the details of your 'story.' You'll have about a week to learn it by heart. Do you think it'll be sufficient for you?"

"It'll have to be sufficient if you don't give me more time."

"We'll see about that tomorrow. You didn't answer about the cable."

"Yes. 'Solange will see Mère Catherine beginning March. Happy to see Octave again. Friendly greetings' or something like that. How will your censors react to such a cable normally?"

"They would check the name and address of the sender, I suppose. If anything seemed suspicious, the police would question the sender."

"In fact, if I were really working by myself, my only risk would be to spoil my sector (filière) 'Sabina Romans.'[4] You don't have to produce an identity card at the post office to send off a cable abroad?"

"No."

"Then, logically, I would have risked it. We can send it off."

"Do you think that, with such a short text, Emile will understand?" says Mariya dubiously.

"I don't know why he shouldn't? He knows the address of Mère Catherine! So that he will know that it's Lisbon. The date is clear. He knows that I am Solange and that he is Octave. What else do you want?"

"And where will he find you?"

"You remember he gave me an address—a man called Rudolph Morgener. I'll call on him as soon as I'm there."

"And if this Morgener shouldn't be there, or were absent?"

"I should send a cable to "Moustache" through Sabina Romans to fix a place where we could meet."

"Good. And now let us go and have dinner in the restaurant downstairs."

This morning Ronnie accompanies Mariya. I haven't seen Ronnie for some time, and I'm surprised to see that he wears a moustache. It suits him about as much as it would suit me!

"It's for the rehearsals—to give you a better illusion that I'm Major Kliemann!" he says, laughing. "There's your 'story,'" he adds, getting to work. "I have noted here the names, addresses and main facts which you'll have to learn by heart. I'll leave you these two typewritten sheets. Now I'll go into the details of your alibi. You work at the M.O.I. (Ministry of Information), in the cinematographic section! Your chief is Sidney Bernstein! He is tall, rather young, has a broken nose and very fine teeth! He generally wears plus fours[5] and dresses in tweeds or in checked stuff! Can you figure the type of man he is?"

"Yes! Approximately."

"You're on very good terms with him."

"How good?"

"In short, you get him to do what you want. He listens to you willingly, is ready to accept your advice and suggestions."

"I see. Go on."

"Your supreme chief is Brendan Brecker. You have never seen him—he is to highly placed."

"So that at least I haven't to know the form of his ears."

"No. Now I'll tell you a few words about the English cinema. The M.O.I. is preparing films which will be shown in the liberated countries: France, Holland, Belgium, etc. But we have a very serious competitors (and this is the truth!) in the Americans, who have more money, more facilities, more actors and larger means for the production of propaganda films. You have suggested to Bernstein the idea of using stage-managers who escaped from occupied countries so as to give more realism to these films, and who will at the same time be better acquainted with the mentality of the enslaved populations, know better their tastes and their wishes, have more exact knowledge of what would strike their imagination or amuse them. Bernstein has brought your suggestions before Brendan Brecker and after discussing them, they have been approved. The chief difficulty was the scarcity of personnel. Nobody was free to make inquiries in the matter. It's then you proposed yourself for the mission, stressing the fact that you were "new" in the Ministry, that your work was not urgent and besides, that being French, you would have all faculties to discuss with Frenchman and Belgians."

"Excuse me for interrupting you. How should I come to hold such a trustworthy position in the M. O. I.?

"Through your cousin, naturally!"

"Yes, of course, but don't you think all the same that Kliemann would deem it strange that the M.O.I. should entrust me with such an important job—and abroad—after having employed me for three months at the utmost? It's the most I can pretend to have been there."

Ronnie shrugs his shoulders. "I'm sure you'll be able to persuade him of the thing being plausible! You've made him swallow pills larger than that! You'll hear about the rest of the details from Mariya (he says: "Mary"). When you're in full possession of your role, I'll come and we'll have a rehearsal."

So now I'm provided with the most incredible alibi, and it's with that I must face the German's mistrust! We write out a rather long message for "Moustache." We skip one number so as to let him think one of our letters did not reach him, the one precisely where I spoke to him about my new "job" at the M.O.I. Otherwise I'm afraid it might seem rather sudden! I tell him that, as I've already written to him (!), it's possible there might be an unexpected opportunity for me to go to Lisbon. This, if it should happen, I would only know about it at the last minute! I would advise him by cable through Sabina Romans. But I ask him earnestly to be prepared to come to Lisbon at my first sign and above all not to forget to bring the transmitter.

We have little hope, Mariya and I, that this letter should reach him in time; but at least it will explain my cable when it reaches him. I'll have to look out sharp!

The sirens howl, filling the night with their piercing noise. They are silent and the silence is heavy. Then somewhere in the distance a gun barks. I have put out the light and gone to the window. London all around as black as an ink blot. Opposite—it must be southeast—a fuse, two fuses go up, lighting up the sky with a red glimmer, and a few instants later I hear the distant crackling of bursting projectiles. The sky is swept by the pencils of powerful search-lights piercing the darkness. By and by the peculiar noise of several German planes is audible and the A.A. enters into action.

I half-open the window so that the glass panes should not be smashed, let the heavy curtain drop and re-enter the room. The next moment an unimaginable noise, like steam escaping from an overheated boiler, but increased a million of times, obliges me to squeeze my head between my shoulders. Then I hear the house coming down. No, it doesn't come down! But the noise is repeated several times, and I remember then what Mariya told me about the firing of fuse-guns, those which are in Hyde Park, at one hundred meters from my house, the same ones concerning which "Moustache" wanted to have information!

The blackout lasts for half an hour. Somewhere, bombs are dropped, but not very near from here. Five minutes after everything has become calm, my telephone rings. It's Louisa, Mariya's friend. "How do you feel?" she asks.

"Very well, thank you! Why?"

"I don't know—this bombardment and you all alone on the eighth floor. So I thought you would be frightened! Did you go down to the shelter?"

"Certainly not! I prefer to fall down from the eighth floor than receive eight floors on the top of my head! But it's sweet of you to ring me up." I like Louise very much. There is something so "cozy" about her. But poor Louisa is terrified by the raids!

Mariya and I study the last details of my "story." I'm supposed to live at 16 Redcliff, Old Brompton Road. The flat belongs to some friends of my cousin. The husband is in the army, and the wife has gone to live with her parents. That's how I could get it. Every two weeks I pay the rent to Miss Collins, the charwoman. Today Mariya has brought a car, and she takes me to see the house and gives me a description of the flat. Then she shows me the bus I'm supposed to take every morning to go to the M.O.I. It isn't a direct one and I'm obliged to change. She tells me the number of sections, the price of the ticket. I change at Hyde Park Corner and get out at Malet Street.

The M.O.I. is temporarily lodged in the buildings of the University of London. Mariya brings me there keeping to the bus's itinerary. We go around the University which was partly in construction, but the work has been interrupted. Mariya draws my attention to the University having been damaged during one of the bombardments and that three floors in the highest part—the one looking like a tower—have been smashed down. "It's there at the top that is the restaurant where you generally have lunch," she says. "You can have a meal for 2/6, or tea with scones and a dish of eggs for 1/6. Will you have a sufficiently clear idea of the place where you 'work' and of the way you go every day?" she asks.

"I would also like to see the entrance. I would like to know in which wings are 'our' offices. I would like to know what they are like and with whom 'I work'; if I'm alone in the room, or if we are several? I would also like to know what my work is. And finally, if a permit is necessary to enter the M.O.I., I should like to know what it's like."

"Good. Let us proceed in order," says Mariya who has parked the car. "There is a permit to enter the M.O.I. Here's mine. Look at it. I cannot give you a description of the offices, as I have never been there. You can invent one. The work you're supposed to do? It could be translations: fragments of dialogues of which you don't know yourself the whole contents. Also corrections of translations."

"I would also like you to give me some titles of films made by the M.O.I. and some documentation on cinema, so that I can at least bring out some technical terms!"

"All right, you'll get it all. Now I'll bring you before the entrance."

"You see," she tells me when we are there, "you pass under this arch. The door is behind, on the left, and you go up to the 2nd floor. Is it all you wanted to see?"

"Thank you. I think it's all."

Again a bombardment. This time it must have come down pretty near. My house has swung and my lamp has been thrown down. I was just about to learn about the métrage[6] of a documentary film, the cost of a "short," etc. I spend all my time with Mariya, going through every detail, imagining all the questions "Moustache" might ask me, all the suspicions which might occur to him.

I have got used to Mariya. She has entered my daily life without my having chosen her, and for a long time I had a feeling of hostility towards her. Now she is part of the daily routine! I even sometimes forget that she belongs to the "gang," as I call the people from the Intelligence Service. Which fact, when I think of it, makes me shrink back into my shell. I distrust even Louisa, when I come to think of it. But there is something about Mariya, in the way she twists her legs in a spiral, the way her stockings come down like a cork-screw, in the way she walks with big strides, swinging her arms and sometimes humming a little melody—as I caught her doing once I followed her for about five minutes without her noticing it, from Green Park to Piccadilly Circus—there is in her something bohemian which doesn't correspond to the hard look she wants to show.

Ronnie clears his throat, passes a finger in his too tight collar and begins: "I'm Major Kliemann. I have received from you a cable summoning me to Lisbon. I meet you. You have just arrived from England. You have a British passport. I have a reason to be surprised—suspicious. Do you follow me?"

"Yes," I say with an effort not to smile and keep serious. Poor Ronnie makes such a funny Kliemann. But by and by I enter my part. I'm no more in Hill Street before a Ronnie holding a questionnaire in his hand. I'm there, in Lisbon, in the presence of "Moustache" and I stake much more than my life: the success of my work. I suddenly realize what the success of a three years long effort represents for me. I thought that the results didn't interest me anymore. It's false! I have still the strength to fight and to gain. I'll go to face "Moustache." I know that the "story" which the English have prepared for me is not much good, but I'll convince him, and he'll believe.

So we plunge into a conversation where I start by giving Ronnie a general version of the unexpected manner in which I obtained this situation in the M.O.I.—a few words about my work; how lucky I've been to find a flat; what rent I pay; the installation of my radio. Then he begins to ask me questions, which appear very harmless, but each one contains a hidden snare. He asks me how I go to my work: by bus. He asks me how long it takes me. Fortunately, I have timed it with Mariya, and I'm able to answer him. I even go as far as to give him a description of my supposed flat, which my imagination has endowed—goodness knows why!—with mauve moquette![7] I go as far as describing to him the non-existent charwoman, Miss Collins. After an hour's time, Ronnie folds up his questionnaire and rises. "I think you held your part. I couldn't catch you. Gosh! I'm tired!"

I'm not. I remark that I'm able to "change skin" with an unbelievable ease. Is it because for three years I have created and personified a being so entirely different from myself? Maybe. I wonder if I should have more time to live, if I were still alive after the end of the war, if I would be able to re-adopt myself to a normal life, to become normal again?

Three bombardments in a few days.

"Mariya," I say this morning, "perhaps we could go to have a look at the results of the bombs. You remember that Graf, in Paris, insisted that every time there was a bombardment in the place where I was, I should try to find out the places that had been touched and let them know. I don't see much sense in it when there are no important objectives. All the same! As they want it!"

"All right," says Mariya. "But I would suggest doing it in a different way. We'll give you information for 'Emile.' I suppose you'll want to write it down. At the same time I'll get you the 'addresses' of the places where the bombs have fallen. You can note it all at the same time. Then you'll have to gather all the papers you want to take with you, and I'll go with you to the censor with those you will take over with you. It's on account of the control the customs. When we're through with all this, we'll go to look at the bombarded places."

"O.K."

Among the information I have to transmit to "Moustache," there is one I don't like. It concerns a factory and an aerodrome near Bristol on the road to Chipping. Mariya makes me a sketch of the disposition of the buildings and shacks on the aerodrome, of the adjacent workshops and tells me the type of motors which are made there.

"If you had only told me about it while I was in Bristol!" I say. "It was so easy to go round there. But to describe all this without having seen it. What colour are the buildings? What are they made of?"

"I don't know," says Mariya.

"How are the roofs?" Mariya doesn't know. "Look here," I say. "It's with such futilities that one is caught. Suppose they know this aerodrome, that they are in possession of air views of it, that they know that the buildings are made of bricks, and that I tell them that they are wooden, or the reverse? Suppose that I pretend that there are slate roofs, when they are tiles, or of corrugated iron? No, I cannot do it. I don't want to say I have seen it. I must invent some excuse to explain how I got the information."

Finally we decide that I got it through a friend of Teddy's, who is engineer and test pilot in the region and who came to spend an afternoon at Wraxall. I have written down all the information and the addresses in secret ink on the last two sheets of a block of paper, and we take it together with my address book and a few other papers to the censor.

"And my camera?" I say, suddenly remembering it. "Do I need a special authorization for it?"

"I don't know, but I suppose so," says Mariya. "It's rather late to think about it. I'll inquire at the office tonight."

I have telephoned Bessie, and she promised to come to see me tomorrow morning.

February 27th 1944

I leave tomorrow. Mariya has just told me Robertson would call at 2 o'clock. I wait for Bessie, but time passes, and she doesn't come. 2 o'clock. Someone "scratches" at my door. It's Mariya's distinctive way. I go to open it. Robertson is following her.

"Well!" he says. "I'm happy to see you up and looking better than last time. How do you feel?"

"Not bad."

"Do you think you'll succeed?"

I shrug my shoulders: "I don't know."

Robertson frowns. "I don't like hearing you say 'I don't know.' Aren't you sure of yourself anymore? Doesn't your work interest you anymore?"

"It isn't that. Before, I had no doubts about the success. Now, now, I feel vulnerable."

"I don't like this," repeats Robertson, and he adds after a moment's reflection: "Would you prefer not to go?"

"No!" I say, shaking my head. "Do you think I'm afraid?" I smile. "If I'm discovered, they'll kill me. And you know, to die now, or to die a little later. But I would prefer, should the Germans guess the truth, that it should occur while I'm there. Otherwise, my parents would have to pay instead of me. Don't be alarmed; I'm a bit out of spirits just now! But when they'll be wanted, I'll have them."

"By the way," says Mariya, "I don't think you'll be able to take your camera. I have inquired. It's absolutely forbidden to have them in the plane. It would have to be sent to you by the diplomatic bag, and you wouldn't have it before two weeks at the earliest."

Robertson gives me more advice. He tells me how much he counts upon me, the importance he attaches to the success of my mission. I notice that his words make little impression upon me. To know that I'm useful doesn't give me the same keen pleasure it did four months ago, when this same Robertson congratulated me upon the work accomplished, when I landed in England. The telephone bell interrupts the conversation. The porter tells me that a lady is waiting for me downstairs, but refuses to go up. It's Bessie.

"Tell her to come," says Robertson. "In any case, I'll have to leave you in a few moments."

I go down, but cannot persuade Bessie to come and see my flat. She isn't keen to meet Robertson. "It looks as if you were afraid for your reputation!" I say, laughing. She leaves me after five minutes!

"I believe I have frightened your cousin away," says Robertson. Once more, he wishes me everything one can wish somebody starting on a journey, on a journey from which one is not sure to come back!

When Robertson is gone, Mariya says to me: "I've got something for you; you wanted to buy a souvenir for Kliemann. I saw it in a shop window and bought it." She hands me a small wallet made of nice leather made by Dunhill's. It just the form of an envelope and bears a blue 2½ d. stamp. "I liked it because of the stamp," says Mariya. "I thought it would amuse and flatter 'Emile' to have a wallet of such unmistakable English origin in war time! It will be like a trophy!"

"Excellent idea! And do you know what I'll do, once I'm in Lisbon? I'll have it engraved, like an address: To Octave
               Souvenir from London
               29th February 1944
                   Solange.

What do you think?"

"It will be very amusing. And now, let's go to work. We'll look up the places touched by the bombs."

FEBRUARY 29TH 1944

No planes are leaving today on account of the bad weather. I take my luggage back home.

MARCH 1ST 1944

Second unlucky attempt. I am told that I'll have to take a plane at Bristol tomorrow, instead of leaving direct from London.

March 2nd 1944

Mariya takes me down to the station and puts me into the train. I feel that she would like to be in my place, because at the moment she doesn't think about all the risks there'll be. She might even wish it in spite of the risks.

Bristol. The same aerodrome where I landed four months ago. The same security captain who comes to shake hands with me and wishes me good luck. Suddenly I catch sight of the astounded face of Mr. Gold (the one who told me: I? I'm from the Home Office"), who looks at me as if he was seeing a ghost. From the corner of my eye I see him rush to the captain at the other end of the room, pull him by the sleeve and point in my direction. The officer probably tells him I'm O.K., because Mr. Gold calms down, but remains there, planted on his short legs and staring at me with round eyes. The captain is in the custom's room when we pass inspection. He is behind the custom-house officer as this one puts his hand on the strap of my suitcase. He tells him two words and my suitcase remains unopened.

Finally we get into the plane. The day seems very long to me.

VI

Lisbon, 1944

LISBON, MARCH 3RD 1944

2 a.m. The sleepy night porter has put down my suitcases and has left. I look around me. The reservation has been made by the British Embassy. The walls of the room are hung with golden paper; the heavy velvet curtains and the silk bed cover are red. I go to the window and open it wide. The streets are brightly illuminated, the sky full of stars. Everything is silent. I remember the cloudy sky of London that I left yesterday morning. I think of the fog that is probably covering everything over there. I don't know what the result of this trip will be. Maybe it is one from which one doesn't return. Death has less importance in radiant surroundings.

"I was expecting you," says Captain Barratt putting out his hand. "Had a good journey? Satisfied with the room?"

"Thanks. Everything is perfect."

"What may I do for you?"

"Nothing for the moment, except that I need money."

Barratt takes three thousand escudos bills out of his wallet and hands them to me. "I haven't received any instructions concerning the money question, but I think this should be sufficient to keep you going for a while. If you'll wait a minute, I will go and fetch someone who wants to see you."

I remain in the tiny reception room furnished with wicker chairs. Later on I shall see "the other one"—the German. But before that I must go to the Embassy to verify my alibi. It is safer to do so.

Barratt returns, accompanied by a slim and fair youngster with pomaded hair.[1] I could easily imagine him at the counter of a draper store, a pencil behind the ear, measuring yards of wool and silk materials, and smiling an artificial and slightly silly smile. "This is my friend who, from now on, will act as contact between us," says Barratt. "I shall be kept informed, but it is better for you not to come back to the consulate. It is possible that you will see me at the Avenida Palace—I go there quite often. Needless-to-say, you will not know me." He smiles. "Now I am going to leave the two of you," he adds. "Goodbye and good luck."

As soon as the door has closed, Cobbe (I only learned his name later on, but shall use it from the start to simplify matters) takes out a note-book and proceeds to interrogate me. "Have you already met someone?"

"No—no one."

"Ah! When will you see 'them?'"

"I don't know."

Cobbe seems disappointed. "Have you made any plans?"

"No. I simply have a name and an address. I will go and see what it is, and then will act according to circumstances."

"Weren't you given any instructions?"

"Yes, I was. They are to bring back a transmitter, a code, and some money."

"It will be better to meet again when the contact is established," says my interlocutor, screwing on his fountain pen's cap and putting away his note-book. "What will be your first move?"

"I have a letter of introduction to the Press Attaché, Mr. Stewart. I'll go to see him right now. I'll be probably meeting him quite regularly. If you need to see me, or have some message for me, let me know it through him."

I leave the consulate, follow the Rua Emenda, stop a taxi and tell him to take me to the British Embassy, Rua San Domingo, to the Press Section. I give the porter the letter of introduction from the War Office, and he takes it to Stewart, who receives me immediately. He is a tall young man, very English in appearance; he examines me with a certain curiosity.

"I suppose I'll need your help," I say point blank. "So I might as well acquaint you with certain facts. I am supposed to be sent by the M.O.I. to meet with the chief of your Cinematographic section about the possibilities of hiring some French scriptwriters to work on the propaganda films in French language. How does that sound?"

"Hum," says Stewart, "it would be perfect if our director of cinematographic propaganda didn't happen to be in London just now."

"Oh hell! Thousand hells! There's my alibi all gone!"

"I came back from London three days ago," adds Stewart.

I am furious with Robertson and all his gang for not being better informed. "I'll have to think it over," I say. "I'll come back to see you tomorrow morning! In the meanwhile, I must find a solution."

I leave Stewart and decide to walk. It is evident that whatever story I give the Germans, it is going to be picked to pieces. So if I tell them that I have been sent to discuss with the director of the cinema production a deal, the similar of which he went to work out in London, they won't be long discovering the bluff. I must find something else—but what?

The streets of Lisbon are gay, animated. The houses are painted in pink, pale blue, yellow, cream, almond green, salmon. The pavements are made of white and black stones that form mosaics. The Place of the Rossio disappears under flowers, pigeons and the beating fountains. If my present situation didn't worry me so much, I would have looked at the shop windows. But time is too precious to lose.

So I go back to my hotel, the Avenida Palace. I lie down on my red silk covered bed and, arms folded behind the head, eyes closed, I start thinking. The first part of my alibi can remain: my work at the Ministry; my salary; the people I see there; my apartment. The second part fails: my mission.

What else could I be doing in Lisbon? Interview French refugees capable of writing scenarios? I would have to do it for good. Stewart doesn't advise it. He is afraid of complications. Anyhow, he doesn't think I'd find any scriptwriters amongst the French immigrants. Here is something I could say. I have come to interview them; I am told that they no longer come to Portugal, because all the French are now sent to North Africa via Gibraltar (which is true). So I am going to write a letter to the British Press Attaché in Madrid to ask him to make a choice among the French scriptwriters who might be there. The answers will take time, which is what I want. When it comes, the Press Attaché will tell me that he is not qualified for that sort of job, and that anyhow he must receive orders from London before he does anything. Then I will write a letter to the M.O.I. asking them to send the necessary instructions and offering, if need be, to make a trip to Madrid.

Of course, none of these letters will be written. It's nothing but camouflage. Tomorrow I'll have to inquire from Stewart how long the supposed letters would take by the diplomatic bag, and the names of my correspondents. I don't want to leave anything to chance. I reckon I'll have to find an excuse to stay a month in Lisbon; therefore, my supposed correspondence will have to cover those lapses of time.

I recapitulate. My story seems to me plausible ... except ... except for: why should the British have used me, an alien, for such an important mission? Me who arrived to England only last November and is only supposed to be working at the M.O.I. since January? I try to put myself in "Moustache's" place—whom the question will puzzle. The answer will be: Thanks to THE cousin, that cousin I have made out to be so important!

If "Moustache" accepts her importance, he'll believe all the rest. My cousin, who knows everybody in all the Ministries has procured me this job, has strongly recommended me. The scarcity of personnel explains that they have made use of me. Being French and having recently arrived from France, I've been judged capable of dealing with the question. What about the British passport? It would have been delivered to me on the demand of the M.O.I. to simplify my travel. Will "Moustache" believe that? There is the question.

I have looked up on the map the street Antonio Augusto de Aguiar. I decide to go there after lunch. The street is near the Plaza Pombal.[2] All the houses are new. One of the sides is not built; it's a public garden. The tree branches that point out through the iron bars of the fencing are already covered with green buds. Spring is near. I pass in front of the N 9 without having made up my mind to go in. I follow the street, but having come to its end, I retrace my steps. What's happening to me? Am I going to be silly? I press the button that opens automatically the door, and go by the porter's lodge without asking anything, because I know it's on the third floor.

I walk up the stairs and ring the bell. A very young servant opens the door. "Herr Morgener," I ask. She answers something very quickly in Portuguese, which I don't understand. "Quissiera a ver el Senor Morgener," I repeat in Spanish. "Esta a casa?"[3] She shakes her head and says he is at the office. I ask her to tell him I'll come back to see him tomorrow morning and go away.

—⚹—

MARCH 4TH 1944

This morning I have a long conversation with Stewart. We adjust my cover story. This is my plan:

1. Stewart is supposed to write to his colleague at the British Embassy in Madrid to ask him to get in touch with San Bernardo, the Free French Committee, to be notified of the presence of any French scriptwriters in Madrid; then to have them sent to North Africa through Lisbon instead of via Gibraltar. On their arrival in Portugal, they will be carefully interrogated by someone of the British Embassy, section of Propaganda.

Stewart's letter is supposed to have left in yesterday's "bag." In it he also asks who will be in charge of the preliminary interviewing in Madrid.

2. Then will arrive the first difficulty. Stewart will refuse the responsibility to decide whether the people who'll be sent to him are able or not to fulfill the part expected from them.

3. I am supposed to have an interview with Collett, the chief of the cinematographic production who will declare himself incompetent to take a decision in the matter.

4. On March 6th, I'll supposedly send a letter to Sidney Bernstein to ask him if it would be possible for the M.O.I. to send someone who would be attaché for a time to Stewart or Collett, with the purpose of examining the cases that might present themselves.

5. On the 14th of March, I'll receive a telegram—"Wait for instructions"—that'll give me time.

6. Meanwhile, an answer from Madrid will arrive saying that it is John Stordy who is taking in hand our affair.

7. I have asked Stewart to give me some place at the Embassy, where I can come every morning and pretend to work. I think it's a good idea, because (1) the German military Attaché has his office just opposite the British Press section, and if "Moustache" chooses to verify my alibi, he can do it easily. And (2) because I can warn the porter of my hotel that should someone ask for me, I am to be found at the British Embassy, and leave him my telephone number.

Stewart accepts my plan. He has put a desk at my disposal. And now that I have made myself a new alibi, I must assimilate it. I must live it.

No, Morgener isn't in yet. But if I want to wait, he won't be late, for he leaves the office at 12 a.m. Apologizing, the little maid issues me into a study. The telephone rings. She picks up the receiver, says a few words, then turning to me: "It is Madame. Do you want to speak to her?"

I take the mouthpiece and say in German: "I would like to see you husband, Madam. It is urgent."

I can feel a hesitation at the other end of the line. Nevertheless, she doesn't ask who I am, or why. She only says: "All right. Have a little patience. I'll let him know."

I wait. Less than ten minutes have passed, when a key turns in the lock, and immediately after, a man enters the room where I am sitting. He looks at me. I look at him. At last I say: "You are Rudolph Morgener?"

"Jawohl![4] Who are you?"

"Does 'Solange' mean anything to you?"

"Absolutely nothing."

"And 'Canuto?'"

"Neither."

"Do you know 'Octave?'"

"Never heard of him."

"Kliemann? Kylburg?"

"No."

"All right," I say. "I simply notice that one has omitted to warn you. It's regrettable. So here is, in few words, what I expect from you. 'Solange,' it's me. I work for someone named Kliemann. I come from London. He is in Paris. I want you to contact immediately your services over there, so that they get in touch with Kliemann. He must come at once—he ought to be here already."

VI. Lisbon, 1944

Morgener doesn't say yes or no. He is thinking, examining me at the same time. He's a tall man with a broad face and accentuated features; his hair is brown, thick, slightly crinkly, parted on the side and brushed back. I sustain his scrutiny without blinking. At last he says slowly: "I haven't the faintest idea of what you are talking about. If you'll be on the Plaza Pombal tonight at 9 p.m., behind the statue, I might inquire in the meantime, and perhaps give you an answer."

I return on foot. The Avenida is so beautiful with its double row of palm trees, its lawns, its tamarisks. I feel tired. I lack enthusiasm. It's bad—the game is on. I need all my dynamism.

I spot an empty bench in the sun and sit down. I look at the white and black pavement at my feet. I gaze along the avenue towards the statue, behind which I'll have to find myself tonight... Tonight... At 9 o'clock. I wonder if it wouldn't be wiser to go back to the Embassy and warn Cobbe of my meeting. What's the good? I shrug my shoulders. He won't prevent anything! No, I must go there alone. Tonight. At 9 o'clock. I am so tired that it leaves me indifferent. I am far from recovered from my illness. At times, my sight is so weak that I can hardly see at a few yards. I get up from my bench and return to the hotel.

I have slept all the afternoon. Now I feel better. I go down for dinner to the restaurant. In the Elevator, I meet Barratt. I go out. He goes in. We don't know each other.

Tonight I find the meal especially good. It seems to me the orchestra plays better. I feel very peaceful. I go back to my room, take off my black dress, slip on a tweed skirt and a brown pullover. I tidy all my things and then brush very carefully my hair. It's nearly time. I put on my heavy coat and go downstairs without waiting for the elevator.

The street is full of people. I mix myself in the crowd and walk towards the Rossio. It's in the opposite direction of where I have to go. But there I take a street car. I get out before reaching the end of the Avenida. Some hundred yard remain which I'll do by foot. I loaf along, the hands deep in my pockets.

The Plaza Pombal is not lighted. The statue of the Marquis disappears in the blackness of the sky. I slowly circle round it and stop behind. The spot is completely deserted. Not a soul in view. It seems to me I can hear the ticking of my watch. I look at the luminous dial; it says 9 o'clock and half a minute.

At that precise moment a car shoots out from a dark street. Its lights are so dimmed that they are hardly more than parking lights. It takes the turn with a screeching of the tires. It's going to pass me. It is passing me. No, the brakes grip. The lights go out. With a jerk it stops in front of me. I am so close to the edge of the pavement that it nearly touched me. The door opens; a hand seizes my arm, and drags me inside. The door slams and the car takes off. I have fallen on the back seat. I sit up and try to make myself comfortable. Having accomplished a complete circle, the car takes the same street by which it came. This part of the town is very sparsely lighted. The glow of the rare street lamps is insufficient for me to see the faces of the two men who accompany me. No one says a word. I too remain silent.

At last the one next to me says in German: "In which language do you desire to speak?"

"English or French."

"Let it be English. What do you want?"

"I want you to contact immediately your services in Paris and transmit the following message: "Solange is in Lisbon. She has to see Octave at once. He mustn't fail to bring the suitcase."

"All right. The message will leave tonight. Is that all?"

"It's all."

"Who is Octave?"

"It's none of your business."

"O.K. O.K. Don't get cross. I only thought I might know him. In that case I could have helped you right now."

I hesitate. But what do I risk, after all? "Killburg," I say.

"What? Kliemann? He's a great friend of mine!"

"I don't congratulate you!"

"Why?"

"Because, Sir, your friend works like an ass. It is not work; it's sabotage! Because he has no order, no method. Because guys like that ought to be shot. Because to have a man like Kliemann in a service is a calamity! And if you want to know more, I'll file a complaint against him to Berlin. I am willing to risk my neck, but it is to get results, not for the fun of someone who doesn't give a damn. I manage to go to England, to write from there, to come back. Two weeks ago, I gave him a rendezvous in Lisbon, and he is not here! Not only isn't he here, but the agent, whose name and address he gave me, has received no instructions. You call that work! Not I! And I am fed up with it, fed up with taking risks and wasting possibilities for nothing. You understand! I am through!" As I speak, I work myself up to a fury.

"I beg you," says my interlocutor. "I am not to blame! I know that my friend Kliemann is sometimes confused, but he is a gentleman."

"I have no use for gentlemen in this kind of a job! When I say I want so much to succeed, I want the money to be there. When I say that I want to see him on such a date in Lisbon, or in Timbuktu, I want him to manage so that he is in Lisbon, or in Timbuktu. I do not ask him to help me to get out of England! But the least I expect from him—when I do accomplish the most difficult—is not to cast stones in my path. On the 15th I must be back in England. Now, it's up to him to be here before that date." I stop talking and back further in the corner of the seat.

"Do you need any money?" asks the man.

"No."

A silence. "How did you manage to get out of England?"

"None of your concern."

"All right."

The car continues to advance slowly along the dark streets. After a while, the man says: "I expect to get the answer the day after tomorrow. When I get it, may I ring you up, so that you can meet me at the same place as today?"

"Yes. I am at the Avenida Palace. Room 61."

"Whom must I ask for?" Although I don't care to do it, I have to give him my name.

"Your first name doesn't happen to be Nina?"

"No."

"You wouldn't be from Kiev?"

"No."

"It's strange," he remarks puzzled. "I have once met a girl. She was called like you. She was very gay. I brought her back from Danzig to Rouen. I wonder what has become of her."

I turn the head towards him, but in the darkness I cannot make out his features. "Take your hat off," I tell him.

He lifts the felt pulled low over his eyes. "Why?" he asks.

VI. Lisbon, 1944

"I just want to see if you have changed, Captain Bücking. What have you done with the Adel Traber?"

"You! Good gracious! If I should have expected that!"

"The world is small," I remark.

Bücking has got hold of both my hands and squeezes them affectionately. "If I could only have foreseen that," he repeats.

It happened long before the war. I had been visiting an uncle in Lettland. I was short of money for the return trip (it often happened to me!). I wrote to the Worms Co. to ask them for a free passage on one of their cargos. The reply said that it was against Company's regulations to take private passengers aboard. But it gave me the name and address of a German company where I could write. I did and received in return a free passage ticket from Danzig to Rouen. The name of the ship was Adel Traber, its captain—Bücking. I was the only passenger. The journey lasted six days, five of which I was seasick. On the sixth day—we were at the mouth of the Seine—the captain and his crew having more time on their hands, I organized a "pillow battle." Feathers flew down the hold and covered the deck. I suppose that's what Bücking referred to as "very gay." When I arrived in Paris, and Bücking returned to the Adel Traber's base in Hamburg, I sent him a postcard I had drawn: it caricatured him in a very old-fashioned striped bathing suit, towing the Adel Traber while swimming behind a coffee pot held as bait by the first mate at the end of a fishing rod. I hadn't put Bücking's name on the postcard, only the Navigation Company's.

"Do you remember the card you sent me?" asks Bücking. "I got it. And how I cursed you! The Company's director had me called in his office and told me: "This is you, isn't it? Very original bathing suit you have! My compliments!" I was highly humiliated and hated you for it. I kept the postcard."

The car stops. The Plaza Pombal is as dark and deserted as when we left it an hour ago. Morgener, whom I hadn't recognized in the driver's seat, opens the door for me. Bücking kisses rapidly my hand. "I will call you tomorrow," he says. "We could have lunch together. I'll speak English on the telephone. It's safer. If I fix you a rendezvous, I shall only say the hour. The meeting place will be here. If I have heard anything from Paris, I'll just mention that your aunt is coming, or is going to come, or is in good health."

"O.K."

"Good bye."

The next moment I find myself alone on the Plaza. I look at the time at my wrist watch; it is five to ten. I walk to my hotel. "Here I am! Yes: I have come back!" I say to the things in my room. And I start laughing very low: this old skirt and used jumper, I had put them on thinking that it would be a pity to have my new black dress ruined by bullet holes, or torn by a knife.

At my desk, at the British Embassy, I write letters and work at my novel "Jean (Fragment of a life)." Stewart comes in. "Someone is asking if you are all right, if there is anything new?" "He" is waiting at the telephone. "What must I answer?"

"That everything is for the best in the best of Worlds. No, he needn't worry—nothing worthwhile."

—⁂—

SAME EVENING, 7 P.M.

Bücking rings me up. "It's about your aunt," he says. "She is in good health and is going to come and see you. I won't be able to have lunch with you tomorrow. I am terribly sorry. But I'll see you on Monday, at 7 p.m., if you are free. So long and good night." He hangs up.

Monday

Cobbe hasn't been able to wait for me to call him. He has come to see me, has written down Bücking's name and said: "Try to discover what he is doing, and where he has been operating lately."

7 p.m. I am punctual at the rendezvous. A few minutes later the same car appears from the same street as yesterday. And as yesterday, the lights go out while it stops. I get in. This time there are three men in the car.

"This is a friend," says Bücking without naming the vague silhouette in one of the front seats. The latter turns towards me, giving me a narrow bony and flabby hand. After many tours and detours, we enter a popular sector of the town. Morgener doesn't seem to be too sure of his way. At last we get into a narrow street, badly paved and dimly lit. A poorly dressed woman stops and starts gazing at us. The street isn't long.

"I better drive to the end and leave the car behind the corner." says Morgener. "It's wiser not to park near the house."

We walk back. In front of N 23 Bücking halts.

"It's here," he says. "But there is no light on the staircase."

He pushes a door that squeaks. The house is dilapidated. One can imagine the dirt on the wooden stairs, although one doesn't see it. The air is heavy with the smell of cooking, grease, lavatories. Bücking, going up in front of us, strikes matches. In the flickering of the little flame, the walls, the steps, the baluster appear still more sordid. Our moving column seems really sinister.

"Here it is: the Fifth Column!" I say to myself.

"It is not very luxurious," ironically remarks Bücking.

The staircase shakes under our steps. At every floor, lights filter under the badly joining doors. Bits of conversations strike our ears. The smell of latrine is stronger. We grope our way. At last we are there. Bücking feels in his pocket, finds a key, opens the door. He turns the switch, and we remain blinking in the aggressive light of an unshaded lamp. "My bachelor quarters," explains Bücking.

The four of us crowd in the tiny room. There wouldn't be place for a fifth.

"If you don't need me anymore, I'll leave you now," says Morgener. He salutes me, then, turning to the other two men, he clicks the heels, lifts his right arm: "Heil Hitler!"

The arms go up in response: "Heil Hitler!"

And we are in Lisbon! And I have come from London!

Morgener gone, we remain the three of us. There is a little more room to move. I examine the stranger. He might be twenty-three or twenty-four years old. He is wearing a light raincoat and a grey felt hat. His narrow face is pale; his chin prominent. I look at his hands. I was sure of their shape from his clasp. He must bite his nails; he's the kind. His fingers are long, narrow, slightly spatulated at the end,[5] and seem transparent. One expects them to be cold; they are. When he takes off his hat, he uncovers a high convex forehead, fair straight hair, parted on the side and brushed back. His eyes are grey.

"Don't you think the walls are rather thin?" I ask Bücking, looking round me.

"No. Have no fear! The flat underneath is owned by a very old couple (they are about 100 years of age). Above us is the roof. There is only one apartment on every story.

I had these heavy drapes hung in front of the door, for I do admit, it doesn't close very tightly."

"Well, let's get to the point," I say. "What is the news?"

"Your message was sent on the same night I saw you. Kliemann was contacted next day. He'll be here in a few days. Meanwhile, not to lose time, he wants you to be taught a cipher."

"What cipher? And what for? I've got one already."

"I know. But yours is no longer good. Anyhow, I believe the new one is much simpler. It is my young friend who is going to explain it to you. He is a specialist in ciphering and all that."

"All right. When do we start?"

"Now, if it's O.K. with you. I'll go in the adjoining room and let you two work. It won't take long, anyhow."

"Let's start."

Bücking leaves us. "You'll see how easy it is," my new teacher, who speaks French and English, tells me. "You have a key sentence that never changes."

"What about the book?"

"You use it too."

"Ah? But then it complicates it instead of simplifying it."

"No, it doesn't, because the ciphering itself is much simpler. The sentence is: 'AUX CHEVAUX MAIGRES VONT LES MOUCHES.'[6] You must learn it by heart."

"It's not impossible."

"The first part of the sentence in unchangeable. The second part changes place. You'll understand immediately. Here is some checked paper. I advise you to always use checked sheets for your ciphering; it's easier."

"I always do."

"Good. Now then, I write down in every other square, the first 16 letters of the sentence: 'AUX CHEVAUX MAIGRE.' Is that clear?"

"Quite."

"On the following line, I use the squares underneath the empty ones of the first line, but starting with the one whose place corresponds to the number of the current month. I'll explain. We are in March. That is the third month. So you'll start with the third square, writing the two last letters of the sentence in the two first squares. If you were ciphering in July, the seventh month, you would start in the seventh square. Do you understand?"

"Yes."

"So let's write (for March):

A U X C H E V A U X M A I G R E

E S S V O N T L E S M O U C H

Then number each letter as it stands in the alphabet:

A E U S X S C V H O E N V T A L U E X S M M A O I U G C R H E
1 625213022 4281118 7172929 21426 831231516 319132710 52012 9

"It is the line of numbers that will serve you for the whole month. If you think you can hide it well enough, so as to keep it without risk, it'll save you a lot of time. But, of course, if there is the slightest chance of a perquisition[7] at your home, it is better to burn the paper after having used it. I'll call your attention to the fact that this row of numbers wouldn't give anything away, even if it was discovered. You'll understand immediately why. Under the number corresponding to the date of your message, you make a mark. Then you cross out horizontally all the squares of that first line, including the marked one, also all the squares vertically under this last one. Do you follow me?"

"Yes, it's very simple. Today we are the 9th. I make a cross under the 9 and bar all the line until the 9, and the whole column under it. But how many down do I cross out?"

"It's of no importance: you can cross them all out. As long as it covers the length of your message. After which you write your message in clear. Let's suppose it to be: 'Suis bien arrive. Vous enverrai nouvelles sous peu. Vous ecoute tous les soirs.'[8] You count your letters and see that their number ends by 0 or 5. If it doesn't you add the difference of letter, so you don't need to add any. Having done that, you prepare a second sheet of checked paper, the same as the first one, except that you don't bar the vertical column. Then you transcribe horizontally the letter, taking them vertically in the numerical order of the columns.

And here is the end. For the last time you transcribe the new columns, in their numerical order, dividing them in groups of 5 letters. Your message is ready to be sent:

1 6 25 21 30 22 4 28 11 18 7 17 29 24 2 14 26 8 31 23 15 16 3 19 13 27 10 5 20 12 9
S U I S B I E N A R R I V E E B O U S E N V E R R A I N O U

V E L L E S S O U S P E U V O U S E C O U T E T O U S L E S

S O I R S
1 6 25 21 30 22 4 28 11 18 7 17 29 24 2 14 26 8 31 23 15 16 3 19 13 27 10 5 20 12 9

S U I S B I E N A R R I V E E B O U S E N V E R R A I N O U V E L L E S S O U S P E U V O U S E C O U T E T O U S L E S S O I R S
S U S E O E E E S N L U E O R P U E I S A U U S R O V U N U V T I E R S R T O E S L R I S E O E V I L I O S A U N O V U B E S S C
STSRE USETU VUISL LEVVE VOSEU BRUPO AIUOU RMSSA NEURE RSLOS SECUE ONEOE IOSII

Do you think you have understood?"

"Yes, of course. It's easy enough."

"Good. Now I am going to explain to you the deciphering."

"Is it necessary? You just work it backwards."

"You've guessed right. Will you know how to do it?"

"Yes. But that's no guess: only logic."

"Well, will you cipher a message of your composition for tomorrow?"

"O.K."

He goes into the next room and wakes up Bücking who has fallen asleep. "We have finished."

"Ah! Fine. Does she seem to understand?" Bücking asks the instructor.

"Oh! Yes. She appears to have a great experience of ciphering."

(If only they could have seen me in London, between Ronnie and Maria, ciphering with difficulty THE only message we had ciphered, and which the German Intelligence in Paris hadn't been able to decipher! It is true they had misplaced the key group. It wasn't entirely my fault!)

"I would like to see Miss Solange tomorrow," says the young man. "Could we meet here?"

"Surely," replies Bücking, amused to hear me called "Solange." Then turning towards me: "I'll take you home."

VI. Lisbon, 1944

It's past 9 p.m. Once more we fumble in the darkness of the stairs. A child is crying somewhere. The cursing of a drunkard... Deep snoring from behind a door. We go down. At last we are out in the street. It's a relief. Bücking's friend leaves us. Having walked a hundred yards, I discover that we are quite near my hotel.

"Why have you chosen the name of Solange?" asks Bücking.

"If I had chosen 'Jacqueline' you would have asked, "Why Jacqueline?""

"That's no answer."

"Maybe. But let's talk about you. No more sailing? Through with the sea? The vast spaces, the far horizons, the storms?"

"Yes. At least 'for the duration.' They wouldn't take me in the Navy when the war broke out: too old. So I got in Intelligence."

"Not a bad choice. It's lovely here, plenty of everything, no bombardments. I had less luck than you. After France, England. In other words, the same restrictions ... and the fog in addition. I wish "they" could have sent me here instead of London! Especially now that I have met an old acquaintance."

"Unfortunately, I am not going to remain here. I would have liked it."

"What! Are you leaving?"

"Yes. I am about to be recalled."

"I hope it's not to Berlin?"

"No, only to Madrid—anyhow to start with."

For a while we walk in silence. "I wonder how you are to work with," I say wonderingly. "You see, Kliemann really discourages me. It doesn't take much to lose an opportunity, to miss a chance. He is slow, slow! Now, take my case, for instance. I am here six days. I can be recalled any time. Then I'll have to leave without having seen him, without having received the T. S. F. and it'll be all my future work handicapped. There isn't much probability that I should find another opportunity of coming back to Portugal. Yet, I have wired him a fortnight in advance!"

"You know," says Bücking, "mail is so unreliable! I have agents in Morocco. Their letters take sometimes three and four months to reach me. First they must find somebody to pass them to Tangiers; then the censor detains them. You don't even know if our friend Kliemann has received your telegram. Maybe it has been stopped by the censor."

"I don't think so. It's more likely his nonchalance. Kliemann has half a dozen watches, but I have never seen him be on time. He fiddles, chats and, with the first delay, gets all his appointments confused. I have known him to arrive at 9 p.m. for a rendezvous he had fixed with me at 3:30 p.m. and to be furious not to find me waiting for him!"

We have reached the Avenida, and Bücking doesn't accompany me any further. I return alone.

"He is about to leave for Madrid where he expects to remain some time. He has agents in Morocco—two agents, as much as I could make out. He complains of the length of time letters take: three or four months, he says."

"Good," remarks Cobbe, who is writing. "Anything else?"

"No. You have the code. I don't know the name of the instructor. And I've given you the address of Bücking's quarters."

Cobbe leaves. I take out of a drawer the novel I have started writing, and very soon I am deep in someone else's life.

X. (I have to designate somehow my instructor!) is waiting for me on the esplanade that dominates, over the roofs, the whole town and faces the old citadel on the other side.

He comes to me, hands deep in the pockets of his loose raincoat, his felt hat pulled low over his eyes. He looks disguised and ridiculous on this lovely sunny day, at 5 p.m. I advance unconcernedly towards the banister that surrounds the square. I don't seem to notice him. He approaches and leans against the iron railing at my side.

"No news," he says. "Herr Bücking hasn't been able to come. Do you want to take a lesson? I've got the key to the apartment."

"I don't think it necessary. I understood everything. Here is the ciphering you asked for."

I hand him a tiny square of folded paper that he slips into his pocket.

"Shall we meet here again tomorrow? Maybe at 6 p.m. for a change? I'll give you the result of your work and will also tell you if there is anything new."

"I'll be here."

March 16th

"It cannot go on. It's grotesque. It is the 16th. I was supposed to stay until the 15th. I have warned you. You say you've done the same for Kliemann. So what is he doing? What? My work over here is so to say finished. I am just waiting for a telegram. If it comes tomorrow saying: 'Return,' what do you want me to do? I can of course pretend to be ill! But if the Embassy sends me their doctor, I'll be done for. No, you mustn't expect to extend my sojourn in Lisbon more than two, perhaps three days after my recall!"

Bücking seems very upset. "I assure you I am as much annoyed as you are. I can't understand what keeps back our friend."

I correct him: "Your friend. For five days you assure me Kliemann is in Madrid. Well, what the dickens is he doing there? If with the passport of a representative of the German Chamber of Commerce he is unable to obtain a visa for Lisbon, it must be that he isn't trying! No, you see," I add shaking the head, "if you have such a lack of organization in your Spying Services, I fear you'll lose the war!"

Bücking doesn't answer. We walk back and forth on the esplanade that dominates the town. Since that first lesson of ciphering I had in his apartment, I haven't seen Bücking. Everything evening I have met X! Every time, it was to learn there wasn't anything new. Yesterday I had expected that Bücking should come in person. He has come.

"So now," I say finally, "this is what we are going to do. There is no sense in continuing these meetings. They are useless and would eventually give me away. No sense in telephoning me either to say nothing. Each one shall keep quiet. The day Kliemann arrives (if he does), you'll give me a ring. If you are told I am no longer there, you'll know I have left."

"What!" exclaims Bücking astounded, "Without even having let me know when you'll be leaving?"

"What for? It wouldn't change anything."

"I'll send another message tonight," he says tossing his head.

March 19th

The telephone ringing wakes me up. I lift the receiver and recognize Bücking's voice. "Your aunt would be happy to see you," he says. "Could you come today at 5 p.m.?"

"Sure," I answer. I replace the mouthpiece and stretch with a yawn. All the same, he has arrived! Now, I regret nearly it! It means that in a few days I'll have to leave Portugal, go back to England. I love Lisbon, the palm trees, the sun, the shops where you can get anything, the gay looking houses.

My cupboard is full of boxes, cartons, packets: all presents for my friends. Silk stockings, underwear, perfumes, gloves, ties, cosmetics! Since my arrival I have been buying without end. After France, where you couldn't find anything, and England, where everything is rationed, Lisbon is a shopping paradise. And then, not to have to bother about money! I don't suppose it'll ever happen to me again—to be able to spend like from a horn of plenty.

I took 3,000 escudos from Bücking, in addition to Barratt's 3,000, and spent nearly everything. I've had two pairs of shoes made, and a pair of soft Chamois leather fur lined crepe soled boots. It's something I wanted very much. I've got them! Shoes to order cost 400 escudos, and if you are in a hurry, you can get them in two days! I have also ordered a pair of navy blue shoes and a bag to match for Mummy. "Moustache" will take back with him a suitcase of presents for my parents.

If I felt a certain anxiety at the time of my first "contact" on the Plaza Pombal, today I haven't the least apprehension. No, they don't know. They haven't guessed anything. Otherwise I wouldn't be alive by now. As for "Moustache," I am absolutely sure of being able to manage him, of finding an answer to any question he might ask. Am I wrong to be so confident? I suddenly feel so strong, so certain of my victory.

Bücking has said 5 p.m. It means that with a bit of luck, Kliemann might be there by 6 p.m. Nevertheless, I decide to be on time. It is X who comes to meet me! While waiting, we wander back and forth amongst the passersby, avoiding children playing with the sand. I rather like this part of the town. Here foreigners don't come (except us!). It's a poor and populous section. And then the view is so beautiful.

X looks at his watch. "I don't understand," he says. "It's already 5:20, and Herr Major isn't here yet. Maybe he hasn't found the place although Herr Bücking was to accompany him."

I laugh: "Do not worry. The major is never in time or always late, whichever you prefer! But eventually he'll turn up." As if by enchantment, I sight the two men at the other end of the esplanade: "Moustache" and Bücking. Bücking looks as shabby as Kliemann is well groomed, in a navy blue suit and a felt hat. Except in rare cases when his fantasy has the best of his taste, I have always known him well dressed.

"Here he is!" says Bücking with a broad smile.

"Hello!" "Moustache" greets me.

"You!" I say, putting in that "you" all the contempt, the disapproval, the irony that three letters can hold. "Ah! You!" I repeat without noticing his outstretched hand. "You. I'd like to shake you like an apple tree—but not even apples would fall from you."

Kliemann raises his thick eyebrows. I look cross—very cross, while I restrain myself not to burst out laughing. "I'll explain; it's not my fault," starts Kliemann.

"Not here," I tell him, "for you are going to hear what I think of your behavior, and there are too many people in the street."

Bücking seems anxious about the turn the conversation is taking and steers us towards his apartment. The staircase, in full day light, appears still more dilapidated and sordid. Peels and dirty papers litter the steps. Half way up Kliemann stops, out of breath. "I have been very ill," he explains, apologetically.

In the lodging, where we have to remain standing for lack of space, Bücking hands the key of the door over to Major Kliemann and, escorted by X, retires leaving "Moustache" and me alone. As soon as the door has closed, Kliemann collapses on the sofa. I examine him, prostrated, sunken in a heap. How he has aged! He gazes up me from under his bushy eyebrows with a beaten dog's expression. Something akin to pity stirs in me—pity for the diminished human being he has become. But it doesn't last.

I seat myself facing him and look at him. For a while we don't talk. At last he says: "I listen. Tell."

Slowly, I sum up all the happenings since I last saw him in Madrid. From time to time he approves with a sign of the head. When I have finished, he asks: "You wrote that you had been ill. You don't look well. What's the trouble?"

I shrug the shoulders: "Doctors have given me six months to live; so I hurry to live them. It appears I am finished."

He wants more explanations. Then he reflects. "Do you want to return to France?" he asks suddenly.

I am seized with anxiety. "Why? Haven't I succeeded up to now?"

"You have! Beyond all our hopes!"

"Well? Do you want me to give up?"

"No! Not I. I must even admit that owing to your success, my position has considerably improved. I wasn't very stable at one time because of … because of … let's say personal matters. (Yvonne! I think to myself.) If you give up now, it'll be the end of me. But don't think of that; think of yourself. If you really feel too tired, I'll fix it so that you can go back to France."

I smile for the first time since he has arrived—perhaps because I am reassured—and squeeze his hand. "Thanks, but it is not necessary. I prefer to go on until the end. What would I do, if I had nothing to think of? No, really, it's not necessary. Still, thanks. Here, I have a present for you," I add, handing him the billfold on which I have had engraved: "To Octave from Solange. 9th of February 1944. London. England." He smiles. He likes it. He is even touched. It'll look good in front of his colleagues, to have an English billfold!

But Kliemann wants more details about my job, my installation, the radio I was able to buy. I recall Ronnie, his question list in hand—Ronnie who has let his moustache grow—sitting in one of the two white armchairs of the Hill Street flat and saying: "Now imagine I am 'Emile.' Emile is interested by your work, the people you see at the M.O.I. But remember that Emile' is suspicious. He'll try to check you."

Ronnie had been satisfied by my answers. Now it's to "Moustache" I give details. Amongst others, I slip a word about my flat's rent, the price of lunches at the M.O.I.'s top floor restaurant. I tell him also that my solitaire has been valued at £120 by a jeweler, so I had found it wiser to exchange it with a U.S. airman against a Hallycrafter Skyrider and £50. "Moustache" thinks it's very little, having paid it 95,000 francs.

My story about the Ministry of Information appeals to him. "You are very clever," he remarks tossing his head, "very, very clever." And he adds: "I have brought along a suitcase with old clothes and the radio, for your aunt."

"A suitcase? For my aunt? What do you want her to do with it?"

"You wrote me: "Leave suitcase with used clothes and wireless at C's. Shall have them picked up by a friend from the Ministry who shall be in Madrid round the 3rd of March." I understood "C" to mean Mere Catherine."

I burst out laughing: "No, truly you ought to choose another profession! First of all, Mere Catherine isn't in Madrid. You know that. And secondly, what was there after the 'C?'"

"A ciphered sentence, but they were not able to decipher it."

VI. Lisbon, 1944

"Why? Because they told me to place the key group 3rd and 10th on uneven days, and 4th and 9th on even days. And where did they look for them, can you tell me? 5th and 7th; 6th and 8th I bet! And no wonder they didn't find them!"

"It's true," he admits. "They must have made a mistake. Anyhow, they worked very badly. We have new cipher experts now."

"Well, if you had deciphered the address that I had ciphered for extra precautions, you would have seen that I was mentioning Carmen E. who lives in Madrid."

"But then you don't need the suitcase and what's in it?"

"I don't."

"And the radio. How do you intend to take it back?"

I pretend to think it over. "That is what I'll do tomorrow. I'll ask Stewart at the British Embassy, if he heard of anyone who'd have a second hand radio to sell. I'll tell him I have been trying to get one in London, but there are none to be had in England—which is true. On the following day I'll tell him I found one, but I wouldn't want to pay duty on it. I'll ask him if he wouldn't be so kind as to send it by the diplomatic bag, to the M.O.I. for me. What do you think of that? After all, I have been sent by that same M.O.I.! There is no reason why Stewart should suspect me."

Kliemann thinks it over. Have I rushed it too much? Is he going to see through the game? His eyes scrutinize my face, as if he wanted to penetrate my thoughts.

And I repeat: "What do you think?"

"You are," he says slowly, without taking his gaze off me, "you are…," and he stops. I am cold with apprehension. "You are wonderful," he achieves at last. I very nearly let go a sigh of relief. "But," he adds suddenly, "what if he refuses?"

I shrug my shoulders. "We'll look for something else. But he won't refuse. He must not refuse."

"Are you always as sure of yourself?" he asks, thoughtfully.

I do not answer. Instead, I take out of my handbag the large yellow envelope sealed by the British censorship, break the seals, and extract the bloc of writing paper from which I tear the two end pages.

"What is it?" asks Kliemann.

"The last information I got you. I have noted them in sympathetic ink not to forget. Have it developed, and I'll give you the additional explanations next time."

"All right. We'll talk it over tomorrow. And Babs?" he asks suddenly. His question revives my grief. I turn away my head.

"He is dead," I say.

"Dead? Oh!"

We remain silent. I know he loved Babs. It wasn't faked. "I regret—I regret a lot. How?"

"An American," I say with grudge. "An airman who had given me his word of honour to bring Babs to London. He said he was coming over the week after I left Gibraltar. It wasn't true. He never did come. He had Babs run over." And I add, looking away to hide my sorrow: "You see, I wanted to avoid the quarantine of Babs. It would have made him too unhappy. He wouldn't have understood."

Kliemann doesn't say anything, and I am thankful for it. Then he thinks of something: "I almost forgot. I have a small letter from your Mother." He takes out from his billfold a fragment of paper hardly larger than a stamp.

"Why is it so tiny?" I ask, surprised.

"Yvonne has telephoned to her, saying that she could get over a 'small' letter for you (not to make her suspicious). So I suppose that Madam your Mother thought it was by means of a carrier pigeon!"

I bend towards the lamp to read. "Ah!" How can such a small piece of paper contain so disastrous news!

"What is the matter?" inquires "Moustache.

I answer automatically: "Solange is dead." And add: "She was a friend." I don't hear the condolences he murmurs. I recall Solange, her face full of laughter, her fair hair.

I open my handbag, take out a post card addressed to Solange de G. I wrote it this morning. "Wherever you should be, we shall soon meet!" Kliemann was to post it in Paris. Now, it's useless. I tear it up.

Mummy says in her letter: "Maybe you know already that poor little Solange died with her husband in a plane crash a week after her marriage." Suddenly, Life appears to me without sense, empty. One fights, one suffers, one loves, one struggles, and in one instant Death wipes out everything. Why do I continue fighting, when I know that soon this body of mine, alive at this moment, this brain that thinks, these eyes that see—all that which is the living me, will soon be an icy corpse? Why?

"I am tired," I say. "Shall we meet here again tomorrow at 2 p.m.? In the morning I am at the office."

―⁂―

March 20th 1944

X2 is present. "Moustache" too. The radio is on the table. It looks cheap and old fashioned. I am disappointed. I wouldn't want one like it, if it was given to me! The Major who has noticed my expression, starts laughing: "It looks worthless, doesn't it? No trade mark. The lamps are made in U.S.A. The instructions are in English. The model is at least five or six years old." He seems proud and happy, and reminds me of a salesman praising some rare merchandise. "And now to work! 'Our friend' is going to explain to you the construction and the manipulation of the set."

"X" shows me how to dismount it and names the different parts. I am totally ignorant in the matter and must concentrate all my attention to remember the details. The five crystals are hidden in a dummy lamp; each one is marked with a number. "X" tells me which one corresponds to which frequency, how to place them and how to use them. "And here are the two holes in which you plug in the key. It's the only exterior sign that could awaken an expert's suspicion, if he examines the set. Of course, we won't give you the key; it would be too risky. But I'll show you how to make one. It's very easy. You take a small wooden board and transpierce it with a nail, so that the point passes ¾ of an inch. Before driving in the head of the nail, you fix round it one of the wires of an electric cord. You place your board the nail point upwards. On the board you put a book in the pages of which you insert the point of a kitchen knife, having round its blade the second wire of the electric cord, whose other end is connected with the wireless set. The knife forming lever is flexible. Each time you press on its handle, the blade touches the point of the nail making a contact. So you follow?"

"Yes. May I try?"

"You'll have to practice a few days before using it, so as to adjust the space between the nail and the blade. It mustn't be too small, and not too distant. Your blade must be sufficiently far in the book, not to wobbly, yet remain sensitive to the least pressure. It's a question of fingering, and has to be adapted by you."

VI. Lisbon, 1944

Having taken the set apart, "X" lets me reassemble it again. I manage it without hesitating too much. "Moustache" follows carefully. When I have tightened the last screw, he asks me: "What will you do, if you are caught?"

"I'll do the one who doesn't understand."

"Meaning?"

I shrug my shoulders: "It'll depend on so much: circumstances, people, inspiration of the moment! How can I say in advance what I'll do? The radio isn't new. I'll pretend I bought it second hand. How could I know what was inside? I didn't look in it! Had I done so, I wouldn't have known what it is! Where I bought it? From a Frenchman I met in that shop where I was buying a suitcase. He needed money, I was looking for a second hand radio. I gave him 200 escudos for it."

"Moustache" begins to laugh: "Very good, that innocent look! Don't forget the innocent look when you tell your story!" Then, recovering his seriousness, he continues: "I think you hold the answer. The idea of the Frenchman isn't bad. What's more obvious for you than to talk to an exiled countryman. What more natural for him than to try to sell you his old radio. Maybe he was using it in France when working in the underground resistance! But he has fled, and now this radio is useless to him. That's good! Very plausible! Still, I hope you won't have to go through with it!"

"I hope so too, because the loss would be losing the set."

"Now then here is the deciphering of the two sheets you gave me yesterday. I don't understand. What are all these addresses?"

"The places that were hit during the last February raids."

"Moustache" begins to laugh. "Do you mean to say you went to see all the spots where the bombs fell? What the hell do we care!"

"I don't know. I acted according to Graf's instructions. Personally, I didn't see much sense in it. But Graf told me: 'We are interested to know the precision of our aiming.'"

"Moustache" shrugs his shoulders. "These aren't strategic bombardments, just to show we still have planes!"

But the position and the description of the air field and of the plane factory interest him. I try not to fumble too much in my explanations, and to render plausible the details I am supposed to have obtained at random of conversations.

March 21st 1944

"How is the radio?" Cobbe is burning with impatience.

I pretend not to understand. "I haven't got it with me."

"Of course you haven't! But what does it look like?"

"Like a radio."

Cobbe looks so disappointed that I stop teasing him and give him all the details. He notes everything pell-mell: description of the set, of "Moustache," of his clothes, construction of a key, etc., etc. "When will you bring it along?"

"The day before I leave."

"You are not afraid they'll change their mind?"

"No. Why?"

"Do you think they really believe your story of sending it by the bag?"

"Sure! If there is one thing true, it's that one! If Kliemann suspects it, he'll suspect all the rest."

Cobbe passes a narrow pale hand over his neatly brushed back blond hair. He would like to think everything is for the best, but isn't sure of it.

"I won't see you tomorrow," I tell him.

"Why?"

"Because 'we' are going to Sintra."⁹

"All right. Next time we meet here again. O.K.?"

By "here," Cobbe means a small house opposite the American consulate. He prefers not to be seen at the British Embassy.

This afternoon, I rehearse for the last time how to take apart and put together the wireless set. When "X" takes leave from me, he shows signs of emotion in wishing me to succeed in my enterprise. I won't see him anymore.

"He admires you a lot," says "Moustache" after he has left.

"Admires me? Why?"

"Well, to have been able to penetrate in England, and to have come out, and to be going back! Do you realize you are the first one to have achieved this exploit? I am very proud of you, Lily!"¹⁰

I pity a little "Moustache."

March 22nd 1944

The hired car takes us to Sintra. It's a wonderful day. I'd like it never to end. I don't feel like going back to England. There are moments when I have no strength left to make an effort. I would like to rest, to think no more. The landscape brushes past. The new fresh greenness is flooded by the sun.

"I am leaving tomorrow," I say without turning my head.

"What? You are leaving? Where?" exclaims "Moustache," sitting up.

"I am going back," I say, giving no details because of the driver who can hear us.

"You are joking?"

"No."

"Since when do you know?"

"For half an hour."

"I thought you hadn't been to the Embassy this morning?"

"I haven't. But I telephoned. A telegram has come for me. I am told to return at once." We remain silent.

It is true I am going back tomorrow. There was no telegram. I have just made the decision. It's better so. The day after tomorrow I'll be back in the cold and the grayness of London. The landscape brushes past: fruit trees in blossom; tender little green leaves; buttercups and dandelions along the sides of the ditches.

We arrive in Sintra and start by visiting the royal castle.

"What about taking a picture here?" I suggest. "It would be a souvenir." I expect him to refuse—at least to hesitate, to be unwilling.

"Excellent idea!" he says on the contrary. "You've done well to bring your camera."

I find a place where to stand my Zeiss, and the automatic shutter does the rest. I can imagine Robertson's face when I give him Major Kliemann's photo! Robertson who didn't want me to take my camera, because it isn't allowed on planes, and he didn't think I'd have the opportunity of using it. I did well to smuggle it through in spite of him.

During the visit I take two more snapshots of "Moustache." I just hope he won't ask

Lily with Emile Kliemann, her German handler, when the two of them met in Lisbon in March 1944 (KV 2/466, The National Archives of the United Kingdom).

me to give him the film. Behind the guide, we are nothing but ordinary tourists, who admire, question, look. But at the terrace of the small restaurant situated in front of the Castle, while we are waiting for lunch to be served, "Moustache" leans towards me: "At what time is your plane?"

"Tomorrow, at midnight."

"That leaves us little time! We'll have to act quickly. Are you still decided to send the radio by the diplomatic bag?"

"I am. I spoke about it to Stewart, and he said that if I managed to buy a second hand radio, I could bring it to him."

"What if he gets suspicious and has it examined?"

"Nothing ventured, nothing gained!" I say in a doctoral tone. "Anyhow, he asked me to give it to him wrapped up, so that he shouldn't have to pack it. I don't think he would have asked that, if he suspected anything. At least he would want to have a look at it."

"Maybe you are right, and I am wrong in being so mistrustful. Let's hope so! Then there is the money question to settle. I was advised this morning that it'll be at my disposal tomorrow before noon. You'll get £1,500. It ought to keep you going for 6 months. How will you take it?"

"It depends. Is it in £5 or £10 bills?"

"I don't know. £10 I suppose."

I ponder: "Perhaps simply in my handbag!"

"You are crazy!"

"Why? When I arrived in England, five months ago, my luggage was thoroughly searched, but not my clothes. I questioned the other French women who were with me at 'Nightingale'; none had her clothes examined. They wouldn't undress me now that I am travelling as 'civil servant!'"

But "Moustache" refuses to let me try. "Find some other way. You're too much in love with risk! This would be playing with fire!"

"As you wish. Then what about this—in a cigar box. You must surely have some specialist who would know how to take off the paper band sealing a cigar box and put it back, without it showing? Buy a large box of 100, lay the hundred and fifty £10 bills at the bottom, replace the cigars over and reseal the case. I'll declare the cigars at the customs and will pay the duty. It's a cinch!"

Kliemann runs the fingers through his hair and pulls on his moustache. "Perhaps it is an idea. But what if the customs want to open the box?"

"I'll protest! I'll tell them it's a present for my boss at the Ministry, (after all, haven't I got official papers?) that the box hasn't been opened as they can see for themselves, and that the number of cigars it contains is marked on the lid. What more do they want?"

"I suppose you are right. Well, anyhow, I must give you the latest instruction on what we expect from you. We've got the whole day for that. But first, I want to hear more about your mission and what brought you to Lisbon. This cinema business sounds interesting. Maybe something can be worked out. What has been the final result of your trip to Portugal? Let me hear it once again."

It is the question I've been waiting for, hoping for! In the details of this question I have built a plan. "Sydney Bernstein, the chief of the cinematographical section at the M.O.I. has sent me here," I explain, "to try to dig up scriptwriters recently arrived from occupied France. The M.O.I. intends to produce a series of propaganda films to be shown in the liberated countries immediately after the invasion."

"Do you believe there will be an Allied invasion?" interrupts Kliemann.

The fraction of a second I hesitate. "Yes!" I say at last.

"I too," agrees "Moustache." "When do you think it'll take place?"

I am perplexed, because when I was in London, I asked Robertson: "If Kliemann questions me about the invasion, must I answer affirmatively or negatively?" He just said: "What do you think yourself?" I replied: "I think it'll be soon." Robertson shrugged his shoulders: "Then tell him so!"

And not later than yesterday, I learned at the British Embassy that the "ban" will take effect in just a few days, cutting off all postal, telephonic and telegraphic communications between Great Britain and the rest of the world. "You haven't much time left," Stewart had warned me.

I don't know if I can repeat it. On the other hand, I tell myself that "Moustache" couldn't change anything if I told him; that he probably wouldn't even believe what he would consider to be a rumour; but that, when the ban will be official, he will remember I warned him, and it'll increase his confidence in me. "I think the landing is imminent," I say, and I repeat to him Stewart's warning.

He frowns thoughtfully and I remain silent. "All right. Keep on telling me about the propaganda films."

"It's obvious that these films, which will treat the German occupation and are designed for the liberated populations who will have undergone this occupation for years and years, it's obvious these films must be strongly realistic, remaining, nevertheless, in the limits of probability. Exaggerated situations that would give the creeps to Englishmen, or Americans, who have not known "occupation," would appear ridiculous to Frenchmen or Belgians, if they were too far from reality. I have been to a few American film presentations offered to the press by the Office of War Information. It was pitiful! The British, who are competing with the Americans for the post war film production, want to avoid such mistakes. That's why they want to use the knowledge of men recently escaped from occupied Europe.

"These are the reasons and the aim that motivated my trip to Lisbon. My mission was to interview French, Belgian and men of other nationalities, en route to North Africa through Portugal; then warn the M.O.I. and send them a brief curriculum vitae if I found individuals capable of helping us. Unfortunately, when I arrived here, I learned that the convoys no longer travelled via Lisbon, but via Gibraltar. I then asked Stewart who was in charge of the Press-Cinema Propaganda Section in Madrid. It appears it's a certain John Stordy. I sent a report to Bernstein and suggested that the M.O.I. should write to Stordy and ask him to contact San Bernardo—you know, the Free French organization in Madrid— and ask them to advise him of all the writers, scriptwriters and movie-people that happened to register at the Calle San Bernardo. Stordy could interrogate them, and if he found anyone interesting amongst them, he'd offer him a job in England.

"The M.O.I., foreseeing an endless exchange of correspondence, instead of writing directly to Stordy, charged Stewart with working out a deal. The latter submitted the idea to Stordy, who answered he could not assume the responsibility of judging the value and talent of artists, much less deciding whether to send them to the United Kingdom. All he could do was to ask San Bernardo to give him their names and to forward the list to Stewart. Exceptionally, he could have these people sent to Africa via Lisbon to give Stewart, or Collett, the possibility of interrogating them.

"Stewart refuses to do it. He says he is Press Attaché and knows nothing about cinema. Collett has also refused, saying he is overloaded with work and that this is an all time job.

So I wrote again to Bernstein, suggesting that the M.O.I. should send someone permanent who'd be attached to Stordy in Madrid, or to Collett in Lisbon, and only in charge of this particular work. It's in answer to this letter that I received a telegram saying: 'Wait instructions' followed by today's recalling me to London. Stewart thinks it's because of the coming ban, and the stop of all communications."

"Do you know what I was thinking? If this business of yours works out, I'll be able to send you scriptwriters! They'd have to get, of course, a good training, even some practice."

"And an alibi."

"What do you mean?"

"Don't forget that if you send over scriptwriters—even very expert ones—they'll have to tell where they have been working. And more competent they are, longer they will have been with such or such firm, and the easier it'll be for the British to verify their sayings. There are quite a number of refugees in London, who have worked in cinematographic companies."

"You are right, but I have thought of that too. We partially control "The Continental."[11] It'll be easy for me to get someone in it. Even to have him work there during a year, so as to acquire the necessary experience and an alibi."

"I've got an idea!"

"Say it."

"Do you remember V.M. whom I introduced to you?"

"Yes."

"V.M. has quite a knowledge of cinema, as an amateur, of course! He has done quite a lot for his own pleasure. It would be nothing for you to give him the finishing touch; he is all trained! On the other hand, you can trust him, as completely as me. You could introduce him in the "Continental." He'd work there for six months. Then he'd leave France. He'd escape to Spain. In Madrid, like all the French refugees, he'd end up at San Bernardo. Or, if you want to save time and have him avoid the Spanish concentration camp, you could have the "Continental" send him, with all the equipment, to take a news reel film or something in Spain. Once there, he'd pass over to the "Dissidence." In this case too, he'd end up at Calle San Bernardo. One way or the other, he couldn't miss Durand, who'd probably take him directly to Stordy. He'd be interrogated. He'd say he only accepted that work to find an opportunity to escape from France. That he doesn't care about cinema. He is a regular army man; he wants to join the Free Forces and continue the fight. 'And what if we offered you a better opportunity to serve the Allied cause?' Stordy will suggest. And he'll tell V. M. about the propaganda cinema which is called to play such a great part in the liberation! V. M. would hesitate; the army appeals more to him. Stordy would insist, would urge him. V. M. would give in."

"What an enthusiast you are!" says "Moustache" smiling. "Off you go! One could think it has all happened!"

"I suppose it's because I can see it all so well! It's such a logical, such a human, enchantment!"

"I think that, maybe, you have got something there, after all," he says, regaining his seriousness. "Let's see; have I got your friend's address?" He consults his pocket book.

"L. M. M. Here it is: Van M. Yes, I've got his address. He has no telephone. I'll tell Yvonne to summon him. I'll see him as soon as I get back. Do you think he'll accept?"

"I told you I vouch for him. Do you think I would have risked introducing him to you, showing him what kind of people I knew, if I were not sure of him?"

"Does he know you work for us?"

"I haven't told him. But maybe he suspected something when he saw me leave for Spain."

"In this case it's better to have him on our side. Anyhow, your scheme is to be considered. Let's see if I have all the names right. You said John Stordy in Madrid, didn't you? Here, in Lisbon, it'll be ... what was the name?"

"Collett."

"That's it—Collett. And your boss, in London, is Bernstein—a Jew! Is he the head of everything?"

"No, he isn't the Propaganda's Goebbels, at the M.O.I. The big boss above him is Brendan Brecker. But in my case, the decisions will come from Bernstein."

The ice has melted in the pail. What remains of the champagne in the second bottle is tepid. We are discussing for two hours. I suggest: "Wouldn't it be better to go somewhere else?" The hostess is getting impatient, peeping at us more and more frequently through the door. In the empty restaurant, the idle waiter is dusting aimlessly the tables, moving flower bowls from place to place.

"O.K.," says "Moustache," and he asks for the bill.

"Let's go and visit the castle up on the mountain before we leave Sintra."

"All right. It's the Castle of the Pena."

The chauffeur is dozing in the driver's seat. We have to shake him to wake him up. The road twists and turns, climbing amongst centenary trees and giant pines. The camellias are in bloom, bordering both sides of the road with their white, pink, red or spotted bushes. High above our heads the Citadel rises in the blue sky.

Once we get there, it's a deception. Everything has been restored and is practically new. But the panorama is beautiful! During a few short instants I forget everything: why I am here, and with whom; tomorrow's departure; everything fades out, and there only remain the warm sun, the sloping hills, the dungeons, the turrets, and flowers everywhere. Kliemann appreciates beauty, too. He admires, gets enthusiastic, gives me details because he already knows the place.

"We'll go back to Estoril," he tells me. "I want to show you the Casino. On the way we can stop in some coffee house, as we have still a lot of things to talk over." While we are driving, "Moustache" speaks mainly about Yvonne!

"How did it turn out after your return from Madrid?" I ask him.

"Better. But still it isn't the way it should be."

"Do you know what's wrong? Your imagination! You see things where there is nothing; it's jealousy."

He shrugs his shoulders. "I hope you are right and that there is nothing more to it." Then, indicating the country that's surrounding us: "This is where I wanted to take her to live. I would have bought her one of these small pink houses with a flat roof and a garden full of jasmine and orange trees. And when everything would have collapsed in France and Germany, I would have joined her here. But she says she'd be bored doing nothing. Then I offered to start her a 'Maison de couture'[12] in Lisbon. She likes sewing; she's got good taste; she would have made a success. She didn't refuse, but she seems far from enthusiastic."

"Were you thinking of a dress shop as a camouflage for something else?"

"No. Yvonne has been sufficiently mixed in my affairs as it is. She isn't made for that. From now on, I want to keep her out of it."

The road has brought us to the sea. We follow the coast, crossing small villages. In one of them we discover a restaurant built in the cliff overhanging the beach. The glassed terrace is empty. "Shall we stop here?" I ask.

"Moustache" orders the driver to stop his car. The landlady looks at us with surprise. She mustn't have many customers at this time of the year. The tables are of rough wood and the whole place seems rather primitive. "I just hope they sell spirits," sighs "Moustache," and is only relieved when he holds his glass of "fine."

"Now let's talk business. You have got already the new cipher. Tomorrow morning you'll find the radio at your hotel. It'll be packed. At noon I'll give you the money. There remains to fix the days of transmission. Do you still want it to be Tuesday, Thursday, and Saturday, or do you want to change?"

"I think we better make it Monday, Wednesday and Friday. On Mondays we generally have quite a lot of work at the Ministry. So it's possible I won't be able to call you before the evening on that day. On the contrary, on Fridays, the translations are often finished early, and I don't get any new ones before next Monday. I can leave the office at twelve o'clock and mostly go away for the weekend on the same day. Generally it is to Bristol. Sometimes to Cambridge. Often I am invited by colleagues from the Ministry to their homes. So don't be worried if I don't answer you on the Friday night transmission. I won't be in London."

"All right. Now which are the most convenient hours for you?"

"In the evening, I don't care; but during the day time, I can only leave the office between 12 and 1.30 p.m. Usually I have lunch at the Ministry. There is a luncheon room on the top floor and I get a decent meal for ⅙. But I can easily come back and be at home at 12.30 p.m. Would half an hour do for the whole transmission? I'd have to leave at 1 p.m."

"It would. I want the transmissions to be as short as possible. The shorter the better. And what time suits you in the evenings?"

"Would 11 p.m. do? People go early to bed in London. When I go out, or if friends come to visit me, parties seldom break up after 10 or 10:15."

"Moustache" notes in his pocket book: 12.30 a.m. and 23 p.m. G.M.T. "It makes it 13:30 and 24 European time," he remarks. Out of his brief case he takes out a few sheets of paper. "Here is our indicative. It doesn't change. It'll always be XRF on the 8650 meters wave length in daytime, and the other one at night. So automatically you'll listen for XRF at noon, and for MLO at night."

"I've got it."

Then "Moustache" hands me a list of frequencies I'll have to use, with their corresponding number. "Read it over a few time when you get home, then burn the paper," he tells me. "Amongst the things that interest us," he proceeds, "is the weather. That is: (1) the temperature; (2) the direction of the wind; (3) the type of clouds; (4) the overcast of the sky; (5) the ceiling. All this is very important for our aviation. But it's no use giving us this information in your midnight transmission, because if there is to be a raid, the planes have left by that time, and for the next day it has no value."

Kliemann explains to me carefully each of the five points which, in the messages, will be no more than one group of five letters. "To take the air temperature, a thermometer fixed outside your window is no good," he says. "Should you take a thermometer with you in a park, and place it on a bench, it would also be false, as it would indicate a ground level temperature, or would be taken in the sun, or in the shadow."

"So what must I do?"

VI. Lisbon, 1944

"The best would be to attach your thermometer to a string and swing it in a circle above your head."

I consider Kliemann with incredulity, wondering if he is pulling my leg. But he seems in earnest. "Don't you think it would look queer and attract people's attention if I went brandishing a thermometer in Hyde Park? It's not a thing usually done!"

"You'll have to do it when there is no one about."

"It's still more risky. Should anyone notice me, he'd report me at once."

"I see. Let's leave this question aside for the moment. Temperature isn't the most important thing. Next comes: the wind orientation. Very important. Of course you can find a building that has a weather vane. But you can also buy yourself a little apparatus that tennis and golf players use to know from where comes the wind. This instrument is of British make. You can choose which ever you prefer. Anyhow, you have eight winds: North, North-East, East, South-East, South, South-West, West, and North-West. They are numbered 1 to 8 and give you the second number of your group of five."

Then Kliemann names the different types of clouds: cirrus, nimbus, cumulus, etc. and gives me the figure corresponding to each one. It'll be the third number of the group. "If the sky is overcast, you'll give us the proportion of blue sky—not of clouds. For instance: ½, ⅕, or ⅐, writing down only the denominator. This will give you your fourth number. And to finish with, the ceiling. This is nearly impossible for you to measure. You have to have experience and a great habit to judge it at eyesight. But if you know airmen, you can pretend to be interested in clouds and ask them how high they are. When you have your five numbers, you replace them with the corresponding letters. In place of the missing numbers, if there are questions which you haven't been able to answer, you put the letter P. For instance:

Temperature: ?
Wind direction: East
Cloud type: Stratus
Sky overcast: ¼
Ceiling: ?

You get the number: .324. and transpose it in letters: P.C.B.D.P.

Do you understand?"

"Yes."

"But you must memorize the order of the winds and clouds. For the ciphering of the temperature, I'll give you a microphoto with an explanatory table. I didn't have time to have it explained to me, but I was told it's very easy and you'd understand it yourself." From his bill fold, "Moustache" takes out a tiny fragment of onion-skin paper, half the size of a stamp. It looks grey. The Major hands me a magnifying glass, and I distinguish columns of letters and numbers. "You'll see it much better under a microscope."

I don't ask any explanations, thinking that the British Intelligence Service will figure it out for itself; also because I am getting tired.

"Moustache" passes me another microphoto: "These are the instructions for the transmitting set, in case you forget anything." I slip the two fragments in the stamp section of my address book.

Evening is coming. The sun has nearly disappeared in the sea. A fishing boat is leaving the coast. Its sails are pink. The sky is pink; the sea reflects the sky. It's pink too. There are pink geraniums in the boxes under the verandah windows. A few small light clouds are sailing towards the horizon. I see the sky with new eyes: these are cirrus and the nine-tenths of the sky are blue. The beginning of my group would be: .19 or P.A.I.

"Moustache" is enumerating the areas that interest him in England and that I must try to visit. "Bristol. Avonmouth.[13] Highly important. Salisbury Plain—you have sent me already information about it that was of great interest. They are very satisfied with you in Berlin. If you see a possibility to go again to Salisbury Plain, don't hesitate. But don't force the opportunity. Be cautious. Bear in mind that it's more important for us to have you in England, even if you send us but a few first rate information at distant intervals, than to get a whole lot of them over a short period of time, and then lose you because of an imprudence!

"Do you remember the description of an insignia you sent in one of your letters: yellow, red, blue triangle, superposed by a 6? It was excellent. It revealed to us something we ignored—that the 6th Armoured Division was in Bristol! So, just send all the information you can pick up, and don't try to decide their importance. Often apparently inconsistent facts can be of great value."

"If I permitted myself to judge of the utility of information," I remark with a smile, "I wouldn't have lost my time running all over London during days to note the damages caused by a few stray bombs! It appeared to me quite useless. But these were Graf's instructions."

"He must have made a mistake, or you misunderstood him." I have picked up Kliemann's lighter and am examining it. I've never seen so small a lighter. "Do you like it?"

"Yes. It's amusing!"

"Take it, if you want it. Or better, here, choose." And he brings out of his different pockets three other lighters. There is a Dunhill and a gold one. The third one is in platinum from Cartier. "Which do you want?"

"I believe it's still this little one that I prefer."

"But it's the cheapest one."

I start laughing: "I don't intend to re-sell it, and I like it!"

"Moustache" observes me thoughtfully. "Sometimes I don't understand you," he says slowly. "You react contrarily to what one would expect. Anyone would have chosen the Cartier lighter. Not you. It's your indifference for money that's perplexing to me. We do not hold you by money. You have never protested or asked for an increase of salary, and you seem to accept what we give you with complete detachment. What hold have we on you?"

"None," I answer. "Unless it is my parents who have remained in Paris, as you reminded me one day."

"You bear a grudge for it?"

"No. It was normal. Only it would be better for you to consider that I am acting freely, rather than under pressure. You'd feel much surer of me."

"Moustache" doesn't answer and calls for the bill.

"Do you know what I'll do? I'll have engraved on the lighter: "Octave to Solange."

"Moustache" laughs: "Everybody shall wonder what it means!"

"It'll be one more mystery!"

It's nearly night! We go back to the car. "Hoppe says," starts "Moustache," but checks himself immediately, correcting his sentence. "The instructor says the radio is excellent."

"How did you call him?" I ask absentmindedly.

"Moustache" hesitates: "I call him "Hop-la" because I always forget his name."

I don't insist but remember the name: Hoppe. We go through Estoril.

"I would have liked to show you the Casino and take you to one of the chic restaurants for dinner, but it wouldn't be wise. The place is full of international gangsters, double agents and Intelligence Service agents. It is better we shouldn't be seen together in public."

It is late when we get back to Lisbon. Nearly all the restaurants are closed. We are obliged to have dinner in a night club.

"I am thinking of this captain," says Kliemann, following the thread of his thoughts. "With the Continental at my disposal, and what you have organized for the recruiting of scriptwriters, by Jove, we ought to be able to stuff England with German spies!" He rubs his hands and smiles at me across the table.

I too think about V.M. I am not afraid of his having the guts, but rather: will he be a sufficiently good actor? Will he be able to lie without blinking, without hesitating? He is career officer, frank and loyal, sometimes violent, and he hates them. In other words, too much of one piece to deceive off-handedly.

Before we part, Kliemann asks: "You are still decided to send the radio by the bag?"
"Yes."
"Then I'll have it at your hotel at 8:30 a.m. When do I see you next?"
"At 9 a.m. I must be at the British Embassy to give Stewart the radio, take leave of him and collect my place ticket and passport. Shall we meet at 11 a.m., if I am not detained?"
"All right. On the Plazza di Commercio in front of the post office?"
"O.K."

—⚡—

March 23rd 1944

"Is that it?" asks Cobbe eagerly, getting hold of the parcel I hand him.
"Yes."

He looks satisfied and places the box delicately on the table. Then he brings out his unavoidable little pocket book. "Have you learned anything new?" And he hurries to add: "You don't have to tell me, and I have no right to interrogate you. All that will be communicated to us from London anyway. But if you'd give me the details now, it would save time."

Not caring one way or the other, I tell him what I know. "The name of the instructor is Hoppe. Kliemann, in other words the German Secret Services, controls the 'Continental' Film Co. They'll probably try to send you some so-called scriptwriters through that channel."

"To whom will they be directed?" asks Cobbe.
"Probably to Stordy."
"Righto. What else?"
"That's about all. At noon Kliemann will hand over the money."
"Under what form?"
"Bills."
"How did you tell him you'd get them over?"
"In my handbag."
"And they believed you? Really, they are too naïve!"
"It's exactly what they think of you British!" I say smiling.
"I suppose so. Are you going to hand us over the money here, or take it yourself to London?"
"I don't care. But I don't think I'll have time to see you again before I leave. I am nearly certain there'll be some mix-up and the money will be only given to me when I'll have one foot in the plane." I leave Cobbe after a warm handshake, congratulations and wishes of success.

Although it's 11.15 a.m., I can't see "Moustache" anywhere. I go inside the post office without finding him. Just for a change, he is late! I walk up and down in the sun. Tonight everything will be over for me! They'll be satisfied, over there. I've succeeded—yes. Nevertheless, it leaves me indifferent.

The esplanade of the "Black Cavalier" is beautiful! I love the large white steps that go down to the Tagus. Tiny short waves clatter against the steps, where of sea gulls await the slightest pretext to shoot up in the air with piercing cries: the landing of a ferry, the sight of a thirsty stray dog, some rushing screaming kids, or simply the deep instinct of every bird: flight.

"Dreaming?" "Moustache" is standing near me. He slips his free hand under my arm. In the other he has a bulky packet wrapped in brown paper and tied around a few times with a string. "Come! Here is the boat."

"Where are we going?"

"Over to the other side of the river. I've heard of a good restaurant."

The restaurant is indifferent. We probably went to the wrong one. Nevertheless we remain. As soon as the waiter has departed, "Moustache" whispers: "It's for you," indicating the parcel he has laid on a chair near him.

"What is it?" I ask, intrigued.

"The money."

I look at him in amazement. The packet is the size of two shoe boxes tied together!

"That?"

"Yes."

"You're joking?"

"No. You find it a little voluminous?"

"A little! I should say so! How much is here?"

"£1,500. In one pound notes," he adds sheepishly.

What can I answer to that? Am I to laugh or get cross? I say: "All right."

"How will you smuggle it in?" asks Kliemann anxiously.

"I'll carry it under my arm."

"Don't joke."

"I am not joking! You don't expect me to hide it in my brassiere, do you?"

"I told them I wanted that money in 5 and 10 pound bills," says "Moustache" disconsolate. "This morning when I went to pick it up, I was told that they had to have it sent from Madrid, and this is what they received. Listen. Immediately after lunch I'll try to change it, even if I had for that to do all the banks and exchange offices of Lisbon!"

"You'll get traced."

"I won't do it myself. I'll put three or four people in charge of it. Now we have one last question to settle. In case something went wrong with the radio, or you were afraid of using it, I'll give you and address here, in Lisbon, where to write."

"What's the matter with Sabina Romans in Barcelona?"

"It's better, for the present, not to send her any more letters! You've made the mistake of writing her every time in a different handwriting and under a different name. Our services got scared; they're afraid that she might be under observation. Just think, a student who suddenly starts getting dozens of letters, not only all from England, but all from different people. No wonder if the police got nosy!"

"I thought you had the Spanish police under control? I only worried about the British side. The censorship might have noticed the name of Sabina Romans, but it would have seen that all the letters were from different people and different places."

"You might be right, but we haven't put the Spanish police on our secret. Of course, if anything had happened, we would have hushed it up, but nevertheless it would have attracted attention to Sabina Romans, which must be avoided at any cost. So here is the new address: Maria Pia Leitao. Rua Luz Soriano 100, Lisboa."

Having written it down, I ask: "Her profession?"

"She gives lessons of Portuguese."

"That's easy. I wanted to take advantage of my sojourn in Lisbon to learn the language. I took two or three lessons. What is she like?" "Moustache" describes her to me. "Where does she live? I mean, what kind of house? On what floor?"

"I don't know."

"Never mind. I'll say she came to give me the lessons at my hotel, or that we met in a tea room."

"That's right."

"Is that all?"

"No. I've got another address for you: Jean Francois Salomon—but you won't write Jean-Francois, you'll put Renee, for instance. A feminine name always attracts less attention. The address is: Florissant, Geneva, Switzerland.

"A Jew?" I ask, surprised.

"Yes! You must admit it's a good camouflage! Who would ever go suspecting a Jew of working for the Nazis? But I don't think you'll need this address; but I am giving it to you in case we had to use it to send you some money when you'll run out of the £1,500. This ought to last for six months."

As I am getting up to leave him, he holds me back by my sleeve and makes me sit down. "I was going to forget. We want all the trumps on our side and must take for that all possible precautions. Suppose the British unmask you. What do you think they'll do? They won't arrest you. They won't prevent you from working. They'll watch you for a short time. They'll register all your transmissions to be sure they know your way of transmitting. Then they'll force you to work for them. You wouldn't be able to do anything but give in under the threat of a revolver, and I'd be the last one to blame you for it. So I want to give you the possibility of warning us by a sign which we'll be watching very carefully. You could, for instance, finish your message by "G.B." (goodbye) preceding the S.K. It's international and wouldn't attract the attention. Or you could repeat "S.K." three times instead of two."

"It would be noticeable. You've said it yourself; before grabbing me, the British would probably have registered a few transmissions. It would all be noted. And if I suddenly changed anything in my way of transmitting, it would be noticed immediately. Here is what I suggest. In head of the message, between K.A. and the number of letters, there is a dash. In Morse it's: -...- . This dash has no importance. Sometimes I used to do it, sometimes not. We'll agree that if I do it twice—that is: once in the message, and once in the repetition of the message—It'll mean I am no longer free. Pay close attention if the dash is there both times, for if it's there only the first time, or only the second time, it won't mean anything. Because now and then I may send it in one of the transmissions, just to render the detail less noticeable. If they register a series of my messages, they will see that it varies, and won't pay any attention to it when I repeat it both times."

"That's excellent!" declares "Moustache," and he notes in his pocket book: "Strich zwischen Anfang und Number."[14] "We'll watch for it," he assures me.

Back at my hotel, I pack up rapidly. A few more hours and it'll be the departure. Yet it leaves me indifferent. I sit down on the edge of the bed littered with packages and linen, and start recapitulating the events of the few past months.

It's only five months ago that I arrived in Great Britain. I was so full of enthusiasm then, so ready to love the British, so eager to help them with all my strength. I admired them. I trusted them. I had faith in the British "fair play." Fair play! I think sarcastically. I was without defense. They exploited me. In exchange for the ready work I was giving them, of the risks I was taking, I was only asking them one thing: to keep my dog. It wasn't asking much, but still too much for them! They wanted everything for nothing. So they promised in Madrid, but once they got me to London, they refused. I was in their power. I couldn't do anything! Fair play!

And tomorrow I'll be in London. I'll hand them over the money, the code, the radio, everything—except a dash! A dash which will enable me to destroy all my work, all their work, the minute I want to! I shall not use my power. I know it. But I'll feel I have them at my mercy! I won't let them steal my work from me, the day they'll feel like it. I trust them no longer. I estimate them no more. I need them, so that France can be liberated, so that Paris is no longer hungry, so that the Hun is defeated. I use them, just as they are using me. And it's I that pay them. I start laughing at the thought of the buffoonery. I pay the British Intelligence Service £200 a month!

Out of an envelope, I extract three photos of "Moustache," the ones I took yesterday at Sintra and had developed this morning. They are good. I had three sets of them printed. One of each, and the films, I'll give to the Major, telling him I prefer not to run the risk of keeping them. It'll make him feel safe. The second set of prints is for Robertson. The third for me.

I watch the time at the clock: 8 p.m. "Moustache" must be pacing in front of the corner shop. I pick up my hat and gloves and go down. He is there. Having seen me, he turns back and walks away towards the Avenida. I follow him. I presume he is going to Bücking's apartment. I catch up with him only in the stairway where he is waiting for me with a match to light the steps. Having hardly closed the door behind us, he drops on the sofa and wipes the sweat off his forehead.

"I wasn't able to change all the money," he says. "I hope you won't be cross and will be able to manage it like that. There is £500 in ten pound bills. Then I have bought you a bracelet of 42 diamonds set in platinum that I paid 69,000 escudos. The remaining sum I'll have to give you in Portuguese money. Will you be able to change it? You could always say you borrowed it from your Portuguese aunt?"

"It's feasible."

"How will you take the Pounds sterling? I haven't been able to camouflage them in a cigar box! The specialist who does that stuff is absent. I had bought two boxes for that purpose. Here they are. What will I do with them? I don't smoke cigars."

"Give me one. I'll put it in the suitcase you'll take back to my parents."

"O.K. What about the other one? Couldn't you take it with you to England and give it to some friend of yours?"

"That's an idea. I'll give it to my boss."

"Moustache" bursts out laughing: "With the compliments of the German Espionage! I'd give my right hand to see his face if he knew it!"

"Now I have to leave you," I say. "I haven't finished packing. I haven't either had dinner. And Stewart, the Press attaché, is coming for me at 11 p.m."

VI. Lisbon, 1944

"Then goodbye. I don't say 'good luck.' But be cautious." He bends over and kisses my hand.

"I am double-crossing him," I think to myself, "and I don't care! I must have changed."

From the top of the last step, the little flame of his Dunhill lights the sordid stairs, the walls with scaling plaster, a whole resigned misery from which I hasten to fly.

One last time I lean out my hotel window. To the right I get a glimpse of the Rossio with its fountains; to the left, the beginning of the Avenida. The streets are brightly lit and animated with people. But the window panes and shop fronts are pasted with paper bands: anti air-raid precautions. Each time I look at those lozanges, triangles, squares, at these arabesques, often artistically combined in different coloured papers, I start to laugh, thinking that it's always the least exposed who take the precautions. Neither in Paris, nor in London, where houses are collapsing under the bombs, does one think so much to preserve the window glass.

The telephone ring makes me jump. Stewart is waiting for me downstairs. The porter gathers my suitcases. The open cupboard doors and the gaping drawers display empty shelves. My glance runs over the gilded walls, the cherry red silk bedspread, the conventional furniture. Here I have spent a fragment of my life, and already it belongs to the past.

Stewart is waiting for me in the smoking room. He has my suitcases placed in his car, and smiles when he sees the huge basket from which stick out the leaves of a pineapple and the end of a banana. "You'll make some people happy in England with that," he remarks.

"I hope so. They haven't seen bananas or pineapples for four years. I am also taking them dates, figs and pistachios."

We are flying for three hours. The monotonous throbbing of the engine lulls, but the cold, in spite of four blankets, keeps us awake. The windows of the plane are blacked out. Inside, the dim lamps spread a yellow gleam. We've been all provided with sandwiches and thermoses containing tea. Time passes slowly. Outside it must be getting light. It's 5.30 a.m.

I still have the impression of being in Lisbon. I expect, when I'll step out of the plane, to find myself in the glowing sun, under a dazzling sky. A shake, a swaying, a sensation of hollowness, of emptiness, a shock, followed by jerks and hits that go on decreasing. The plane taxies, then comes to a standstill. We have arrived.

Shuffling. Each one collects one's belongings: a book, his handbag, a magazine, his remaining provisions. The door at the front of the plane opens, and the pilot followed by the co-pilot appears. Outside steps are running, orders are being shouted, something is rolled against the side of the plane. Bolts are pushed; the door opens. A dense grey day light seems to hesitate on the threshold.

VII

England to Paris, 1944

I meet the eyes of the captain in charge of the pass control. He smiles at me discreetly and says a few words in the ear of the sergeant. The latter comes towards me: "Will you please follow me?"

The officer awaits me in his office where we are now alone. He rises and shakes hands. "Pleasant voyage?"

"Excellent."

"Can one congratulate you?"

"You can."

His smile broadens. "That's fine! I'll have you escorted to the hotel at once. You're expected there. Let's first go to the customs. Have you got a radio with you?"

"No. It has been sent directly."

"O.K. Money?"

"Yes."

"You'll say "no" at the control."

"All right."

We go to the custom house. At a sign from him, not only are my suitcases not opened, but I'm not even asked any questions. In twenty minutes everything is finished and a quarter of an hour later I'm at the hotel. I inquire at the reception if Maryia is there.

"She hasn't come down yet," I am told.

"Will you please let her know that I am in the dining room?"

I order breakfast and look in surprise at the tiny square of margarine and half the spoon of marmalade which are served to me. In three weeks time I have lost the habit of being rationed! Mariya has come in without my hearing her. She wears her eternal leopard coat. The smile with which she gratifies me is her usual one. She pulls up a chair and sits down. "Morning," she says.

And suddenly I have the impression of having seen her the day before. Nothing has happened since. I haven't been anywhere. I have dreamed it all. To make sure, I have but to look at Mariya. I stretch out my hand towards my cup and my glance falls on the diamond armband. Mariya has noticed it also.

"Not bad!" she says. "Is it all?"

"No."

"Tell me how it was there. I mean: life, people, the town, the climate. But we'll speak of it 'at home.'"

VII. England to Paris, 1944

I begin to describe Lisbon to her: the flower market, the bazaars, the fruit stalls, the orange and fish merchants, their large baskets which they carry on their heads, hands on the hips and walking barefoot in the evening; and shoes which are made for you on order in two days; and the zoological garden with its palm trees, its arbres de Judée[1] full of blossoms; and Lisbon's white and black mosaic pavements; and the streets where all the ground floor windows and doors bear numbers, the same house having three, four or five numbers! And while I'm speaking, I forget I'm in England.

"I should have liked to be with you," remarks Mariya with envy.

We take the London train at 11 o'clock. Mariya continues to ask questions and I to tell. "I've got something for you," I say. From my handbag I take the three little photographs of Kliemann and hand them to her.

"Who is it?"

"Emile."

She looks at me bewildered. "Why? Did you have your camera?"

"As you can see!"

"And he let you photograph him! What a fool! But the Colonel will be glad."

The train enters Paddington station. The journey has seemed shorter than usual. Mariya comes with me to Hill Street. "We have got a surprise for you," she says. "You didn't like the flat at Rugby Mansions. Colonel Robertson has decided to give you this one."

That makes me really happy. Mariya helps me to unpack. I hand over the parcel with the pounds sterling and, unfastening the bracelet at my wrist, give it to her. She puts everything away in an envelope and leaves me. I light the standing lamp, draw the curtains and open wide the radiators. "And that is that," I say to myself. So much finished.

Everything seems to come off easily. I try to imagine Paris. It probably rains. The wooden soles slip on the wet and shiny pavements, splash at every step. The water makes stains on the bare legs, covered with paint that is supposed to make up for the absent stockings. The officer was standing. I was sitting. He was exactly on my way to the door and his right foot was protruding exactly as much as needed. I prayed to Heaven that he should not go out before me. And Heaven heard me! Putting all the weight of my body into my foot clad in heavy wooden soled shoes, I carefully posed it obliquely on his small toe. His boots were of thin leather. He screamed in anguish, swearing loudly. I turned round, pretending to be surprised and looking at him questioningly. And noticing only then the foot he was rubbing: "Oh! That was it!" I said getting out of the metro.

Paris! How I should love to be there. A Paris without Germans, without croix gammees,[2] without hate. Again, I think about my dear ones who have remained there, and I remember Kliemann's face bending towards me and saying slowly: "No, I can trust you, because your parents have remained in Paris."

And besides privations, hunger, cold, they have to fight against the anguish of thinking me in danger. Shall I ever see them again? They've told me at the hospital: six months. Three are passed. Three more to live! Shall I have time?

―⚍―

March 20th 1944[3]

The telephone bell wakes me up. I am surprised to find myself in London. By mistake, I snatch the wrong receiver and get the interior telephone, then remember that the private line is in the drawing room.

"You sleep soundly," I hear Mariya saying. "How long will it take you to dress?"

"It depends. Why?"

"The Colonel wants to call upon you."

"I'll be ready in twenty-five minutes."

Robertson never takes the trouble to come unless on important occasions: my arrival in England, my departure for Lisbon, and now my return. I have just finished dressing when I hear scratching at the door. I know it's Mariya; she always scratches. Robertson follows her.

"So, there you are back again!" he says, stretching out his hand to me. "We didn't quite expect you to come back."

"I know."

"Did you suspect it? In short, everything turned out well. So much the better." Robertson sits down in one of the white armchairs. Mariya takes the other one, and I sit on the sofa. I report in detail about my mission. Mariya takes notes.

"Do you know from where comes the money you have brought back—the pounds sterling?"

"Kliemann exchanged the £1 notes which were given him by his people in Lisbon for £10 ones at different stock brokers. In any case that's what he told me. Why?"

Robertson hesitates. Then: "Because thirty-nine of the fifty banknotes are false!"

"False!"

"Yes. Do you think Kliemann knew it? Do you think that it could be a trap?"

"Certainly not! What would be the aim?"

"He might want to know how you will react."

"Do you know how one knows a real pearl from a false one? You put it in vinegar. If it dissolves, it was real. Suppose that Kliemann has given me false banknotes to test me, but I really work for them (Which he wants to ascertain). What would happen? At the first note which I would try to exchange, I would be arrested. There would be an inquest, and Kliemann would risk very much to lose his agent. No, that makes no sense whatever!"

"You might be right."

"If you're not convinced, I could after a while send a message to Kliemann telling him that I've had a lot of trouble with the first ten pound note I tried to exchange and that I don't dare to try with the others."

"No, it isn't worthwhile! Let us leave it at that." After an hour's time, Robertson rises: "I'm obliged to leave you, but Mary will remain and you can go into details."

"Wait, I have a present for you from Major Kliemann!"

"Are you sure there is no explosive inside?" he says not without misgiving.

"Have no fear! Kliemann said to me: 'You'll give it to your chief. I'd like to see his face if he learned who is sending it to him!' He was thinking of Sydney Bernstein: it's a spoliation!"[4] The fact that Kliemann should offer cigars to Robertson strikes us as being so comic that we all three of us burst out laughing.

"Fine cigars!" remarks the Colonel with satisfaction, putting the box under his arm. "Has Kliemann been as appreciative of OUR gift?"

"Yes, he was delighted with the wallet."

When Robertson is gone, Mariya asks me a few more questions, notes certain particulars. Then: "About the flat, we'll retain £4.10 per week. It naturally doesn't correspond to the actual lease price of this flat which is much higher, but we want to help you and the War Office will pay the difference."

I find it difficult to hold back a smile. If they could squeeze out the last penny out of me, they would do it. Nevertheless, I don't protest.

"Do you agree?" asks Mariya.

I make a sign of assent. I figure it out for myself: the weekly trip to Bristol, with taxis and tips, cost me four pounds, which makes sixteen pounds a month. About ten shillings daily for the meals: fifteen pounds a month. I have to add to it telephone, laundry (6/- a week), electricity: let us say three pounds. No, that cannot do. I'm two pounds short! "I'll have to go begging," I say sadly.

"Begging? What do you mean?"

"Walk about in the streets with dark glasses and a wooden bowl, to scrap up the missing two pounds. Unless I can manage to spend four days every month without eating." And taking a pencil, I add up the figures and show her the total.

"I'll keep this note and show it to Colonel Robertson. He'll see what to do about it."

March 26th 1944

Ronnie comes to fix all the details regarding the radio: how to use it, the frequencies, the hours of the transmissions. He is accompanied by a certain Russell Lee, or Leigt, whose job it is to see about the transmission, ciphering, code. Russell seems to be a good boy, with pimples on his face, round eyes and an upturned nose. He is peaceful, scrupulous and I expect to see him munch and to ruminate every single word I utter. His digestion must be slow but sure. He finds the sentence—"Aux chevaux maigres von les mouches"[5]—ridiculous and wants to know why it has been chosen. He is of the type who wants a reason for everything. Unfortunately I cannot satisfy his curiosity and, with a heavy sigh, he accepts—The leanness of the horses and the flies!

Mariya, an unavoidable witness to our meeting, tells me that I will now work with Russell. "When do we start?"

"As soon as the radio has been mended."

"Mended? What has happened to it?"

"It has been slightly squashed during the transport. Nothing serious: the dial and a lamp. They can be substituted."

"In any case, 'Moustache' doesn't expect to hear me before ten or fifteen days."

"We don't need more."

After Ronnie and Russell have left, Mariya, who has remained, tells me: "We have determined the question of your salary; we shall reimburse you all your travelling expenses."

"All right," I say, smiling, as I've decided to say "yes" to everything.

"What amuses you?"

"Your extraordinary accounts. I should have expected the Intelligence Service to be above that!"

"But it's only a question of bookkeeping."

This time, I laugh frankly. "Mariya dear, do you know how much you cost me: £200 + £18 = 218 pounds per month. That is what I pay for the honour of working with you! The pleasure is rather expensive, but I own that the satisfaction I derive from it is worth the price. It isn't given to everybody to pay the Intelligence Service!"

Mariya doesn't appreciate my sarcasm and passes to another subject. I had figured out the total value of my clothes stolen in the suitcase as amounting to one hundred sixty-two pounds and their value in coupons to 130 points. Mariya tells me that the War Office grants me one hundred pounds and that she hasn't been able to obtain more than ninety coupons!

I don't like London. Maybe it's due to the circumstances; maybe on account of being lonely. I don't see anyone. I'm forbidden to see French people. My cousin J. is absent. Bessie is always on weekends when I want to go to see her at Cambridge. I had reckoned very much upon Bessie during my stay here. She is my favorite cousin. I had hoped to see much of her. I would have felt less lonely.

Mariya does all she can for me. We often go to theaters, to the movies! Sometimes Louisa joins us. I'm very fond of Louisa. If I could get over this feeling of mistrust I have towards everyone, we would be friends. But it's impossible for me to trust her, or Mariya, or Robertson—not when it comes to feeling. I expect that if I lived for a long time in England, I would become like the English: cold, reserved, impersonal.

I have now traveled several times from London to Bristol and back. It takes about four hours. Not once have I exchanged a single word with any of the passengers. Yes, once, a three year old little boy came near me in the compartment and putting his little hand on my knee said to me: "We are going to see Granny." That was all. His mother snatched him by his pants, made him sit down beside her and told him: "One doesn't speak to ladies one doesn't know." So that I don't care for these trips where everyone seems to protect oneself with one's newspaper.

It's only with my friends at Bristol that I become myself again. With them, no need to "pretend," to be on one's guard, to mistrust. I'm allowed to relax, and I don't think I could otherwise keep up any longer. The great joy is the letters from Paris. I know what a privilege it is for me to be allowed to communicate with my family. Mummy writes to me by the diplomatic bag in Madrid, where one of the attachés transmits the letters to the British Embassy, and from there they are sent over to me, again by the diplomatic bag. It takes eight to ten days, which is really not long.

I also write through the intermediary of Swedish friends. Mummy uses the same way. Now and again one of my letters is returned to me with the mention that "although it is not an offense against His Majesty the King of England, it is contrary to regulations to communicate with the enemy, or with countries occupied by the enemy." The post reimburses me the cost of stamps. I have only to change the envelope and to send it off a second time, hoping to be more lucky this time. As a rule, it goes through.

"Moustache" had also asked me to write to him via Sweden addressing my letters to Annick le Guean. He was supposed to send Annick's address to my friends who would have forwarded these messages of a supposed fiancé. But "Moustache" forgot to give the address! I received in Lisbon a letter from my friends saying "We receive very passionate messages from a certain Maurice Le Feuvre, in London, addressed to a certain Annick. Do you know who it is? What are we to do? Could you fix us? We have sent one to your Mother, but she doesn't know anything about it."

The War Office got concerned. What if my friends made inquiries through the Swedish consul in London and if this one should telephone to Maurice Le Feuvre! They made me send a letter saying that it was a misunderstanding, that everything was now settled and would they tear up the letters. But I'm vexed. I took so much trouble writing these love letters. I had created a personality for this name destitute of a face; he had become a plucky little Britton (Annick is from Brittany), not very learned, but very straight and very much in love. He came to join de Gaulle. In London he has found comrades. But he longs for his Annick. He hopes to see her soon.

VII. England to Paris, 1944

That is what he (I) said in these letters. It was fine; it brought tears to your eyes. The message in secret ink across the first page spoke of guns, of airplanes, of a new type in the 6th armoured division, which had landed in Bristol, of the 1st Army arrived recently. I'm vexed that these letters had to be destructed.

WRAXALL, MARCH 29TH 1944

I have returned to have a rest at Wraxall, at my friend's, until Mariya warns me that everything is ready to begin the transmissions. It has been decided that then I would spend half of the week in London and the other half in Bristol. It's fine in the country. Everything is green. It's spring. All the neighbours are talking about my journey to Portugal, but Mary and I have gratified them with the "M.O.I. version." And if they don't believe it, they make as if they did. Mariya rings me up. She wants me to return to London.

APRIL 13TH 1944

This morning Russell and Mariya come to fetch me by car at Hill Street where I'm going to live and take me to see the place where we shall work. They show me the installation of the radio. It's in the suburbs of London, near Hampstead, in the house of a War Office employee. The barrier round the tiny little stretch of garden in front is shattered and badly needs a layer of paint. A bush is covered with pink blossoms. The shutters and the front door are painted royal blue. Russell has got the key. The house is empty. We go up to the first floor. The room which is put at our disposal is just at the left. On the table I recognize the post given to me by "Moustache" in Lisbon. The room is small and thronged with a bed, a cupboard with a mirror and chairs.

"I'd like to try the manipulation," I say. For over a year, I haven't touched it. I take a book and for ten minutes I form letters. No, I haven't forgotten. It's O.K.

"We would like to send a message tonight," says Mariya. "Do you feel strong enough to do it?"

"Yes. Why not?"

We return to Hill Street. Russell leaves us, but Mariya comes up with me. "We're going to word the text of the message. For the first time, we'll make it short. Then I'll bring it to the office to have it okayed. Russell will come back tonight for the ciphering. What do you want to tell Kliemann? We won't send him any information this time."

"Well, I can always tell him that I have safely arrived as well as the radio, that the M.O.I. has been satisfied with my work in Lisbon. Tell me. Don't you think that if, in the future, I have to send him all sort of information, I had better change my job and find one which allows or requires frequent moving about, or at any rate accounts for it?"

"That's a good idea! But I don't think we have to bother about it just now."

"On the contrary, I think that we could allude to it now. Later on, we might have a large number of information to transmit, or else we'll be in a hurry and we'll have no time to lose with "staging up." We could for instance tell Kliemann that I try to get at the M.O.I. a part time job which would leave me a few free days in the week. That would account for many things in the future."

"All right," consents Mariya. "After all, it doesn't bind us in any way." She takes my text to the War Office and returns to have dinner with me. Russell arrives straight after dinner.

The ciphering takes us quite a long time, because it's the first time we do it, because twice we make mistakes and have to begin all over again.

I'm terribly tired. Since I have been in hospital, I nearly always went to bed before dinner, which I had in bed, or else immediately after dinner. It is ten o'clock when Ronnie joins us and we take the car. I can hardly keep my eyes open, and my head feels so heavy, so heavy. The house in Hampstead is in complete darkness. Russell rings the bell, but nobody answers. We knock, but without result. "I can't understand," says Ronnie. "He said he would be here!"

We listen tensely. Whoever "he" might be, he must be asleep, because through the half opened window on the first floor, the sound of a mighty snoring reaches us. One after the other, Ronnie and Russell call, whistle, throw handfuls of gravel against the window pane. Nothing doing!

"I know what I'll do," says Russell. "I'll go and ring him up from the first telephone box I find." And he leaves us. Ten minutes pass. At last the bell starts ringing inside the house. We wait. In the intervals of silence, we can hear the snoring, deep and steady. The telephone rings, rings, rings, rings. The sleeper snores, snores, snores. It's incredible, but it's true. After twelve minutes, Russell gives it up and the ringing stops. Ronnie begins to get nervous. Time passes.

"It's ridiculous," I say. "One could simply break one of these little window panes, open the window and get in. He'll have it fixed tomorrow." Ronnie seems shocked.

"You cannot get in by the window. And you're not supposed to break the panes."

"You're not supposed to snore like that either!" I say.

Russell then returns and we start knocking. Unfortunately we cannot knock very hard on account of the neighbours. As it is, it's wonderful that we haven't roused the whole place. Trying not to be too loud, we hold council.

"What's the matter there?" says a voice over our heads. "What's all this whispering?" Our sleeper has at last woken up and opens the door for us. We have just time to rush upstairs.

I fix the helmet. Russell puts the quartz. On a second set he tries to hear M.L.O. on 5100 meters. "They're not there," he says shaking his head.

I have before me the sheet of paper with the message in cipher. I don't think of anything. My head seems to be empty; tongue is cold! I'm tired, very tired. Mariya holds the watch and waits for my turn to come. "Get ready," she says.

I take the manipulator, and suddenly I'm seized with a terrible panic. "I'll never be able to send this message. I'll never get to the end."

"Go on," says Mariya.

My indicative is written down before me. I know it. But panic paralyses my hand.

"Well," says Russell, "go on!"

I make a supreme effort and, clumsily, manage to strike the three letters. "It isn't difficult," I say to myself. "Three letters to repeat during ten minutes!" By and by, my cramped fingers relax. I tell myself that probably the Germans won't even hear me. And that gives me courage. But a vice tightens round my head, and I feel the sweat coming down my temples. And then, this unconquerable need of sleep! "Not now, not immediately, not while I'm sending off this message," I say to myself trying to concentrate my attention on what I am doing.

"I begin," I say. I make a pause, then send KA. KA. "No dash," I say to myself, no dash. And I give the number of letters, which I repeat a second time, then I begin the text.

Towards the middle, the letters begins to get blurred, and I'm panic stricken. I know this symptom; it has happened more than once to me lately. First the letters divide themselves in two, after which an opaque glass seems to get over the middle of the page. Then everything becomes grey and milky. I hurry so as to finish before I cease to see. I pass my hand over my eyes as if I could remove the veil from before them.

Mariya bends over me: "What's the matter? You're not well?"

"My eyes," I say. "I don't see well."

"Don't get nervous," she says.

My whole will is bent on finishing the message. Behind me, Ronnie, Russell and Mariya are restless. If they only could go away. I'm obliged to interrupt the broadcasting. I send A. S., stop and close my eyes.

"You're not going to faint?" asks Mariya.

"No. Excuse me. It will pass."

I reopen my eyes. No, it isn't better. I'll try to get to the end. I must.... I finish. I take off the receivers, put down pencil and paper, leave everything for the others to put away and stretch myself on the bed. Then, stupidly, I feel two tears run down my cheeks: weakness, nervousness, and also vexation—a deep vexation at not to have been able to hide my weakness before these people. I didn't notice Mariya leaving the room. She returns with a cup of tea.

"Drink. It will do you good."

When I hand her back the empty cup, she has a smile which is almost friendly. "Are you better now?" she asks.

London seems to me terribly empty. My cousin Janio has left for Italy. I have called Bessie several times. I wanted to go to see her on a weekend. But every time she told me she was invited somewhere, or that she had someone staying with her. If it were not Bessie, I could have believed that she is trying to avoid me! But Bessie wouldn't do that.

We have decided that from now on we would work during the day. I don't feel strong enough to begin again in the night. That's what I have come to: no strength! It makes me furious! And if the doctor is right, I have two more months to live—sixty days. I have time enough to fix the broadcasting, and later they'll be able to continue alone. I know that Vogel and Grün have both asserted that there is as much difference between two ways to transmit as between two voices. Even I could recognize when it was Roger who was emitting in the next room, or the fellow who was studying Spanish, or Richard's wife. Now, of course, they were beginners.

I wonder if the Germans will notice it on the days when it won't be I who will transmit? If it's always the same one who receives my messages, yes. But I suppose they have numbers of people who take turns, in which case it won't attract their notice.

I'll have no regret leaving the work to the English. I'm too tired to be able to go on for very much longer. My aim is actually attained. I have succeeded! All these plans laid in Beyrouth, when at night I lay awake in bed, and which, in the morning, seemed so absolutely fantastic, all these schemes of which I had dreamed have been realized one after the other. I have paid them with many deceptions, but one cannot have everything without giving something in return. I must be content with having succeeded. I must be content with being the stronger. Yes, every time I transmit, I know that I can ruin the work of three years, that I can do harm, much harm. Just a dash, and the Germans will know that I work under the control of the Intelligence Service, and the British won't even suspect anything! This is my revenge for the faith I had in them to whom I brought my work, and which they have ruined; for having taken advantage of my being helpless, for having promised and not kept their promise. I might be bad—utterly bad—but I feel a strange voluptuous pleasure to feel them at my mercy!

I remember having once said to Mariya: "It's very difficult not to take advantage of one's strength, when one is the strongest." It isn't difficult for me. I will never make use of the weapon I detain. I would never help the Germans out of personal revenge, and above all in harming the British I would wrong the French who are awaiting their liberation. That is the reason why the British have nothing to fear—but that is the only reason.

I have left a note at Mary's, in Wraxall, which she is to give Mariya if anything should happen to me. In this note I explain to her the key of the transmission. When I'm not here anymore, they will be able to continue without me. But they cannot deprive me of my work by force; they would destroy themselves! These three years spent "between" the fighting parties have taught me one thing: that the only spying of which one can be sure is the one dictated by patriotism. There is no price which cannot be over bidden, and one can never totally rely on someone one is holding by terror or blackmail. Hate is very ingenious!

I take the underground to go to Hampstead. It's very far, and I think the War Office could extend his prodigality as far as taking me there by car, even if they had to retain the cost from my salary! But as I don't protest, they must be glad of this extra economy. I suddenly think of the most fantastic tales, which were circulated in Paris and according to which Intelligence Service men, under various disguises, left rings and diamond brooches to good people who had brought them over. The idea seems highly comic to me.

Mariya and Russell have arrived before me. We have luck today. The Germans send us a message. Immediately after them, I send my indicative and transmit the message we have ciphered last night for today. When I have come to the end, instead of sending S.K., S.K., I send K.K. (S.K. means the end of the transmission; K means "come" i.e. "your turn now").

"Why?" asks Russell who is following with attention.

I repeat K before answering: "I want to know if they hear us. They should answer O.K.—S.K." We wait, but there is no sign to show us that we have been heard.

Russell takes the message away to decipher it, and Mariya comes home with me to prepare another one for tomorrow. The German message is of no interest: simply a confirmation that they are listening on the agreed hours and days and are awaiting news from me. Mariya and I find the transmission hours very unpractical. We decide to change them as soon as the Germans will have confirmed having received our messages. We decide upon 11 a.m. and 10 p.m., local time. This would allow us to be through by lunch time, and if we have to work in the evening, it doesn't keep us up too late.

Still nothing to prove that the Germans hear us.

My weekends at my Bristol friends' give me strength to pursue my work. Mary is everything for me here in England: my family, my friend, my home. Today, when I arrive, she takes me in her arms, looks me over and says with shining eyes: "Oh! Lily, now I'm sure that you will live!" These words show me how deeply concerned she had been and what a source of unrest I had been for her.

I send a minimum of three messages a week, but sometimes there are two at a time. We still don't know if we are heard. We haven't therefore been able to change our transmission hours.

May is in full bloom. Hyde Park and Green Park are a jumble of blossoming shrubs.

Mariya has asked me if I preferred another place than Hampstead where to work. "You're not very enthusiastic about our installation," she says, smiling. I don't protest.

VII. England to Paris, 1944

This morning we go to see another place. It's quite near, on the other side of Hyde Park: Palace Gardens Terrace. From Kensington Road, we turn to the right on Kensington Church Street, which we leave almost at once for Brunswick Street. Brunswick Street turns at right angle and ends exactly in front of the entrance of the house we have chosen as our H.Q. This time, the door is painted light green; green is supposed to be the colour of hope! The street is bordered on both sides by tall cherry-trees; their branches are covered with white blossoms and bees are humming around.

We have moved. I prefer working here. Besides, Russell and Mariya come to fetch me with the car without my having said anything about it.

We don't receive any more receive messages from the Germans, and Russell begins to feel uneasy. He fears the installation in Palace Gardens might be bad, and we return to make a trial at Hampstead, but with no result!

―⚘―

May 10th 1944

At last, today, we take a message. I'm full of pep when sending mine. I finish it by a serial of K's. And suddenly—Oh miracle!—We hear O.K.—G.B.—S.K., S.K.

"They have answered!" I scream.

And we look at each other, the three of us, with a deep joy, as if ... as if this success belonged to us, as if this work were our work, as if victory, when it would come, would be our victory!

I look at my hand with a sort of curiosity, and I say to myself: "These are the fingers which, a few minutes ago, have established the contact between the Intelligence Service and the German I.S.! It's I who have spoken to them." No, it isn't pride. It's joy about this material personal victory in the tremendous entanglement of the war. It's the right to tell myself—I haven't been completely useless.

This time the Germans tell us they have received several messages of which they give us the numbers! They ask to repeat two of them and those which are missing.

"What do they imagine," I say, "that I keep a file with copies of the messages I send them! Besides they would have to be re-ciphered according to the date of transmission."

We decide to send a long message in which we say that the two messages they want to have repeated are without any military interest. We propose the new transmission hours and add some information.

I first write down the message in French, in block capitals. Then we cipher it on sheets of lined paper brought by Russell. He dictates to me; I write it down. It's rather rapid. Between the two of us, we're less subject to making mistakes.

The contact is now regularly established. I send an average of six messages a week. We work at 12 on Tuesdays, Wednesdays and Thursdays. On Thursdays at 4 p.m., I take the Bristol train at Paddington Station and go down to my friends until Monday morning. When I return to London after my weekends, my first question to Mariya is: "Well, where have I been this time?"

And she answers me, laughing: "You have stayed with a colleague from the Ministry at Salisbury Plain," or "You have been at Cambridge, at your cousin's."

I take other imaginary voyages, in places the existence of which I ignored, and from there I bring back rich harvests of information, the number of which sometimes frightens me! In this world of fiction, I spend my time in trains, clubs, messes, canteens. And I transmit pell-mell descriptions of badges, vehicles, tanks, planes and airports, the whole adorned with conversations overheard, from which the Germans cannot fail to derive the desired conclusions.

"Today you're going to describe that to them," says Mariya putting before me a drawing she has made in pencil. "The original is red," she adds.

I ask: "What does it represent?"

"What do you think it represents?" she answers.

"A flower pot with a chimney on top."

"Well, just describe it that way! If I told you what it represents without your having guessed it by yourself, it would show that you don't know this object, and the Germans might get suspicious."

I hesitate between the precedent description and "reversed isosceles trapezium with small rectangle at the base." Gosh! I'm no geometer! And I finally describe this geometrical figure as "flower pot surmounted by a short and wide chimney," hoping that the German would show an imagination with a poetical tendency and understand what a flowerpot adorned with a chimney might look like!

When the message is finished, Mariya tells me: "It's a keystone."

How could I have known? I'm no architect!

Soon after I returned from Portugal, the ban has been established and all postal communications with the outside have been suppressed. But I continue to receive letters from Mummy through Madrid and the English diplomatic bag. I know that something is going to happen and am worried about my parents who live in a town quarter, which is likely to be bombarded.

I ask Mariya to send a "personal message" to "Moustache" asking him to tell my parents, through Yvonne, to move into my studio. It's less exposed, the house is stronger (of reinforced concrete) and it's far from any objective. Mariya says that she'll ask the authorization from the office.

My message has gone. I insist upon its confirmation.

—⁂—

May 18th

The pigeons crowd on my window-sill, coming to get bread out of my hand. The largest, Adolf, whom I have called that so on account of the "vital space" of which he always seems to be short, strikes out with his beak right and left, defending the approach of my hand. Sally, his wife, makes haste to swallow all the bread, nearly choking with the largest bits. The other day I found Sally in the recess which serves me as a kitchen, sitting in a dish of warm milk rice. She seemed perfectly contented, pecking around her. I had to get her off the rice and put her out with a little slap. When I'm alone, Adolf and Sally come into the room, walk about on the desk, jump onto the back of the armchairs and partake of my tea. They are my companions, my friends, during the three week days I spend in London.

Mariya looks at the pigeons. Today she wears a bordeau[6] suit with golden buttons. She pretends it makes her look like a general.

"Mariya," I say suddenly, "I should like you to know one thing; you mustn't try to work without me. I didn't have the intention to warn you. I'm not concerned with what happens to your people. I don't owe them anything. They have hurt me without any necessity. I promised myself to repay them. I have the means to do it, and I shall do it. When I put myself into your power in November last, I was helpless. I trusted you. You know the result! But it doesn't mean I'm beaten—not by you, not even by you! I had the intention to bring our work to a point of perfection and then to ruin it. This would perhaps have shown to your services the price they would have to pay for my dog. Or else I could have said nothing and just withdraw leaving you to work alone, and have the sadistic pleasure to watch you achieve your own destruction and put you into the hands of the Germans. But I have given it all up. You are warned."

"Do you realize that it would not be us alone you would harm, that the landing is very near, that from our possibility to deceive the Germans depend thousands of lives? That among the landing troops there will be French units. That in France your countrymen await their liberation. If we have been at fault towards you, I'm sure you wouldn't want them to suffer for it?"

"Why, in fact, do you suppose I have given it up?"

Mariya doesn't answer. "You were very fond of Babs?" she says after a while.

"Very." And I add: "But it's much more you have destroyed. It's the faith in your country, in your honour, in your loyalty. For three years, I have been fed on hatred, in contact with the Germans. When I arrived here, I thought it had come to an end! I suppose you cannot understand."

"I believe I do," says Mariya. "And now?"

"Now? Nothing. It's for you to decide. My decision is taken. I shall continue to work."

May is nearly through. Bristol knows an unusual agitation: military drive past in every direction; convoys arrive from Avon-Mouth; long files of truck go southwards, thronged with British and American soldiers. One can hardly sleep at night because of the noise made by armoured vehicles on this generally so very quiet road. London also is almost emptied of Americans. Before one hardly saw ... and heard but them. Now London streets appear very empty and still. One waits.

I've made a bet with the driver of the taxi who takes me twice a week from Bristol to Wraxall and back again. I said the landing would take place in the first week of June. He thinks it'll be in the third. He is more cautious.

"Moustache" has not answered my personal message and it has made me cross. I have written a new one where I insist upon an answer. Otherwise there will be no more information. Mariya smiles, because she knows my threat doesn't mean anything.

"How about presenting them something about combat gas? It's one of the points of my questionnaire we haven't touched yet and which interests them."

"I'll ask at the office," says Mariya.

This time I'm supposed to have my information from a high ranked General Staff officer who has the bad habit of drinking too much! My message could bear the title: "Hold back, or else." According to the information obtained, the Allies have no intention being the first to apply gas. But they are quite ready to answer by using them in vast air attacks, should the Germans begin. The allied aviation is so much superior to the Luftwaffe, that it should make the Germans think it over. The German Information Service seems entirely satisfied with the information I supply them. From time to time there are congratulations in the messages.

Message on a type of parachute supplied with a lifeboat bearing an aerial and a radio, used by the Costal Command to help ships in distress. A telephone call from the War Office interrupts us in the middle of the drawing up of a message. I'm about to pass the information that in case of an invasion tow gliders will be used for the transportation of men and material. I say that I have seen a great number of them in an aviation camp; they were all provided by a camouflage consisting of black and white stripes. Tanks will be parachuted.

Mariya, who has taken the communication, puts down the receiver and turning round towards Russell and me: "Stop. No information about the tanks must be given."

"Gosh!" I say. "It obliges us to re-cipher the whole message."

Russell looks at the watch with annoyance. "Let's hurry, or we'll never be in time!"

I now send three messages a day. We also work in the evening. Russell takes the German messages while I just take it easy. Why make the same work, as he is taking them in any case. These messages mostly ask for a repetition or a precision.

Today I pass on imaginary revelation which General Konig, who is actually in London, is supposed to have made to Nelly. "Do you expect the Germans to know who Nelly is?" I ask doubtfully.

"Surely not. But the fact that you name her will make them think they are supposed to know of her existence, and they won't search any further."

We've had a night transmission at which Ned, a young American has been present. It appears he is going to do the same work in France where he will be landed. Mariya was afraid his presence might inconvenience me, but I've passed this stage a long time ago. Heavens! What a funk I had the first time, and how ill I was!

Mariya and I go to see "Gone with the Wind" near Leicester Square. When going out, I notice that her nose is red, her eyes swollen and that the front of her leopard skin coat (or is it ocelot? I haven't yet been able to situate the "nationality" of the animal when he was alive!) is wet.

"Mariya! What's the matter with you?" I say, amazed.

"I've cried, of course!" she retorts with dignity and a last sniff. "Don't you? I always cry at the movies," she adds.

I burst out laughing, and putting my arm through hers, I give her a squeeze. "What a funny old thing you are!" I say.

Mariya crying at the movies! Could she be human after all, this Mariya with whom I'm working for seven months, trying to discover in her that which will allow me to consider her like as a live being and not as an automaton! How often, when she began to laugh, I wanted to say: "Go on! Laugh, laugh straight out!" But it always was but a polite little laughter, cold and restrained, what I called to myself—a miser's laugh.

May 28th 1944

At Paddington Station, the crowd is unthinkable. Thousands of Londoners stand in line to try to get a seat in one of the trains leaving the capital. It's Whitsunday[7] in two days. After having waited for two hours, I give it up and go home with the awful prospect of a solitary weekend in London. Perhaps I could go to Bessie on Sunday? There won't be the same crowd then, the holidayers having already left. I ring up Cambridge. Bessie is at home, but tells me she will be away on Sunday. I sadly hang up.

"I'll warn Mariya that I haven't been able to leave," I say to myself. And I telephone her at the War Office, room 0.55.

Mariya calls me back after dinner. "Have you got a pair of sheets?" she asks me.

"Sheets? What for? Yes, I believe so."

"In this case, pack a bag. I'm taking you with me tomorrow morning to my sister!" And she rings off.

"It's sweet of her," I say to myself, and I feel quite cheered up.

VII. England to Paris, 1944

MAY 29TH

Three days in the country. Marvelous weather and really warm. I discover a Mariya quite different from the one I have known so far: gay, full of spirits, natural. The first morning she brings me my breakfast in bed and as I protested, she grumbled: "Be quiet, you need a rest. I'll take care of you." She continues to be brusque, as if she were afraid that I could take her kindness for weakness. Funny Mariya! I like her, she can be very sweet.

During these three days, waves of planes have passed day and night over our heads. One feels that the "great day" is approaching!

MAY 31ST 1944

The messages become longer and longer. Since the conversation I had with Mariya concerning our work, I haven't heard anything about the subject.

JUNE 2ND 1944

"I'd like to ask you something," says Mariya. "You might refuse to answer, but the other day you said you could ruin the work we are doing. How?"

I look at her in silence. "You think that I was bluffing?"

"No."

"I didn't bluff. There is a sign of security."

"I see. But perhaps we know it?"

I begin to laugh. "Oh! No. You can have registered all my transmission, and compare them, and go into mathematical calculations. You won't find it."

"What is this sign?"

"Mariya, dear!" I say reproachfully. "This question astonishes me coming from you."

"It's obvious; you won't say." And she pursues after a while: "You are aware that I'm obliged to warn Colonel Robertson about it, don't you? You can guess he won't be pleased."

"I know," I say, sadly. "I'm only surprised you haven't done it yet."

JUNE 5TH 1944. WRAXALL.

I'm in bed again. Hemorrhage. I'm tired, tired of existing, of waiting. That it should be finished, once for all! I ring up Mariya and tell her I'm incapable of making the journey to London.

"Do you think that if I came to fetch you with the car, you could stand it? Try to!"

I say, I'll try.

There reigns a funny silence on the roads today.

JUNE 6TH 1944

"It's done! They have landed," announces Teddy as I come down for breakfast.

"Ah!" I say.

"Yes, in Normandy, on several points!"

"Landing has begun." I repeat this to myself since this morning, without being able to realize its full sense. From hour to hour the radio gives us news about the development of operations. But it doesn't waken any echo inside me. Maybe I have waited too long for this moment. Maybe I've desired it too much, dreamed of it and felt it too much to allow these simple sentences make me understand what has happened.

And then, suddenly, truth flashes up like a light: "Liberation has begun! The Germans are being driven out of France! They are fighting in France! Paris will be free! All these thoughts rush like a torrent to my brain. I'll see France again. I won't die here. But what am I doing here? I want to go away."

All at once I remember Nelly told me she was going through a course of lectures in order to enlist. She is going to leave. I will... I suddenly remember that I'm held here by my work. That I shall have to return to London, continue to send stupid messages from a tiny room now that the whole game will be played in France! Let them do their work themselves! Let Russell take my place, Russell, or another one, and let them allow me to go, that I should be free once again!

Mariya has come with Louisa to fetch me. They both have lunch with Mary, Teddy and me. Mary likes Louisa very much. Who wouldn't?

The distance from Wraxall to London seems to me endless. The least jerk makes me feel as if needles were driven into my kidneys. It's dark when we arrive at Hill Street.

"Lily," asks Mariya, "could you make an effort and just send off a message tomorrow?"

"All right," I say.

"After that I'll take you to the hospital and get you X-rayed."

"All right," I say again.

—⚜—

June 11th

At St. Mary's Hospital, I have been given another room than the one last time. My six months are over: the six months that were given me to live, when I was so ill at the beginning of January. I'll live longer. There is need of more than stones to kill me. I'll go home, I'll see France free. I'll have the strength to live that long.

The radios[8] don't show any change. I'm leaving the hospital tomorrow.

—⚜—

Tuesday, June 14th 1944

Mariya rings me up early. "We won't work today. But be at home. After lunch I'll come round to see you." Scratching at the door. It's Mariya. I go to open and am surprised to see Colonel Robertson behind her.

"You!" I say. "What is the great event which is bringing you?"

"I have to talk to you," he says.

Here it is—the big scene of the third act! Robertson sits down in one of the white armchairs and I settle down on the sofa with my legs under me. Mariya remains standing against the window. I cannot see her; she is behind me. I look at Robertson. He doesn't smile.

"I'll talk to you in private and with severity," begins the Colonel. "I'll be brief and go straight to the point." He pauses.

I say softly: "G.A."

Robertson lifts his eyebrows. He probably doesn't know that in Morse G.A. means: "Go on," but he doesn't ask any questions. He continues: "Mariya (he says "Mary") has informed me of what you have plotted in Lisbon, and we have accordingly decided that you were not trustworthy any more. In the future, you won't transmit anymore; we'll do it ourselves. For your information, we have already begun to work without you." Another pause. He probably expects a protestation on my part. But I know he is lying; they have not transmitted without me! I don't move.

Robertson resumes again: "Mariya has told me you had gone to Lisbon in order to agree about a sign of security. True or not, I chose to ignore it. We have also learned you had arranged to communicate secretly from us through Portugal."

I have an imperceptible smile. Robertson must have noticed it, because the red of his nape extends to his cheeks and rises to his forehead. "The situation is then presently as follows: You cease to work for us. We shall continue to pay you five pounds a week for your maintenance. As soon as possible, but without any obligation on our part, I shall see that you return to Paris or Algiers to your sister. In the meanwhile, you'll leave this flat. You have two weeks to clear out and look for a room. Should you in any way displease us, or talk, or getting annoying, you shall go to prison and be given over to the French authorities to be tried by them. Keep that well in mind. Now, what have you to say?"

I look at him in silence. His eyes are blue and seem still more so in his red face. He has a badly made darning on the left leg of his checked trousers. I try to imagine his looks when he made this tear! His hands are laid on the armchair's elbow-rests. He has ugly red hands with a ball-shaped thumb. His fingers hold fast and cling so much to the armchair, that his knuckles are white.

I notice all these details without lifting my eyes off him. I remember the rehearsal I had with Ronnie, in this same place, before I left for Lisbon. Ronnie occupied this same armchair. Robertson looks to me like a bad actor in a bad melodrama. All at once, I'm fed up with the staging up. I'd like to yawn.

"What do you have to say?" repeats Robertson.

I become aware that I've forgotten to answer his question. I say slowly: "Your first allegation is right. Your second is false. Your money, you can keep it."

"This money will be paid to you! You can then throw it out of the window. It doesn't concern us anymore."

"I won't take it!"

"Yes, you will take it. You won't be supported by the British Government."

"If I need money, I'll accept it from my friends, not from you."

Robertson changes the subject: "You acknowledge the rest?"

"Who told you I had arranged to communicate through Portugal?"

"I don't have to answer your questions."

"You cannot answer this question, because you know it's false." He doesn't say anything. "Now what concerns me being sent home, thank you. But I have left France without your help. I'll return there in the same way."

"I suppose," he says at last, "that you don't wish to give us the sign of security?" I only shrug my shoulders. He rises, pickup his cap. I notice that he needs to go to the barber. "That's all I had to tell you," he concludes. "Should there be anything you wanted to let me know, you can tell it to Mariya. If we need you for anything, referring to the work you have been doing and we should not understand, we'll send for you."

That's the limit! Does he imagine I'm going to wait here for a sign from him?

He stops in the middle of the room: "It is still 'no?'" he asks.

"You said a while ago I was not trustworthy. What security would you have, should I give you the sign, that it was not exactly the opposite?"

"It isn't said we would believe you."

I look at him, smiling. He waits. "Go away!" I say very softly.

He opens the door suddenly and goes out. Mariya crosses the room and closes the door behind her without giving me a look. I had forgotten Mariya. I'm sorry for her. All this must have been painful to her. I pick up the book I was reading when Robertson arrived and pursue my lecture, but in spite of myself, my thoughts return constantly to that which is now of the past. I see the incessant efforts, the three-year's patience, the success, the deceptions … and then "this." To have struggled so much, hoped, believed so much to finally end like that.

I'm not beaten, I tell myself. But what a poor comfort, if I know that I have myself destroyed my work, or at any rate have rendered it useless. I feel confusion getting the best of me. I must make them realize the danger they would run if they worked without me. They don't believe it; they think I'm bluffing. But they'll be lost, and the worst is, the Germans will know. The telephone rings.

I take up the receiver and recognize Mariya's voice. She sounds hesitating. "Do you want me to come? Don't you need me? I thought you might have something to tell me."

"I have nothing to tell you, Mariya. Everything that had to be said was said."

A silence. Then: "Do you hate me?" asks Mariya.

"No," I say, surprised. "Why should I hate you?"

"I'm glad you don't hate me," she says. "You know I couldn't do anything else!"

"I know, Mariya. You were obliged to act as you did."

"Are you sure you have nothing to tell me?"

"Quite sure."

"All right. I just want to add that should you ever need me—in a personal way—I'll be happy to help you." She hangs up.

I return to my upsetting thought—prevent the War Office to make a false step. And to be alone—quite alone—and not to know what to do. There is only Louisa to whom I could go. I could explain to her; with her, I could speak. I ring her up. It doesn't take her long to come. I tell her everything although I know she already knows everything; she works at the War Office.

"Why did you do it?" she asks, reproachfully.

"Because they cheated with me, so I cheated with them."

"What do you want of me?"

"That you should tell them that they cannot continue transmitting without me. They must give it up. I promise you I don't lie!"

"Why don't you tell them what there is to do?"

"Why should I tell them? They have taken everything from me, and I should help them?"

"Wouldn't you be satisfied to have accomplished a great work? That this work will help to liberate your country?" I don't answer. "Are you so very keen to continue working a manipulator?"

"It isn't that, Louisa! But I have worked very hard and I refuse to be vanquished by them, by your damned Intelligence Service!

Louisa puts her arm round my shoulder: "Ducky, that's just pride!"

"Maybe," I say. "But I won't give in!"

Louisa gets up: "I must return to the office. I'll tell them. Supposing they'll give up working, would you be satisfied?" I remain silent. She pats my shoulder, smiling. "I believe I know you better than you do yourself."

VII. England to Paris, 1944

When I am alone again, I stretch myself on the sofa and close my eyes! I'm so very tired. Suddenly, I start up. I must leave, leave without delay. There is only one place where I could go: Mary. If she still wants me. This flat is an object of horror to me. Everything connected, from far or near, with the Intelligence Service, is hateful.

I take up the telephone and ask for Bristol. I'm told I'll have an hour to wait. I hang up. Five minutes later, the telephone rings. Already!

"It's me again," says Mariya's voice. "Can I come?"

"If you want."

"Then I'm coming. I'll bring a cake for tea." She hangs up.

At last I have Bristol and Mary on the wire.

"Darling," I say. "My work is finished. Can I come back to you?"

"But naturally," she says. "What an absurd question!"

"Do you want me, even if I'm in disgrace?"

"Stop your nonsense and come."

I'm ringing off when a familiar scratching at the door warns me of Mariya's arrival.

"I have telephoned to Bristol," I tell her. "I return to my friends tomorrow."

"What will you do now?" she asks.

"I don't know. For the moment I don't want to think. When I know, I'll write you."

"Do you think you could consider me as your friend, or would it be difficult for you?"

"You are my friend." It's funny, but I completely dissociate Mariya with all that has happened this afternoon.

We have tea and talk of this and that. At 6 o'clock she rises to leave. "Accompany me," she says. "It will do you good to walk." We walk along Piccadilly. "You haven't forgotten that I have taken an appointment with the doctor for you for the day after tomorrow," she reminds me. "You cannot leave tomorrow."

"To hell with all appointments! I'm in a hurry to leave London."

"No, you must go there. Promise me. And tomorrow we'll go to the movies."

I promise. But on the way, my thoughts are elsewhere, and we walk without speaking. A terrible struggle is going on inside me. I don't want to capitulate. At the same time, I see France occupied, the hungry look on the faces of people standing in lines; fire-places without fire; hands covered with chilblains; the dreary despair of those who wait for four years, of a defeated people. It's for them, for us that I have struggled, for them that I must give up today what is my right. But will that help them? Is it for France that I have worked after all? I can see the Chamber of Deputies, the Ministere de la Marine, the Tour Eiffel adorned with the swastika. I see the Germans sitting around tables at Maxim's on the terrace of the Café de la Paix. I can see them stuffing themselves with lobster, chicken, drinking champagne. If some day a doubt should arise that I have served France when I came to England, one won't be able at least to doubt that I have served against these. It's for them, for those who are not free yet, that on the shelter of Piccadilly Circus, while we are waiting for the cars to allow us to pass, I say to Mariya: "O.K. You win. I'll give you the key."

"Yes?" She takes out a bit of paper and a pencil. I tell her. She notes. "Is it all?" she asks. She puts paper and pencil back in her bag.

"I won't go with you any further," I tell her. "I'll leave you here."

She holds out her hand and smiles without saying anything. I go home. I try to imagine Mariya arriving triumphantly at the office and announcing: "I've got it! She has told me!" And Robertson congratulating her. As he congratulated me several times, probably with the same words! It'll be a success for Mariya. I'm glad to be the cause of one of her successes. I feel affection for her.

June 16th 1944

A quarter past midnight. Sirens begin to howl. I'm not in bed yet. I have just finished packing. I put out the light and go to the window. The sky is full of stars and cloudless: not at all a night for raids. The search-lights reach far away, sweeping the sky. They soon become motionless on a definite imperceptible point which appears white in their light: a plane. It flies very high and—how strange—in spite of the ack ack, in spite the search-lights who have caught it in their crossed pencils, in spite of the projectiles which burst around it, it doesn't seem to make the least effort to avoid them and pursues its flight without deviating. It comes down, comes nearer, becomes larger. Soon I have the unpleasant feeling that it comes straight towards the house. Over my head, on the roof, I hear the watchers getting uneasy.

I know that in a few moments all the fuse-guns of Hyde Park will shoot together. I wait with apprehension for the crash they will cause. The plane is very low. It comes with an ear-deafening noise, similar to a monstrous and hatched purring. I suddenly can distinguish a long trail of fire which seems to escape its fuselage. "It's touched," I say to myself. It will crash down. It will be terrible for the house on which it will fall." It speeds over what seems to be Berkeley Square, not very high, just over the trees.

At this moment the fuses go off. It's too low! They pass over it. For a while the noise of explosions covers the noise of the motor. All at once I have the impression that the fire trail, which follows it like the tail of a comet, goes out and simultaneously, the sound of the motor stops. One cannot see anything in the dark. A few seconds elapse, and then the explosion—a dull explosion, different from anything I heard so far. I saw no flame, maybe the houses have hidden it from me, but in spite of the darkness, I can see an enormous column of very black smoke going up in a straight line to the sky.

I don't wait for the "All clear" and go to bed. From time to time I'm awakened by similar deflagrations! The anti-aircraft guns are doing good work tonight. It's past 9 o'clock when "All clear" is given.

In the street, I learn astonishing news. London has had its first attack by the V.I., Hitler's secret weapon. The newspapers are full of descriptions of these pilotless planes and by the enumeration of the precautions to be taken.

4 p.m. I'm taking the train to Bristol.

Wraxall. June 17th 1944.

I tell Mary about my "last adventure."
"At least I have you," I say, "and Bessie, and I know I can rely upon my friends!"
"Bessie!" exclaims Mary. "Don't compare me with Bessie, please."
"Mary, what's the matter? What has Bessie done to you?"
"What she has done to me? What did she do to you? I'll show you." She looks furious as she leaves the room. She returns and throws an envelope in my lap. I recognize Bessie's handwriting. "Read," she says.

I unfold the letter and read. I have finished. I look at the horizon in the distance where one distinguishes the sea, fields shielded by hedges. I don't say anything. Mary observes me in silence. I lift my eyes to her and try to smile. I should like to pretend that it has no importance, that one deception more or less, but it hurts!

Suddenly, Mary bends over to me and takes me in her arms. "I shouldn't have shown it to you," she says. "I've hurt you. You needn't have known. But it made me cross to see how much you trusted our cousin and the way in which she returned it to you!"

"It doesn't matter," I say. "It's better I should know. I should have understood. I could have guessed long ago. But I had such a high opinion of her. So much the worse, don't let us think about it anymore."

But at night, before going to sleep, I remember the sentences written by a cousin I loved very much: "I want to make it clear that although Lily used my good name to come to England, she has done it without my consent or my approbation, and I don't wish to assume any responsibility on her behalf. It wasn't to see her cousin that she came to England, as you no doubt know." And further: "Besides, to be quite frank, I don't want to be mixed in any way in her activities, and for this reason don't invite her to come to Cambridge. I find it deplorable that Lily should be in England and hope that her health will hold until the end of the war, when she'll be able to return to her family. I can't do anything for her, but I'm sure that you're of great help to her." And she ends with these words: "All I can do is to pray that God should protect her." If she only had told me this, to me! I would have understood her. I have the impression of having something very bitter in the mouth.

—⁂—

June 19th

My decision is taken. I have told Robertson that I will return to France without his help. It's up to me now. Nelly is in the Army. I will enlist too. When I told Mary of my plans, she looked at me doubtfully. "You'll never have the strength to do it!" she told me. "A week ago you were in hospital!"

"Oh! Yes, I'll be strong enough. I want so much to go to France, that I'll have the strength to do it."

I write Mariya to tell her what I've decided. I don't know how the War Office will take my decision. I hope for myself, and for them, that Robertson won't object to it.

—⁂—

June 24th

A telephone call from Mariya: "I've got your letter. They agree. But I must first see you. Can you come to London?"

"Yes. Tomorrow."

"All right. I'll wait for you at the flat at Hill Street. Will you take the 11 o'clock train?"

"Yes."

"O.K. See you tomorrow."

—⁂—

June 25th 1944

The porter greets me with a bright smile. It's funny to be in a place where yesterday you were at home, and where, now, you are a stranger! The parts are reversed. It's I who knock at the 83rd and Mariya who opens.

"How goes?"

"It goes."

"Now about what concerns you, I have shown your letter, and 'they' agree to let you do what you want. We can count upon your silence, can't we?" I make a sign of assent.

"You wrote me," continues Mary, "that you will probably have to undergo an interrogation by the French Security, and that you will have to explain to them your stay in England of which they know nothing. That's correct. We will therefore communicate them your dossier file which I will now read to you." Mariya takes out several typed sheets and reads me a brief resume of my work in France, giving the names of Kliemann and Yvonne Delidaise. It is said that my journey to England has been organized by the Intelligence Service who mentions my work—without saying what kind of work—with the War Office and ends with the declaration: that this work came to an end on June 14th 1944.

Having finished her reading, Mariya looks up at me: "Are you satisfied?"

"Yes. What do I do with it?'

"Nothing. We'll transfer it to Captain Vaudreuil of the B.C.R.A.[9] It's where you'll be sent to pass your security visit. He'll be warned. Telephone him beforehand and tell him at what time you'll go to see him. That's all."

"Thank you," I say.

"Lily," asks Mariya, "you're sure you are not making illusions to yourself about your strength?"

"No illusions whatever! I feel able to swim across Channel! May I use 'your' telephone?"

"Go on."

I ring up Nelly. "Nell," I say. "I must ask you a great favour. Can you take me up for a few days?"

"Sure. But what happens to you?"

"I am homeless."

"You!" I hear Nelly's astonished voice. "Well, come."

Before leaving Mariya, I say: "Everything seems to come down on me at the same time! Read this letter from Bessie."

Mariya runs it over. Then she looks at me: "You didn't expect it?"

"No."

"Neither did I!" And she adds: "You must hate England?"

"No, it could have happened to me elsewhere."

"I would like you at least to be sure that what you have done has served its purpose."

"I'll try."

JUNE 26TH 1944

The alerts follow one another without interruption, while the V.1.s tumble down without stopping on London. They already have a familiar name. They are called the "robots" or "doodlebugs." Life continues in spite of the houses which collapse.

I go to Dolphin Square. I enter my name in something called M.M.L.A.[10] I have been told what it meant, but cannot remember what it is. At Dolphin Square reigns an incredible mess, but I'm happy to be again among French people.

Nelly told me to ask for Madame Margry or Madame de Rotschild. I've got hold of one of them on the stairs. I don't know which. "What do you want?" she asks me.

"I want to enlist in the M.M. something."

"In what capacity?" she says.

VII. England to Paris, 1944

"I don't know. Anything."

"You cannot get into the Liaison anymore; the course has started. There only remains to be a secouriste."[11]

"I don't mind." As if I cared. I fill in a quantity of papers. In return I get a slip.

"Go to Portman Square to pass the security visit. Then come back here," she tells me.

I return to Nelly, take up the telephone, ask for the number Mariya gave me, and when I have it, inquire about Captain Vaudreuil.

Then a voice says: "Here Captain Vaudreuil."

I tell my name, tell him that I'll come round to see him at 3 o'clock and hang up. Perhaps I should have asked him if it suited him," I say to myself. I didn't think of it. Perhaps it would be just as well to get into the habit of paying attention to ranks.

3 p.m. A taxi puts me down at Portman Square. At the door, I have to fill in a slip. There is no waiting room, but, on the other hand, a great disorder. Employees hail each other from the top to the bottom of the stairs. People shout. A young girl in slacks passes carrying dirty cups. After twenty five minutes, a man comes and tells me: "Follow me."

We go down to the basement, pass through what must be another house, go up stairs newly made, and my guide leaves me in an office, after which he retires. Two men are seated at a table. One of them wears the uniform of a captain; the other one has civilian clothes.

I ask: "Are you Captain Vaudreuil?

He hesitates slightly. "Yes, that's it, as you have been given my name." I sit down in front of him and wait. We look at each other. "I would like to ask you a few questions," he says at last.

"You have seen my file?"

"Yes! I should like a few more details."

"Ask."

He starts questioning me about my work in France, about Kliemann, Richard, Yvonne, about the way in which I was recruited, about my training. I feel at ease with him. His face appeals to me. When I have told him everything and he doesn't know what else to ask, he tells me: "You've done a good job—very good. If there could be anything to reproach you, I could only see one thing."

"What?"

"You've done it out of love for France, isn't it so?"

"Yes."

"Why did you go to the British instead of coming to us? We were in need of people like you."

I look at him in surprise. His question astonishes me. "For two reasons," I say. "The first is that I didn't know anyone in the Resistance."

He shakes his head without convictions. "You've done something more difficult than that. I cannot believe that you wouldn't be able to find our organization."

"I don't think I could have had confidence. The risk was too great!"

"You want to make me believe you're afraid of risk?"

"Not for myself: for the result of three years' patience. And this is the second reason: The German's work was directed against England. If I had come to you, you couldn't have employed me. You would have been obliged to pass me on to the English. The information I was to transmit had to come from the War Office. So, what difference that I went straight to them?"

"Nevertheless," says the Captain, "just for a question of principle." And he adds: "Why did you leave the Intelligence Service?"

I look him straight in the eyes. "Because my work is finished," I say slowly.

"Yes, that's what is said in your dossier. Well, let's admit it. I would like you to render me a service. Could you make me a resume of the methods of working, of recruiting, paying, etc. of the German espionage? Everything you could have observed. It's only for myself. You can write it down in pencil."

"All right. When do you want it?"

"Tomorrow? Could you bring it to me at 11 o'clock?"

"You'll have it."

He gets up as I do and holds out his hand. "And I want to congratulate you," he says.

"Thank you," I say.

He's the first Frenchman who has congratulated me!

"And naturally," he adds, "there is no objection to your enlisting in the Army. On the contrary!"

June 27th 1944

This morning I return to Portman Square. I hand over the paper to the Captain. We chat for a moment. "You couldn't tell me why your work is finished," he insists.

I hesitate, and then tant pis![12] "I didn't get on with the English. Before I started working with them, I have asked for a favour, or put a condition, as you prefer. I asked to be allowed to keep my dog. It was granted to me. I trusted them. I may seem ridiculous to you, but I need to trust in order to be able to work. When they had me here, they didn't keep their promise. I didn't forgive them. When they sent me to Portugal, the Germans gave me a new cipher and we agreed about a security sign so that I could warn them in case I was discovered by the British. I didn't reveal the existence of this key, because, without it, the transmission was not possible and I wanted to remain maitresse[13] of my work. But I warned them, so that they should not try to work without me if anything should happen to me."

I am silent. He seems to consider the matter. "So they have fired you?"

"Yes. And then they came to ask me to tell them the security sign," I say, smiling.

"What did you do?"

"I gave it to them."

"Why?"

"They're not alone in the squabble. There is France."

He doesn't say anything and looks at me. Then: "You're right! I'm glad you told me all this. What I wanted to hear you say is that you didn't get on with the British."

Camberley, July 1st 1944

I have put on the thick khaki cotton stockings, the skirt which is too wide, the blouse with the sloping shoulders. There is no mirror to look at myself, so that it makes no difference what I look like. I go to the refectory to occupy a place on the narrow bench. I'm going to eat tepid soup from a mess-plate, with a tin spoon. I'll sleep on a hard bed in a corrugated-iron barrack. I'll learn with the others to march in time—one, two … one, two

VII. England to Paris, 1944

... to turn, to salute, to say: "Yes, sir." I'm N. "75,054." I've lost my personality. With it, I've lost my solitude! I'm no more alone. I've got the whole Army. I'm part of it.

September 2nd 1944

We returned to Paris six days ago. I have found my parents alive and well, and my joy has no end. I shall always remember Paris on the day after her liberation. Nothing in my life will be able to make me forget it: the flags in the streets, the delirious crowd, women, girls, children dressed up in their best clothes; thrown down barricades, now useless; here and there, the last German tanks finishing to burn. I have found Paris intact, the Paris I had left fifteen months ago, so mournful under the Nazi domination, the Paris to which all my thoughts converged, from Madrid, from Lisbon, from Gibraltar and London. The Paris I doubted to ever see again and whose walls and houses I'd now like to caress, and the asphalt of the pavements, the tree trunks, so great is my happiness at seeing them around me!

One of the first friends I meet is Van M. whom Kliemann has not employed and who has not left Paris. He has taken part in the liberation of the capital. We go together to have a fruit juice at Fouquet's. We have such a lot of things to talk about.

"I believe I'll want your help," I tell him.

"You can dispose of me," answers Van M.

"I must get to know what the British have done about people as Kliemann, Yvonne, Richard and the rest of them. I want to be sure they have been arrested. They are not a danger for England, but left at liberty, they are one for France. And the Intelligence Service might very well, if they don't have an immediate interest in it, take no trouble about Kliemann's gang. That's why I must know about it. But I don't know what to do about it. I would like to avoid getting in direct touch with the Intelligence Service. You might perhaps, as you're in the Military Security, be able to tell me whom I should see?"

"Yes, I could arrange you to meet one of my friends. It's a very fine fellow. He'll help you or, in any case, will tell you where to go. It's Captain M."

"Could we see him today, now?"

"We could try."

Van M. and I drive to the Avenue Foch, to the house where the Gestapo had its H.Q. and where now the Allied Security has temporarily established its quarters. It seems very difficult to see anyone. Nevertheless, we finally succeed.

When at last we see Captain M., he doesn't even look at me but says to Van M.: "My dear friend, excuse me, I cannot see you now. I'm over head and ears in work."

Forgetting my crumpled uniform, my condition of private, I stand up before Captain M. "Captain, you must listen to me!" I say forgetting the regular way to address a superior.

Captain M. seems surprised. I don't wait to hear him tell me he has more important business to attend to than to listen to me. Briefly, I tell him my story. I tell him what I want. He has given up showing us out. He offers us seats. When I have finished, he thinks the question over: "The best would be," he says, "to see Captain Vaudreuil, especially as you have already met him in London and he knows about your work. The B. C. R. A. is in touch with the Intelligence Service and Vaudreuil will be able to get you the information you require. You'll find him at the Majestic."

That's all I wanted to know. Without losing a moment, Van M. and I go to the avenue Kleber. The Hotel Majestic offers a sight of intense disorder, the disorder left by the Germans in their hurried retreat. For two hours I wait for Captain Vaudreuil. At last, an office boy shows me into an office and I'm met by a tall man I have never seen before.

"I should like to speak to Captain Vaudreuil," I tell him.

"I'm Captain Vaudreuil," he says.

I look at him in silence. "What's the joke?" I say at last. He begins to laugh.

"I know," he says. "In London you have seen someone else who introduced himself under my name, but I know all about you. What can I do to help you?"

"I would like to know what has been done on behalf of Kliemann and his gang. I have the right to know. I have worked in order that they should be arrested. It might not interest the British any more, but it still interests us, because they are harmful."

"I'm about to leave for London," says Vaudreuil. "I'll be away for two days. I'll inquire, and as soon as I'm back, I'll give you an answer."

I give him my telephone number and leave him. I have no confidence in his promise.

November 9th 1944

Our detachment has been sent to Verdun on the _th September to organize and run a D. P. camp.[14] I'm in Paris on a week's leave. Of course, Vandreuil hasn't telephoned on his return from London, and I have left in September without knowing anything. So I have decided to go through the matter myself. Van M. will help me.

First step: we go to Villa Boileau, Yvonne's former address. The concierge doesn't make any difficulty to give us the address Yvonne has left with her: rue des Muguets, at Louveciennes (Seine-et-Cise).

"No," I say, "we won't find anything there. It's in Paris we must look for her." I think it over. "I have the names of two intimate friends of Yvonne Delidaise's and Kliemann's. One is a certain Madame Marty-Chanclos, the other one a Madame Gorlier. We try to find them in the telephone book but without success. "Do you have a possibility to discover their addresses?" I ask.

"I don't know. I could try."

"Wait. I believe I remember something. This Marty-Chanclos was a mannequin, or a saleswoman in a well know Maison de couture."

"Try to remember the name!"

I try desperately. Where did Yvonne order her clothes? From where did she tell me her clothes came? "I go to Madrid, she told me, to show the collection of … of … Heim." I've got it: Heim Jeunes filles."[15] "At Heim's?"

"Splendid. I know someone there who will get me the information. I'll bring it to you tomorrow."

November 10th

I meet Van M. at the Etoile.

"Good morning, sir," I say saluting.

"Will you stop making fun of me! I've got the addresses."

"Both?"

"Yes, both. Mme Marty-Chanclos, 9, rue Boileau. Mme Gorlier, 19, rue Lecomte de Lisle."

"Will you help me?"

"Sure. What are we doing?"

"We'll begin by calling upon Mme Marty-Chanclos. She was a great friend of Yvonne's. They have been together in Spain."

Fortunately, Van M. has a car. We arrive at 9, rue Boileau, and Van M. shows the concierge his Military Security card. He asks where Mme Marty-Chanclos is.

"She is travelling," answers the woman.

"Where?"

"She didn't tell me."

"Did she leave an address?"

"No. And she has sub-let her flat."

"What are you doing with her letters?"

"There haven't come any."

"When has she left?"

"Two days before the Liberation."

"And you don't have her address?"

"I don't have her address."

We are out in the street again and look at each other. "It's not very convincing," I say.

"No," says Van M. "But we're going to do things legally. We'll go to the commissary to take and bring a policeman with us. We'll come back and search the concierge's lodgings.

The commissary puts himself at our disposal and lends us a young policeman who asks if he'll have to use his gun. We reassure him. Van M. tells the commissary that he might have to arrest someone, and this one tells him to send the suspicious individual over to him. They'll keep him.

We return to rue Boileau. We have not to search for a long time. Under a blotting paper, we find a dirty copybook containing addresses. The last one entered is Mme Marty-Chanclos's: 24 rue Francois I. That's all we wanted to know. For principle's sake, we send the concierge to pass the night at the commissary.

"And now?" I say, when we are once more alone in the car.

"Let's think it over before we do anything," says Van M. "I think the best would be to have her come to my office and to get her through a regular interrogation."

"O.K. Will you ring me us as soon as you know something."

—⁂—

November 11th

When I take up the receiver, I recognize Van M.'s voice on the line.

"'The person' will be at my office in twenty minutes. Will you come?"

"I'm coming." It takes me far more than twenty minutes to get from home to the Champ de Mars. When I am there at last, Van M. has already begun to question Mme Marty-Chanclos. She says she effectively knows Yvonne and has already been questioned on the subject. She says she cannot understand why this poor Yvonne should have been arrested! In any case, Yvonne has been released. No, she doesn't know her address, only her telephone number. She gives it to Van M. That's all. She can go.

When the door has closed behind her, Van M. comes into the next room where I am. "Here is the telephone number," he says, giving me a slip of paper.

"Thank you. Now we must act rapidly. This woman will very soon tell everything to Yvonne. Has Yvonne ever seen you?"

"No."

"But she probably knows your name. She knew the names of all those Kliemann saw. Did you tell your name to Mme Chanclos?"

"Yes, I introduced myself."

"It's a pity. You're too polite, old boy! I'll ring Yvonne up. I cannot understand why she has been released."

I dial the number Van M. has given me and after a while recognize Yvonne's voice.

"Hello, Josephine!" I say.

I hear her catch her breath, then: "You! Where are you?"

"In Paris! You seem surprised!"

"Yes. Yes, I didn't expect! How did you get my telephone number?"

"That's a long story."

"Come to see me."

"With pleasure, but I don't know where you live."

I feel her hesitate. At last she makes up her mind. "65 Boulevard Malesherbes, first floor, right. Go straight up. I'm always at home."

"O.K. I'll see you soon." I hang up and note the address. "At last, I shall know," I tell Van M.

―〜〜―

November 12th

I walk to the Boulevard Malesherbes. I have prepared a story for Yvonne.

Answering when I ring, she opens the door herself. She sticks out her head in the opening and asks: "Who's there?"

"I," I say.

She utters a scream and starts: "You've frightened me. I didn't see you." Then her first question is: "From where did you telephone me?"

I lie: "From a 'bistro.' Why?"

"No, it's nothing. I have the impression of being watched. But you? This uniform? And how did you find me?"

"I'll answer your questions, after which I will ask you some. One of your damn V.Is has fallen on the house where I lived in London. Result: no radio to transmit with and not a shirt left. I couldn't be of any use to "Moustache" any more and had no choice but to leave. I have enlisted in the Army. Yesterday I went to see a friend—he is in the Military Security. He is making investigation on the gold traffic between France and Spain. He was just questioning a woman in the next room. I could hear everything. I didn't specially pay attention, when I heard your name. Then I listened. The woman gave your telephone number. She said she didn't know your address. That's when I rang you up from a 'bistro.' Now, it's your turn."

"What do you want to know?"

"First and before all, tell me how and when you have been arrested. Have you been questioned?"

"Several times."

"Did you mention my name?"

"No." I give her a hard look. "I swear, I didn't!" she asserts.

"All right. I'm willing to believe you. Now tell me everything."

"I had moved to Louveciennes."

"I know. 'Moustache' told me about it in Lisbon. You were about to do it."

"It's there we have been arrested by the F.F.I.s—he, myself and Annick. The house has been plundered."

"Where is 'Moustache?'"

"Last time I saw him, he was at Fresnes."

"Do you know if he has spoken?"

"You mean about you? No, he didn't say anything. You know, immediately after his return from Portugal, everything began to turn wrong for him. He lost his job, had to hide. The Gestapo was looking for him. But he managed, before that, to send all his papers, documents, photos to Vienna. So you have nothing to worry about. There is no trace left of you!"

"So much the better," I say. "And Richard? And your sister in law? And Annick?"

"They're all arrested. We must have been denounced."

"How does it come they have released you?"

"One of my mother's husbands was American, so she claimed the American nationality. She is under American protection."

"I see."

I get up to leave her. "Where will you be?" asks Yvonne.

"Far! As far away as possible!"

Returning home, I find an urgent summons from the Renseignements Generaux[16] for tomorrow, / o'clock. Gosh! What's that again? I ring up Van M. and tell him about it. "I won't go," I say. "And the day after tomorrow I'm returning to Verdun."

But Van M. insists on my going to the Quai des Orfevres.[17]

"Why," I say, suspiciously. "Do you know what's it about?"

"I can guess," he says reticently. And he adds: "I'll take you there with the car."

November 13th 1944

I'm an hour late when I arrive at the Renseignements Generaux and hand to the office boy my convocation. I'm ushered in at once and approach a desk behind which sits an employee. I know there are two more people in the room, but I didn't look at them. "You wanted to see me?" I say to the civilian.

"Yes," he says. "Sit down. You are," and he reads to me my name, surname and profession. "Your address?"

"The Army."

He looks up with displeasure. "That isn't an address. Your permanent address?"

"I have none. I always change."

"Well, let's proceed," he says. "The Captain here is from the Intelligence Service. He would like to question you."

It's only then that I examine the other occupants of the room. The British officer is at my right. In a corner, clad in leather, I recognize Captain M. I turn to the civilian: "In what capacity does he want to question me?"

"I'm aware you have worked in England?"

"Yes, and in this case you must know, I have nothing whatever to do anymore with the Intelligence Service. Finished!"

"We thought so," says the Englishman, "but we learn you have tried to resume relations with certain German agents."

"You mean Yvonne Delidaise?"

"Quite right."

I look at him for a while in silence. "Why 'tried?' I went to see her."

He starts violently. "You have seen her? So our information is right. You have left our Services and will try to return to the Germans."

I turn round, furious. "You're a fool! Do you imagine that if I wanted to join the former members of the German Secret Service, I would take my appointments by telephone? Your opinion of me is not flattering, but it's nothing to me. I don't want to have anything to do with you anymore, nothing. Do you hear me! I don't owe anything to you. It's I who have paid you, not you. It's I who have conceived the work, not you. It's I who have executed it, not you. But it's your services who have stolen it from me when everything was done. And now I want you to leave me in peace."

He is very red, the British Captain. "In this case, could you explain to me for what reason you went to Yvonne Delidaise?"

"I don't owe you any explanation. Nevertheless, I'll give it to you.

Last September I saw Vaudreuil and asked him to tell me what had been done with Kliemann's people. He was to ask you about it. I haven't had any answer. Then I went myself to ask it from Yvonne. Does it satisfy you?"

"What did she tell you?"

I tell him about my visit Boulevard Malesherbes and by and by his anger passes. When I have finished, he says: "We have released Yvonne Delidaise, but she is tightly watched. We hope to discover other accomplices through her. Are you now satisfied?"

"It was so easy to warn me beforehand."

"And now you will promise us to keep out of all this. Otherwise we would be obliged—he turns towards M.—to take measures." For an answer, I only shrug my shoulders. "You'll sign a paper," says the Englishman. And he dictates to the civilian a declaration in three copies, according to which I promise—Oh supremely ridiculous!—not to try to contact German agents! "Sign!" he says, when it's done.

"What name?" I ask.

"Yours, naturally!"

"I've had so many of them! If my intention should be to take up with the Germans again, I should be a traitor. And if I'm a traitor, what would my engagements, my promises, my signature mean to me? On the contrary, if I'm honest, my work should be enough. One way or the other, your declaration is ridiculous and useless."

The Englishman doesn't answer. He keeps a copy and hands one to each of the other men. "That's all," he says. "And no grudge." We shake hand and I leave.

Van M. waits for me in the car. "Now I can tell you everything. On the evening you rang up Yvonne, my secretary was alone at the office and was preparing to go home, when she heard the doorbell ring. She heard men's voices, lost her head and tried to escape by the back stairs. They were policemen who had been sent to inquire about your telephone call which had been traced to my office. The policemen must have heard my secretary on the stairs, and they caught her in the street. They thought they held the author of the telephone call, that they had caught a German agent, etc. The poor girl spent the night at the commissary. I had to have things out with M., who asked me not to speak to you about it before he had seen you. That's the whole business!"

"You sneak!" I say.

VII. England to Paris, 1944

MARCH 15TH 1946

Two years have passed. I haven't died. Contrary to the doctor's prophecies, I continue to live. In four days I leave for the States to join my husband. Yesterday I received an urgent summons to report to the Palais de Justice, at the office of the examining-magistrate A, room 42, to be heard personally as stipulates the yellow paper. There are many people on the benches at the entrance of the passage guarded by a constable. Barristers come and go. At last, it's my turn. The office I enter is dark and smells close, of dust and dried ink.

The magistrate points his chin to a chair without moving. His complexion is pale and discoloured. His hair is the tint of spider web usual to people who live among piled up papers and seldom see the sun. "It's about the "Delidaise affair." You know?" I nod affirmatively. "I would like to ask you a few questions. Do you think she knew of Kliemann's activities?"

"Yes."

"Did she work for him?"

"Not officially. She made errands for him. She fixed and arranged appointments with the agents. I believe she must have known most of them. As far as I'm concerned, it was she who handed me money every month. It's up to you to decide if you consider it as working for Kliemann or not."

"And her sister-in-law?" asks the examiner. "Did she have any activity?"

"I knew her very little. I only saw her at the radio lessons, which I had at Richard's (Yvonne's brother) apartment. Other pupils came there. Richard's wife naturally must have known them. At the beginning of my course, when I was but a beginner, in the absence of her husband, it's she who, several times, sent from the next room the Morse I was to take. She wasn't a professional and did it badly."

"Do you know who the other pupils were? Have you met them?"

"Only one. His Christian name was Roger. I've been told later that it was Roger Ardouin. In any case, I didn't know it at the time."

"All right," says the examining magistrate A. "I will now confront you with the accused."

The next moment, the door opens and Richard's wife enters, accompanied by her lawyer and escorted by a policeman. She seems haggard and old and looks ill. She doesn't even look at me and sits down on a chair which is shown to her. Her advocate takes a seat between her and me. The magistrate asks her if she knows me. She leans forward, looks at me and says she doesn't. "Are you sure?" asks the judge.

She shakes her head and black stray hair falling down in disorder brushes her face. She throws another look at me; her mouth opens a little. "Ah!" she does. And she adds: "Yes, I know her. I didn't recognize her."

The magistrate reads my evidence to her. She shakes her head in denial. "I have never 'sent' radios."

The magistrate turns towards me: "Do you maintain?"

"I maintain."

"Excuse me," says the advocate of Richard's wife. "Will you please note that the witness is contradicting herself, gets confused, shortly, doesn't know what she says."

I raise my eyebrows: "How?"

Addressing again the magistrate, the defender persists: "Now the witness speaks of radio, now of transmissions, now of Morse! We should come to an agreement. Which is it? The witness doesn't seem to know it herself!"

"May I ask you, Sir, what you mean by 'radio,' by 'Morse,' and by 'transmission?'"

"How should I know? I'm not a specialist!"

"Exactly! So I will tell you. I mean by radio lessons, the teaching that was given me in order to take and send sounds called "Morse," by the means of a manipulator and of a receptive—emitting post. And it's the fact of 'transmitting' these sounds that I call 'transmission.'"

"Well, I don't mind," says the defender. "I don't know anything about it. I thought there were buttons to turn."

She, whom Richard called Love (pronouncing Leuve), denies having known Roger.

"That will do," says the magistrate. And when Yvonne's sister-in-law has left the room, he says to his secretary: "Get the other accused."

Yvonne enters. She stops when she sees me. "Oh!" she exclaims. She looks at me with round eyes and her cheeks become paler.

"Do you know Mrs. Collings?" asks the magistrate.

"Yes. No. That is I didn't know her under this name," and her pallor increases.

Again the examiner reads my deposition.

"It's false!" protests Yvonne. "I was Kliemann's mistress, but I didn't know anything about his activities. I have never arranged any appointments between his agents and himself. I have never transmitted any money."

The magistrate asks me: "You maintain your deposition?"

"Yes," I say.

"It isn't true," objects Yvonne. And addressing me directly: "You know perfectly well that it wasn't I who paid you. If I did it once, it was out of my own pocket and out of kindness."

I don't want to argue with her. I have been asked to give evidence. I have told the truth. I have no personal feeling against Yvonne. I'm not the one who has to judge. I'm not interested in crushing her. I said what I knew. Now it's up to the Judges to do the rest.

Her defender says: "All this is very uncertain. I should like more detail. How many times does the witness pretend that my client has given her money?"

"I have been paid for the first time in December 1941. I have left France in June 1943. I have been paid every month. You can add to it four voyages I made in the Free zone. If you're a medium good mathematician, you will be able to find the solution."

That's all. Yvonne has been taken away. Now, I also get up to leave. The magistrate thanks me. "It was very unpleasant," I remark to him. "I prefer a hundred times to face these people when they are the strongest."

Editor's Notes

Part I

1. Field gray. Unless otherwise indicated, Google Translate is the source of all translations.
2. Beirut. This is misspelled throughout the text. I have left the misspelling.
3. Sergueiew was in Syria when World War II broke out. She stayed in Beirut where she took a nursing course.
4. -14°Celsius = 6.8° Fahrenheit.
5. In the published version, this is Paris, December 1, 1940. While Sergueiew boarded the train to Paris on 1 December 1940, she did not arrive until the next day.
6. In September 1938, Sergueiew left Paris on a bike trip. Although her final destination was Saigon, the outbreak of war derailed her travel in Syria.
7. -17°Celsius = 1.4° Fahrenheit.
8. The Lyon Station.
9. Three Areas (Quarters).
10. Hermann Goering was commander in chief of the German air force (Luftwaffe).
11. Oh! You dear friend!
12. Moussia was Sergueiew's younger sister. She was married to Guillaume Sauty de Chalon and the mother of two daughters—Corinne and Irène.
13. This phrase is misspelled in the manuscript. The author probably means "God willing" or something similar.
14. Writing with invisible ink.
15. -24° Celsius = 11.2° Fahrenheit.
16. In the published version, the date here is February 4, 1941. See Lily Sergueiew, *Secret Service Rendered* (London: William Kimber, 1968), 25.
17. The Tcherkess are from the Caucasus Mountains. Philibert Collet, born in December 12, 1896, in Sidi Bel Abbes, volunteered from the infantry in World War I. Wounded twice, he received four citations, including the Knight of the Legion of Honor on the battlefield. In 1919, Collet volunteered for operations in Palestine-Syria, where he again won four citations. In April 1941 under the leadership, the Tcherkess rallied to the Free French Forces and participated in a campaign in Syria.
18. Chilblains are small, itchy swellings on the skin caused by cold temperatures.
19. Patter or talkativeness.
20. This is Sergueiew's first meeting with Emile Kliemann, who would be her contact and frustration from this point on.
21. "Special Message" to "Special Message."
22. Although the date in the memoir is January 30, 1941, Sergueiew obviously meant June 30, 1941. Two entries in a row have the same date. The second has been deleted.
23. This date may be incorrect. The next two entries are dated July 5 and July 6, 1941.
24. This date may be incorrect.
25. In Belgium.
26. In the memoir, this date is incomplete. The entry suggests, however, that Sergueiew wrote it at the end of July or early August 1941.
27. Minsk fell to the Germans on 26 June. Four days later after a second failed attempt by the Soviets to breach the encirclement, the Germans succeeded in closing the circle around the city completely.
28. Pierre Laval was head of the Vichy government. During the assassination attempt, both he and another collaborationist, Marcel Déat, were wounded. Laval recovered. After the war, he was tried and executed for treason.
29. Czechoslovakia.
30. A type of wimple or head covering worn by a nun.
31. Schlüsselburg is 35 km east of St. Petersburg.
32. Depression or melancholia.
33. Yevgeny Viktorvich Tarle was a Soviet historian.
34. On 4 September 1941, the USS *Greer* became the first American naval vessel to fire on a German ship.
35. Justification for acts of war.
36. The Fried Rabbit.
37. Sergueiew is probably referring to the statue dedicated to the Maréchal de Moncey.
38. Soldiers' dining hall.
39. Vanves is in the southwestern suburbs of Paris.
40. Janio is Sergueiew's diplomat cousin.
41. Charenton was an insane asylum.
42. Tver is a city in Russia. Mojaisk is a Russian city on the Moscow River between Moscow and Minsk.

43. No smoking.
44. How are you?
45. Military medal.
46. The dates are mixed up here. I have removed the incorrect date.
47. Very well. From now on we speak in German.
48. One moment, please.
49. Who is speaking?
50. Literally, Soldatenkino means "cinema soldier" and Herrenvolk means "master race." In the first instance, I think that she means that they had to wait for the German soldiers to exit the cinema.
51. This should probably be "Foui. Foui. Pien Sur. Voulez-vous voir?" This translates to "Foul. Foul. Of course. Would you like to see?"
52. English week.
53. Favorable review.

Part II

1. Next.
2. Birthdays.
3. A victory for the Allies.
4. Cheers.
5. Attack or assassination.
6. April 16, 1943, was a Thursday, not a Tuesday. The correct date is probably April 21, 1943.
7. Have received telegram 15.2. Madrid. Letter follows. Solange.
8. He wanted to leave.
9. Mothballs.
10. l'Oiseau means bird.
11. Invisible.
12. Kilometer mark.
13. Audacity—much audacity.
14. Secret.
15. Literally means boar's head. She might mean pig's head.
16. Avonmouth is a port and a suburb of Bristol. It is located on the Severn Estuary at the mouth of the Avon River.
17. Ferryman.
18. Hendaye is a Basque town in the southwestern part of France.

Part III

1. Literally means "It is!"
2. Please, miss, come with me.
3. A stranger! A stranger!
4. Holy Mother of God.
5. Ring.
6. Yes! I am. Who is this?
7. Yes! Yes! Very good! Address? Address? Telephone?
8. We shall be obliged to check your story.
9. She probably meant to say, "I want a few clarifications."
10. Emile Kliemann's aliases included Ernest Killburg, von Kaerstaedt, and Octave.
11. Very good, very good. Tomorrow at 11 at Lys.
12. In the first English translation of this memoir, which was published in 1968, the word "queens" was replaced with "decorations." Lily Sergueiew, *Secret Service Rendered* (London: William Kimber, 1968), 87.
13. "You speak Spanish now," remarks Miret. "It is very good."
14. This date and the date for the previous entry are probably incorrect. It is more likely that the date for this entry is September 17, not September 19. Kliemann says that he is leaving in three days—on the 20th. In addition, the next entry is dated September 18.
15. She was a shop girl at some confectioner's.
16. Tomorrow.

Part IV

1. Mothballs.

Part V

1. Influenza.
2. Uremia refers to kidney (renal) failure.
3. Roughly.
4. She probably means the communication channel.
5. Plus fours are loose knickers bagging below the knees. They were worn for sports, such as golf.
6. Length.
7. Carpet.

Part VI

1. Pomade is a substance used to style hair. It makes hair look slick, shiny, and neat.
2. Plaza Pombal, or the Marquess of Pombal Square, is an important roundabout in Lisbon between the Avenida da Liberdade (Liberty Avenue) and the Eduardo VII Park.
3. "I wish to see Mr. Morgener," I repeat. "Is this his house?"
4. Yes!
5. Flat, blunt ends.
6. The leanness of the horse and flies.
7. A thorough search.
8. Am coming. You send news shortly. You listen every night.
9. Portuguese town outside of Lisbon.
10. Kliemann wasn't completely correct. At least one other double agent—Dusko Popov—who was based in London traveled to Iberia several times to meet his German controller. Lily was, however, one of a very small group of double agents who met their controllers there. For more on this agent, see Mary Kathryn Barbier, *D-Day Deception: Operation Fortitude and the Normandy Invasion* (Westport, CT: Praeger Security International, 2007).
11. Kliemann was referring to Continental Film Company, which was under the control of the German Secret Service.
12. Fashion house.
13. The port Avonmouth is a suburb of Bristol.
14. Line between the beginning and number.

Part VII

1. Judas trees.
2. Crossed lines.
3. This date, although in the original manuscript, is incorrect. Lily was still in Lisbon on the 20th of March. In the 1968 English version of the memoir, the date was changed to March 25, 1944. This date is probably the correct one. Sergueiew, 193.
4. In the 1968 English version of the memoir, this phrase is changed to "Of course, he meant Sydney Bernstein: it's robbery!" Sergueiew, 194.
5. The leanness of the horses and flies.
6. Burgundy.
7. Pentecost.
8. X-rays.
9. Central Bureau of Investigation and Action (B.C.R.A.) was established by General Charles de Gaulle in 1940. The B.C.R.A. handled intelligence and covert action for the Free French during the Second World War.
10. Mission Militaire de la Administrative (Military Mission of the Administration).
11. First aid worker.
12. Too bad!
13. Mistress.
14. Displaced persons camp.
15. Heim girls.
16. General Information.
17. Goldsmith's Dock.

Editor's Bibliography

Primary Sources

KV 2/464, KV 2/465, and KV 2/466, The National Archives of the United Kingdom (TNA).

Masterman, J.C. *The Double-Cross System in the War of 1939 to 1945.* New Haven: Yale University Press, 1972.

Sergueiew, Lily. *Secret Service Rendered.* London: William Kimber, 1968.

Secondary Sources

Barbier, Mary Kathryn. *D-Day Deception: Operation Fortitude and the Normandy Invasion.* Westport, CT: Praeger Security International, 2007.

Crowdy, Terry. *Deceiving Hitler: Double Cross and Deception in World War II.* Oxford: Osprey, 2008.

Haufler, Hervie. *The Spies Who Never Were: The True Story of the Nazi Spies Who Were Actually Double Agents.* New York: NAL Caliber, 2006.

Levine, Joshua. *Operation Fortitude: The Greatest Hoax of the Second World War.* London: Collins, 2012.

Macintyre, Ben. *Double Cross: The True Story of the D-Day Spies.* New York: Crown, 2012.

Twigge, Stephen, Edward Hampshire, and Graham Macklin. *British Intelligence: Secrets, Spies, and Sources.* Kew: The National Archives, 2008.

West, Nigel, ed. *The Guy Liddell Diaries.* London: Routledge, 2005.

Editor's Index

Algiers 42, 71, 73, 75–8, 80, 83, 103, 131–2, 143, 148 153, 229–30, 289
American Consulate 65, 260
Ardouin, Roger 48, 52–3, 281, 303–4
Avenida Palace 243–4, 248

Babs 5, 7–16, 21–2, 24, 30, 40, 46–7, 55, 57, 62–4, 68, 70–2, 76, 80, 102–3, 106, 122, 130, 135–9, 142–4, 146–9, 156–9, 163–5, 168, 177, 181–2, 184–4, 207–8, 213, 218, 221, 223–4, 227–32, 257, 285
Barratt, Captain 243, 247
B.B.C. 22, 25, 49, 54, 75, 78, 80, 90–1, 179
B.C.R.A. 294, 297, 307n
Benton 149–53, 155–6, 158, 160–1, 165, 175–6, 179, 181–2, 184–5, 187, 191, 202, 207, 221
Berlin 6, 14–20, 23–7, 31, 34, 37, 41, 46, 50–2, 77, 101, 115, 171–2, 202, 248, 253, 268
Bernstein, Sidney 236–7, 246, 262–5, 276, 307n
Bessie 31, 43, 144, 150, 152, 161–2, 212–4, 223, 229, 232–3, 237–8, 240–1, 245, 278, 281, 286, 292–4
black market 12, 30, 43, 46, 49, 53, 57, 59, 63, 72, 78, 82, 91, 131, 135, 146, 151, 214–6
Boris, Madame 42, 50, 111–2, 154–5
Brecker, Brendan 236–7, 265
Bristol 64, 126–7, 143, 197, 199, 212, 214–9, 228–31, 240–2, 266, 268, 277–9, 282–3, 285, 291–2, 306n
British Embassy 6, 16, 181, 243–6, 249, 257, 260, 263, 269, 278
Brown, Miss 201
Bücking, Captain 248–55, 272

Canuto 128, 142–3, 151, 246
Carmen E. 232–3, 257
Champollion 7–9
La Ciotat 65, 71, 82, 86, 128, 143, 145, 156
Cobbe, Mr. 243–4, 247, 250, 253, 259–60, 269
Collett 22, 30, 246, 263–5
Collins, Miss 238–9
"The Continental" Film Company 264, 269, 306n

Darling, Mr. 193
Dassel, Felix 6, 13–29, 36, 41, 46, 58, 148, 171–3, 202–3
Dassel, Sigrid 18, 26–9
de G, Solange 70–1, 129–30, 132–3, 258
De Gaulle, Gen. Charles 29, 35, 52, 78, 91, 104, 144, 153. 278, 307n
Delidaise, Love (Leuve) 48, 304
Delidaise, Richard 2, 42–54, 56–7, 61, 68–70, 135–6, 169, 281, 295, 295, 301, 303–4
Delidaise, Yvonne (aka Gertrude Walter) 2, 22–5, 30, 38, 40–6, 49–51, 57, 59–60, 62–4, 67–8, 70, 74, 77, 79, 88–90, 93, 99–100, 111–2, 114–5, 122, 125–6, 150, 168–71, 173–9, 256–7, 264–5, 284, 294–304
de Rotschild, Madame 294
de V., Nelly 201, 204–5, 208, 223, 228, 286, 288, 293–5
Diegez, Senor 179–81
Dieppe Raid 68, 76
Durand, Monsieur 144, 146–7, 153, 264

"Eye of Moscow" 204–6, 208–9

F.F.I. 301
Fingado, Gerardo 154–6, 160, 203
Francine 201, 204, 208

French Embassy 22, 66, 179, 182

Genty, Mr. 89–90, 98, 150–1
German Embassy 32, 177
German Espionage Paris Branch 24
German Information Service 285, 302
German Secret Services 60, 64, 269, 302
German Service of Information (S.R.A.) 2–3
Gestapo 48, 80, 130, 137–8, 172, 175, 203, 297, 301
Gold, Mr. 197–8, 202, 242
Gorlier, Madame 298
Graf, Herr 2, 115–25, 146, 159, 239, 259, 268
Grün, Herr 69–70, 74, 76–8, 93, 106–12, 115, 141, 281

Hampstead 279–80, 282–3
Hill Street 234, 239, 256, 275, 279, 288, 293
Home Office 197, 242
Hoppe, Herr 268–9

Intelligence Service 31, 60, 130, 219, 228, 239, 267, 269, 272, 277, 281–3, 290–1, 294, 296–7, 301

Janio 43, 47, 190, 223, 281, 305n
Jones, Dr. Hanfield 225–27
Joris, Mrs. 208
Josephine (aka Yvonne Delidaise) 62, 89, 300

Ken 188–92, 223
Kliemann, Major Emilee (aka Herr E. Killburg; Kylberg; The Major; Moustache) 2–3, 25, 41–2, 46–7, 50, 57–63, 67, 70–1, 74, 77–81, 87, 89–90, 93–4, 97, 99–104, 106, 111–6, 121–30, 132–9, 142, 145, 148, 150–2,

154–6, 158, 160–79, 203, 211, 214, 229–33, 235–41, 245–6, 248, 251, 253–72, 275–9, 284–5, 294–5, 297–8, 300–4, 305n, 306n

Lane, Major 218
Laval 30, 59, 72, 77, 89, 92–3, 95, 305n
Lee (or Leigt), Russell 277, 279–83, 286, 288
Le Feuvre, Maurice 217, 278
Leitao, Maria Pia 271
Lépinard, M. 98–9, 102–4
Le Quean, Annick 49, 59–60, 62–3, 88, 102, 111, 114, 128, 145, 217, 278, 301
La Linea 178–81, 184
Lioubinski (Lioubinsky), LouLou 190, 192–3
Lord, Clifford 190–4, 208, 213, 218, 221, 223, 228–9, 232
Louisa 214, 237–9, 278, 288, 290
Lucas, Captain Derryck 184–8, 190–1, 193

M., Captain 297, 301–2
Maisonnette 42, 50, 111, 122, 154–5
Marcel 65, 82, 84–6
Margry, Madame 294
Mariette-Pacha 7–10
Maritza 209, 211–2, 214, 219, 221, 223–5, 229
Marseille 2, 9–11, 64–5, 71–2, 74, 81–2, 87–8, 150
Marshall, Larry 219, 221
Marty-Chanclos, Madame Mary 64, 126, 176 298–300
Mary (Lily's childhood friend) 215–6, 218–9, 228–33, 282, 288, 291–3
Maud, Mrs. 200–4, 206, 208
Mercier, M. 24
Mère Catherine 143, 236, 256–7
Miller, General 171–3
Ministry of Information (M.O.I.) 236–9, 244–6, 256–7, 262–5, 279
Miret, Luis 128, 142–3, 145, 150–4, 160–2, 178, 181, 306n
M.M.L.A. 1, 294
Morgener, Rudolf 128, 236, 245–7, 249–50, 306n

Morse code 41, 43–5, 49, 57, 69, 121, 141, 159, 271, 288, 303–4
Mouki 24, 40, 49, 59–60, 62
Moussia 15–6, 21, 76, 231, 305n

Napoleon (aka Lily Sergueiew) 62, 89
Nightingale Lane (Nights-in-Jail) 204–5, 208–9
#19 Rugby Mansions 210–1, 219–20, 229, 234, 275

Octave (aka Emilee Kliemann) 128–9, 154, 177–8, 236, 241, 246–8, 256, 268, 306n
O'Shaga, Mr. 187, 191–5, 197, 202, 207, 221
Ottondo, Miguel 128, 156

Page, Dr. 222, 225, 227
Palace Gardens Terrace 283
Petain 33, 44, 51, 76–7
Portman Square 295–6
Portuguese Consulate 38, 157–60
Prefecture of Police 21, 38
Press-Cinema Propaganda Section 263

Ration 11–2, 46, 72, 91, 102, 106, 123, 211–2, 215–6, 255, 274
Reichart, Herr Doktor 18–21, 46–7
Roberti, Jacques 132, 143, 145–6, 148–9
Robertson, Colonel T.A. (TAR) 209, 211, 217, 227–8, 240–1, 244, 260, 263, 272, 275–8, 287–91, 293
Romans, Sabina 167, 212–3, 217, 229, 236–7, 270–1
Ronnie 214, 229, 236–7, 239, 252, 256, 277, 280–1, 289
Rugby Mansions 210–1, 219–20, 229, 234, 275

Salomon, Jean Francois 271
San Bernardo (the Free French Organization in Madrid) 144, 245, 263–4
Sherer, Mary (Mariya) 202–4, 206–9, 211–9, 221–3, 225, 227, 229–42, 274–95
Sicily 104, 156
Sintra 260–5, 272

6 Nightingale Lane (Nights-in-Jail) 204–5, 208–9
Skyrider Hallicrafter 167, 229–30, 256
Solange (aka Lily Sergueiew) 1, 108, 129, 145, 151–2, 157, 159, 177–8, 213, 236, 241, 246–7, 252–3, 256, 268, 306n
Spanish Consulate 80–1, 107, 111
Spanish Embassy 74
S.S. 17, 85
Stevens, Colonel 132, 145–9
Stewart, Mr. (Press Attaché) 244–6, 249, 257, 262–4, 269, 272–3
Stordy, John 246, 263–5, 269
Suzanne 45, 49
sympathetic writing 20–1, 115–6
Syria 5, 13–6, 19, 22–4, 27, 41, 52, 103, 122, 151, 196, 305n

Teddy 216, 218–9, 229, 240, 287–8
39 Hill Street 234, 239, 256, 275, 279, 288, 293
Tramp *see* Solange
Treasure *see* Solange
Tremaine, Dorothy (aka Lily Sergueiew) 192–5, 197, 199–200
Tunisia 52, 77–8, 104

Vaudreuil, Captain 294–8, 302
Vichy 31–3, 64–6, 68, 70–4, 79, 81, 87, 89–98, 145, 149–50, 156, 179, 182, 305n
Villa Boileau 63, 100, 128, 134, 298–9
V.M. (Van M.) 103–7, 113–4, 123–4, 129–30, 264, 269, 297–302
Vogel (aka l'Oiseau) 45, 68–70, 93, 112, 281, 306n
von Buch, Hans 152–3, 155, 159–65, 168, 170, 178, 203
von Winter, Colonel 31–8, 40–1, 46, 58

Walter, Gertrude *see* Delidaise, Yvonne
War Office 31, 197, 213–8, 222, 228, 230–1, 235, 244, 276–9, 282, 285–6, 290, 293–5
Wraxall 198, 215–7, 229, 233, 240, 279, 282, 285, 287–8, 292